Weddings

Weddings

by

Martha Stewart

Text by

Elizabeth Hawes

Photographs by

Christopher Baker

Design by

Ellen Burnie

Clarkson N. Potter, Inc./Publishers

To my husband Andy:
Our wedding will always remain my favorite
and to my daughter Alexis,
whose wedding I look forward to with pleasure.

———

Published by Clarkson N. Potter, Inc., 201 East 50th Street,
New York, New York 10022

CLARKSON N. POTTER, POTTER, and colophon are trademarks of
Clarkson N. Potter, Inc.

Manufactured in Japan

Library of Congress Cataloging-in-Publication Data

Stewart, Martha.
Weddings.
Includes index.
1. Weddings—United States.   2. Weddings—United States—Planning.
3. Marriage service—United States.   4. Wedding etiquette.
5. Cookery—United States.   I. Hawes, Elizabeth.
II. Baker, Christopher.   III. Title.
HQ745.S78   1987   395'.22   86-12182
ISBN 0-517-55675-8

10 9 8 7 6 5 4

Acknowledgments

—

No well-published book is a solitary effort. A book of this complexity is the product of the efforts of many people who worked, in this instance, together with a sense of beauty and harmony.

This book begins with the brides and grooms and their families, who let me into their private lives during a time of great intimacy and personal consequence. Their images, and their names, appear throughout this book. I hope the warmth and gratitude that I feel toward all of them are reflected on these pages.

The president of Crown Publishers, Alan Mirken, has been my patient friend and supporter throughout the long and arduous project from the moment it was conceived.

My editor, Carolyn Hart Gavin, has been deeply interested and involved in this book and its subject matter, as she was in all my previous books. Her care and precision help make this book a pleasure to read and easy to use. Carol Southern, Michael Fragnito, Bruce Harris, Nancy Kahan, Harvey-Jane Kowal, Amy Schuler, and Barbara Peck all helped tremendously in making the publication as free from worry as possible.

Gael Towey worked tirelessly with the editors and the design and production departments to make this project as beautiful as possible.

Susan Magrino has been in almost day-to-day contact, devising creative publicity for the book and scheduling appearances all over the country for its promotion.

Many others have been of tremendous help—Kathy Powell and Cathy Killeffer offered a great deal of editorial assistance and even culinary skills. They often left the office and typewriter and the light box to don aprons and help in the kitchen.

Marsha Harris, Amanda O'Brien, Susan Ward, and Jennifer Levin helped immensely with the preparation and styling of the food, and Joan Stephanak, Wendy Bartlett, Marinda Freeman, Wendye Pardue, Marlene O'Brien, and Rafael Rosario offered their professionalism at many of the actual weddings.

Lisa Krieger, with the assistance of Marian Barnes and Jody Thompson, did much of the actual floral work at the weddings.

Necy Fernandes helped with many of the weddings and often with the styling of the pictures, finding props and arranging flowers.

Anne Campbell and my sister-in-law Rita Christiansen ran the office with smooth efficiency and calmed clients while I wrote.

Celso Lima offered a great deal of help by maintaining our gardens and helping me grow many of the flowers and vegetables that were used throughout the book.

Elizabeth Hawes Weinstock worked with me on the text of *Entertaining*, and has again lent her beautiful prose to this work.

Ellen Burnie, the designer, uncannily chose the perfect pictures for each page. Her skill with typefaces, placement of pictures, and her sense of aesthetics have helped make this book extra special.

Christopher Baker worked tirelessly and selflessly on the photographs for this book. He is an artist beyond measure.

Table of Contents

——

Working on this book has been a wonderful adventure, which has filled the course of two and a half years and taken me to many lifetimes of weddings. Each wedding brought a different story, which became a new world to absorb, study, and reflect upon. Watching and learning from the legions of wedding professionals, I sometimes felt like the Little Prince, visiting the planet of the baker, the planet of the dress or tent or music maker, each with its own focus and special energy. My work was enriched by its collaborative nature, which joined the sensibilities of a writer, Elizabeth Hawes, and the eye of a photographer, Christopher Baker, to my own. We all became much more involved in the subject than we anticipated, for it is a deep one, full of surprises and poignancies. Betsy and I often had tears in our eyes at these weddings, and Chris, who is younger, cooler, and always professional, expressed his feelings more subtly, lingering on late into the night to catch a last glimpse of a scene, or rising early to witness the intricacies of a setup.

Weddings bring so many ingredients to bear that we all had new experiences: riding in a Coast Guard vessel, breathing the fire of a hot-air balloon, hearing our first loon cry, seeing Victorian Central Park anew, learning a Greek dance, meeting a Moroccan dress designer, tasting authentic deep Texas barbecue.

We began with the idea of documenting a rich sampling of events in order to capture the wedding experience as it happens from beginning to end, in city and country, home and club, the first or second time around, to real people in real times. At the start, I had a variety of weddings to cater myself and a network of professional friends who, as caterers, florists, decorators, or tent men, wanted to share their experiences in catering beautiful weddings. When I lectured around the country, I told my classes about the forthcoming book and encouraged them to call me with ideas, which they did. The Temerlin wedding derived from my appearance in Houston; the Carpenter wedding from a call from the florist Renny; the GarDianos wedding in Central Park from a young caterer who used to work in my kitchen. As we traveled to Martha's Vineyard for Mimi Dabrowski's wedding, held at the bed-and-breakfast inn of Betsy's friend Beth Flanders, we spied another tent en route, investigated, and added the Kontjes to our wedding group. There was a wonderfully spontaneous, somewhat random quality to our news sources that we came to realize was as descriptive of the wedding scene as a carefully controlled researcher's poll. Toward the end of our publishing schedule, wedding leads were cropping up like wild flowers—one on waterskis in Maine, in a fort in Bermuda, in authentic eighteenth-century style in Newport, or the ultimate hotel production in Beverly Hills. It was difficult to stop, yet we had to, for after more than two years, we had ninety thousand words and more than twenty thousand photographs from which to refine a 384-page book. And by then we knew that we had covered a world and established a spectrum, and anything more would be an embarrassment of riches.

The generosity of the people who agreed to share very personal moments, who opened up their private wedding dramas for the benefit of future weddings, was one of the joys of this book. From them, and from all the cake makers, florists, and lighting experts, came a phenomenal wealth of firsthand information that creates not only a unique documentary but also the richest sort of reference work. Sometimes we found ourselves involved in the inner workings of a family, and the resulting text catches intimate details in the evolution of decisions. At other times, we enjoyed a close view of a finished production, which afforded other, more objective insights. Many of the most enlightening conversations came several months after a wedding, when we visited the newlyweds and family to show them our photographs and look back on the day together, the pressures dissipated, the memories deepening, the course of events clearer in hindsight. The universal feeling was one of relief, pride, triumph, and general euphoria.

One of the questions we invariably asked a bride or groom was what in the day they remembered most clearly. Their answers, of course, were unpredictable—"the goofy expression on his face," "my grandmother's tears," "the sound of rain on the tent," "our dance." The whole process of inspection and introspection made Betsy and me very thoughtful about our own weddings, which happened twenty and twenty-five years ago, respectively. Both Betsy and I did our weddings ourselves, in New York, far from our hometowns in Ohio and New Jersey, in a bit of an unsophisticated haze. Both of us were marrying men of a different religion, which was a more complicated matter in the 1960s. Both of us had the desire for a classic, beautiful wedding, but had no time, no money, and little of the self-awareness that we recognized in almost all the brides of today.

I was a naïve nineteen-year-old, still a student at Barnard, and Andy was beginning Yale Law School, so it seemed appropriate to be married in St. Paul's Chapel at Columbia in an Episcopalian service, mainly because we didn't have anyplace else to go. Our families were somewhat overcome at the prospect of our marriage, but we were strong-willed enough to just go off and do it. Andy chose the music (Purcell's "Trumpet Voluntary"), and in the three weeks after final exams my mother and I made my dress from embroidered Swiss organdy we found on West Thirty-eighth Street in New York's fabric district. We fashioned four layers of fabric into the gown, and then saved a length to cover a pillbox, the hat Jackie Kennedy had made so fashionable at the Inaugural earlier that year. I carried a bunch of field daisies. There were no formal invitations (I wrote little cards to the family), and no formal portraits. I had arranged a simple lunch for eighteen in the Barberry Room of the Berkshire Hotel that ended with an ice-cream cake. Then Andy and I changed clothes at my in-laws' apartment in the Ritz Towers and drove off for a weekend honeymoon in Vermont, for we both had summer jobs and had to be at work on Monday. I suppose it was very basic, but I didn't feel that way. I felt very special.

In reconstructing her wedding, Betsy recalls, "I went to see a prominent Episcopalian bishop who had in fact known my grandmother and baptized me, who said that he *might* marry us after six months of instruction for my groom, so we moved on and eventually found a wonderful, liberated Greenwich Village preacher who said that if Davis believed in love, hope, charity, and fidelity, that was enough for him. I wore my matron of honor's wedding dress, which was a bit small, as she is five four and I am five eight, but I was trying to be economical. Only recently did I discover my mother's wonderful satin tunic gown in a corner of our attic in Ohio. I remember the recep-

Garlands of full-blown pink roses cover trellises in our garden. One day I hope Alexis will be married in this beautiful and romantic setting.

tion site, called the Georgian Suite, run by a sweet Frenchwoman; the French accordionist who roamed through the ballroom like a street musician; and the wedding cake, which was made by a French baker—all tribute, I suppose, to my years in France. A friend's mother took the wedding photographs, but she left the camera with the film in a taxi. Davis's grandmother, an imperious opera singer, dominated the receiving line, and when I dressed to 'go away,' my godmother cried because I wasn't wearing a hat."

With our newfound enlightenment, Betsy and I now have very concrete dreams for the

next generation, and we stand ready to be called into action one day for our children's weddings. Betsy has three sons, but given the flexibility that rules weddings now, she knows that maybe she will be able to contribute to the planning, or perhaps to pass on her mother's satin gown to one of their brides. Her middle son, who is fourteen, has already picked out a site in their backyard, a lovely knoll where he sees deer stop to graze in the early morning, and from which he can still see the basketball hoop where he spends his happiest hours.

My friends are impatient to see how my twenty-one-year-old daughter Alexis will be married, but I already know it will be an event beyond my present imagination, because her individualism and style will be expressed in some surprising new way. Nonetheless, I fantasize about a background of roses and a benediction of apple blossoms, and continue to perfect a possible setting for her. In the last two years, on the grounds at the back of the house, Andy and I have designed and built a network of trellises, inspired by the ironwork at Monet's Giverny. Soon they will be covered with garlands of old roses, completely enclosing the garden and creating an ideal private and perfumed world for 150 wedding guests. In the front yard, Andy has been religiously pruning the apple trees that line the path to the house so that, over the years, they have begun to grow together to form a Romanesque arch, like those remarkable pleached lime *allées* in France. Every spring Andy announces that his trees are *almost* ready. This year, the arms of the arch are just beginning to touch, suggesting a covered walk for Lexi's processional. Perhaps she will find this scene as beautiful and romantic as I do. If so, my only remaining problem will be how to get the apple trees to bloom at the same moment as the roses.

Introduction

Of all the events in the course of a human life, a wedding may be the richest—in fact, in folklore, in spirit. By almost any measure—the dreams extended, the energy and funds expended, the planning, the paraphernalia, even the quality of tears shed—it emerges as monumental. It is curious to think that the wedding ceremony lasts somewhere between four and sixty minutes, its celebration between one and six hours, and yet its preparation consumes months, if not years, of frantic time; that for all the careful choreography of dresses, flowers, cakes, singing strings, special shoes, lace garters, calligraphy pens, Jordan almonds, rose petals, items borrowed and blue, what remains behind is a dress, a folio of photographs, and memories. Memories so strong, so well preserved in mind's eye and imagination that thirty-five years later, the scent of roses blooming or the sound of a harp playing will evoke the full-blown scene.

In spirit, the wedding experience begins in childhood, when weddings register as the most magical, most fanciful events conceivable; in wide and dancing young eyes, one can read that all the costumery, pageantry, and tangible joy appear as extraordinary excursions into the realm of storybooks and fairy tales. In America, and in most countries in the world, bride and groom grow up nurtured by wedding lore, bride dolls, play houses, the romantic sagas of literature, film, and news coverage, even the old "Bride and Groom Show" and the new "Newlywed Game." From changing vantage points, a wedding is anticipated. "I want to be married in the woods by a raccoon minister," a young boy announced to me recently. "I want a top hat and James Taylor," a slightly older brother declared. By the time they are eighteen, most girls have a gauzy image in their head of their wedding dress, their wedding site, their wedding day, based on the most personal fancies. Years later, in middle and old age, they have relived the wedding day countless times, revived it in part with anniversaries, and passed on its stories and mementos to other generations.

A wedding is many things. Foremost, it is a rite of passage, an end and a beginning, a fulfillment and a promise. It is one of the three watershed events in the life of man and, in the company of birth and death, the only one that is voluntary, premeditated, undertaken in full consciousness. Every culture throughout history has commemorated the transition of a human being from one state of life to another, and the wedding is anchored at the very heart of civilization. Its components, irrespective of nationality and religion, are legacies from primitive times: the veil (emblem of chastity and submission); the wedding ring (a vein was thought to go directly from the fourth finger to the heart); the bridesmaids and groomsmen (reinforcement from the days of marriage by capture); the flowers (symbol of fertility); the food (celebratory feast). Indeed many of the

ABOVE: A heart-shaped petal from an extraordinary old rose named Charles de Mills. OPPOSITE: Andy and me on our wedding day, July 1, 1961.

trappings of today's wedding ceremonies are moored in magic and paganism and predate the church's first involvement in the thirteenth century. A wedding is also a proclamation, a public announcement of a new relationship between two members of society. In light of all this, a wedding is a ritual and celebration of the highest order.

Weddings speak volumes about human behavior, values, history, fashion. Indeed, a wedding is a microcosm of the dreams and facts of American life. What other event results in the single-minded attention of whole families for as much as a year; an expenditure often greater than that allotted for education; a transformation of character from nonchalant libertine to concerned traditionalist; the suspension of all reality in the moment the bride, swathed in lace and net, floats down the aisle. For many

brides and grooms, a wedding is a chance for a perfect event on which to build the rest of their lives; for some, it is the rite that sanctifies their marriage; for others, it is a grand party, as expressive as the union it describes.

Looking back on the fifty-odd weddings attended in the past several years, I realize that I was in the unusual position of being both an outsider and an insider. As an outsider, unknown in any intimate sense to the principals, I had the advantage of objectivity. What I took away from weddings was sometimes a general impression—the beauty of the day or site, the closeness of the family, the carnival of music and dancing. It was some small, and unpredictable, detail that will always stand in memory—the bride's arrival at the reception in an old Mercedes roadster, veil flying in the wind; guests wandering into the fields to talk to the horses; the solemnity of the vows; a single flute playing serenely while a church filled with high-style guests. As an insider, I saw how weddings come together, how well-laid plans bring their own rewards, and the myriad ways in which personality can assert itself. Because I was there in the wings of weddings, inadvertently I observed intimate moments generally reserved for the family: talking with a flower girl to help her relax; peeking in a window at the groom primping; being a part of the bustle of dressing the bride; the behind-the-scenes anxiety of "is there enough salad?" and "are the flowers wilting?"; the adjustment of the bride's train; and her last happy-but-scared look back before stepping out into the processional aisle.

More than ever now, I find weddings exciting, evocative, and inspiring. To convey that is the aim of this book: to recapture firsthand the wedding experience; to enlighten and enrich thinking; and to celebrate the nature of one of society's oldest and most important events.

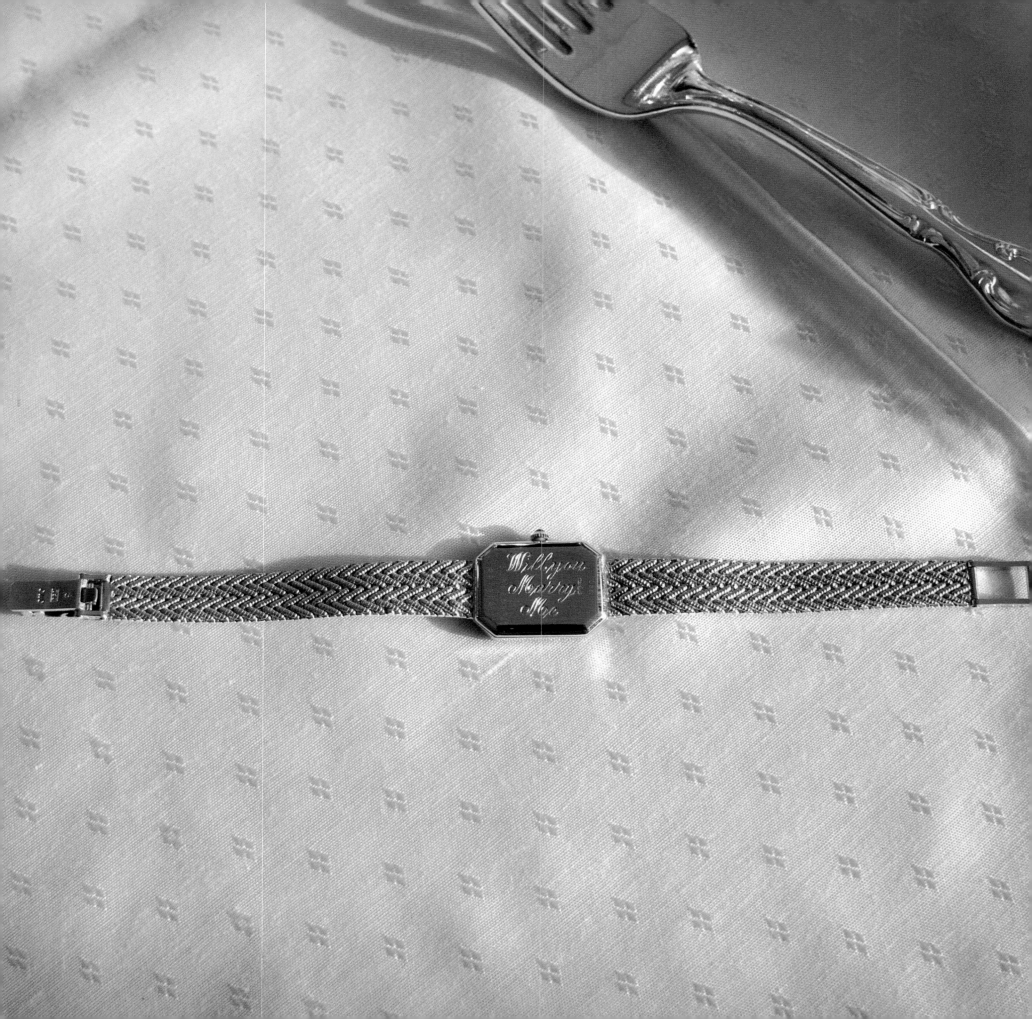

Style

Visions of long trains and lacy fingertip veils; baby's breath, roses, and cymbidium orchids; little wicker baskets of rose petals, and five-tiered chocolate-almond cakes fill my head. My ears continue to echo Mendelssohn and Purcell, Handel and Bach, with a counterpoint of Gershwin and Porter, "The Girl That I Marry," and "You Are the One." It feels as if the whole country were getting married, which, of course, millions of its population are doing each year. In June, the statistics are almost visible, when every other home in the countryside or cityscape seems to reveal a cloud of pink and white balloons tied to a mailbox, or a policeman waiting to direct park-ing, a telltale crowd on the steps of a church, a glimpse of a backyard tent, a limo idling in the shade, or a homemade banner flapping from the trees.

Now when I try to summon up the image of a precise event, I receive instead a composite of myriad events: a quiet country church in Wilton, Connecticut; a flowering chuppah in Deal, New Jersey; a huge barbecue in Texas; a scalloped tent dripping in Massachusetts rain; a launch bound for Church Island, on Squam Lake, in New Hampshire. I think of wedding newsmakers like Timothy Hutton and Debra Winger, who were quietly wed on a bluff in Big Sur and then sped off to a film location in South Carolina; twenty

PRECEDING PAGE: Jacquie Van Den Berg had been hoping for an engagement ring at Christmas and admitted a feeling of disappointment when she opened her present and saw this watch. Upon closer examination, she burst into joyful tears and accepted.
LEFT: A Scottish paisley shawl and landscape painting on top of a crisp white linen cloth transform an ordinary table into a stylish serving bar for a wedding at the 1730 Colony House in Newport, Rhode Island. RIGHT: The bride and groom bid farewell to the coachman, a family friend.

thousand Orthodox Jews gathering in joy in the Coliseum on Long Island for the wedding of the children of two Old World rabbis; Caroline Kennedy and Edwin Schlossberg, American royalty in the public mind, who succeeded in safeguarding their privacy while supplying the press with information, and celebrated with Carolina Herrera gowns, Glorious Food, and George Plimpton fireworks at the family compound in Hyannis. I also remember my friends Ursula and John, who married in a meadow on Martha's Vineyard, reading their love letters to the small group of friends gathered there, beautiful meditations on friendship by two strong-willed scientists, written over the course of their long-distance courtship.

There is no stereotypic wedding; I knew that before this book, but I have learned it again. One night, overwhelmed at the diversity of weddings I have witnessed in the last several years, I asked my daughter Alexis how she would be married in her dreams, and she responded that she would have as her attendants all the animals of our barnyard—cats, dogs, chickens, turkeys, and sheep—and would

dress them in doll clothes and bits of lace and frou-frou.

The more weddings I attended, and the more I heard about—each wedding seemed to elicit dozens of stories about memorable weddings I had just missed—the more I realized that each one was a wonderful drama in itself, steeped in personality, family history, and a kind of folklore. From a distance, there is a sameness to weddings, for the white dress, the tall cake, the rings, and the flowers are always there. Back in 1900, a sociologist named L. J. Miln, who in *Wooings and Weddings in Many Climes* studied nuptials around the world, from India to Bali, concluded, "I've found the marriage customs of most peoples strangely alike." That, indeed, is the strength and beauty of one of the basic events in the life of mankind. And yet, within the structural sameness of ritual, there is something very special about each wedding. In my experience, nothing has been predictable: an event that promised to be a simple at-home affair turned out to be an old-fashioned country idyll; a traditional ceremony evolved into a religious songfest; a funky party was warm and personal. In almost

every case, this freshness and individuality had to do with the participants, their priorities, their feelings, their taste—in other words, their style.

Style too often carries a trendy connotation. Yet style is much deeper than fashion. Like its Latin antecedent *stylus,* it is a manner of expression, descriptive of the character of an individual, and like handwriting, it derives from innate rhythms and expresses something personal and unique.

Style is a complicated matter. It resides in large decisions about whether a wedding is to be essentially a ceremony, a show, or a party. And it is a sum total of smaller decisions about the number of guests, the color of the bridesmaids' dresses, and even whether to shower the couple with rose petals (real or paper), rice, wheat chaff (a French custom), or, in the case of Sandra Leo-Wolf's winter wedding, birdseed. Style is practical, but at the same time, it is idealistic. It is a focus, a spirit, and a point of view.

The common cry from a couple first confronting the prospect of planning a wedding, from the shy and uninformed to the sophisticated and radical chic, is "I want to do it right." A wedding seems to bear all the weight of history, tradition, and fantasy. Any public library boasts enough shelves of books on wedding etiquette and planning to render even the most self-confident rather meek. Bridal consultants and bridal magazines—*Bride's,* older and more traditional, and *Modern Bride,* among the most successful ventures in publishing history, exist for the sole purpose of advising. And they are emblematic of

the huge wedding industry that has grown up in America since World War II, a consortium of dress salons, jewelers, bridal registries, florists, caterers, photographers, orchestras, honeymoon travel agents, engravers of announcements, bakers of cakes, that shares a twenty-billion-dollar-a-year market. Weddings are big business, and the pressures exerted by commerce and fashion are very real.

Not too long ago, in a *New York* magazine article on the wedding of the eighties, the reporter, a single woman in her late twenties, posed as a bride-to-be and set out to research

A nineteenth-century silver-shot shawl covers the dessert table. The silver coffee set and candelabra were the bride's mother's.

the subject in a rational way. Skeptical at first of all the traditional fuss and frills, she soon succumbed to their lure and, by the end, opted for expensive and impeccable convention. It was a good case study, and yet, had she *really* been about to marry, with her grandmother's wedding dress preserved in a trunk, her groom's loft available, and a newfound inter-

est in Big Band music, she might have made more personal choices. The lessons of recent times have offered a valuable perspective and made it poignantly clear that the right style is your own style, informed, perhaps, by the industry, enriched by tradition, but defined by your fancy.

The changes in style and in the attitude toward style of the last two decades have made us thoughtful. Looking back on times gone by, it is easy to see that changes come in response to the recent past and to social conditions. The sixties and seventies, with their sexual liberation and their lessons in individualism, which resulted in barefoot brides and home-made vows, were a response to the fussy institutionalism of the fifties, which was probably a response to the austere, unpredictable forties. *The Bride: A Celebration,* written by Barbara Tober, editor-in-chief of *Bride's Magazine* since 1966, has a chapter that characterizes the bride by decade, to show that she is ultimately part of the larger truths of changing times: the wartime bride, who often made plans around a weekend furlough, insisting nonetheless on a traditional ceremony as an anchor in chaotic times; the spendthrift fifties girl, liberated from a wartime economy, emerging as part of the Silent Generation, dressed in a frothy dress with a hoop; the sixties and seventies flower-children brides, rejecting the obvious and pretentious in favor of the natural and sure, celebrating love in its simple, homespun, and honest forms.

A friend has described his archetypical wedding of the sixties for me: The bride and

groom, she, white and Jewish, he, black and Baptist, had been in the Peace Corps in Africa together, and had taken the names Ashanti and Kamante. For their wedding in Baltimore, they created an earthy ceremony, celebrating primarily the gift of life, for which all guests (including many members of the black and white academic and financial upper-class establishment) were bade to dress in swathes of African cotton and join in a reception to share exotic dishes of wild roots and rice and vegetables. The matchbooks at the wedding were engraved ASHANTI AND KAMANTE, and the

Plantation Catering of Newport, Rhode Island, set up this raw bar using Dutch copper skuttles and masses of fresh seaweed.

reception included native dances. Afterward, however, the bride's family invited a large group to their hotel suite, where everyone dressed in tuxes and designer gowns. Smoked salmon and caviar were served on silver trays and the matchbooks read MARCIA AND MARK.

Through the process of trial and error and energetic self-expression, the sixties and sev-

enties taught us perspective. At first rejecting tradition as empty and institutional, couples sought substitutions, and improvised personal wedding ceremonies, sweet and intimate and profound and occasionally metaphysical, illuminated by Kahlil Gibran, gurus, and the romantic poets: "Sing and dance together and be joyous, but let each one of you be alone"; "We hereby commit ourselves to a serenity more flamboyant and more foolish than a petalfall of magnolia." Weddings were invented and idyllic moments, and, more important, acts of a new self-awareness. Now, two decades later,

the self-awareness has grown larger and less egocentric and has led to a reexamination of tradition, a recognition of its beauty and strength, and a respect for things that last. As a *Time* magazine essay by Lance Morrow reflected several years ago: "If a bride and groom repeat the same vows their parents repeated, the vows they may expect their children to repeat; and if the same tears are shed now that were shed five generations before at the same rite, the ceremony has its continuity and resonances."

It is increasingly difficult to define a traditional wedding, such is the diversity of styles in play and the complex composition of couples today. Interfaith and interracial marriages, second and third marriages, often with several sets of children involved, late marriages, marriages after years of housekeeping together—all are common enough to have sharpened our sensibilities and altered the rules. A white dress is traditional, but it can also be ivory or champagne, long or short, bare-backed or high-necked, a cocktail suit or a sailor dress. As far as the old virginal connotation, white is a state of mind, and, in any case, in its Victorian origins, it was chosen to signify not purity but joy, like the Easter lily, and brides now wear white the second time around. Although some couples embarking on a second union exercise restraint, thinking it befits their experience and maturity, and plan small family affairs or large impersonal parties, others have learned that they want to indulge this special moment, and to make up for the past with bold articulate show.

Traditional is also a church ceremony, but the preponderance of clergymen of all religions are willing to confront the times and the ERA by omitting "obey," and they welcome the addition of personal readings, musical selec-

tions, and reflections. Annie O'Herron's wedding on Cape Cod combined the best of Catholic and Baptist traditions to forge a thoughtful and thought-provoking ceremony under the aegis of two clergymen. "God will understand" is how the Episcopalian minister at Hilary Cushing's wedding on Long Island explained his deletion of references to the Trinity in order to soothe a Unitarian groom.

Tradition is a tall white cake, but the white may be white chocolate, camouflaging a macaroon-scented, raspberry-filled sponge cake. That there is no blueprint for weddings, including traditional weddings, makes their planning more personal, more pleasurable, and often more complicated. Recently I spoke with a mother who was planning her daugh-

LEFT: A green meadow was the dance floor at Mimi Dabrowski's wedding reception on Martha's Vineyard. BELOW: At the Cook wedding in New Hampshire, pigs Häag and Dazs slept all day.

ter's wedding on the tenth anniversary of the day they decided to live together, and was as nervous about the organization as she would have been if she had not known the groom's family intimately. The mother of a bride who was to be married in June after a honeymoon on a sailboat in the Bahamas in January and the birth of a baby in May declared, "Things are not like they used to be. I am learning to cope," she said, "but it seems rather complicated."

The stories in this book celebrate diversity and personality. Many of the events have the aura of the classic, because they were beautifully articulated, and their ingredients chosen for meaningful personal and practical reasons. A Barbra Streisand song was the right choice for the processional at one young couple's wedding, because it suited their sense of romance; the restaurant Le Zinc, chosen for a reception, was at the center of Joyce Roquemore and Paul Hanly's courtship. A wedding is not a casual event, as all those who have planned one know, and the more personally gratifying each decision is, the more memorable and meaningful it will be.

Determining your own style means assessing your situation as well as defining your own taste and fancies. One of the first realistic questions to ask is "Whose wedding is it?" for it is a day of fulfillment for mother and father and family, who have nurtured a child up to this point, as well as for the bride and groom. Some brides are happy with a wonderful send-off, for it is indeed the last chance for such dependence, and they are comfortable simply to approve decisions. Others have idiosyncratic dreams in their head, and the energy to support them, and want to do it themselves. The latter seems to be prevalent enough for Tiffany's, the traditional arbiter of good taste, to have broadened their stationery format this

year with an informal invitation in which the bride and groom are hosts. One of the most visible effects of the sexual revolution of the sixties and seventies is that the groom is a frequent partner in all the planning decisions. The whole subject matter of weddings—design, ritual, entertainment—is, in fact, more interesting to men than in days gone by. Recently, in the wings of a wedding, I overheard the videotape crew musing about their ideal weddings; they agreed on a free-form barbecue, with Frisbees, volleyball, and a can full of

ABOVE: A hot-air balloon ride up Golden Pond was the culminating event of a full and fabulous wedding day for Debbie Cook and Tim Legge. OPPOSITE: At another wedding, tables are dramatically set with blue linens and bright garden flowers in the middle of an expanse of lawn.

golf balls to hit into the lake at which the future event would take place, and also agreed on formal attire, including top hats, although one young man wanted to underlay his tux with a Hawaiian shirt.

I have often wondered about the role of bride as central figure in a matriarchal totalitarian event (the groom doesn't even make an official entrance, and there is no *Groom's Magazine*), and wondered if it were a trade-off for her relinquishing of name, the responsibility of childbearing, the implicit consent, until recently, to follow her mate wherever fate might take him. Times, of course, have modified this blind arrangement, and in terms of weddings, it is acceptable and even desirable now for the groom and the groom's family to contribute their ideas, and even to share expenses. A woman with whom I have worked on three weddings provided an example of the most graceful manner of sharing. All her children wished to be married at home, a lovely sprawling estate in Greenwich, and so, in the case of her sons, she gave her home openly to the bride's family, offering to contribute the tent and equipment and any necessary help or moral support, and leaving the design decisions to them. It worked out beautifully. On the other hand, however, I know a wealthy grandmother who made a generous offer to finance a wedding and yet imposed conditions that in the end created an affair that was formidable and awkward and made the bridal couple miserable. A wedding is an event that calls for magnanimity and flexibility.

Although wedding costs accelerate as rapidly as the wedding industry proliferates, and the wedding budget is an element that must necessarily shape the day, there are notable exceptions to a formidable outlay of savings. Not necessarily for reasons of budget, but rather for

a sense of community, Mimi Dabrowski's wedding on Martha's Vineyard was a model of the act of friendship, with some friends contributing their organizational skills and others bringing their favorite food, to create a groaning board of extraordinary proportions. A wedding is a time to call on friends, and everyone does in some way—for moral support, for advice, sometimes for physical assistance. Hilary Cushing, whose wedding was a model of fashion, called upon her old comrades at Sotheby's—the chef, the florist, and the caterer—to aid and abet her efforts, because she was confident of their talents and of their friendship. When the opposite case occurs—an impersonal hired-out wedding, dictated by the guidelines of fashion—the result is often spectacularly cold. A family I knew drew upon their unlimited resources to employ the latest in wedding services, in fact hiring a phalanx of

New York's most successful and eccentric artisans to do their own thing, and the result was an odd show of talents, glossy, self-conscious, unrelated to the real drama at hand. Another family invited their wealthiest and showiest friends—to create an exciting guest list and to ensure extravagant gifts for the bride and groom—and found themselves with a stiff and dispassionate ensemble. It is important to remember that a wedding is a send-off from one stage of life to another, and that those who have shared intimate moments with the couple are the ones likely to appreciate the occasion. So many brides, even Sophie Desmarais in Montreal, who had the theatrical setting of a gala state wedding to distract her, look back from the most sumptuous of weddings and remember most clearly the faces of people dear to them.

So the answer to the question of budget is

an old-fashioned one: that money makes it easier to make free choices, but that money is not the arbiter. Half a century ago, in the 1925 edition of Emily Post's *Etiquette*, after an entry on "The Most Elaborate Wedding Possible" and "The Average Fashionable Wedding" and "A Small Wedding," she recounted "The Wedding of a Cinderella":

Some years ago there was a wedding where a girl who was poor married a man who was rich and who would gladly have given her anything she chose, the beauty of which will be remembered always by every witness in spite of, or maybe because of, its utter lack of costliness.

It was in June in the country. The invitations were by word of mouth to neighbors and personal notes to the groom's relatives at a distance. The village church was decorated by the

OPPOSITE: Loose branches of pink flowers adorn a table in a hall-way. RIGHT: An elegant interior—perfect for a reception. BELOW RIGHT: This gorgeous nineteenth-century stone house was a wonderful location for a wedding.

bride, her younger sisters, and some neighbors, with dogwood, than which is nothing more bridelike or beautiful. The shabbiness of her father's little cottage was smothered with flowers and branches cut in a neighboring wood. Her dress, made by herself, was of tarlatan covered with a layer or two of tulle, and her veil was of tulle fastened with a spray, as was her girdle, of natural bridal wreath and laurel leaves. Her bouquet was of trailing bridal wreath and white lilacs. She was very young, and divinely beautiful, and fresh and sweet. The tulle for her dress and veil and her thin silk stockings and white satin slippers represented the entire outlay of any importance for her costume. A little sister in a smock of pink sateen and a wreath and tight bouquet of pink laurel clusters, toddled after her and "held" her bouquet—after first laying her own on the floor!

The collation was as simple as the dresses of the bride and bridesmaid. A homemade wedding cake, "professionally" iced and big enough for everyone to take home a thick slice in waxed paper piled near for the purpose, and a white wine cup were the most "pretentious" offerings. Otherwise there were sandwiches, hot biscuits, cocoa, tea and coffee, scrambled eggs and bacon, ice cream and cookies, and the "music" was a victrola, loaned for the occasion. The bride's "going away" dress was of brown Holland linen and her hat a plain little affair as simple as her dress; again her only expenditure was on shoes, stockings and gloves. Later on, she had all the clothes that money could buy, but in none of them was she ever more lovely than in her fashionless wedding dress of tarlatan and tulle, and the plain little frock in which she drove away. Nor are any of the big parties that she gives to-day more enjoyable, though perfect in their way, than her wedding on a June day, a number of years ago.

After these big questions are answered, the aesthetics come into play, one decision leading to another and building up pyramid-style until a real event begins to take shape. For some brides, it is a joy to have an arena in which to

ABOVE: Mädderlake decorated sections of this tent with pulled, pleated tulle; Glorious Food served as hors d'ouevres shellfish from a fantasy carved ice bar. RIGHT: Party designer Carole Gordon handscripted this menu for a very elaborate and interesting wedding.

display their taste and pleasure, their love of Art Deco, their secret fancy for a French wedding dress, or their fondness for their summer home. Many mothers, too, have kept a corner of their heads reserved for wedding ideas to act upon when the moment arrives. For others, however, the artistic freedom to create this important event is paralyzing, because it is difficult for them to do their own thing. No one should take it for granted that everyone has an innate sense of style, because it often only comes with age. I met a young woman at Tiffany's open house for prospective brides and grooms who had been married for ten years and was just then choosing her dishes and crystal because at last she knew what she wanted. Decisions come gradually, with honest appraisal of likes and dislikes as well as dreams. But it is not a time to be afraid to express yourself, even if your mother's beautiful long Empire dress is preserved in your name, and

you look spectacular in short, simple designs or if your family loves huge gatherings, but you feel shy and tongue-tied in crowds. Indulge your fancies: a love of Dixieland bands or baroque music, a fondness for peach ice cream or picnics or barbecues or the high-tea ceremony. At several of the weddings in this book, the bride and groom concentrated their efforts on the ceremony, for that was the most meaningful element to them. At others, the choice of site suggested a theme—a yacht club and a seaside home led to nautical themes, articulated with sailor dresses, flags, a get-away boat; a farm inspired the idea for a picnic on the grass and a buggy ride. If you are really at a loss, it is a time to think about friends' weddings, what you liked and disliked, and to call upon close friends, particularly creative ones, for advice as well as coordination.

Despite a possible awe in the face of design decisions, the typical bride today is better in-

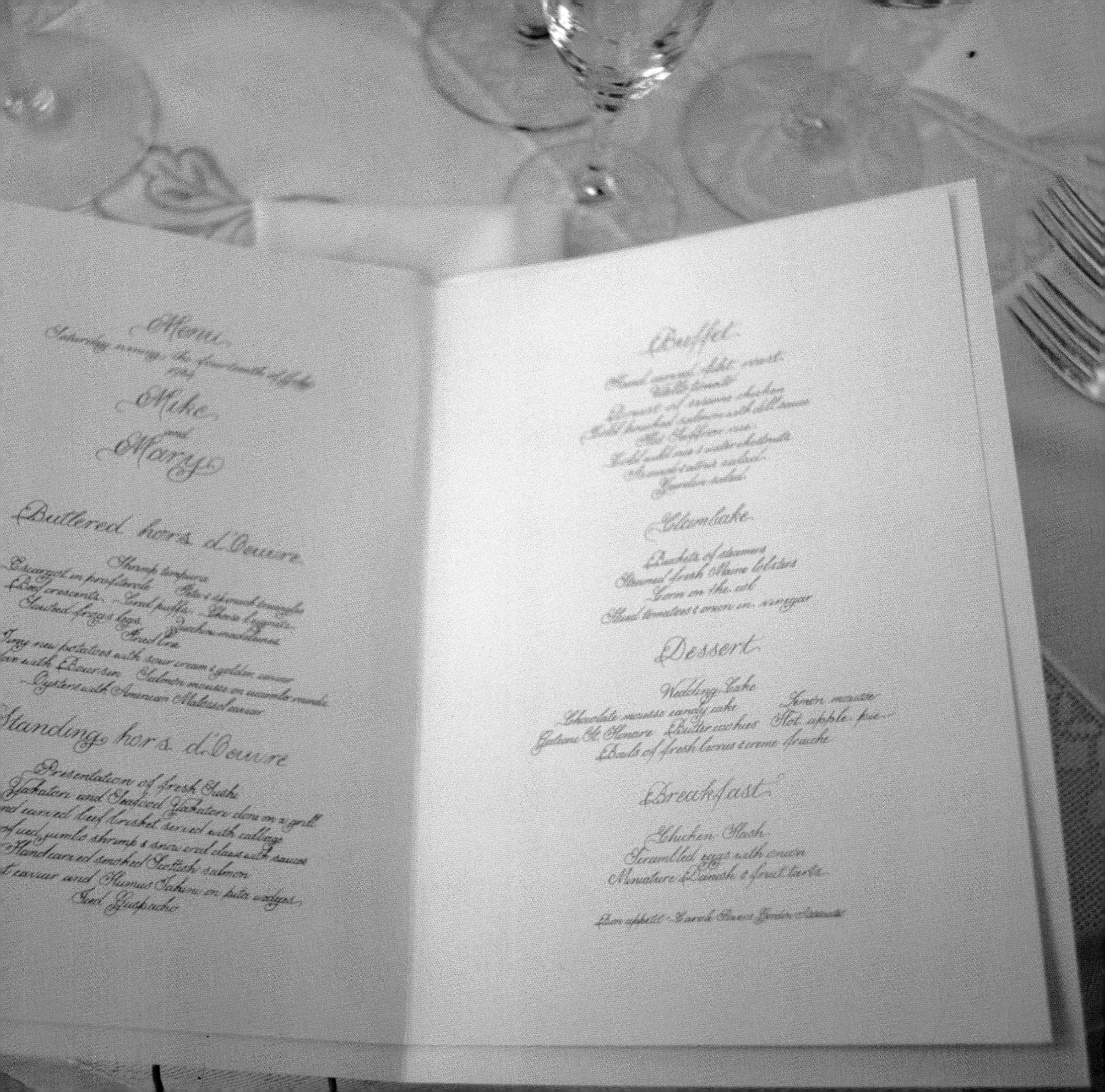

Menu

Saturday evening, the fourteenth of September
1985

Mike

and

Mary

Buttered hors d'Oeuvre

Shrimp tempura

Escargot in profiterole — Pâté skewered triangles
Beef crescents — Crab puffs — Cheese baguette
Seafood frogs legs — Chicken medallions
Fried brie

Tiny new potatoes with sour cream & golden caviar
Brie with Boursin — Salmon mousse on cucumber rounds
Oysters with American Malossol caviar

Standing hors d'Oeuvre

Presentation of fresh Sushi
Yakatori and Seafood Yakatori done on a grill
Handcarved beef brisket served with cabbage
Fried jumbo shrimp & snow crab claws with sauces
Handcarved smoked Scottish salmon
with caviar and Hummus Tahini on pita wedges
Iced Gazpacho

Buffet

Hand carved filet roast
Veal filet roast
Breast of savoria chicken
Filet broached salmon with dill sauce
Flat Shelltow rice
Wild wild rice & water chestnuts
Steamed entree cocktail
Garden salad

Clambake

Buckets of steamers
Steamed fresh Maine lobsters
Corn on the cob
Sliced tomatoes & onion in vinegar

Dessert

Wedding Cake
Chocolate mousse candy cake   Lemon mousse
Gateau St. Honore   Butter cookies   Hot apple pie
Bowls of fresh berries & creme fraiche

Breakfast

Chicken Hash
Scrambled eggs with onion
Miniature Danish & fruit tarts

Bon appetit — Carole Peace Gordon, Sarasota

formed and more educated in the decorative arts than her predecessors, and it shows in weddings. Sometime in the early seventies, it registered on the national consciousness that understanding beauty was in large part taking things at face value. The interest in urban restoration, the popularity of arts and crafts, the fact that the Cooper-Hewitt Museum now has master's and doctorate programs in the decorative arts, with equal numbers of male and female candidates, all attest to this trend. To me, the success of my first book, *Entertaining*, says that people are paying attention to details and are confident about expressing themselves in their own way. Taking pride in a table setting, thinking it not frivolous but expressive, also means taking pride in a wedding dress, bouquet, or cake, as an extension of yourself. Pride in these details reflects an affection for the simple rhythms of life, which are not trivial at all. So many people have forgotten but are rediscovering the satisfaction of planting a garden, decorating a house, planning a wedding, and finding them important forms of expression. The end result is liberating, for it means that you will wear the white linen suit of your dreams (because you are a career woman and love wide lapels and also forties movies), or will serve hot dogs or tempura, or use an old ice bucket for a flower vase, because it suits you and pleases you. And because it is your day, others will be pleased at this willful choice, too. The wedding stories here are full of such decisions, which, in small and large ways, added up to happy events.

There are smaller considerations that con-

tribute to style, too. In the weddings I have attended, it has often been thoughtfulness that played a part in the way a wedding unfolded, such as Meg Hester's decision to dance immediately so that others would not have to wait around ceremoniously. In the most stately and

ABOVE: Reflected in a windowpane is the main glass conservatory of the Bronx Botanical Garden, where the Hester wedding took place. OPPOSITE: Musicians greet Sophie Desmarais and her new husband at their reception at the Museum of Fine Arts in Montreal.

high-powered of weddings, Madame Jacqueline Desmarais, in Montreal, made sure that the gypsy violinist serenaded every table with equal force, spent a disproportionate amount of time on seating arrangements to ensure lively matches, and provided floor cushions for late-night respite. Small touches—trays of champagne lining an entrance path, a cocktail table placed at a central location to guarantee conviviality, corsages and boutonnieres for each guest at a small wedding—these were all important grace notes in a celebration.

The excitement of weddings is in vogue. Wedding statistics are up, confidence in the institution of marriage is up. Everyone seems agreed that a wedding is a time for a big effort, for doing things in an idealistic, energetic, and individualistic way. If not, it may be the moment to slip away, to elope to old Quebec or Venice, and expend efforts on a gala celebration later. But as the experienced know, weddings are wonderful affairs, poignant human dramas. Each one stands alone, because there is always something unpredictable that hangs on in memory, often something small but significant that celebrates the way human beings are—a group of young children dancing by themselves on a bandstand; unexpected tears from a bride; a garden of flowers suddenly caught in a celestial light. A wedding is a microcosm of human affairs, the commercial and the ritualistic, the dreamy and the fashionable, but, in the end, it is a drama of two people, with all their ideas and fantasies, celebrating the continuum of life.

The Dairy in Central Park

Kathryn GarDianos and George Furlan

Even to the most world-wise of New Yorkers, the Dairy in Central Park is a small wonder, a surprising bit of nineteenth-century whimsy tucked away in the green oasis that sprawls at the heart of their fast, tall city. Though located only several minutes' walk north of Fifty-ninth Street, this gingerbread cottage, built in 1870 as a milk dispensary for the young and elderly, is as far removed from the Manhattan streetscape as Hansel and Gretel's house. An unabashed romanticism is spelled out in its gables and fretwork, its porch sheltered by lacy arches, its setting on a quiet knoll under lofty pines. Park-goers catching a first sight of the landmark have been known to rub their eyes in disbelief.

On most days, the Dairy, which has recently been renovated as an exhibition space by the Parks Depart-

ment, is closed by dusk. But on June 3, 1984, as the sun went down, its lights came up dramatically, and when a crescent moon rose in the sky, it found a place directly above the illuminated tower, making a magical scene in the dark park. Late joggers were drawn to peer into the high, arched windows of the Dairy, where lights, voices, music, and a generous joy spilled out of the cottage. The spectacle inside had a storybook quality: a wedding scene, with familiar elements—a happy bride in white, a proud groom in a tux, a cake on a pedestal—and yet more vivid, more animated than the traditional. Indeed, framed as it was in Victoriana, the scene looked like a unique bit of folklore, unmistakably modern, and yet as charmed as something from the past. Flowers grew everywhere: in window boxes, in baskets, on tables, and in lapels—delicate blushing shades of violet, peach, and rose. A cold feast was laid upon a long table, around which a parade of people lingered: young men and women, wearing long wide-cut jackets, vintage dresses, big hats cast at stylish angles, mingling with an older generation dressed in more somber European fashions. Around the perimeter of the room, and outside on the porch, too, were small round tables, draped in pastels, where convivial groups were illuminated by candlelight. At center, a band played funk rock, as its leader sang out in a high falsetto voice. When the music turned Greek, the dancers broke into a circle, and the groom,

PRECEDING PAGES, LEFT: Hidden in a verdant hollow next to the Central Park Zoo is a charming little cottage known as the Dairy. RIGHT: George Furlan escorts his lovely bride Kathryn GarDianos down a path toward their wedding reception.

ABOVE: An openwork basket filled with a profusion of stock, roses, lilacs, and freesia.
BELOW: I offered my help as flower arranger.

BELOW: Shane Kennedy makes one of the centerpieces for the dinner tables, using lilacs, stock, and sweet peas.

holding a napkin in his mouth, improvised bold, high-sweeping steps. The bride, tiny, dark, and animated, took his hand and beamed.

"It was a great party," the bride, Kathy GarDianos, now Mrs. George Furlan, says with a smile that collects around big deep dimples. "We didn't want a traditional wedding—a receiving line, dinner on a dais—so we planned a party, in our own style. And I think everyone enjoyed themselves because they just came to our party."

It was inevitable that "style" would be key at this wedding party, for both the bride and groom are successful young fashion designers, with a sure sense of their own aesthetics. Since their student days together at the Fashion Institute of Technology, George first established himself as a designer of textiles for Jeffrey Banks menswear and now is a menswear designer at Alfred Surf, and Kathy, after several years in womenswear at Bill Blass, has recently begun designing her own collection of young evening wear, soft and drapy, inspired by her love of Art Deco. "The twenties' style is so simple it is still modern today," she commented. Not surprisingly, the essential elements of Art Deco were in evidence in all of the wedding plans.

To a passerby the GarDianos wedding just seemed to happen that night in the park. Its organization seemed spontaneous, even happenstance. There were no orderly notebooks and files, no mastermind coordinators, no meticulous blueprints—only a fixed date three months off; a guest list of 130; two traditional families, one Greek, one Italian, to be taken into consideration; a well-defined set of personal aesthetics; and a sense of fun. When they first decided to marry, Kathy and George had planned to elope to Venice. Then, realizing

ABOVE AND BELOW: Atop the fretwork balustrades, wicker baskets filled with Gerbera daisies, begonias, and impatiens are the bride's version of window boxes.

their families' desire to be part of the event, they began to formulate ideas nearer home. "George thought about a Circle Line cruise around Manhattan, then investigated lofts and catering places in Manhattan. Meanwhile, my family, who is Greek, was researching big halls with flocked wallpaper in Sheepshead Bay. I wanted a country wedding though, and looked at hotels and old mansions in Westchester County, which seemed inconvenient and somehow inappropriate. We had heard of the Dairy because Perry Ellis had done some fashion shows there, but we had never seen it.

The day of our first visit was dark and rainy. It was early spring—mud season, no greenery—and the Dairy was only a bare shell, but I immediately saw it as an enchanted rustic cottage. I had just been to London, on a buying trip, and I had been very affected by the English-garden mentality—all those quaint streets spilling over with flowers and plants. I thought: I'll make it look like an English garden."

In her mind's eye, Kathy had composed a dreamy pastel garden, but it was with Jody Thompson Kennedy, a free-lance floral designer at *House Beautiful,* who educated her

A guest in straw bonnet and antique dress looks perfectly at home in the Victorian setting of the Dairy.

The hand-beaded antique white skirt of Kathryn's tea-length wedding dress falls gracefully toward her silk slippers.

White-shirted waiters, lining the path to the reception, serve champagne in flute glasses.

with books of flowers, that she found her exact color palette of washed shades of cream, peach, rose, purple, and yellow, and identified the blooms she wanted—impatiens, begonias, primroses, petunias, African Gerbera daisies. To convey a true sense of garden, Jody searched early-morning markets in the flower district for live plants that could "grow" in hanging baskets and window boxes, all spray-painted a creamy white. For full effect, table linens were conceived in the same palette, and when Kathy couldn't find the right rental fabrics, she arranged for her sample maker to cut twenty tablecloths and two hundred napkins out of the pale linen left over from her spring collection.

On that plucky trip to London, Kathy had found her wedding dress, too, as much a factor of circumstance as the table linens. She had already made a sketch of her dream dress for her seamstress, but then, wandering on Fulham Road, a chic quarter where all the wedding boutiques displayed dresses like Princess Di's, she saw its incarnation—tea length, with dropped waist, hand-beaded in antique white. To this she added a skull cap, hand-beaded, to which she attached a silk tulle veil decorated with pearls, and threw away a hat she had bought prematurely in Paris. Kathy, who as a size four had long before resorted to sewing her own clothes, proceeded to make a dress for her maid of honor, taking the idea of a man's

dinner jacket from the twenties and elongating it in silver silk charmeuse and setting it off with a period hat, worn atilt. For her mother she made a dress in silver-gray silk, with a hand-beading of swirls, like big petals, on the shoulders. Both dresses articulated her passion for a bygone era, and elaborated her now-established theme.

With the bridal party dressed in silver and cream, George determined to make his trousers from gray morning fabric, and pair them with a vintage white jacket. In the end, however, he settled for an alternative period look, achieved with an oversized black cotton tuxedo from Italy, worn with an antique shirt with a piqué bib and wing collar, and a silver jacquard tie. George engaged Rinaldo, a Brazilian funk-rock street musician he had met playing on Seventh Avenue, for the dance music at the reception. But when the first family argument erupted over his choice—forecasting the importance the dancing would play in their wedding festivities—George decided to tape other music—Greek for Kathy's family, who had been hinting about a Greek band, and early Motown and New Wave for friends, to supplement Rinaldo's high-powered samba. Surrendering to sentiment, he and Kathy agreed that their actor friend Michael Leslie would sing "their" song, "My Funny Valentine," for "their" dance.

Invariably, one decision led to another, suggesting and imposing ideas. Kathy's garden-esque color palette was extended to include the invitations, which she had printed on pastel rice paper; when she received them and thought them too plain, she bought a silver-ink pen and added a decorative floral motif. (She had printed the RSVP on Art Deco postcards to facilitate responses.) Because the Dairy lacked a kitchen and proscribed heating devices, the supper would have to be cold, and Kathy began to look for adaptable caterers. Word of mouth led to Sara Foster, a young, newly independent caterer and food stylist in Greenwich, Connecticut, whose sample menu touched off their imagination, notably because of her innocent inclusion of stuffed grape leaves and leg of lamb—foods to bring relieved joy to the Greek contingent. As neither Kathy nor George were passionately involved eaters, Sara was left to her own artful devices (although George requested a tortellini salad, homage to his roots and his favorite dish). Sara's affinity for fresh, light "supper" food, and her talent for graceful innovation, were proven perfectly suited to the young couple's

Black lacquer trays of hors d'oeuvres are passed among the guests.

vision of a resplendent but informal summer feast, and the buffet was as eclectic and spirited as the crowd that gathered the night of the wedding. The grape leaves, in a new incarnation, were stuffed with grapefruit, rice, and duck breast marinated in a walnut vinaigrette; the lamb, trimmed and shaped to a delicate roll, was filled with rosemary and raisins; the tortellini salad garnished with proscuitto. The wedding cake, subcontracted by Sara to pastry chef Jane Stacey, was an original confection of Kathy's favorite combination of tastes—a dark chocolate cake, with a raspberry–Grand Marnier-laced filling, frosted with white chocolate and decorated with curls and leaves of chocolate. ("My mother was afraid chocolate

brought bad luck, though," Kathy remembers.) George's father was proud to choose the wine for the meal, a Pinot Grigio Santa Marguerita. Kathy, who has a diminutive appetite, had promised herself that she would eat a lot that night—unlike the traditional bride, who forgets to—and she did; George, in his strongest wedding memories, conjures up the buffet table in full color.

The location of the Dairy also posed the problem of transportation. With limited parking on site (and a permit required for each vehicle), and the uneasiness many people suffer in the park at night, it was important to escort guests directly to the Dairy. When hansom cabs (the obvious period choice) proved too expensive and difficult to find, and the union rules too stringent (they had to tour the whole park before depositing passengers at the Dairy), a limousine was hired to shuttle guests from a Fifty-ninth Street drop-off and back. As for the wedding couple's trip from church to reception, a silver Bentley was *de rigeur,* dictated by F. Scott Fitzgerald and the color scheme.

The week before a wedding is alternately easygoing and euphoric, peripatetic and pressured. Kathy's wedding dress had finally arrived from London. George had decided to make ties for the reception waiters out of silver-striped black silk—"We got a little crazy"—a finishing touch he had yet to finish. Kathy scrutinized the guest list, composed of their conservative families and their artistic friends, white and black, gay and straight, flamboyant, sensitive, and modern, and said, "How are they all going to get along?" On Thursday night, bachelor dinner night, George had a quiet glass of champagne with a few friends, and was presented with a beautiful tie piece by his best man. Friday night, re-

LEFT: The bride and groom dancing a traditional Greek wedding dance. OPPOSITE: With a crescent moon above and soft candlelight below, the Dairy seems enchanted.

hearsal dinner night, Kathy took her godparents out for a lobster dinner. (George was still working on the ties, and looking for wedding shoes, and his flowers.)

The wedding day dawned wet and gray. Kathy had tears in her eyes all morning, as the telephone rang hourly with a worried George on the other end. By three o'clock, however, the rain had ended, leaving the park newly washed and smelling sweet. A friend's gift of a salon coiffeur to do Kathy's hair, however, had not materialized on time, and Kathy, in pink bathrobe and wet hair, paced until his arrival at four, mourning the elegant dressing scene she had planned to photograph at a beautiful Art Deco vanity, her most recent birthday present from George. A few minutes past five o'clock, when the religious ceremony had been scheduled to begin, George telephoned to say

that he was at the church and had already been sent down the aisle to the altar and been recalled. At five-twenty, the GarDianos party, in its crosstown run from Kathy's apartment on the Upper West Side, encountered a boisterous parade on Fifth Avenue. At five-forty, Kathy GarDianos entered the old domed Greek Orthodox Cathedral at Seventy-fourth Street and First Avenue where she and George Furlan exchanged vows and crowns and were wedded in the age-old manner.

For the rest of the evening of June 3, a splendid serendipity seemed to hold sway. En route to the Dairy, sipping champagne in their Bentley, Kathy and George spied an Art Deco building in their neighborhood in the midst of renovation, stopped the car to admire it, and, on a whim, dispatched their photographer, with a twenty-dollar bill, to ask the

doorman if they could take some pictures in the lobby. "For both practical and personal reasons, I had dismissed the idea of formal wedding portraits. But the building in that late-afternoon light reminded me of Lalique glass," Kathy recounts. "The lobby was fanciful, and we posed on old marble benches, shot several rolls of film, and then piled back into the car and continued on our way." In the park, George and Kathy strolled to the Dairy like Sunday promenaders of an earlier day, and near the site, found a fanfare of waiters lining their path, bearing trays of champagne, their formal tux shirts gleaming, their hair Tenaxed and glistening according to George's fondest wishes. As the Dairy filled with guests, their clothing created a swirl of romantic color and their collective spirits established a festive and informal mood. There were many hats and dresses designed by Kathy in the crowd. A dear friend arrived late, making apologies for the fact that he had been finishing the jacket on his back. The dance music began early, and as a few elegant hors d'oeuvres were passed (Sara favored a choice few over a voluminous, appetite-diminishing assortment), the group flowed in and out and around, unhampered by a fixed timetable or agenda. Dinner was laid without great ceremony, to avoid a sudden shift of mood and a long queue, and was served casually for hours. When the Greek music was introduced, the momentum of the reception intensified; the energy of Kathy's family spread like a happy contagion; and George danced like a native. "I invented the custom of dancing with a napkin in your mouth," Kathy admitted, "but George looked great. It seems very telling that in most of the wedding pictures I have my dress hitched up to dance."

As night fell, the magic of the Dairy became apparent. Far away, the lights of the metropolis came up on Fifth and Central Park South and Central Park West, like distant corridors of tiny Christmas lights to surround and insulate the scene. Nestled in its isolation in the woods, the Dairy felt small and private and quite enchanted. The security men provided by the Parks Department gently warded off the few curious souls who

came to investigate the merriment; before the evening's end, at midnight, according to park rules, all security men, waiters, and guests were dancing.

The GarDianos wedding lingers on in memory, for it suited its principals to perfection and sparkled with originality. Kathy and George had a fresh approach, to which they re-

mained committed, down to the thank-you notes, which Kathy wrote on copies of a photograph of their procession down the path to the Dairy. To have found the country in the city, the modernity in the old-fashioned, the folklore in the New Wave was a feat of personal vision, with a generous touch of invention and ambition. "Somehow we found a way to do exactly what we wanted to," is Kathy's explanation of their wedding preparations. Inevitably, there were adjustments to be made to their initial budget. The flowers, unexpectedly, were their largest expense, not the liquor, which comprised only wine, beer, and champagne. In many instances, costs were modified by their own involvement, and that of friends, in the work of the wedding, which of course added to its personality. The Furlans, for example, have a wonderful but idiosyncratic folio of wedding pictures, for the photographer, who was a friend of a friend and works in fashion, involuntarily produced a study of the beautiful dresses and visual effects of the day. And although the church service remains a blur to them—George retains only a mental picture of walking around the altar three times in a traditional ritual—there is a Betamax videotape of the ceremony, executed by a friend "with a lot of floor and ceiling shots," to refresh their memory.

Montreal sparkles in the fall, a city of many facets, with its clean new skyscrapers, its cobbled quaint old quarters, its sprawling green McGill campus, its chic couturier shops and austere *antiquaires,* its royal mountain on top and the great St. Lawrence at base. Sophisticated, chic, modern, it is also relaxed, historic, warm-hearted. Montreal is one of those big worldly cities that feels small and accessible, like a hometown, whose moods are almost visible and rhythms almost audible. And within minutes of arrival there during the first week of September 1984, it was easy to feel a special excitement in the air. It was bigger than that seasonal crackling of energy that comes upon cities in the fall, for that week was seeing a remarkable confluence of important, even historic events, and the city

Montreal Grand Bal

———

Sophie Desmarais
and
Michel Kaine

was abuzz with news of it all: tickets for the first local Michael Jackson concert had gone on sale; Jesse Jackson was in town; the pope was arriving in a matter of days; Brian Mulroney, that very Tuesday, had swept the Conservatives into power; and on Saturday night the eighth, Sophie Desmarais, youngest daughter of one of Canada's most powerful and prestigious families, was to be married to Michel Kaine at the Basilica of Notre Dame, and feted at the Museum of Fine Arts. All these happenings seemed part of the supreme sense of well-being afoot in Montreal. A cab driver explained it easily: "Everyone knows the Desmaraises—they're like the Kennedys— rich, powerful, young, beautiful. Paul Desmarais fishes with Trudeau and Mulroney. This is a little like a state wedding for us. Important people are arriving

PRECEDING PAGES, LEFT: Sophie's attendants dressed in white silk taffeta with teal blue sashes and hair bows. Each carried a large spray of rubrum lilies. RIGHT: The Museum of Fine Arts silhouetted against a backdrop of September cumulus clouds. LEFT: The family retainers dressed in their best uniforms await the arrival of Sophie and Michel. RIGHT: The grand staircase of the Museum of Fine Arts.

from all over the world, and the papers say it will be Canada's wedding of the century."

It is natural for townspeople to feel proprietary about their public figures, because they are emblems and examples, and their lives, when they open to public inspection, have a fairytale quality. Long before it actually occurred, and long after it ended, the Desmarais wedding held Montreal's fancy. The city's most prominent professionals were involved in its planning—caterers, couturiers, florists, theatrical designers—and in the weeks immediately prior to the wedding, the cathedral and the Museum of Fine Arts, both public landmarks, were being readied for the festivities. At the museum, where a very popular Bouguereau exhibition was in progress, any art patron could peer beyond the heroic tableaux to witness the gradual transformation of the central halls into an extravagant setting for a *grand bal.*

The man responsible for the complete design of the wedding was Jean-François Daigre, a Parisian who is the partner of preeminent interior designer Valerian Rybar, and who has been described as the most talented party designer in the world, with Rothschild and Louvre balls to his credit. At the museum Daigre, cool, nattily dressed, and a little forbidding, was most often stationed upstairs, center-front, surveying the scene critically.

"This will not be a wedding atmosphere," he said. "The traditional French wedding is a garden party, but this will be a *fête.* Jackie, Sophie's mother, had a vision from *La Traviata,* and I was directly inspired by the salon of the Empress Josephine at Malmaison. In their specifics, however, my design decisions were based on the personality of the Desmarais family—strong, traditional, neither wild nor extravagant. They wanted something lasting, and a warm color, so I thought of orange and

red and gold (everyone loves gold) and pure Empire. With this concept in hand, I then had to go with the structure of the museum itself. Jackie led the way, which involved sophisticated thinking." Daigre moved through the reception space, which, for him, began at the base of the flight of steps outside the museum, and entered the wide double front door, where a grand central staircase swept upward to a wide courtyard landing overlooking the ground floor. Hors d'oeuvres and drinks were to be served here, conceding later to an orchestra and dancing and cake cutting. For dinner, guests would proceed downstairs by way of a wide graceful back stairway into three lofty rooms. And then, in the wee hours of the morning, the cavernous corridor outside these rooms would be set with a champagne buffet.

In Daigre's mind, the most important feature of this setting was the imperial front staircase, for it would provide the first impres-

CLOCKWISE FROM THE LEFT: Chefs preparing the dessert of chocolate-coated profiteroles; a fan handpainted with "Sophie" and "Michel"; a mirror from the museum's collection reflects the immaculate and organized temporary kitchen; violin cases stored for the evening in one of the painting galleries.

sion and, in one grand perspective, establish the mood of the evening. Architecturally, it commanded a large pivotal space that could not be wasted on mere effect, and was central to his design, which was based on the ennobling effects of symmetry. Consequently, Daigre used the staircase like a *coup de théâtre,* and announced his design at the door. In one ascending glance, his essential elements were stated: a rich persimmon carpet, hand-painted with a gold classical motif, which covered the stairs and led the eye up to the landing, where a pair of statuesque golden candelabra, set with bouquets of flowers, framed the back wall, which was hung with swagged deep-orange velour, and at center affixed with a large mirrored wreath etched with MS, for Michel and Sophie, entwined in ornate script. The effect of this one panorama was transporting—even "*choquant,*" according to Daigre.

On Friday afternoon and evening, the scene at the museum was reminiscent of the preparations for a medieval pageant, with small guilds working away feverishly at their artistic tasks. The wedding team was bigger and more specialized than usual, and more carefully orchestrated, as the magnitude of the event demanded. Upstairs, the theatrical decoration, directed by Marcel des Roches, under Daigre, was under way. Velvet was hung on the main walls, framed at intervals by Greek columns with pineapple finials, all sculpted out of

polyester mousse. Doorframes were being painted to match. The flower design firm Eric van Horn and Roberge wrapped the brass railings of an adjacent loggia area with glossy camellia and magnolia leaves, placed potted palms at corners, and began to position the other massive candelabra strategically. Downstairs, in a room filled with buckets of flowers, they made dozens of wreaths of magnolia leaves, and began to arrange orchids, lilies, roses, tulips, and ferns in the smaller candelabra that would adorn each table at dinner. A dozen pails of white calla lilies went unattended, for they were designated for the ends of the pews at the church. In the dining rooms, round white wooden tables and chairs were in place, and a mound of chair cushions, hand painted with the MS motif, continued to grow as groups of women hemmed away on the floor. At the back door, trucks unloaded cases of champagne, announcing their deliveries

Former Prime Minister Pierre Trudeau
arriving alone for the wedding at Notre Dame.
Onlookers clapped and bodyguards followed.

through a walkie-talkie before being cleared
by the security force.

Friday evening, while the museum preparations continued late into the night, Sophie
Desmarais and Michel Kaine, snug in a crowd
of 150 friends and family, were attending
their rehearsal dinner in the Salle Bonne Aven-
ture, an intimate nightclub in the Queen Elizabeth Hotel. By comparison to the wedding
celebration for 340, it was a small and closely
knit gathering. The evening featured perfor-
mances by the impersonator Jean Guy Moreau;
Robert Charlebois, a famous French Canadian
rock star; and Dinah Shore, a family friend
who flew in from California with her accompa-
nist and who had personally translated "Yours
Is My Heart Alone" into French to sing to the

bridal couple. Although Madame Desmarais, a one-time jazz singer with a rich, bluesy voice, did not perform, Sophie sang her own rendition of "I've Got a Crush on You" to her father (and everyone cried), and Brian Mulroney, in a wonderful baritone, responded to the moment with "Paper Doll."

Saturday, the pitch at the museum was intense. Daigre's stage set was in order, majestic and opulent, the museum walls indistinguishable behind three thousand yards of draped, handpainted velvet; the feather-weight polyester-sculpted candelabra, for all appearances immense golden relics from French royalty, placed at dramatic posts. Yet his eye continued to scrutinize the scene nervously, while his attention focused on small crucial details, like ensuring the timely lighting of candles in the candelabra, which would provide the only illumination at the reception.

Downstairs, handlettered cards were arranged before place settings by a social secretary, following elaborate blueprints. The kitchen was in a frenzy, with Réné Pancalla, a popular Montreal caterer, flying about like a madman, punctuating his preparations with bellows of alarm. Pancalla was organizing a multitude of elaborate hot and cold hors d'oeuvres and the champagne buffet, while the Desmaraises' young provincial French chef, Roger Duret, planned dinner, founding his menu on his own creative impulses and dishes dear to the family: artichokes stuffed with lobster, a duck casserole fashioned into a crown and called Pompadour de Caneton, vegetables from the Malbèque region of the Desmaraises'

Serge Sénécal and Réal Bastien adjust the ruffled tulle veil of Sophie before she walks down the aisle of the main nave of the basilica.

country house, and Profitéroles Sophie for dessert.

By five o'clock, the Ritz Carlton Hotel was a press photographer's paradise, with important people, in important clothes, marching into limousines two by two. They made even grander appearances at the church, where a crowd of hundreds, behind police lines, applauded celebrities, withholding their loudest reception until the arrival of Trudeau and Mulroney, who was making his first public appearance since his election. Inside, Canada's largest and most beautiful cathedral was serene, decorated only with a new carpet in celestial blue to match the painted vaulted ceiling and the large stained-glass window above the altar. Tall lilies were positioned like

Paul Desmarais escorts a veiled Sophie up the crowded sidewalks outside the cathedral.

royal guards on the aisle. "The church is a neo-Gothic *folie*," Daigre had explained earlier, "extravagant in itself, and besides, we had to be careful, for the pope arrives here on Tuesday. All traditions are being respected; we will roll out a white carpet for the bride to walk on, a beautiful ritual."

From the balcony, Les Petits Chanteurs de Mont-Royal, with their ethereal boy-soprano voices, sang the words of Lohengrin's wedding march in the original German as Sophie Desmarais, dressed in a confection of dotted swiss, trailed by many, many yards of tulle, floated down the aisle on the arm of her father to meet Michel Kaine. At the altar, dwarfed by the grandeur of the church, bathed in the light necessary for video cameras, the amplified voice of the priest bid welcome in French and in English to the international audience. A traditional French Catholic *messe de mariage* was then celebrated, accompanied during the signing of the registry by Bach's "Magnificat," and then Mozart's "Laudate Dominum" and Verdi's "Ave Maria." The priest's formalities concluded with a "*Si vous voulez embrassez . . .*" which received a spontaneous round of applause. Upon exodus, the swelling crowd outside renewed their affectionate cheers.

At six o'clock, Jean-François Daigre and his chief assistant, Guy van de Hove, were positioned inside the front door of the museum like expectant children. Opposite them, three young chambermaids from the Desmarais home, who had been assigned responsibility for the coatroom in order to allow them full view of the festivities, whispered excitedly. Singing violins from the dozen musicians lin-

Sophie being escorted down the aisle of the basilica by her father.

ing the stairs filled the hall. When Sophie and Michel appeared in the doorway, and Sophie's eyes swept over the decorations and then filled with tears, Daigre bowed his head in gratification. "That's all I wanted to see," he said. "It is like theater, and it worked."

As the Desmarais family greeted the last of the guests on the receiving line, and then retreated downstairs for a portrait session with the photographer, stealing a few warm moments en route to hug their cook and maids, the kitchen moved into high gear. A fleet of artichokes were already arrayed on the long work tables, and Roger Duret began to unmold his duck, while René Pancalla dispatched waitresses in frilly uniforms with

silver trays of hors d'oeuvres, "No, no, *no,*" the taskmaster shouted time and again, "where are your napkins? That tray is not right!"

As the candelabra were lit in the darkened dining rooms, and as they cast their arclights down on the array of wineglasses on the tables and up through their flowery headdresses to create magic on the ceiling, another more intimate drama began. Gypsy violinists played from the back landing as the wedding party swept down to dinner, two by two in amused formality, to set in motion a long noisy feast. The violinists then circulated between rooms, focusing wistful melodies on heads of state and college friends alike, and diminished their attentions only when Bill Harrington's orchestra struck up above.

As is the wont with grand balls, the evening of September 8 did not seem to want to end. Brian Mulroney danced many times with his wife Mila. Dinah Shore danced many times with Pierre Trudeau. The Chinese ambassador danced with Jacqueline Desmarais. Couples settled down on cushions against the staircase to watch the show. At eleven o'clock, to an orchestral fanfare, a trio of chefs rolled out a monumental five-tiered, star-shaped Empire wedding cake for a ceremonial cutting. As Sophie recounts, "The chefs looked so proud and proper in their high starched hats. Mama apparently whispered to me, 'Remember, it's a fake,' but I didn't hear. I put my hand on Michel's wrist as you're supposed to do; we smiled and cut together, but it resisted, and I said to Michel, 'My God, it's stale!' The knife was stuck there like King Arthur's sword and everyone had to laugh, for the cake was Styro-

LEFT: Prime Minister Brian Mulroney and his beautiful wife Mila arrive at the museum for the reception. BELOW: Violinists play triumphant, joyous music as guests arrive. RIGHT: Suzy Knickerbocker and Estée Lauder gather with friends for the reception.

foam and its edible twin was already cut, ready in the wings for serving to the guests." Cake gave way to many more hours of dancing, and eventually, replenishment at a buffet table, laid with pâtés, hams, salads, scrambled eggs with Iranian caviar, brioches and marmalade, and giant strawberries, raspberries, and blackberries. Long after midnight and long after the sleepy departure of Sophie and Michel, guests wandered out of the museum only to find the street still filled with a band of well-wishers. "Vive Sophie, Vive Michel!" a tiny elderly woman with an Instamatic camera cried out at 2:30 A.M.

The Sunday morning edition of *La Presse* carried a front-page photograph of Sophie and Michel above the banner *"Un Mariage Princier pour Sophie Desmarais."* It had indeed been a regal wedding, involving superlatives—one of Canada's first families, Canada's largest and

most beautiful church, Canada's oldest museum—and drawing upon the most successful international professionals for its design, decoration, food, and music. Many hundreds of workers had contributed their skills, orchestrated by many distinguished subchefs, and at the top, by Jacqueline Desmarais, whose reputation as a master organizer and inspired party-giver was given its ultimate test. The decisions were sophisticated, the plans elaborate and carefully annotated in meticulous notebooks, the execution expensive. And yet in reviewing the eight months of preparation, there is one homey image that illuminates: that of Jacqueline and Sophie Desmarais sprawled together on a bed, planning and dreaming.

Sophie, a lithe, pretty, dark-haired twenty-four-year-old, whose clothes, gestures, and conversation reveal a secure sense of style and

self and an easy exuberance, still likes to talk about her wedding. And every time she goes home she takes a peek at her dress, which hangs in her mother's room. Her bonds to family remain strong and active: her introduction to Michel came from her brother Paul; after a honeymoon in Europe (where it rained every day), she and Michel joined her parents for a month's trip to China; upon their return, they moved into a new home in West Mount, above the city, near her parents and brothers and, in fact, next door to the house in which she was born. Michel is an engineer whose design for a new plastic manual water pump is being tested now in underdeveloped countries, and Sophie, who earned her B.A. in foreign languages (she speaks five) is contemplating a business degree and a career at *La Presse*, one of the newspapers owned by her father.

"When I think back on the wedding, I remember concentrating very hard to be relaxed at the church; I remember walking up the stairs to the museum and seeing the carpet leading up to our monogram—*cela m'a touché au coeur*—and [laughing], I remember cutting the wedding cake. I knew what the wedding would be like because I had planned it with Mama and seen many of the details but...I didn't really know."

"The idea of the museum was improbable," Madame Desmarais said, "because it had never been done, and the Bouguereau exhibit was scheduled. But the director was impressed by our blueprints for the party and agreed to let the decorators work at night. People will be curious and it will be fun, I pointed out, and as it happened, it all worked together like a positive force."

Sophie had fantasized about her wedding and her wedding dress since she was twelve years old—about the age she first met Serge Sénécal and Réal Bastien, her latter-day couturiers. Early the morning after her engagement was announced in January, she knocked on their door and described her dress to them: dotted swiss, tiny satin bows at the elbow, a long detachable train, billows of material (as it turned out, 120 meters in all). Within a matter of months, Serge and Réal had also made the six white taffeta, turquoise-sashed bridesmaids' dresses and a long amethyst taffeta gown for the mother of the bride. In March, Sophie and her mother spent several weeks in Paris assembling her trousseau, and, in June, shopped in New York for the house. Over the summer, they fussed over the details of the dinner, meeting with the fastidious cake-master M. Caban of the Patisserie de Gasgogne more often than with the couturier. ("He always came dressed up in his suit and bowler

ABOVE: Sophie and Michel make their appearance at the top of the staircase to invite guests to dinner. BELOW: Elizabeth Hawes taking notes on the wedding for her text. OPPOSITE: Carefully placed candelabra, votive candles, and soft ethereal flower arrangements on the tables transform the museum into a more intimate setting.

hat. 'A heart shape in chocolate,' he'd say. 'Well, not exactly,' we'd say. And then he'd come back.")

Madame Desmarais admits to being very organized; she also had supreme confidence in the genius of Jean-François Daigre, who, with Valerian Rybar, had already decorated their new Palm Beach house and masterminded ambitious soirées there. For her, the most difficult task of the wedding turned out to be the seating arrangements at dinner, which had to be sensitive to the diverse personalities, nationalities, egos, and political alignments in attendance. The invitations were completed by June, but up until the last moment, she and Sophie were tinkering with their charts, sorting out names, and reflecting. Madame recalls, "We had all the different prime ministers, victors and losers, the Chinese ambassador who didn't speak either English or French, and the dilemma of the different rooms. In the end, we put all the young people off in the third room because they would have more fun; all the corporate people and good friends in the second room because they'd understand; and all the heads of state in the first room. It worked out beautifully."

The "mistakes" of the Desmarais wedding seem inconsequential in light of its triumphs. "The lilies in the church were too high," Madame says, slightly distressed. "They looked like lovely soldiers, but you couldn't see around them. And I was furious at the video crew, coming into the cathedral with their harsh lights, after we had carefully planned the gentle illumination of thousands of votive candles. In the video, all you hear is my saying, 'Turn those things off!' And they had promised to wear tuxes. But then Sophie has seen the tape at least twenty-five times, and I show it to everyone who visits us."

Organization

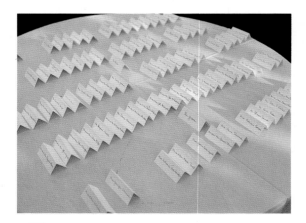

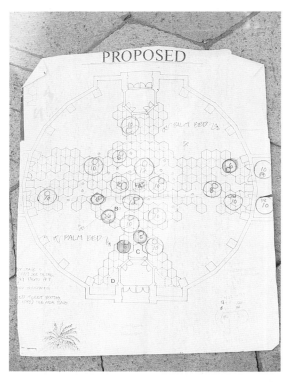

Sometimes when I see the bride and groom, bridesmaids and grooms-men, mothers and fathers posing serenely under a mellow old maple tree for the official postwedding photographs, I think of other significant portraits, too. One would assemble a larger group, dressed in a variety of work clothes, and would include the engraver of invitations (and perhaps the stationery store salesperson), the wedding dress designer (and a row of seamstresses), a shoe salesman, the hotel (or club or restaurant or rental space) manager, the caterer (and a dozen cooks in aprons), the florist, the tent man and helpers, the photographer, the judge or clergyman (and organist), the bandleader and members of the band, the limousine and chauffeur, and possibly a dozen other specialists (the lighting man, the video crew, the landscaper, the hairdresser and makeup person, the carpenter, etc.)—a veritable theatrical crew. Another photograph might be a landscape of sorts, shot with slow film like those studies of the Place de la Concorde at night that swirl with the time-exposed taillights of traffic, and it would show all the steps taken to bring a wedding into existence. These photographs, in effect, would be angles on the organization of a wedding, all that happens before the event actually takes place.

Good organization is crucial to the success of a wedding; not only can it guarantee its grace and individuality, but it can also moderate the anxiety and pressure that come with

For this country wedding, we had to deal with complex logistical problems—no convenient source of water, no refrigeration, no on-sight cooking equipment, and only portable sanitary facilities.

PRECEDING PAGES, LEFT: The place cards for dinner seating at Meg Hester's wedding reception are lined up in alphabetical order. MIDDLE: A floor plan makes the placement of tables easier and allows one to move tables around on paper, rather than physically, until the plan is complete and satisfactory. RIGHT: The mother of the bride used alphabetical lists of the guests and tacked them onto the barn doors. Each name was followed by a table number assignment. FAR RIGHT: I often use cordless telephones, walkie-talkies, loudspeakers, and even a hand-held horn to issue instructions and communicate with workers when setting up a party.

We have had to learn how to work around photographers and video crews.

the day. There are exceptions to the rule—the last-minute bride who, with a flurry of telephone calls, seems to will a perfect wedding into existence; the mother of the bride who operates on instinct rather than foresight and throws together, here and there, like bits of a patchwork quilt, the ingredients of a model wedding. But for most people, a well-laid structure is essential; the number of wedding planning books in the library, the existence of an industry founded to advise and coordinate brides, and even the checklists published every month in brides' magazines all attest to that fact.

The planning of a wedding can take a month or a year, and whatever time is allotted is likely to be filled, for planning, like a ground cover, always seems to claim available space. Five or six months is the usual time frame, although a year's advance reservation may be necessary for popular clubs and bandleaders on Saturdays in June or September, and a month's time may suffice for a small event given flexibility about rentals and invention with invitations. Even a small wedding, however, has so many ingredients to consider and coordinate that it has to be conceived, produced, and directed in the spirit of a theatrical event.

Organization is ultimately coordination, and the exact method of organization depends on personality. One bride or mother of the bride may be comfortable with casual procedure, while another will mastermind her operations like a general attempting to make history. One will hire a crew of professionals and delegate all but supervisory responsibilities, while another will take pride in deciding and articulating every detail herself. Etiquette, fashion, experience, ambition, and imagination serve variously as guiding stars.

The trend today is to the do-it-yourself wedding, yet do-it-yourself describes the spirit as much as the hard labor. It means personal interest and input, a handmade contribution, a guiding aesthetic, and for a select few, the literal elevation of a tent or construction of a bandstand. The dictates of personal expression have to a large degree supplanted those of etiquette, although the times are not rebellious, only thoughtful and informed. There are insecurities, of course, that accompany a first venture, and there are questions that terrify. But as with any first venture, one learns the terminology and the terrain, and then confidence grows, and the decisions are true, sensitive, and pleasureful.

It all starts quite simply and sweetly with the news of a forthcoming event. There is a wonderful moment of joy and pride and excitement, and then a flash of panic, a visionary flood of pending responsibilities that may wash out the first night's sleep. As Margot Olshan recounted to me, "I called my parents to tell them our news, and they were so happy for us. 'Ohhh, you're getting married,' they said, jubilantly, and then, midsentence, my mother's voice cracked, and she croaked out, 'You're getting married? We have to put on a wedding!' " Face to face with the reality of a wedding to plan, almost everyone suffers an attack of anxiety. And at this moment, perhaps the best response is to set out on a long walk, to think about all the beautiful weddings fixed in memory, to dream freely. For it is important, right from the beginning, to treat a wedding as a very personal event, and to take prideful note of who you are and what you want.

Soon enough, the mechanics of organization will take hold. They begin with the basics. A brides' magazine or one of the many planning

Bridal coordinator Flora Bryant offers last-minute instructions to Beth Gardella and John O'Connor.

books can provide an overview. A notebook, as simple and straightforward as a schoolboy's copybook, divided into categories by index tabs and headed with a table of contents, to which every bit of minutiae is committed, will chart your course. Notebook and lists are essential, for the humdrum list is a form of control, a visible log of the responsibilities and intentions in your head.

The primary list encompasses all the elements of a wedding. These are the dozens of ingredients, large and small, that have to be considered, elaborated according to your traditions and taste, executed according to your own timetable. Whereas etiquette books and brides' magazines set forth precise calendars to be followed, I have found that a larger logic and more personal rhythm animate most successful weddings. One buys the groom's present or the attendants' gifts when one sees something appealing and appropriate; these days, one mails wedding invitations anywhere from three to eight weeks ahead of time, depending on the season, or the size of the event, or the nature of the guest list. And sometimes, the right choice of musician surfaces unpredictably, from a random encounter in a jazz club or musical bar. In other words, with the flexibility of the times and the ascendance of personal expression, a precast or iron-clad timetable is inappropriate.

Answering the first basic questions—the date, time, place, size, and budget—establishes the basic structure of a wedding. With this foundation in place, you can address yourself to the aesthetics of the setting, and to the refreshments that will be served in that setting, thereby giving specific shape to the day. One decision quite naturally leads to another and decisions interlock. The hour will suggest a general menu, the menu, certain rentals,

which, in turn, will help define decoration.

Mrs. Flora Stebbins Kendall Bryant, a distinguished bridal coordinator, or a self-described "social secretary and entertainment consultant" who since the late 1940s has organized some thirty-five hundred weddings and parties in the New York area, compares planning a wedding to building a wall. Detail by detail it grows up until it has a shape and a strength. For example, in a first session with clients, she may establish the basic choices of place, caterer, and music; the particulars are then spelled out in a series of meetings with the respective service people. Mrs. Bryant, who has written a book about weddings called *It's Your Wedding,* and under the nom de plume Peregrine Pace, a lightly autobiographical novel entitled *No Gloves for the Groom*—"I always say that because they are in the way"—casts an eagle eye on each phase of the planning, thereby avoiding later unexpected problems.

Early on, she finds out what the daughter wants and what the mother doesn't want ("You don't meet the subsequent flare-up head-on; you use persuasion, an acquired art."); if she gets a call in December for a spring or summer wedding, she immediately sends her tent man to the site, before the cover of snow; she inquires about the location of the septic tank, in order to foresee a need for additional facilities; she considers the use of a stand-by generator. Mrs. Bryant makes three checks on everything—ice, toasts, garbage pickup—"because you *have* to." And at least one week before the wedding, she conducts briefings with the parents and bride and groom, in which every detail of the event is laid out, "so that I don't have to give cues, which bothers me."

Mrs. Bryant has decades of original advice

and perspective to share. "If you publish an engagement announcement, leave town for a while, because the telephone will ring incessantly with soliciting merchants." "Evening weddings are a dream and preferred by most men; if Saturday is taken, why not Friday or Wednesday or Thursday, for in the past, posh weddings took place in the middle of the week." "Mail invitations on Thursday so that they are received on Saturday, for if a woman receives an invitation on a Monday, Tuesday, or Wednesday, she puts it in the desk where it becomes part of the décor." She speaks of the mothers "who come to me like Jell-O, because they have read too many etiquette books and are confused; and I say throw them out—I've never read one." She continues, "I'm the one to worry about organization; all I need from the bride and family is the approval of estimates and a reasonable head count. I don't want anyone to feel overorganized, because that can be dreadful. We have briefings so that the bride and groom will feel natural." In the

Setup for a big party is done in advance by a special crew that arrives on site before the kitchen and service crews.

case of nerves or mishap, Mrs. Bryant carries her Panic Bag to weddings, where she sits unobtrusively in the background. It contains safety pins, smelling salts, needle and thread, a spare wedding ring, and "everything but a spare groom."

Everyone needs some form of support system in planning a wedding, be they friends and relatives, or professionals, for advice, energy, and assistance. A bridal coordinator or a Mrs. Bryant is a traditional source of organizational skills, and few other professionals put themselves so completely in the service of the bride. Yet in recent years, more through circumstance than through original intent, the caterer has become a very useful consultant in wedding matters, sensitive and experienced in areas related to but larger than food. In these days of lavish and expressive entertaining, food and drink are central elements in a wedding's character. Quite naturally, table decoration and flowers, and then tents and lighting, the general timetable and even the overall color scheme have become extensions of the concern with food. And consequently, the caterer has emerged as an important figure in wedding plans, as someone who knows your style and point of view, and can be a valuable resource. From my own experience, I know that my involvement with food and flowers has led to the creation of the bridal bouquet, advice on appropriate linens and rental equipment, the subcontracting of a tent man and a band. When I am there in the home and friendly with the family, sometimes I find myself fussing with a bridesmaid's resistant sash, or helping to stage the receiving line and the toasts. Caterers also have valuable inside advice to offer on how to negotiate a rental space and how to shop for rental items, and can offer ideas and perspective on weddings in general.

Most caterers make it a point to get involved in the overall planning, at least in order to coordinate their services with others'. And many caterers now specialize in decoration as well as food.

Carole Gordon is an example of a new breed of caterer who is flourishing in San Francisco, Dallas, Chicago, and, indeed, in most major U.S. cities. After ten years in the entertaining field in New York and Philadelphia, she has created a "total business," based on her talents with food, flowers, design, and calligraphy, and masterminds Broadway opening parties and corporate soirees. Like her peers, she has learned that weddings are organized much like theatrical productions, and can profit spectacularly from the new theatrical mode in design. Her style is dramatic, lavish, and lush, sometimes baroque, sometimes Hollywood, and she wants "the most gorgeous, breathtaking event one has ever seen." In composing a scene, sometimes Carole draws upon her extensive collection of antiques and theatrical props and sometimes she stirs her imagination and then invents—the fantastical silver lamé, tulle, and satin scene that supplanted a tennis court, for example, or the bacchanalian silver-painted melons and grape clusters that garnished outdoor cocktail tables.

For another wedding and reception, out-

doors on a beautiful new estate on Long Island Sound, Carole was given free artistic rein. With extensive grounds, she envisioned the event as a series of small dramas—the sushi bar, for which she hired a sushi chef; the raw seafood bar, for which she filled a rowboat with ice; the buffet dinner by the pool; and then dancing to Peter Duchin on the bandstand she had built. For a wedding in New Jersey, Carole took her cues from the house, a great white Moorish palace, and continued its look with columns and Art Deco motifs in the yard and tent, planning the ceremony and dinner setting to capitalize on its dramatically appropriate features. "People talk about bringing back the old glamour," she says, "but I think it has been here all the time; we've just updated it."

Occasionally I will get a request for catering or a consultation from a woman who I soon realize not only could, but really would like to do her party herself. I have been called in for support and corroboration because she is unsure of herself. Insecurity and stage fright are commonplace and natural—inverted forms of a desire to succeed. And the fact is that many people have such a strong sense of organization that they could and should mastermind their wedding themselves, calling for support and service and assistance only where needed.

Serge de Cluny, one of New York City's most famous party executives, explains to his well-trained Glorious Food staff the intricacies of the day's reception.

T-shirts with printed job titles clearly indicated who was what at the Cook-Legge wedding.

Making decisions means articulating what you really want and then going after it, which may take perseverance. It necessarily involves a budget, which is a major factor in determining the size of the wedding and the type of meal to serve. It is important to be a careful consumer, for a wedding is high-level consumption. Rentals should be organized carefully, for with special needs, they can cost more than the food. The prices of sites and bands in great demand have risen. And flowers can be astronomical—a good reason to cultivate your own garden or borrow from roadsides and meadows. Do not accept the first estimates blindly, and remember to figure in tax, tips on food and service, and food and transportation for a catering crew. And remember that if well organized, a wedding doesn't have to be extravagant. It hurts to spend money on fleeting goods; six months later, even the worldly wise can often be found slumped in an armchair, shaking their heads over a pile of bills.

In this book there are many models to emulate and examples to follow. For her daughter's large fairytale wedding, Jacqueline Desmarais carefully chose a staff, headed by interior designer Jean-François Daigre, that was talented, familiar, and dedicated to her ideas and to the success of the day, and yet no detail was

Liener Temerlin, who organized his daughter's wedding with precision and style.

too small for her own consideration and supervision. Janet Hester, well seasoned at entertaining, and happy with a very special new opportunity, worked out of a single manila folder; she remained relaxed enough to bring to life the meaningful past (adding treasured bits and pieces of family weddings to her own daughter's) as well as the active present (calling on friends to assist with the organization of transportation).

Perhaps the most impressive illustrations of good organization came from the Cook and Temerlin families, one in the country, one in the city, both of whom had to operate on a large scale, bringing guests long distances to their weddings, housing and entertaining them. Babs Cook undertook her mission as stepmother of the bride with the unflagging drive and energy she brings to all the family events and adventures; Liener Temerlin, as father of the bride, took charge in corporate style and ran his weekend in New York like a

merry version of an important board meeting.

To examine Mr. Temerlin's notebook is to understand the careful and complete thinking he applied to wedding arrangements. It is also to see the orderliness of the wedding, for, once committed to paper, each item stood as if done. Along with a copy of the words of the wedding ceremony, written by the groom, and a guest list with appropriate identifications, and, for the bridal party and families, travel arrangements, there is a thorough directory of all wedding services, arranged alphabetically by category (buses, cake, caterer, florist, hotels, limousines, etc.) with names, addresses, telephone numbers, and specified orders, and including copies of the letters to transportation companies that instructed their procedure; a list of hotel reservations, specific accommodations, and arrival and departure dates; and, perhaps most significantly, an exact rendering of the wedding itinerary, beginning on Monday, with the first arrivals in New York (times and flight numbers), encompassing all appointments, meals, dress requirements, and transportation arrangements, and ending on the following Monday, with Liener and his wife Karla's departure for home. With each step of the celebration foreseen, mentally rehearsed, and duly logged, the family was liberated from anxiety and free to enjoy themselves. With 102 guests in their care in a major city, the Temerlin organization was not only thoughtful but necessary.

For Babs Cook, the logistics were even more challenging—accommodating 125 guests in a small resort town in New Hampshire at the height of the season, and transporting all goods and services via motorboat and the good raft *Beatrice* to the family island. Her planning began a year in advance, and indeed filled 365 days. And as a result of her organization, in the first days of August 1985, a casual tourist found all motels and inns in the area booked, and Golden Pond afloat with strange objects—port-o-johns, grills, musical instruments, cases of tomato juice, all making their way toward a distant island.

Babs was "The Little General," as her custom-made T-shirt read, and accordingly, she mapped out ambitious plans for the three-day wedding, which, because thirty-five friends and relations of the English groom were visiting America, in reality extended to a week. Her freezer was an indication of the many meals foreseen, with dozens of packages of French breads and muffins and fruit butters, for example, homemade over recent months, labeled according to the day and time they would be needed. The refrigerator was posted with the wedding week's calendar, noting pickups and deliveries, arrivals, and events.

Every detail of the Cook wedding spoke of its organization; indeed, such an ambitious wedding could only have succeeded with iron-clad plans. And yet the timetable was thoughtful and precise, one that allowed guests extra moments to enjoy the woodsy peace of the ceremony site on Church Island; provided for a very leisurely boat trip, with champagne and bloody marys stashed in coolers, to the reception at home on Kent Island; and encouraged many hours of dancing. The mood was summertime casual and expansive, and the day a series of unforgettable adventures.

RIGHT: Hilary Cushing was married in the same tent in which her sit-down buffet was held. After the ceremony, the temporary altar was removed and tables rearranged while guests enjoyed cocktails and hors d'oeuvres in the house.

ANATOMY OF A WEDDING

Basic decisions:

Date
Budget
Ceremony site
Reception site
Guest list
Clergyman or judge
Wedding party or witnesses

Then you'll need to consider:

Caterer
Musicians
Tent men
Lighting men
Bandstand
Wedding menu
Beverages
Ice
Wedding cake
Rental tables and chairs, china, silver, glassware, linens
Wedding dress and shoes
Bridal bouquet
Bridesmaids' dresses and shoes
Bridesmaids' bouquets
Mothers' dresses
Groom's clothes
Groomsmen's clothes
Boutonnieres
Invitations and informals
Bridal registry

Notebook for gifts
Wedding rings
Trousseau
Attendants' gifts
Ceremony music
Reception flowers
Receiving line
Transportation
Guest accommodations
Rehearsal dinner
Bridal luncheons
Bridal showers
Bachelor dinner
Blood test and wedding license

Things to remember:

Hair and manicure appointment
Wedding notice to newspapers
Display of gifts
Name changes on official documents
Parking for reception
Seating plans
Babysitter for reception
Corsages for mothers
Party favors
Garter to throw
The old, new, borrowed, and blue
Toasts
Rice or rose petals to throw

LAUNCH CLOSED
BY OWNER
WEEK OF JULY 29 – AUG. 5
Due To Wedding

SEA
TRANSPORTATION
AND
CLEANUP

On Golden Pond

Deborah Cook and Tim Legge

Although few have been there, the scene is familiar to millions of Americans: a lake, seven miles long, of dark cold water, clear and like liquid marble to the touch, cut into an endless shoreline of peninsulas and inlets; and planted with dozens of small green islands of every size and shape, some little more than the toehold of a single pine tree, others sheltering rambling rustic camps behind their foliage. Mountains impose on the northern and western edges of the lake, creating a sort of sanctuary, and when the sun sets, it casts its last light sideways through the mass, like a vision. When the sun rises, its first pale rays penetrate the early-rising mist in a way that illuminates the water in gold, and families of loons,  moving out from shallow reefs, greet the day with eerie, heart-quickening warbles. The lake, quiet, spotted with canoes but few other visible signs of humanity, is a world unto itself, in which it is easy to lose track of the twentieth century.

This is Golden Pond, in the backways of New Hampshire, an essentially private summer paradise to a handful of longtime, mostly interrelated families and two boys' camps. A few summers ago, there was a lot of commotion on the lake, when Katharine Hepburn and Jane and Henry Fonda settled into a small camp here to film *On Golden Pond.* But the residents stipulated that no publicity be given their spot, to guard against the encroachment of tourism and camp followers that has

ABOVE: Timothy Legge shares a private moment with his best man before the ceremony. RIGHT: Debbie Cook and her father, Charles Cook. OPPOSITE: Debbie and Tim take their vows.

PRECEDING PAGES, LEFT: A collage of images that highlight the three-day wedding celebration. RIGHT: Sunrise on Golden Pond, and an old straw boater tilted carefully against a stone wall on Kent Island.

threatened adjacent summer areas that now buzz with motorboats and motel trade. Last summer, there was commotion of a more indigenous nature, and the sign at the town landing again read LAUNCH CLOSED, but beneath it, FOR THE WEEK OF THE WEDDING.

During this week, motorboats and a motorized raft known as *Beatrice* crisscrossed the lake hundreds of times between Kent Island and the mainland, transporting supplies needed for the wedding. Kent Island, formerly called Cook's Island, has been in the Cook family for five generations. And so on Saturday, August 3, 1985, they celebrated the marriage of their oldest daughter, Debbie, to Tim Legge, from London, England, with a ceremony on Church Island, and a luncheon at home. The wedding, however, was far bigger than a ritual and reception, for Friday brought a dinner and dance

at the Woodshed Restaurant in town, and Sunday, a huge country brunch and sports day on the lake, and in between, a gala flotilla, a hot-air balloon, and fireworks. For many, the wedding activities had opened early in the week when Tim's family and friends began to arrive from abroad, and ended the following weekend after the annual three-day athletic party.

The Cook wedding added up to an extraordinarily rich slice of life on Golden Pond, served up family style, with uncommon imagination, energy, and organization. Descriptive of the event were the bright green T-shirts worn by the family on Friday, emblazoned with their respective ranks: BRIDE and GROOM for Debbie and Tim; SEA TRANSPORTATION for siblings Andrew, eleven, and Rachel, nineteen, who were manning motorboats; GROUNDS AND BOOZE for Rachel's twin brother Chas; SUPERVISOR for father Charlie ("Supervised," he corrected); THE LITTLE GENERAL for stepmother Babs. Labels seemed to be the outward sign of inward energy and drive, transforming order into merriment. At the house, a large rustic camp built of stone and wood from the area in 1894, set a steep climb from the boathouse and dock, there were other helpers. The kitchen staff, two local ladies and a Bahamian housekeeper, and the calypso band, four Bahamians imported from the family's winter turf on Eleuthera, also had T-shirts. (At Babs's suggestion, the band, on their first trip outside their flat homeland, went to climb a mountain.) The refrigerator door had charts, lists, and schedules, and the freezer contents were described according to day, hour, and meal. Off the back porch, perched high above the lake, the barnyard animals (pigs Häag 'n' Dazs, ram Brooks, cow Coco Chanel, and goat Emma) were housed in a combination ring-woodpile marked THE O.K.

CORRAL. And next to the chicken coop, the portable water closets were divided between "Roosters" and "Hens." Typical of Cook-style fun and games, the front of the doghouse belonging to golden lab Lover held a series of removable plaques inscribed with all the family's nicknames (Meow, Bugs, Weezie,

ABOVE: Debbie and Tim, newly married, lead the post-ceremony procession. OPPOSITE, ABOVE: The photographer attempts to arrange the wedding party in some semblance of order for formal portraits. OPPOSITE, BELOW LEFT: Mr. and Mrs. Charles Cook; Mr. and Mrs. Timothy Legge. OPPOSITE, BELOW RIGHT: Mr. and Mrs. Timothy Legge flanked by the English parents of the groom.

Twerpie, Pedro, Poodles, Mrs. Poodles), any one of which could be hung over the door in the event of disfavor.

The direction and drive of the wedding celebration came from Babs, who had invested a year in its planning and long hours in preparing the homemade brunch for Sunday, which included wahoo and tuna flown up from the Bahamas, not to mention the dozens of other incidental meals for twenty-five or thirty—yet the execution came from all. Charlie had built the smoker and smoked the wahoo; Andrew was in charge of the launches and attended to special errands (including waking me at 5 A.M. to catch the golden sunrise); Debbie designed the place cards, official menu, and seating chart for the wedding luncheon, and a map for all invitees. Several days before the wedding, when the tent, specially designed to abut the wraparound porch, arrived on site in a discordant green and white, the whole crew set about painting the green stripes in a more melodious hue.

As if on special order, the day of the wedding dawned warm, unusually dry, and brilliantly clear, hung with a few great cumulus clouds that looked like maps of the British Isles. Babs served her fruit muffins and fruit butters, sticky buns, and last year's home-cured bacon to early risers at six, and set about last details, her inner motor racing, her facade cool and casual. The barnyard was carpeted with fresh straw, the animals scrubbed and adorned with flowery straw hats and pink bows. By nine, the tables had been laid with chintz and leafy glass plates and garden flowers, and the young chef of the day, Curt Chesley, who used to preside at a local restaurant called the Curtis House, was in the kitchen, surrounded by bowls of salads and trays of oven-ready veal, chopping herbs and deftly

CLOCKWISE FROM UPPER LEFT: The bride, Debbie Cook, dancing to the music of her favorite musicians; after hours of dancing, the bride and her attendants took off their shoes; a place setting for lunch; Andrew Cook and two friends discussing the wedding with Lover, the family's Golden Lab; a tiered wedding cake decorated with daisies, baby's breath, and roses; an ivory and silver filigree flower holder once belonging to the bride's great-aunt held Debbie's bouquet; the resident burro with her wedding hat; an old bathtub was filled with ice to cool the champagne.

rolling sushi. Embarkation for Church Island began at ten, to allow a fleet of ten motorboats, manned by friends and family, to carry the 118 guests in their party clothes across the lake in time for the eleven o'clock nuptials.

Since 1903 and the days of Chocorus, the first boys' camp in America, Church Island (from "Chocorua," the Indian word for church) has held regular nondenominational summer services outdoors in the lap of nature. Guest ministers, who come by canoe, preach in a small glade where a gathering of wooden benches looks out to a tall birchbark cross, set before a clear view to the lake. In the serenity and abiding beauty of this spot, the first wedding guests seemed happy for the moments to wander about, get acquainted, and take in the quiet. A young English cousin of the groom, flushed with happiness, announced her intention to stow away in America. Guthrie Speers, the local minister, who has known the family "always," was wearing heavy homespun white robes and a wooden cross, which, with his black hair, square jaw, and high color, gave him the appearance of an early Native American, and he seemed to glow with benediction. When a boat flying British and American flags appeared in the clearing, the ready congregation moved to the shore to watch the approach of bride and groom, and, at that moment, like a wonderful omen, a family of loons sent a volley of cries into the air. A sense of moment unified the group, and when, during the vows, Tim declared a strong "I do" too early, everyone laughed, and when asked to support the union, they responded as one.

At the end of the ceremony, Debbie and Tim walked down a narrow path through the pines and found a horse and carriage, generously supplied by a farmer friend, waiting to carry them back to the dock. Like a figment of Magritte's imagination, they set forth in the faithful raft *Beatrice* for the reception at Kent Island, riding on water, trailing a bunch of

The luncheon menu.

pink-and-white balloons and a flotilla of wedding boats, each of which had been provided with balloons, champagne, and a gallon of Charlie's clam juice bloody marys (he had made seventeen gallons in all) to encourage celebrating. The sun was sunburn hot, the

lake sparkling, and the pace very leisurely, a factor both of *Beatrice*'s putt-putt speed, and a plan to arrive near home at the precise moment a hired plane flew the banner THE LEGGE IS COOKED. WELL DONE. BAWK. BAWK. By the time the message had materialized, flown backward at first, boats had circled back to the party launch for refills, and the prologue to the reception seemed like the real thing.

After their voyage, the wedding parade settled into the reception. Drinks and passed hors d'oeuvres whiled away an hour, while the official photographer posed the family before old trees, and guests mingled, admired the wedding cake (a five-tiered confection from the local cake lady, Minerva Willoughby, the whole supported by swans and boasting a tiny iron horse and carriage on top), sat in rustic chairs in the shade, or visited the barnyard to watch Emma the goat eat the straw hats off her peer group. Between courses of the elegant buffet lunch, which was served two tables at a time to avoid congestion, Charlie toasted his daughter, who had always wanted to be married in this special place, and the Anglo-American families danced to the Bahamian band. In the aftermath of lunch, already late afternoon, the band, Debbie's favorite, to whom she had sent tapes of her special songs, revived the crowd with music that coaxed all ages into a circle for showy dance routines and break-dancers' acrobatics. At six, a mellow crowd adjourned to the dock, where they caught sight of a rainbow-hued hot-air balloon making its way out of the cove at the town landing. As it drew nearer, it grew

Debbie and her father dance one of many dances.

THE LEGGE IS COOKED-WELL DONE BAWK!BAWK!

ABOVE: As a surprise and a family joke, Mrs. Cook arranged to have this banner flown around the lake right after the ceremony took place. BELOW: The bride and groom cut the cake.

to several stories tall, and its hot-air guns, roaring like dragon fire, awed the gathering. Charlie stepped up with a bottle of homemade vintage wine (circa 1973), tucked under his arm and Debbie and Tim drank to the health of everyone. With Debbie singing "Up, Up, and Away," and a gentleman in the crowd querying, "Isn't the bride afraid of heights?" Debbie and Tim climbed into the basket and with a few shots of air, floated up and out over the lake. Clouds of small balloons were released, and bridesmaids and family leaped into boats to follow their course, which would eventually ground near home.

In all the images of the Cook wedding that remain in memory, the lake presides: balloons and the American, British, and Bahamian flags flying on the docks on the lake; motorboats on a mission scuttling the lake; the lake in mist and in dusk; the lake illuminated by the fireworks shot into the sky by the father of the bride, after the departure of the bride and groom.

LEFT AND ABOVE: Debbie and Tim gaze down from their perch in the hot-air balloon and wave to the guests gathered on the dock.

LEFT: Esther Ferguson and I gaze at the majestic skyline from the stern of the *Entrepreneur*. ABOVE: Newlyweds Hayden and Dana Crawford.

Dallas in New York

Dana Temerlin and Hayden Crawford

Dana and Mr. and Mrs. Stanley Marcus pose for pictures in the late afternoon sun.

Texas is famous for its big sky, its big hats, its big heart, and its big weddings. In 1976 Karla and Liener Temerlin's daughter Lisa was married in Texas in a candlelit ceremony that reflected in their garden pool and a Camelot-inspired reception at a grand hotel. When their daughter Dana became engaged to Hayden Crawford in December 1984, they realized they all had another dream. What transpired the following June 1 was an evening I remember as Dallas in New York, for it brought the Texas flair for the spectacular to bear on the most beautiful resources Manhattan has to offer.

Mr. and Mrs. Jack Boettiger enjoy the view of lower Manhattan. TOP: The Brooklyn Bridge at twilight.

53

ABOVE LEFT: Dana dresses for the wedding ceremony helped by sister Lisa and dress designer Milo. Lisa holds her baby daughter Cary. ABOVE MIDDLE: Dana making up in a dressing room of the townhouse. ABOVE RIGHT: Completely dressed, Dana powders her nose.

ABOVE LEFT: Dana and three young guests enjoy a private moment. ABOVE MIDDLE: A view into the city garden of the Peebler townhouse. ABOVE RIGHT: Hayden Crawford and his father waiting for the ceremony to begin. BELOW, LEFT TO RIGHT: Lisa and her son Blake descend the lily-decorated staircase, followed by the bride and her father.

LEFT: Hayden and Dana in a warm and spirited embrace at the end of the ceremony.
BELOW LEFT: The Crawfords and Temerlins in a family portrait.

For the Temerlins, a wedding in New York was an adventure and an inspiration. The family knew and loved the city to which they traveled almost as often on pleasure as on business—Mr. Temerlin is chairman of Bozell, Jacobs, Kenyon & Eckhardt, a prominent international advertising agency at which Dana has also forged a career in public relations. Their friends thought the prospect of a weekend there promised excitement and fun. When they decided on a water-borne dinner reception on the yacht *Entrepreneur,* the number of guests was dictated by the boat's maximum capacity of one hundred and two, and the romance of the city skyline at night was built into the trip. Charles D. Peebler, Jr., the chief executive officer of the agency, offered his distinguished townhouse on the Upper East Side, still known to many as the old

Gimbel mansion, for the ceremony, and John Teets, another friend and chairman of Greyhound, promised three brand-new buses to deliver guests dockside. Dallas florists Colleen Womack and Peter Harris, photographer Gary Blockley, and dress designer Milo agreed to journey to New York for the weekend, and the stage was officially set.

In traditional wedding history, the father of the bride is cast as a noble figurehead, wistful at the notion of relinquishing his daughter, poignant and proud at the moment of giveaway, but uninvolved in the details. Spencer Tracy, the bemused and beleaguered payer of the bills, remains the lovable prototype. As father of the bride, Liener Temerlin revised Tracy's role dramatically. Charging himself with the well-being and entertainment of 102 dear friends in a major city far from home, he

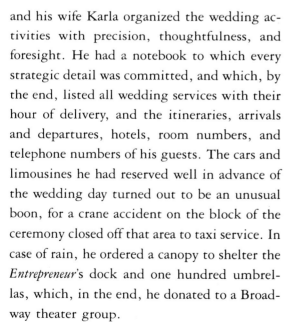

THIS PAGE: A brand-new Greyhound bus transported guests to the dock on West Twenty-Third Street. On board the yacht, Hayden, Dana, their families, and friends enjoyed the breathtaking scenery. OPPOSITE: The Statue of Liberty, still in scaffolding, stands guard over New York harbor while the *Entrepreneur* glides by.

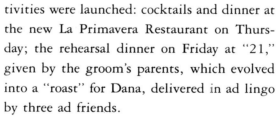

and his wife Karla organized the wedding activities with precision, thoughtfulness, and foresight. He had a notebook to which every strategic detail was committed, and which, by the end, listed all wedding services with their hour of delivery, and the itineraries, arrivals and departures, hotels, room numbers, and telephone numbers of his guests. The cars and limousines he had reserved well in advance of the wedding day turned out to be an unusual boon, for a crane accident on the block of the ceremony closed off that area to taxi service. In case of rain, he ordered a canopy to shelter the *Entrepreneur*'s dock and one hundred umbrellas, which, in the end, he donated to a Broadway theater group.

At the beginning of the wedding week, Dana and her sister Lisa flew to New York and settled into the Pierre Hotel to relax and handle last-minute changes and details.

As friends and family descended, the festivities were launched: cocktails and dinner at the new La Primavera Restaurant on Thursday; the rehearsal dinner on Friday at "21," given by the groom's parents, which evolved into a "roast" for Dana, delivered in ad lingo by three ad friends.

Back at the townhouse, the florists were building a small elevated platform in the living room to allow the guests a full view of the ceremony, and entwining it, and the three-story staircase and two mantelpieces, with ivy, white lilies, roses, and orchid sprays. Many of the flowers had been sent directly from Holland.

Well aware of the uncertainties and delays inherent in New York traffic patterns, the Temerlins greeted each guest at the townhouse on Saturday with a glass of champagne. With the furniture removed and the addition of the new ivy-carpeted stage and a twelve-piece orchestra, the living room was a natural theater

for a black-tie ceremony. Hayden wore the tux Dana had purchased for his birthday, and Dana, a sophisticated beaded and backless gown designed for her by her friend Milo from Casablanca. Drawing upon Unitarian liturgy, Hayden had written their service to celebrate both their love and the traditional Jewish wine ceremony. At the moment when the ceremonial glass was shattered, fourteen violinists playing "On a Wonderful Day Like Today" descended the stairs. More Dom Perignon and Beluga caviar were served while the families moved into the garden for photographs.

At Twenty-third Street and the Hudson River, the *Entrepreneur* lay quietly at its pier. A 120-foot charter yacht, specially redesigned for social and corporate functions, and attended by a Cordon Bleu catering staff, it breathes intimations of days in Newport and Palm Beach, Monaco and St. Tropez. As it set out into New York harbor, where the great lady

still prevails, albeit then caged in restoration scaffolding, hors d'oeuvres circulated fore and aft: barquettes with smoked salmon and salmon mousse, smoked trout, lobster pieces with beurre blanc, beggar's purses, artichoke hearts with bacon, slices of tiny beefs Wellington. The late sun backlit the great stand of buildings at the tip of Manhattan, and offshore breezes tousled hair and whipped flags in the bow. "Water and boats have such romance," sister Lisa had said, "and there we were *captured* on a boat." For hours, Lisa's four-year-old son Grant presided at the wheel.

With many decks and all the wonderful odd niches intrinsic to a boat (behind the bridge, under the bridge), and with lounges, salons, and a dining room below decks, the *Entrepreneur* seemed spacious. The look of the crowd afloat on the East River was high-fashion-formal, yet the mood was warm, relaxed, and informal. An elegant dinner was served buffet-style, and enjoyed out on the decks in the warm night; it ended with Harlequin strawberries, dipped in white and dark chocolate, and a stately rubrum-lily-festooned cake made by Sylvia Weinstock, the cake lady of New York. From the Crawford family's Collin Street Bakery in Corsicana, Texas, came a Deluxe Fruit Groom's Cake, studded with small rich pecans native to the region. Hayden now runs the pecan portion of the business.

After dinner, the wedding guests left the deck and the city skyline for the grand salon, where there was a trio and pianist, mellow lights, a plush red carpet on which to sit, and a sing-along featuring dear friends and songwriters Sammy Cahn and Johnny Green. Sammy Cahn, who has written many of the great Frank Sinatra hits, sang the wedding song, his personal revision of his "Love and Marriage." ("Try to rhyme anything with Hayden and Dana," he said.) And everyone chimed in for "The Tender Trap," "Come Fly with Me," "High Hopes," "It's Been a Long, Long Time," and other songs.

There was no question that the evening of June 1, 1985, was charmed. The weather was perfect, the moon was full, the skyline was breathtaking, and as the boat sailed under the Fifty-ninth Street Bridge, its lights came up. They passed the *QE 2,* and later in the night, on a routine inspection, they were boarded by the Coast Guard, just for a little excitement. Dana remarked later, "It was magic. If you ordered it you couldn't get this sort of scenery for your wedding. The lights of the city were like Disneyland." Hayden added, as he thumbed through the wedding album, "It was as if the whole city was celebrating with us." And then he pulled out a photograph taken by a friend that through a coincidence of images showed the full moon and the Statue of Liberty caught in the bowl of a glass of claret.

Mr. William Sylvester Cargill
and
Mr. and Mrs. Harris Edward Russell
request the honour of your presence
at the marriage of their daughter
Martha Lyons
to
Mr. John Hayden Crawford
on Saturday the first of June
Nineteen hundred and eighty-five
New York

Invitations

Over the past several years, I have collected wedding invitations as documents of style as well as commemoratives of events. And when I open up the file, I see, as if written in code, suggestions of personalities of dozens of brides and their weddings: the perfect engraved elegance of Sophie Desmarais (St. James style) and Hilary Cushing (Belgrave); the complete thinking of the Temerlins (with three enclosures covered with three tissues, a reception card for the black-tie dinner, return envelope, and a card announcing private transportation to the yacht *Entrepreneur*); the individuality of Kathy GarDianos's pastel rice paper; the romantic white-on-pink of Caroline Damerell. For a second marriage, Sandra Leo-Wolf chose to announce her wedding celebration with the formality she missed at her first, while another older friend, with a large, fun-loving family, elected to write her own message on a card of Brueghel's village wedding scene from the Philadelphia Museum of Art. The invitation to Jacquelyn Van Den Berg's marriage to Stephen Myers, white engraved with brown, began, "Thanking God for His Goodness to us, we invite you to share in our joy. . . ."

The choice of wedding invitation today is a much more interesting matter than it was not too long ago, when etiquette restricted all but the libertine to the traditional creamy paper engraved in a variety of type styles. (For economy, there was thermoplate, but then the receiver could run his fingers over the face and detect a facsimile.) It is significant that in June 1985 Tiffany & Co. enlarged its longtime standard fare—three proper invitations—to include informal invitations, engraved on white or ecru paper or card stock, in twelve different colored inks and linings. The decision was made in response to changing times, with a wide new variety of wedding circumstances and styles demanding more relaxed and decorous, albeit proper, designs.

I chose to speak at length with Tiffany's, for while there are many fine stationers and engravers across the country—notably Cartier's—Tiffany's, since its founding 140 years ago, has remained a citadel of good taste and, in fact, has set a standard for social correctness. And Tiffany's private watermark endures as a unique mark of distinction. Dina Clason, the head of the stationery department, mused

PRECEDING PAGE: A grouping of traditional and semi-traditional invitations, many for the weddings in this book.

that people often copy the store's example erroneously. Tissue inserts, for example, originated to protect a pen's ink from smearing in the mail, and were already obsolete when Tiffany first opened its engraving and fancy goods emporium; now the store supplies tissues only upon request. "Many things here are very fussy," she continued, "because we know we can provide the greatest social accuracy."

Most of Tiffany's advice is based on the word of Amy Vanderbilt, which has changed little in many decades. One requests "the honour of your presence" at a religious ceremony, but for a wedding at home, in a club or hotel—in other words a social occasion—the proper phrase is "the pleasure of your company." A small reception card must be enclosed if the site is different from the ceremony's; otherwise, an RSVP may be written in the lower corner line. In the event of a small ceremony, it is proper to reverse the sizes and enclose a small ceremony card. Occasionally, a

couple will also enclose an at-home card, with their new address; a response card, which Tiffany does not recommend, but allows; a directions card. In the rare case of a large and lavish church wedding, a request to special friends might be enclosed to sit "inside the family ribbon," meaning in those special pews reserved for family. This basic format, executed on the large "embassy" size or the smaller "classic" size eighty-weight ecru paper, engraved in one of the nine typefaces (many of them bearing names like St. James, Belgrave, and Windsor, that conjure up English royalty) has been consistent since the time of Edith Wharton and social arbiter Ward McAllister. Yet the more contemporary realities of divorce, and the new variety of wedding situations, are reflected in wording (in the case of divorce, the "and" is omitted between the parents' names, and sometimes children host their parent's wedding) and in the recent proliferation of informals. Remarriage, once considered an event

unfit for announcement or public celebration, is treated in the same way as marriage, and its invitations are subject only to taste and style.

Many of the situations suggesting an informal invitation are commonplace today: when the wedding couple is giving their own wedding ("Joyce Pierce Roquemore and Paul James Hanly, Jr., request the pleasure of your company"), or when the wedding takes place outside a house of worship, at a garden party (Caroline Damerell and Carmine Santandrea), or a country lunch (Sharon Nelson and Harvey Siegel). Yet these days the most traditional of nuptials may be announced with lighthearted stationery if it pleases the couple. A wedding involving two old Yankee families, held at St. James Church in Manhattan (an old society church) with a reception at the River Club (terrain of the elite), brought a lovely long accordion-folded invitation splashed with a pale-green-and-peach Oriental design; a stately high-tea wedding party, an invitation en-

OPPOSITE: Engaged couples waiting at the Fifth Avenue entrance to Tiffany's to attend its annual open house for brides and grooms. RIGHT: An informally attired couple choosing very traditional wedding invitations at Tiffany's.

graved inside a card of a French floral etching from the Metropolitan Museum. There are other choices to suit almost every personality or sentiment, available at stationery stores and wedding supply firms. Leafing through the books at a local printing store, I was amazed to find invitations in every shade of the pastel rainbow, folded, scrolled, and peek-a-boo, embossed with satiny bells, hearts, spring blossoms, rings, rainbows and clouds, inscribed with many messages: "Today we begin sharing not just love but life"; "Our joy will be more complete if you share in the ceremony uniting our daughter . . ."; "Happily we two have chosen the first day of our life together on Sunday, August 9 . . ." In the face of excessive sentimentality, however, I usually find myself favoring the simple and old-fashioned.

In ancient and not so ancient times, a wedding invitation was a public proclamation posted on the town bulletin board, addressed to the immediate world. For many couples today, the time most fraught with anxiety and argument involves sorting out the world, selecting guests, numbering relatives, dear friends, good friends, business friends, and neighbors. At this moment, it is important to choose those persons to whom the event is meaningful and whose presence will warm the gathering. Weddings that fulfill social obligations threaten to be dull and impersonal; weddings that embrace close new friends together with important past associations remain engraved in a couple's memory.

Wedding invitations generally require four weeks for printing and should be ordered at least eight to ten weeks before the wedding. Amy Vanderbilt decrees that they should be mailed as many as four and no fewer than two weeks before the event, allowing more time for out-of-town and faraway dispatches.

Most engravers will supply envelopes in advance of invitations to facilitate addressing them. Addressing invitations takes time, and to be appropriately pleasureful rather than mere drudgery, it requires the assistance of a friend or two, or perhaps the services of a local calligrapher. The most beautiful script I have ever seen adorned Barbara Carpenter's invitations. Elegant, ornate, and yet fluid and unstudied, it came from the hand of a local eighty-year-old Texas friend. Everywhere there are instructors or fledgling artists to be found who might welcome a free-lance job. I know several brides who have indulged in a calligraphy course for the sake of their wedding invitations. And I know many who have at least invested in a calligraphy pen.

It is deeply pleasing to receive a wedding invitation that not only announces a happy event, but expresses it in a manner that seems personal, whether formal or informal. It is an extra flourish to find a romantic stamp on the envelope, for the smallest gesture is meaningful with weddings, and it is worthwhile to buy a supply of festive stamps commemorating love, or hearts, or Queen Victoria, or Art Deco, if they might be appropriate. (The post office always has special issues of one kind or another.) In the fifties and sixties, it was customary to frame a wedding invitation in gold, and set it out on an end table for years to come as a decorative object, a memento, a coaster. Although that custom has passed on now, the invitation retains a symbolic importance that is worthy of thought.

A group of unusual, non-traditional invitations, which reflect personal taste and style.

The Farmhouse Wedding

s the twentieth century enters its late prime, and cities grow faster and taller, it is not surprising that more and more weddings seem to take place in the country, where the mind senses the natural continuum of life, the eye can find the horizon, and time can sometimes stand still. Here are long pastures, rolling stone walls, split-rail fences, and aged trees, cow barns, and old farmhouses—natural theatrical space, and the intimacy that comes with the pastoral. For three couples with three different styles and stories, farms were sites of great personal meaning, in which it seemed most appropriate to be married or celebrated, and to gather together dear friends as witnesses.

LEFT: Daughter Lake and nephew Matthew climb down from the carriage after a ride with their friends. ABOVE: Harvey and Sharon Siegel share a quiet moment together after their wedding ceremony.

I arrange masses of flowers in an old wheelbarrow.

Harvey and Sharon seal their vows with a kiss.

A true-to-life Norman Rockwell scene.

My staff preparing the wedding lunch.

A field of mustard brightens the spring landscape.

Sharon Nelson

and

Harvey Siegel

"The day of the wedding, my five-year-old daughter Lake said she felt as if we were all fairies," Harvey Siegel remembers a year after his marriage to Sharon Nelson under an enormous willow tree behind their eighteenth-century stone farmhouse in tiny Califon, New Jersey. "It was as if a famous director had put it together." It had poured rain the morning of Saturday, May 19, 1984, so that when the sun broke through the haze several hours before the ceremony, scheduled for 2 P.M., the gentle countryside of meadows and hills, dogwoods and apple blossoms, was freshly washed, and smelled sweet and new. A horse and buggy had brought the bridal couple to the ceremony—the transportation inspired by a one-horse-sleigh found in the barn. Cocktails flowed into a late lunch, elegant yet countrified fare of the groom's favorite foods. Tables

Wild flowers in copper teapots adorn the tables.

Friends chat while lunch is being served.

The antique-filled interior of the farmhouse parlor.

Harvey and daughter Lake embrace during lunch.

Rhododendrons, azaleas, and other spring blooms.

ABOVE: Sharon and Matthew. BELOW: Apple blossoms and an old rope swing evoke country.

set in a courtyard enclosed by old stone walls were conveniently positioned off the cellar, which had been recently transformed into a new kitchen. Backed up to a stone wall, Jan and Bob, young musicians discovered in a local restaurant, made music until almost dusk, he on the bass, she singing love songs with her fresh raspy folk voice. In the mellow, easy spirit of the day, after the guests had left, the bridal couple, kids, and family, still in wedding dress, piled into a white Jeep and took off for more fun at the local pizza parlor.

Harvey and Sharon's wedding was fanciful, in part because much of their life together is subject to the pressures of commerce (he is a commercial real-estate developer) and of urban living (they spend their weekdays in a sleek co-op on the East Side of New York). Both had been married before, in more stereotypical events. When they first met, Harvey had just acquired his tumbledown farmhouse, and when Sharon became more than a business friend, structural changes had been completed, and she was involved in the decorating. The farmhouse was their special place, and they wanted to be part of its history, and wanted people dear to them to share a memorable country day.

ABOVE: A hand-stenciled sign hangs at the entrance to the farm. BELOW: The lovely bride.

Guests relax after lunch in the shade of the newly leafed trees.

Most of the planning decisions of this wedding derived from the choice of site. In a local antique store, Sharon found cards stenciled with a farmhouse reminiscent of theirs, which she used for invitations, and had lettered by the instructor of a local calligraphy class. Although Sharon had envisaged an old-fashioned dress, she didn't want to worry about a fragile antique, and so chose a new cocktail-length off-white lace design that still suggested former times, which she wore with ballet slippers. ("Heels don't function well in meadows," she reminded us.) For decoration, wild flowers were amassed in baskets, in Harvey's collection of copper teakettles, and, quite spectacularly, in an old wooden wheelbarrow that had been found on the place. Sharon's bridal bouquet was a loose bunch of blue delphiniums, pale roses, and white stock.

Other decisions, fastidiously annotated in Sharon's notebook, were both spontaneous and practical. Children—Harvey's young son and daughter, Luke and Lake, and nieces and nephews—were central to the celebration that day, their needs anticipated with babysitters and peanut-butter-and-jelly sandwiches as backup. An early site for the ceremony, on a hill with a view to the mountains, was rejected in favor of one nearer the house, in deference to Harvey's best man, his father, who was eighty. A close friend made the basketweave cake as a gift to the couple. And the couple's present from the local Presbyterian minister, who presided over the ceremony, was an "Historic Califon" T-shirt.

For Jacquelyn Van Den Berg and Stephen Myers, a farm was both home and fantasy. Their lives together had centered on their house and horse farm they had built on a large promising property in South Salem, New York, surrounded by five thousand acres of wildlife reserve. From a barren hilltop, in one year they created a farmhouse, paddock and

Jacquelyn Van Den Berg

and

Stephen Myers

——

barn, pond, and geometric pastures in which hopeful thoroughbreds grazed. It was something of a dream, far removed from Stephen's work in cable television. As the plans took shape for their wedding on Saturday, August 18, 1984, it became clear that their property was an ideal site. The tent, rented to cover a dinner and dancing space, transformed a grav-

THIS PAGE: Mary Jane Russell designed the flowers and tent decorations, which were simple and countrified. Clear glass napkin rings held single blossoms on the tables, and embossed white fabric was used for tablecloths and napkins.

PRECEDING PAGES, LEFT: The bride and groom emerge from South Salem Presbyterian Church. RIGHT: Daybreak Farm—a country paradise newly created by Jacquie and Stephen Myers—was the site of their wedding

el driveway off the garage (a perfect service space for my catering crew) into a graceful esplanade, banked by flowerbeds, rising into a hill and back pasture. Below the adjacent space allotted for cocktails and champagne, the land spilled down toward the pond and beyond. Guests arrived in an important procession that snaked up the long dirt drive. Immediately they seemed to catch the aura of the place, and while young children danced to the early music, couples wandered off to visit the horses or toured the new farmhouse, with its massive stone fireplace, antiques, and twig furniture. Dinner was leisurely, punctuated by Top Forties music, which later became the whole show. As the moon rose, as full and white as a wedding balloon, spirits soared. Then, in the hours after midnight, in the spirit of all-American fun, the bridal party was thrown into the swimming pool.

Stephen and Jacquie masterminded the wedding themselves, with their own defined taste, as they had done the house and land.

Families were affectionately included but had no responsibilities for the event. Jacquie proudly wore her mother's wedding dress—a beautiful scoop-neck confection of net pulled up at the hem with bows—but changed into another, less formal and more comfortable, dress of similar design for the reception. The couple's serious focus was on the ceremony at the South Salem Presbyterian Church, which they had carefully planned to be a personal collaboration of ministers, with hymns sung by church friends. They didn't seem to worry about the reception, trusting that with friends and good food, it would be happy and buoyant, which it was. At 2:30 P.M., half an hour before the ceremony was to start, as the resident crew was placing baskets of summer flowers on tables and stringing Christmas lights along tent poles, Jacquie casually wandered by in street clothes and bridal veil, looking for the best man's shoes. Then she disappeared upstairs to dress, reemerged as the bride, and floated out to the limousine.

RIGHT: Some of my staff, formally dressed, prepare for the guests' arrival from church.

BELOW: A view through the horse paddocks toward the large white dinner tent.

LEFT TO RIGHT: Outdoor gear and straw cowboy hats hang on pegs in the front hall; a Texas pie safe full of Beverly Jacomini's home preserved relishes, pickles, and vegetables; the Winedale ranch, where the wedding reception took place.

ABOVE, LEFT TO RIGHT: A pair of mud-encrusted boots left on the porch; an old Pepsi cooler used to chill drinks and even strawberries; friends chatting. BELOW, LEFT TO RIGHT: Rockers lined up on the porch; family doll; buckets of flowers and weeds.

ABOVE AND BELOW: Tom Jacomini's Moosewood Smoker barbequed 150 chickens.

BELOW: As a guest, I always find myself helping with flowers or decoration.

Patricia Morrison

and

Ed Fleming

Mid-April is prize week for wild flowers in southern Texas, when bluebonnets and Indian paintbrush cover the land like a Persian carpet. The Jacomini ranch in Winedale, a small town some three hours northwest of Houston, is set in the midst of eighty-eight acres of this landscape—a big log cottage, both inside and out an extraordinary showcase of southwestern American history. For a year, Tom and Beverly Jacomini, along with friends Nona Wise, Lucia Bryan, Cathy Malone, and Marjorie and Sandy Parkerson, planned a reception in the local style to celebrate the marriage of Patricia Morrison to Ed Fleming, and 150 close friends had put aside the day. True local style being barbecue, and Tom Jacomini being a barbecue nut, he had designed his Moosehead Smoker, a twenty-foot wood-fired barbecue pit, constructed simply out of steel drums, massive enough to cook hundreds of chickens.

ABOVE: Guest of honor Patricia Morrison in her country casual white dress and straw hat.

ABOVE: Gingham-covered tables were moved outside. BELOW: Some of the food offerings.

75

ABOVE: The front porch, with its steep overhanging roof, offered a shady place to sit and talk.
BELOW: Guests were given patchwork quilts to spread on the grass for the buffet lunch. RIGHT:
Kay Khale, a Houston caterer, created this beautiful getaway basket for the bride and groom.

Tom's 150 chickens, cooked in his own three-step process, and served with his secret barbecue sauce, were the heart of an elaborate country meal created by friends: huge Texas cheeses; carrot bread with chicken salad; avocado-crab mousse with black bread; spicy tortilla chips; giant bowls of popcorn; brownies and pound cakes; potato salad and asparagus; corn breads. La Verl Daily, the cake lady of Houston, had made her famous basket wedding cake filled with deceptively realistic wild flowers. And, as if in tribute to the unending joys of local culinary heritage, Kay Khale had assembled a going-away basket for the couple, too—an offering of fresh crawfish-tail salad, a medley of vegetables in Stilton vinaigrette, Texas bobwhite quail with jalapeño

and red currant glaze, heart-shaped bread puddings with caramel glaze, and a bottle of Perrier-Jouët champagne to wash it all down.

Shortly after 9 A.M. on the glorious clear day of April 14, 1984, Tom began his operation and then opened the first beer. Recent heavy rain had left behind mud, but had puffed up the wild flowers. Soon friends began to wander in, dressed in country dresses, jeans, and boots, beer flowed, and country music from tapes played. At two, lunch was served; mounds of quilts piled under live oak trees were scattered and set with blue-and-white dishes and twig baskets. It was a gathering of Texas best friends, who see each other all the time and yet have so much to talk about. The warmth and affection were almost tangible.

Wedding Dresses

The Brooklyn Museum has a collection of wedding gowns in its Costume and Textile Department. The Metropolitan Museum, too, has been collecting wedding gowns; among them, its prize possession is the dress worn by Wallis Simpson when she married Edward, abdicated King of England, the Duke of Windsor. Someday soon, I hope one of these institutions will organize an exhibition of wedding gowns, for they have many stories to tell, of the times, of position and personality, of style and culture. In the meantime, the wedding gowns worn by brides in this book constitute an exhibition of sorts, for they tell of ceremonial life in the 1980s, of the romantic visions of contemporary young women, of personalities defined in ageless fashion.

In America, and indeed in most countries of the world, the wedding gown is much more than a fancy dress, for girls grow up with bride dolls, are affected by wedding scenes in classic literature, films, and contemporary news, and in idle moments, spin out fanta-

PRECEDING PAGE: A selection of dresses designed by Ada Athanassiou hanging in her Seventh Avenue showroom. The fabrics include taffetas, silks, and handkerchief linens.

OPPOSITE, TOP ROW, LEFT TO RIGHT: Sophie Desmarais's bridesmaids wore dresses of white taffeta with teal blue silk sashes; Hilary Cushing's bridesmaids wore Mary McFadden designs; Susan Ciesielski, Sharon Nelson's matron of honor, wore a tiered lace dress and a wreath of fresh flowers in her hair.

MIDDLE ROW, LEFT TO RIGHT: Mrs. Gardella, the bride's mother, having the sash of her Laura Ashley dress tied by her daughter; Margot Olshan making last-minute adjustments to her traditional lace dress from Ada Athanassiou; Meg Hester's attendants wore flower-decorated shoes.

BOTTOM ROW, LEFT TO RIGHT: Shirley Childs's attendants all wore original designs by Koos van den Akker; Sara Solis-Cohen's cousin, Jane, wore a striped Laura Ashley flower girl dress; Barbara Carpenter's creamy lace dress with a twelve-foot train and veil was designed by Enid Morris; Emily Arth, in a pensive mood, wears a tulle gown by Nancy Vandenboorn.

THIS PAGE, TOP: Mrs. Temerlin, mother of the bride, in a white silk James Galanos gown.

sies of their own scenes and their own gowns. On her wedding day, a girl, whoever she is or has been, is celebrated almost like a pagan goddess, and she dresses appropriately. The shy are for a moment flamboyant; the plain and practical, sweetly frivolous. And yet for all its implicit romanticism, the dress invariably describes the bride, sometimes her daily fashionable self, sometimes a dreamy self. I have been frequently surprised, rarely disappointed, and always reassured to see the bride's choice of dress. It was in character and in appropriate style that Sissy Cargill and Annie O'Herron wore their mothers' dresses, and that Meg Hester wore family old lace and shoes, but chose the simple dress of her favorite neighborhood dressmaker. Hilary Cushing, tall, lithe, and composed, chose her exact fashion counterpart in Mary McFadden's coolly perfect columnar dress. As Kathy Gar-Dianos and Joyce Roquemore are involved with real fashion, so their dresses were original statements. Sophie Desmarais, though she wears tailored silk dresses during the day, has

a dramatic high-fashion personality, and knew that dotted swiss and yards and yards of tulle were right for her. Debbie Cook, celebrating her affection for a lake in New Hampshire along with her marriage, chose a simple taffeta tinted with pink embroidery—informal, country, old-fashioned.

It is rare fun to have the opportunity to dress only for yourself on your day. It is a chance to express hidden dreams and desires, the private, sometimes secret, knowledge of exactly who you are and how you should look. Leafing through bridal magazines and studying store racks, it becomes clear that wedding dresses are in a category by themselves, true confections that have more to do with theater or make-believe than the regimen of fashion. Alfred Angelo, one of the largest manufacturers of wedding gowns, has pointed out that the dresses that sell least well are up-to-the-minute fashions. Aesthetically, there are few restrictions imposed on the wedding gown. Since Victorian times, it has been white, the color of purity and, in earlier days, joy, a strictly American tradition; red, an expression of happiness and permanence, is still the color of Hindu and Chinese wedding dresses (red was worn briefly by brides here during the American Revolution as an act of defiance); green, in Norway. Since the Dark Ages, the wedding dress has been a ceremonial gown, that is, a special gown, rich, important, momentous in the eye of the beholder.

Some girls, like Sophie Desmarais, have a precise vision of their wedding gown and simply set about realizing it. Others may favor a particular style or designer. The majority of future brides probably have both a vision and a style, which are as yet unarticulated in their minds, and they embark on a course of shopping and enlightenment. According to Pris-

RIGHT: Entering St. Francis Episcopal Church in Stamford, Connecticut, Heather Bartling's maid of honor wore a white Laura Ashley dress. The hat was bought to match the dress in New York City's hat district.
BELOW RIGHT: Sara Solis-Cohen, wearing a voluminous handkerchief linen dress by Ada Athanassiou, steps into the garden with the help of Amanda O'Brien, her dresser.

OPPOSITE: Heather Bartling, wearing a tissue linen dress with hooped petticoat by Ada Athanassiou from Saks Fifth Avenue, is escorted into the church by her father and stepfather. Heather sewed her own silk flowers on the sleeves.

cilla Kidder, the Priscilla of Boston, the average bride visits ten to fifteen stores. One of the popular destinations in the environs of New York is the Bridal Building on Seventh Avenue, where there are twenty-four floors of boutiques, and thousands of dresses at less than retail cost. It is a rigorous course, however, leaving many girls confused and exhausted, with heavy heads full of beadwork, lace, and embroidery, and spirits diminishing to the level of supermarket shoppers. With the brides I have known, the range has been smaller, and the experience more pleasant, and ultimately the decision rested with two or maybe three dresses, not twenty. An attack of desperation in the search for a wedding dress should be interpreted as a signal to seek out one of those serene, velvet-walled bridal salons

that cater in a sympathetic, motherly way to individual taste and style, and that understand many points of view.

"I have girls tell me they wish they could be married in jeans; reluctantly they begin to try on dresses, and then they are transformed and become traditional brides. If they feel pretty, they look pretty and project it. There is magic in the air." This is Irene Worth, the head of the bridal salon at Neiman-Marcus, in White Plains, New York, who has accumulated nineteen years in the business, first at Milgrim's and Schulman's, and who, according to dozens of brides I have met, is one of the most helpful salespersons in the field. "I don't pressure, but I don't want brides to be nervous at the end, and ordering can take ten to sixteen weeks. We usually have two or three fittings; al-

though most manufacturers will make changes, on sleeves or necklines or trains, most girls prefer the alterations here. Sometimes I walk around with the bride, looking for shoes, or I recommend florists and photographers. Brides are excited and nervous, and if you can save them time, it is nice, like being a surrogate parent. I get a sense of the girl; it's a study in human nature. Petites, for example, don't want to be dressed as littly baby dolls, particularly if they are marrying men six foot seven. And yet one tiny girl recently asked me how I would describe her in her dress and I said 'cute,' and she said, 'Good, that's me.' Even when they can't decide, brides really know what they want to express this day; it's like a role: what mood do they want to be in.''

Mrs. Worth spoke of the new market in wedding gowns, the moires, the taffetas, the lightweight fabrics designed for comfort. She remembers a time when a very young designer, Ada Athanassiou, shared a small studio in New York with Richard Glasgow ("They have come a long way.''), and she knows the ways of all the top designers. "Bianchi will always be known for her gorgeous beadwork, and her silk and silk organza. Ada's dresses are youthful; one wants to be a bride and an individual, too, with simplicity and elegance." She brings out a dress by a Japanese designer named Umi Katsura, which is two pieces, and distinguished by a jacket with a big crystal-pleated flounced jabot, and says, "It is exciting when you see the right girl in this: tall, glamorous, and a bit avant garde." She shows me a traditional formal gown by Bianchi, in satin, with an extraordinary teardrop-shaped train (which can be bustled later for dancing), and points out the embroidery, centered on pearls and flecked with iridescent sequins. Then she presents the new styles, inspired perhaps by *Gone*

Frances Schwartz being fitted at Rubicon in her fiancé's grandmother's dress, originally made in 1901 from Princess and Venetian laces.

with the Wind: taffeta ballroom gowns by Richard Glasgow, with short, full sleeves, an elasticized, possibly off-the-shoulder neckline, a touch of beading, and a full, full skirt with no train. "This, at the moment, is avant garde." She speaks of veils and then headpieces, the various forms (floral wreath, derby hat, picture hat) and veil lengths, from shoulder, elbow, and fingertip, to court and the ninety-two-inch cathedral. "Some girls don't want to wear anything on their heads (Martha Washington didn't) and then I suggest a little baby's breath on a comb."

"When I begin," Mrs. Worth explained, "I think about the time, the site, the season, and the appearance of the bride. But I do believe bridal etiquette is determined by the bride, because it is her day. To be wrong, the choice would have to be in supreme bad taste. Re-

cently I helped a girl select an airy chiffon dress. As she left, she said, 'Picture me running down a beach in this, for that's what I am going to do.' It is their day, and you help them create it."

Most fine department stores have bridal salons with distinct reputations: Neiman-Marcus in Dallas, Sak's in San Francisco, Marshall Field in Chicago. In New York City, Bergdorf Goodman's is quiet and refined; Henri Bendel's is chic, individualistic, and expensive—60 percent of their dresses are exclusive, and Monica Hickey, Bendel's bridal buyer, discovered the Emmanuels before Lady Di did. The bridal business is booming, and bridal shops flourishing. Josie's, in Westport, Connecticut, has tripled its store space in the past several years; antique clothing shops, with their treasures from grandmothers' trunks, have become popular sources for brides, too.

Fine textiles, both old and new, have inspired many young designers. Pat Kerr, a former Miss Memphis and Miss Tennessee, who had run beauty pageants around the world, and collected textiles as a hobby, first began selling wedding gowns made from her expensive antique laces in 1979. Now, from her penthouse bridal salon in Memphis, she creates as many as several hundred dresses a month, and, a year ago, designed the bridal gown pictured in the ads for Estée Lauder's new perfume, Beautiful. Part of her collection are off-the-rack designs sold across the country in specialty shops like Neiman-Marcus; others are customized gowns incorporating heirloom lace—a train fashioned from a grandmother's veil, for example—made for a cross section of brides that range from rich Texans and South Americans, who love lace, to quiet Boston old stock and dreamy young couples who save their money for a once-in-a-lifetime indulgence. All of her dresses are one of a kind.

There used to be a small, charming shop on Madison Avenue called the Rubicon Boutique that specialized in creating original, one-of-a-kind dresses of new and antique lace. The owner, Peggie A. Krasner, haunted old flea markets and auctions for beautiful fabrics, and occasionally had even cut up old curtains and tapestries for her "special occasion" dresses. The shop had the look of a small museum, with gowns hung on walls and on dress forms as well as racks: short, long, tea-length, beaded, appliquéd, embroidered, frilly and slim, puffy-sleeved and sleeveless, lace of every shade of white and every shade of age, as well as dyed in many colors, for bridesmaids or mothers of the bride. The Rubicon's demise was sudden and sad, but given the growing interest in textiles as an art form, I know that it was a prototype, setting a course, and that other such shops are cropping up all over the country and should be sought out.

I watched a fitting at the Rubicon late one afternoon, the hour when brides-to-be slip away from their jobs. I met Anita Wallace, who had made a mental note about this shop, but until her daughter Kim announced her decision to be married, she had not found the occasion to investigate it. This day, they had arrived for the third and final fitting, two weeks before Kim's wedding to Alf Aaronsen, a Norwegian like her mother. Two fittings are the norm; the first, called a virgin fitting, is for measurements, after which the dress is designed and cut. Then there are adjustments. Kim's dress, which she had chosen from an original selection of six, then four, two, and one, was "a killer dress," difficult to alter because of its scalloped hemline and dropped Juliet point at the waist. Also, Kim is a tiny size 4 or 6, and her dress had been a size 8 or 10.

ABOVE: The back of Sophie Desmarais's beautiful dress, designed by Serge Sénécal and Réal Bastien, made from yards and yards of dotted swiss, tulle, and net. BELOW: Kim Wallace being fitted in her lace dress, an original Rubicon design. Her veil was silk tulle.

She had seriously considered a swirling dramatic dress, similar to Princess Di's, but she had decided that it was too much for her wedding ceremony at home.

An assistant brought out Kim's white crinoline petticoats with a swoop, and, in a few moments, Kim reappeared shyly, nonetheless visibly pleased with herself in the dress. French lace on the bodice, with Swiss embroidered net for the sleeves and the skirt over heavy wedding satin, the dress was one of Mrs. Krasner's collages. Kim twirled on request, as the fitter tucked in a shoulder, and admired the recent heightened poof to the sleeves. The wedding veil appeared next, three yards of filmy tulle, and everyone in the shop gathered around. Just as the sighs for Kim were dissipating, another young bride, tall, slim, and serene, arrived to try on her dress, of another style and era. It was two-piece, a long-sleeved high-necked Victorian lace blouse over a long straight skirt. "This look is returning," a helper offered. "It's feminine, elegant, and versatile. After the wedding, you can wear the top with anything—a red taffeta skirt or a prairie skirt. It can also be dyed any color, so it could suit the mother of the bride."

It is not the norm, but perhaps the most gratifying experience of all is working one-to-one with a designer on a wedding dress. Sophie Desmarais had thought about her wedding dress for almost as many years as she had known Serge Sénécal and Réal Bastien, and, in fact, when she knocked at their door, she had only to describe it to effect its realization. Meg Hester and Dana Temerlin, too, had long-standing relationships with their designers, and turned to them with the utmost confidence, borne of experience and trust. Dana's friendship with Milo of Casablanca was such that he accompanied her from Texas to New York for the wedding, rushed out to the garment district to purchase new tulle when her veil was irreparably crushed in transit, and minutes before the processional march, was with her behind the scenes, fussing and fitting. Mary McFadden had made previous dresses for Hilary Cushing and her mother Robin, and although she rarely does other than "turnkey" jobs, she seemed pleased with

her detailed involvement in both the dress and train, patient with Hilary's cosmetic concerns, and generous with advice.

McFadden's studio, in the garment district of the West Thirties in New York City, is a big stylish loft, where below the tall back windows a line of sewing machines hum away at matters as pressing as Barbara Walters's red dress for the next night's special show. The dresses for Hilary's bridesmaids and her mother were finished and draped on dummies nearby, similar but subdued relations of the wedding gown, in white, and apricot silk, respectively. Hilary's dress was long, straight, and stately, cut from the designer's famous pleated silk, accompanied by a floral princess headband attached to five yards of net. Its tiered elbow-length sleeves, of off-white organza, were cut on the bias; its bodice was attached to the skirt at a dropped waist suggestive of the twenties and thirties and, perhaps, Zelda Fitzgerald. When Hilary stood in her dress, the pleats sat on the floor in a perfect formal arrangement; when she walked, the dress moved with her in a way that was supremely dignified and yet a little bit seductive.

Hilary was pleased with the dress, but worried about the headpiece, which, for full Isadora Duncan effect, called for a more studied hairstyle than her usual, and which, trailing an unusual volume of net, was also heavy. "What do I do with my hair?" Hilary fussed.

OPPOSITE: Hilary Cushing looks statuesque and beautiful in her columnar Mary McFadden creation. Her bouquet was composed of cimbydium orchids.

At Mary McFadden's studio, Hilary tries on her dress and veil.

ABOVE: Mrs. Cushing's pleated silk dress in pale apricot. BELOW: A bridesmaid's dress made to order.

"Try it to the side the way you sometimes do," her mother suggested. "Will the headpiece fall off?" "The hairdresser has to secure it." "The train?" "The matron of honor will have to manipulate it; be sure to talk to her." Miss McFadden advised against any jewelry except pearl earrings. Mrs. Cushing suggested a very light lipstick. Lili, a seamstress, circled Hilary many times, carrying pins in her mouth, and beamed. Miss McFadden said that she likes to do wedding dresses, had done about twenty to date, including more frivolous ones in lace for the Medici collection, but favors simplicity, which suits Hilary.

As bridesmaids are attendant to the bride, so their dresses are attendant to the wedding gown. Like bridesmaids, they are meant to be intermediaries between the bride and the scene around her, relating in color, style, and mood to both. A pink bridesmaid's dress may match the roses on the table and the frosting on the cake; a red velvet and lace gown may underline the fact that it is an old-fashioned Christmas wedding. The choice of bridesmaids' dresses is even freer than that of wedding dresses and, in fact, offers an opportunity to articulate the theme of the wedding, to unify the color scheme, or to add a personality that might seem overbearing in a wedding dress. Thus Sissy Cargill and Anne O'Herron, who married in their mothers' dresses at sites on the water, chose sailor dresses from Laura Ashley to elaborate their nautical themes. Thus Sophie Desmarais's bridesmaids wore white taffeta dresses bound with sashes that matched the royal turquoise blue of Notre Dame's brilliant ceiling. Thus Joyce Roquemore's two attendants in their velvet ballgowns verified the presence of the eighteenth century at her wedding at the restaurant Le Zinc.

Bridesmaids' dresses, as a rule, are designed on the principle that they are costumes for a day, unlikely to endure as fashion or to be worn again. Fortunately, they are usually quite reasonably priced, but this often means factory made and poorly constructed. Yet unless bridesmaids' dresses are exceptionally useful and beautiful, or the bride's mother is making a gift of the dresses, as did Shirley O'Herron, it is inconsiderate to select more expensive dresses. For this reason, many brides become inventive, choosing Laura Ashley dresses that can be worn many times; re-creating a favorite evening dress, as Meg Hester did for her bridesmaids; finding a lovely fabric and making their own designs. Kathy GarDianos, herself a young designer of evening wear, was inspired by an antique men's dinner jacket, and elongated it in silk charmeuse for her maid of honor. Sissy Cargill, with the help of her godmother, designed hoop skirts in French provincial cotton.

For footwear, classic pumps have been supplemented with ballet slippers (as comfortable as bare feet, well-adapted to receptions on the soft ground of meadows and lawns, and graceful with short or tea-length gowns). Rosebuds or floppy bows on plain shoes, tiny polka dots on sheer stockings also can add romantic touches to a costume.

In attending a panorama of weddings in the last several years, I have realized that the look of the groom and groomsmen has changed, too, and that now there are choices wider than the formula cutaway, morning suit, or white tie and tails. Formal dress is elegant, and bestows a classic grand dignity on almost every type and physique—the drama of black and white, the lore of the aristocracy. Yet on hot days, a cutaway is uncomfortable, and al-

The maid of honor and best man at the wedding of George Furlan and Kathryn GarDianos. Her dress was an original design by the bride.

though sometimes it is called for, at other times it may be at least as appropriate and more original to wear a blazer and bright tie, carefully coordinated to the wedding scheme. In the country, by the sea, in a relaxed familial gathering in summer, a blazer with a white or striped shirt and white pants seems a natural choice, in its way as evocative of the good life as a tuxedo and pleated shirt.

The weddings in this book indicate the range of choice and the role of personality in that choice. White tie graced the Desmarais wedding; morning clothes, the Zucker wedding. At the weddings of Hilary Cushing, Anne O'Herron, and Sissy Cargill, the blazers

the men wore contributed to the special aura of the day. For his wedding in Central Park, George Furlan, a designer who had first planned to make trousers of gray morning fabric to wear with a vintage white jacket, ended up with an oversized black Italian tux (for a period look) and an antique shirt with a piqué bib and wing collar. John Clapps revised his idea of a red tux into a more subdued pink.

Indeed, in the 1980s, dress rules are much looser than in the past, and a rigid code is antiquated. There is no circumstance, for example, in which a morning suit or white tie and tails, or even a tuxedo, is absolutely essential for decorum's sake. In general, however, a morning suit is worn at a formal morning wedding, up to and including a prelunch event; white tie is worn at a very formal late-afternoon or evening event; and a tuxedo, whenever it suits the mood of both the event and the groom. A business suit or blazer may be worn at any daytime wedding; a dark suit at night. To me, the most beautiful male dress is white tie, and yet it is the least frequently worn. The best-dressed and most comfortable grooms and groomsmen photographed for this book were wearing beautifully tailored suits or blazers, or their own tuxedos.

Only the rare male owns a morning suit. But more and more men own their own tuxedos or dinner jackets, as indeed they should. And everyone certainly should invest in a beautiful cotton or linen dress shirt, with a pleated or piqué front (reserving ruffles for the tango palace). An impending wedding presents a perfect opportunity to have such a shirt made to enjoy for many years to come. Unless you plan ahead as carefully as many women do, rental tuxes can be horrendous looking—true penguin garb, shiny, ill fitting, and obviously the "borrowed" item of wedding ritual.

And there is something demoralizing about renting a tux for your own wedding, especially when the bride is spending vast sums on a confection that is likely to be worn only once. I have a friend who wants to go into business renting extravagant wedding gowns, which may be a more sensible practice, perhaps even the way of the future.

ABOVE: Andrew Cook chats with another young guest at his sister Debbie's wedding.
RIGHT: Sissy Cargill's bridesmaids wore Laura Ashley blouses and homemade flounced hooped skirts. The groom and groomsmen all wore white flannels, navy blazers, and red and white striped ties.

The Social Wedding

Hilary Cushing and John Block

In the annals of weddings, it seems that every thirty years or so, history repeats itself. In Edith Wharton's day, in the Roaring Twenties, in the frivolous postwar fifties, and now in the respectable eighties, the social wedding is in style. It all has to do with conservative times, with a renewed respect for tradition, an affection for order and security, a confirmation of the good life. The pages of newspapers and trendy magazines are full of stories of weddings in the grand style, unions of blueblood brides and corporate grooms played out in society's clubs and century-old estates. They seem to be blessed events, Gothic romances come to life. Suddenly "society" has resonance, and young people barely out of funk and punk are finding manners, wealth, and aristocratic behavior fashionable and exciting. It could be the stuff of Henry James, and yet it is the late-twentieth century, when titles and inheritances coexist with distinctly modern life-styles, couturier gowns, and social clubs with blue jeans and dual careers.

PRECEDING PAGES, LEFT: The portico, towering columns, and shingled facade of the Cushing "cottage" in Quogue. RIGHT: Place cards indicating seating arrangements for dinner at Hilary's reception were given to guests on the way to the ceremony tent.
LEFT: Elizabeth Hawes and Mrs. Cushing look on as Hilary is fitted for her wedding gown in the atelier of designer Mary McFadden.
RIGHT: Hilary Cushing's bedroom the morning before the wedding. Place cards, seating arrangements, and other last-minute details are in evidence.

Hilary Cushing, composed, confident, tall, willowy, blond, with a distinguished New York society family behind her, and a career at Sotheby's ahead of her, well describes the new breed of socialite. And, perhaps appropriately, she wanted to set her June 22, 1985, wedding, Gatsby-style, at her summer home in Quogue, on the shores of Long Island—as it happens, hallowed society ground since the revels and novels of F. Scott Fitzgerald. Hilary's reasons for the choice were nostalgic, however, for Quogue felt most like home to her, a child of the city, and the gracious country mood of Belle Meade, the family cottage, matched her visions for the day. Its great lawns invited fun and ease, its pillared porches and spacious rooms evoked a formal but comfortable, suggestively southern way of life. Although the house sleeps twenty-eight, Hilary had arranged for bridesmaids and friends to stay at old inns nearby, for she wanted the house to herself that last weekend.

Apart from the site of her wedding, the common denominator in most of Hilary's plans was Sotheby's, where she has supervised special events for the past five years, masterminding gala auctions and benefits. The groom-to-be was John Block, confirmed bachelor, a vice-president and head of jewelry in North America at Sotheby's; the minister-to-be, Hugh Hildesley, currently rector of the Church of the Heavenly Rest on Manhattan's Upper East Side, formerly head of appraisals and estate work at Sotheby's; the caterer for the elegant French dinner for two hundred, Bernard Mignot, chef in residence at the auction house; the floral decorator, Jennifer Cohan, also a daily presence at Sotheby's. In the course of her professional life, Hilary designs formal sit-down dinners for five hundred as easily as small receptions, and, like her mother, Robin Cushing, who organizes lavish charity affairs for Irvington House, has become known for her brilliant parties. Together, the mother-and-daughter team decided to split the wedding duties and share their basic coordination. After interviewing a range of favorite sources, they came away convinced that it would be most comfortable and memorable to rely on Hilary's own in-house network; Ber-

nard, who would grant her favorite dishes from the repertory she knew well; Jennifer, young, amiable, with wonderful eclectic aesthetics; me, for the wedding cake, and my service staff, familiar faces from the receptions I had done with Hilary; as well as resources well seasoned at Sotheby's to provide tents (creamy white), dinner rentals (natural bamboo chairs, round tables, white tablecloths with a lacy beige overlay), liquor, and music (Vince Giardano's swing band).

Like many young women on the modern scene, and curiously like women of bygone eras, Hilary had waited for marriage to set up housekeeping ("Living together is out," one reads in the pages of fashion magazines), and she had enjoyed a long friendship with John and a flourishing career, together with all the comforts of her family's home in Manhattan (including occasional breakfasts in bed). In a dramat-

Side apartment; for the wedding, Tiffany invitations ("the big folded ones"), Tiffany bridal registry (their Audubon silver pattern, Limoges china), Mary McFadden gowns for the bride, bridesmaids, and mother of the bride. Throughout the late spring, fittings with the designer, who had made other dresses for Hilary and would finish this very special one after her fall collection was presented, and consultations with the team constructing new bathrooms and kitchen were interlaced with parties (beginning with three friends' black-tie affair at Doubles, the private nightclub at the Pierre Hotel), and the demands of Sotheby's spring schedule. As the season grew warmer and the wedding nearer, Hilary, like June brides all across the country, slipped off to Quogue on weekends to work on her tan.

In the flat saltwater farmland of the southern shore of Long Island, rambling

ic sweep, she and John were doing everything at once: marrying, buying an apartment, reconstructing it, and decorating, all in the stylish neoconservative way that reflects a proper regard for quality and a bow to tradition well mixed with storybook charm. English antiques and chintzes for the new Upper East

LEFT: I examine the bridesmaids' dresses in Hilary's bedroom, which had been designated the "dressing room." ABOVE: The Cushing Maltese, Saga, freshly groomed for the wedding day. RIGHT: The back of Hilary's illusion veil and head wreath.

summer cottages like Belle Meade materialize from behind tall hedges like great Victorian dowagers. Built in 1906 by Stanford White, the brilliant bon vivant whose designs were favored by the elite of New York and Newport, Belle Meade is immediately imposing, for the romantic classical elements are present in abundance: tall white Corinthian columns and a fanlight at the entrance, a high roofline with dormers, a closed hexagonal porch to the side, and, behind, a sweeping deck and open-columned porch. Discreetly landscaped at the back of the house, adjacent to a long lawn, are a tennis court, pool, and, under heavy pine boughs, a tiny guest chamber that might have once been used as a children's playhouse. The proportions of Belle Meade are generous, but not extravagant, its feeling comfortably aristocratic, tended rather than manicured, pleasure-giving rather than pretentious.

The morning of the wedding, Belle Meade was quiet, suggesting the calm before the storm, the hot silence of summer broken only by an airplane's buzz and the occasional hum of a nearby lawn mower. No one was in the pool or on the lawn or court, or in evidence in the main part of the house. The spacious rooms here, decorated in a formal country style resplendent with chintz, each with its own dramatic color, were gracefully appointed

LEFT: Silhouetted against a bright window, Hilary looks elegant in her columnar dress. ABOVE RIGHT: One of the many richly carved mantels in the home, decorated with fresh flower arrangements by Jennifer Cohan.

with large vases of spectacular flowers. Casually, an old friend of John's settled down in the dark wainscotted dining room to write out place cards. ("Now, what about the cards?" she had ventured to Hilary, who wandered through sleepily in a very short tennis dress.) Mrs. Cushing appeared with a response, and then Hilary's older brother, the first sign of nerves, steamrolled through with urgent missions. Gradually, all the Sotheby helping hands arrived—Bernard with a station wagon full of lobster salad, veal roasts, racks of lamb, and garden vegetables; Jennifer Cohan with a van full of June flowers; my service crew, who were to assist Bernard in the kitchen and serve dinner; the Reverend Hugh Hildesley, who adjourned to the tent to create an altar for the marriage ceremony. The back porch filled with cases of soda and champagne, the yard with canvas bags of rental chairs and tables. Robert Cushing, Hilary's father and an eminent New York obstetrician, pulled into the drive in his green Jeep, which sports a pink-and-white-striped top, and wandered idly about the yard, in and out of the large white tent that had been set up off the back porch, by way of a long canopy leading down the steps. "For months, so many people have been here fixing up the interior and the exterior," he said, "that I feel like the head of a huge corporation. But I'm not. I'm a simple man." Was he excited? "I'm afraid at this moment I don't know what I feel."

It is a study in theater to watch the final preparations for a wedding like Hilary Cushing's. First the tables were set up with chairs and draped with lacy cloths. Then came the white plates and sparkling crystal, and a frill of phlox, peonies, roses, campanula, and Dendrobium orchids in glass bowls, and suddenly there was romance. Then, with the final gar-

OPPOSITE: A collage of important wedding-day photographs—the bride and her father, the flowers, the wedding kiss, the receiving line, the smiles, the champagne, the trays and tables, and, of course, the musicians. ABOVE: The fanciful cake, with pleated icing to reiterate the "Fortuny"-type pleated fabric of Hilary's dress, has a tall narrow shape and decorations of old garden roses and white sweet peas.

nish of silver-filigree Art Deco lamps (which would illuminate a circle of happy faces when night fell), there was potential magic under the tent: a makeshift arrangement had become a stage ready to be animated. Likewise, a buffet table looked matter-of-fact until Jennifer began to layer it with swirls of flowers to cre-

ate a background tableau for the food; likewise, a white-draped bar table looked like a white-draped bar table until Allen Acosta, my maître d', began to fuss and improvise—shirring, pulling up and pinning pleats and swags—until it became a respectable altar, ready to be laid with the cross and candles transported for the occasion from the Church of the Heavenly Rest. In the wings, my crew organized itself—table and bar assignments, timetable, and, even at a society wedding and especially at a society wedding, "sanitation" arrangements (garbage cans stashed out of sight under draped tables)—then they moved out, smoothed their formal shirts, and stood ready for the event. The band assembled under the tent, tuned up, and, for practice, played a few bars of Handel's "Water Music," another few of Mendelssohn's wedding march, and then drifts of the dance music that later would set the mellow mood of the evening.

Upstairs in a very feminine bedroom, Roma from Nardi's on Fifty-seventh Street was styling hair, the mother of the groom first, and then "everyone she could fit in before the ceremony began at four-thirty." Mrs. Block seemed effusively happy, both with her hair and with Hilary, whose composure and self-sufficiency she declared the perfect match for her electric and high-strung son. By four-fifteen, guests were drifting in the front door past the Corinthian columns, through the Great Hall, out the back door, under the canopy, and into the tent, where Vince Giardano, a master at Gershwin and Porter, but unaccustomed to the traditional music for which he had sheet music, was playing "Jesu, Joy of Man's Desiring." At four-fifty-five, the groom, best man, and minister were standing together gazing up at a bedroom window where the bride and bridesmaids were still

dressing, inquiring about the time of arrival. According to my observations, 90 percent of brides are late, and no one ever minds or remembers, so time began only when Hilary, proceeded by a flower girl, matron of honor, and four bridesmaids and followed by a long, long tulle train, moved into sight from the door of her home.

OPPOSITE: In the dinner tent, tables were covered with white cotton undercloths, lace overcloths, Art Deco lamps, centerpieces of roses, and hand-blown crystal. ABOVE: The pointed roof of the crisp white tent outlined against the tall trees on the Cushing property. RIGHT: The cake table was strewn with specimen roses from my rose garden. One of my favorite old roses, Charles de Mills, has multitudinous petals, some of which are perfectly heart-shaped.

Bridal Bouquets

In the beginning there were gatherings of herbs, potent combinations of garlic, chives, rosemary, and dill, whose aromas were meant to drive off evil spirits; and orange blossoms to recall Juno's offering to Jupiter on their wedding day. In the 1930s and 1940s, there were calla lilies, the Art Deco favorite; and then there were formal sprays of prescribed white flowers— lilies, orchids, freesia, stephanotis, and, perhaps, lilies of the valley. Now gardens and minds have expanded, and the bride's bouquet might be an armful of pink snapdragons, a single giant calla lily, a nosegay of rich pastel tea roses wrapped in lace and streaming curly ribbons, or a branch of flowering quince. Some brides gather their own handful of field flowers like clover and Queen Anne's lace; others seek out the advice of one of the rapidly growing band of new florists, who

101

have artistic styles all their own and shops full of unusual and indescribably beautiful blooms to express them.

There are no rules to dictate a bride's choice of bouquet beyond its harmony with her personality, her wedding dress, and her setting. A single spectacular flower can be as theatrical and flamboyant as a massive formal bouquet. A simple handful of flowers may be in order when the bride is wearing flowers in her hair or hair combs decorated with fresh flowers, which is in vogue. Another bride may wish to rediscover an old tradition and choose a bouquet of silk flowers, which either she or a lucky bridesmaid can preserve as a lovely keepsake. I think it is in the nature of flowers to go with anything, and, therefore, a bride rarely makes a serious mistake. Yet, although almost any florist can provide a respectable bridal bouquet, it is more fun and more meaningful to make the choice a thoughtful and personal one. The shape, the contents, even the fragrance of a bridal bouquet all contribute to its special beauty.

When Princess Di caught the fancy of the world in her romantic bouffant bridal gown, she carried a cascade of white roses in the formal English tradition. It was an extraordinarily beautiful creation, extravagant, massive, and structured, and although it has come to represent the ultimate bridal bouquet, it was also a bouquet that was hard to hold and exorbitantly expensive to make, reputedly requiring the labors of several florists over several days. Many brides these days have gone in the opposite direction, asking for unstructured, loose armfuls of flowers tied together gently with double-faced satin ribbon. This gardenesque informality has become a prevalent style with many florists now, although most of them tend to do some wiring, to prevent

PRECEDING PAGES, LEFT: A green glass flower "ring" holds blossoms of stephanotis, acknowledged as *the* wedding flower. RIGHT: A cascade of freshly picked white lilacs, wired together and tied with creamy satin ribbon.

OPPOSITE: Renny created this bouquet of roses, Dendrobium orchids, peonies, and ixia. ABOVE: A copy of the bouquet I carried when I married Andy in 1961. He bought the bouquet, but it is very easy to create with home-grown flowers.

bruising of the flowers and to help keep a bouquet fresh and beautiful throughout the ceremony and reception.

Formal or informal, a bouquet may take any number of shapes. The age-old classic is an all-white combination of stephanotis, freesia, white roses, and carnations, gathered into a

sphere, either full and slightly floppy, perhaps trailing a curl or two of ivy, or smaller, compact, and tightly wired. Smaller still is the nosegay, a sweet handful of flowers of a single kind, like delicate pansies or sweet peas, which has Victorian overtones. There is the armful of garden flowers, and there is a single spray, of calla or rubrum lilies, or of the long-stemmed roses so many brides like to carry, which can be easily assembled and then tied together prettily at home.

Comfort is a factor to take into consideration, along with the style of the wedding gown. If a dress has a full swinging skirt, for example, a smallish bouquet with lots of gracefully cascading ribbons is a lovely complement. If a dress is straight and severe, a strongly shaped bouquet adds drama. If she wishes, a bride may take cues from her dress. Thus Beth Gardella chose calla lilies that repeated the appliqué work at her hemline, and Joyce Roquemore chose calla lilies because their rich texture matched that of the heavy satin of her gown.

Although it seems to be the most frequent choice of brides, an all-white bouquet is not the predictable palette one might imagine, for white is also the ivory, champagne, and cream of old roses and ranunculus, as well as the pure snow of lilies of the valley and white orchids. Color, however, is incorporated more and more often in bouquets, for it can offset a dress, and is particularly appropriate to a less formal gown. A subtle touch of color can also serve to unify the bridal party; thus, Margot Olshan chose to carry pink as well as white roses, because her bridesmaids were wearing deep pink. Green foliage is a popular addition, too, for a backing of ferns or a trail of ivy not only adds a bright note of freshness, but also defines the flowers and shape of a bouquet.

BELOW: Red and yellow tulips were wired, taped, and then tied with lace and satin streamers.

LEFT AND BELOW: A loosely structured bouquet of long-stemmed French tulips. Love knots and stephanotis are used in the satin streamers.
OPPOSITE: Long-stemmed giant Swiss pansies tied with tatted lace and silk streamers make a unique Victorian nosegay.

The Rose Bouquet

My own favorite bouquet of the moment is a plump, round, and lightly wired mass of beloved garden flowers, particularly roses and stephanotis, which to me epitomize weddings, garnished with tulle, old lace, and lots of beautiful ribbons. Like many brides of today, I am also very fond of herbal bouquets, which offer the advantages of being very long-lived and carrying a meaningful message: rosemary for remembrance, sage for wisdom, lovage for strength. The language of flowers, of course, extends far beyond herbs: violets symbolize modesty; ivy, fidelity; honeysuckle, faithfulness; white lilac, innocence; and Juno's orange blossoms, fertility and happiness.

I love to make bridal bouquets, and I like to use my own garden for bouquets if possible, but until recently, I had never opened up fully to its possibilities. I had never made a bouquet of daffodils before, but I tried, and found it easy to make—because of the rigidity of the stems—long-lasting, and, tied with contrasting ribbon, very colorful. Then I made bouquets of rhododendrons, those great pink clusters of small individual blossoms, surrounded by stiff glossy leaves, and they had an impressive, important, permanent sort of look. I worried about including allium and chive flowers in my medieval herbal bouquet, but the aroma soon dissipated, and the sweet fragrant greenness remained for more than a week. I experiment a lot out of my own curiosity, but also to show brides that they can go out into the garden and make an inspired bouquet of their own.

OPPOSITE: The finished rose bouquet.

The elements of a structured, wired bouquet: roses, florist's wire and tape, and other supplies in readiness.

Wire is inserted into the rose stems and wrapped around.

The stems are then wrapped with light green floral tape.

Wired roses are gathered into a cluster to form the center of the bouquet. As roses are added, floral tape is wound around the wire stems to hold each flower.

The taping together continues as more roses are added.

All the flowers, roses and lilies of the valley, gathered together and taped.

Lace is drawn with a piece of floral wire and gathered; a puff of tulle is also placed around the head of the bouquet.

The stems are tightly wound with satin ribbons. The bride will hold this smooth, finished "handle."

For those who have visions in their heads, but are unfamiliar with specific names, particularly the Latin names often used, I have made a list (page 117) of my favorite flowers that are in common use for bridal bouquets, and then a second list of other favorites that are less well known but nonetheless well suited.

All of these flowers are candidates for bridesmaids' bouquets, too, or centerpieces or church arrangements. The choice of bridesmaids' bouquets is virtually unlimited, the only considerations being that they should not overshadow the bride's and should be complementary at least in spirit. Vibrant color can come into play here, and originality should be encouraged. If a bride carries white tulips, her attendants might have those exotic specimen tulips striped red and white. The single pink lily carried by the lacy bridesmaids at Allison Zucker's wedding; the upside-down straw hats filled with red, white, and blue flowers carried with sailor dresses at Sissy Cargill's—both offer provocative examples of originality and style.

Flowers are present in other forms at weddings. Sprigs of delicate blooms may be attached to hair combs for the bride or attendants; on a headband, they provide a lovely anchor for a wedding veil. Sweet wreaths of blossoms or myrtle leaves give a medieval touch to the heads of bridesmaids and a flower girl, and can be made by any good florist. For boutonnieres, select at least one of the flowers found in the bridal bouquets, and for the groom, the most beautiful example. The days when corsages and wristlets were shunned are long gone, and almost everyone likes to put on a flower at a wedding—in the lapel for men, at the neck or waist or in the hair for women. Babs Cook tucked a freesia behind her ear at her daughter's wedding. San-

dra Leo-Wolf honored all her nineteen guests with tokens of flowers.

Florists everywhere, even in unlikely rural outposts, have become very sophisticated, are paying more attention to their aesthetics, and enjoying artistic invention. In selecting bou-

OPPOSITE: This herbal bouquet consists of lavender chive flowers, lamb's ears (*Stachys olympica*), clematis, and tansy, tied with a wide pink satin ribbon bow. ABOVE: Long-stemmed, fragrant sweet peas, simply clustered and tied with silk ribbons, are kept fresh until just before the ceremony in a glass of cold water.

quets and wedding flowers, it may be that you can simply discuss your desires, or select the perfect arrangement from his portfolio or refrigerator. For the sake of clarity, however, it is often useful to take along a sketch of your dress, a picture of a favorite bouquet, or some knowledge of flowers you like. There is such variety in flower shops today that a little prior self-education can't hurt, and might, indeed, add to the fun of the day. If your local florist is not very knowledgeable, then show him a picture of what you want and direct him to make it, or, if necessary, ask him to special order your flowers and create it yourself. In either case, be specific, so that after all the soul-searching, you get what you want. Most florists make up bouquets the day of the wedding, and deliver them to the site of the ceremony, and, should there be an interlude that could threaten their freshness, will provide detailed instructions for their safekeeping. Bouquets with exposed stems can be placed in a glass of water to keep them fresh, but flowers with wired or wrapped stems are usually enclosed in a clear cellophane bag that is gently misted inside. In case of very hot weather, it is usually best to keep them refrigerated.

It is difficult to know which came first, the new aesthetics in flowers or the creative new flower shops sprouting on street corners everywhere, but they reinforce one another and enrich our lives. I asked nine of the legion of new flower people practicing their artistry in the New York area today to create signature bridal bouquets for me, drawing upon whatever vision inspired them. The results are formal and informal, sumptuous and fragile, nostalgic and romantic, and together document the wonderful state of the art into which the bride will dip for her wedding day.

English Bouquet

To begin with, a juniper branch for a stiff base; a flourish of rock ferns and delicate grasses; then a heart of blush roses, lilacs, and quince, cradled in Queen Anne's lace, white wax flowers, and traditional stephanotis; the result, a bouquet full of fragrance, texture, and interest, gently Victorian in its touches of subtle purples and pinks among the white, elegant in its full elongated shape, rather lighthearted and free in its components.

Charles Case describes his bouquet as English, and like most English things, it is sturdy and can be made the day before, if its stems are set in water and its head misted and covered with a plastic bag. Charles Case has made a wonderful reputation for himself in Westport, Connecticut, where he works out of a clapboard shop called The Flower Basket, in which his love of flowers and the decorative arts is conspicuous. Since he arrived here from Boston in 1979, I've watched him evolve from a young newlywed who had no idea of the depth of his abilities with flowers, to a deeply involved artist (with four young babies). Charles pays fastidious attention to the freshness of his flowers and is always pleased to pass on some of his special techniques (from him I learned to add gin to the water for tulips and peonies, bleach for stock, hot water for feverfew). He also loves weddings and families, and because he likes to do very different things for different brides, he provides enlightening consultations, nice personal, unhurried conversations, sometimes over a glass of wine.

OPPOSITE: Charles's finished bouquet, tied with picot-edged satin ribbon bow and streamers.

Charles Case begins by wiring the individual flowers he will use in his creation, here a rose.

After passing the medium-gauge wire through the stem, right beneath the flower head, he tapes the wire stem with floral tape.

Twirling the wired rose so that the tape encloses the wire stem.

Every piece of ivy is wound with wire to give it body and malleability. Charles uses thin wire, sometimes doubling it for strength.

Specially fabricated stephanotis stems are inserted in each blossom. The stems are then wrapped with floral tape.

Lilies of the valley are wired, then a small piece of wet tissue is wrapped around each stem and covered with floral tape.

Charles starts to cluster some of the flowers together, using light green floral tape.

A juniper branch, which has been soaked in water to make it more flexible, is wired for use as the base and structure of the bouquet.

The finished bouquet's thick "handle" is wound with satin ribbon and tied in a simple bow. Streamers are left to move with the bride.

LEFT: Lengths of antique white silk faille and pea-green satin ribbon shape this bouquet to the hand.
BELOW LEFT: Another exquisite bouquet designed by Mädderlake—a combination of hybrid tea roses, tuberoses, lilies of the valley, sweet peas—tied, bare stemmed, with cascades of pink ribbons.

Spring Garden Bouquet

Under the direction of Tom Prichard, Billy Jarecki, and Allen Boehmer, Mädderlake, which takes its name from an artist's pigment called madder lake, is a highly individualistic florist, less intent on creating a real show than an interesting personalized accumulation of seasonal woodland, perennial, and wild flowers. Located in Manhattan on East Seventy-fourth Street, it is in fact a floral studio, a gathering of men interested in doing informal and unstudied groupings of flowers, in all their varieties. For final touches to their bouquets, they like to add unusual ribbons, bits of crochetwork, and lace.

The bouquet above, made by Billy, was designed to evoke a favorite spring garden of the bride's, and combines delphinium and sweet peas with two types of showy clematis and white star-of-Bethlehem. It is informal in its mood, in its gardenesque beauty, and in its absence of wiring.

RIGHT: Paul's stunning bouquet, of immense proportions.
BELOW RIGHT: The complex French-braided stem.

French Braided Bouquet

Tucked into a corner of Bleecker Street in Greenwich Village there is a tiny charming shop, appropriately named Twigs, where Paul Gregory Bott, a friendly young florist, plans terraces and arranges flowers for homes, parties, and, in this case, weddings. His desire is to create something beautiful and showy, but not ostentatious, and to that end, he emphasizes the presence of the individual bloom.

When I gathered his bouquet in my arms, I

was affected by its wonderful weight, which made me feel important, and rather regal, like a princess. He pronounced it a French braided bouquet. It brought together an extravagant collection of beautiful perennials, each one full and perfect—white coquette roses, pink ramblers, peonies, delphinium, bishop's weed, lilacs, astilbe, ranunculus, campanula, star-of-Bethlehem, lysianthus, and grape leaves. It was a cascading exhibit of June.

Late Spring Bouquet

In Zezé's seven-year-old shop on East Fifty-second Street, the interior, as well as the flowers, changes totally from season to season. Out come the paint buckets, and there is spring—turquoise walls, sporting a folly of butterflies. Zezé, with his long black hair curling like that of a courtier to Louis XIV and his soft-spoken manner, is Brazilian, and obviously a romantic. It is not surprising that he chose an all-white bouquet for a bride, but lightened its solemnity with little touches of pastel. For the groom's lapel, Zezé plucks out one very special bloom from the bride's bouquet.

Zezé's beautiful bouquet called for pastel poppies, sweet peas, lilies of the valley, white ranunculus, spirea, roses, and ixia—emphasizing all the delicate, fragrant flowers of late spring. It was contained in a plastic bouquet holder, filled with florist's oasis for security, which eliminated the need for elaborate wiring and supplied water for the flowers to drink.

Charmed at the prospect of a wedding, Zezé also fashioned a bridesmaid's bouquet of vivid colors—orange, purple, and pink—using lilacs, sweet peas, roses, lilies, and azaleas, which cascaded down, lending a touch of both formality and frivolity, which seemed to sum up the bridesmaid's point of view.

Distinctive Modern Bouquet

Salou has a large, intriguing modern shop on Columbus Avenue in New York, brimming with equally large and intriguing flowers. The guiding aesthetics therein are modern, which is to say spare or "less is more," and they convey confidence, simplicity, and serenity, and in that suggest Oriental influences.

Here Salou has taken two branches of corkscrew willow, sprayed silver, taped them together into a handhold, and added large lavish examples of white cattleya orchids. The effect is a portrait of strength and serenity, subtly offset with a flash of contemporary silver.

BELOW LEFT: Zezé made this bridesmaid's bouquet with bright-colored flowers and ribbons, setting it to rest in an antique iron urn that he keeps at his shop for this purpose.

BELOW: The resident white pigeon at Salou's flower shop posed serenely for this portrait, with the striking bouquet created for this occasion.

BELOW RIGHT: Jennifer's romantic, loose, unstructured bouquet was photographed on her terrace in the late afternoon sun.

Romantic Country Bouquet

When she isn't arranging the flowers on the premises of Sotheby's, Jennifer Cohan is working out of her home on Bank Street, where she is fortunate enough to have basement space in which to stash her large personal collection of vases, baskets, and other decorative containers in which to display her art form. A true thriving free-lancer, with well-defined aesthetics, she likes unstructured simple bouquets—"a garden tied into a handful with a ribbon"—and she is pleased when the bouquet moves a little as the bride does.

Jennifer's studies were in art history, with a strong peripheral interest in dance, but she says that flowers ended up the best and most expressive of the three. Her favorite flower at this moment is lysianthus, although tomorrow it may be something different, which is one of the joys of the flower profession. With very little wire, and consequently very little formal structure, Jennifer gathered together lysianthus, Queen Anne's lace, and white delphinium, using nylon and real Victorian lace to tie the stems into a romantic country bouquet.

Silk Rose Bouquet

A silk flower bouquet, with care, will last forever. This bridal bouquet, created by Diane Love, is composed of delicate shades of pink and white roses, which will gather nostalgic dust and pale slightly, like a Victorian lady.

Diane knows and uses the aesthetics of silk flowers as does no one else in the decorative arts. For a number of years she had a shop on Madison Avenue full of beautiful decorative objects—Oriental vases, exquisite laces, unusual Eastern rugs—but her background is in silk flowers, and she has a particular understanding of the art form. Silk flowers are not artificial flowers, but handmade flowers, and they have an aura and a delicacy all their own. They have a soft, age-old quality and a rarefied color, and would complement an antique gown especially well. Diane's bouquets call to mind the paintings of Redouté; they also would make a lovely, lasting memento to give as bridesmaids' presents.

Meadow Bouquet

The bouquets of Perriwater, at 900 First Avenue, look as if they had just been picked, perhaps from a pampered English meadow. The color, the variety, and the randomness seem to be Nature's own, and in this natural spirit, the bride is meant to hold the stems without wrapping. Ferns, roses, baby gladiolus, alstroemeria, chive flowers, dendrobium orchids, ixia, brodiaea, white allium, and phlox create a breath of country air.

BELOW LEFT: Full-blown pale pink silk cabbage roses make up this important bouquet.
BELOW: A loose bouquet of country flowers designed by Perriwater.
BELOW RIGHT: Rita Bobrey's great round nosegay of roses, sweet peas, and Queen Anne's lace tied with satin ribbons.

Delicate Feminine Bouquet

Whenever I enter Spring Street Florists in Soho in downtown Manhattan, I feel happy, expansive, and animated. It reminds me of those French and Italian sidewalk florists whose wares spill out under your feet. Adapted to the life-style of the sculptors and painters in residence in Soho, the shop opens late, toward noon, but then becomes a lively marketplace at the end of the day, when the walk-in neighborhood crowd comes to browse or to select a flower or two to take home for the dinner table. Flowers seem really to live in the place, and in their midst, here and there, stands a special prop, like an old wooden wheelbarrow.

In the shop, Rita Bobrey made a delicate feminine bouquet for a bride. Rita creates her arrangements by instinct, by whimsy, and by dictum of what is most beautiful in the early morning flower market that day. This particular day, she had found dream and porcelain roses, rambler roses, Queen Anne's lace, and sweet peas, a combination of delicate pastels she worked into a tight arrangement. For her distinctive touch, she caught the bouquet in an old-fashioned paper doily, and then indulged in yards and yards of thin white satin ribbon, which curled down frivolously.

ABOVE: Sara Solis-Cohen chose Laura Ashley striped dresses for her bridesmaids and flower girl, and her florist, Jean Carte, made each bouquet from different flowers and in various color combinations.

OPPOSITE: Sharon Nelson's matron of honor carried a loose bouquet of lilies of the valley, roses, blue salvia, and lavender sweet peas tied with blue and white ribbons.

My Favorite Flowers for
Wedding Bouquets

Alstromeria
Astilbe
Azaleas
Baby gladiolas
Bachelor buttons
Brodia
Buttercups
Calla lilies
Campanula
Clematis
Curly willow
Daffodils
Dahlias
Daisies
Delphiniums
Eremurus
Ferns
Feverfew
Flax
Freesias
Hemlock
Herbs (allium,
Bishop's weed, chives,
dill, lamb's ear,
physotegia, rosemary,
sage, tansy)
Hyacinths
Hybrid grasses
Ixia
Laceflowers
Larkspur
Lilacs

Lilies of the valley
Long-stemmed
pansies
Lysianthus
Narcissus
Nerines
Orchids (Cattleya,
Dendrobium)
Pansies
Peonies
Pinks
Poppies
Queen Anne's lace
Quince blossoms
Ranunculus
Rhododendrons
Roses
Rubrum lilies
Scabiosa
Schizanthus
Scilla
Smilax
Stars of Bethlehem
Stephanotis
Stock
Sweet peas
Thistle
Tulips
Variegated miniature
ivy
Wax flowers

The Yacht Club Wedding

Sissy Cargill
and
Kelsey Biggers

Clubs, those comfortable little pockets in society that offer both a sense of belonging and a sense of occasion, have always been popular settings for weddings. Among the ranks of country clubs, social, athletic, historical, and professional clubs, perhaps the most colorful is the yacht club, with its waterside base, its nautical trappings, its resident sunburnt, windswept, topsider spirit.

The yacht club in Southport, Connecticut, is housed in a small, rosy-brick Victorian commercial building, perched on a quiet inlet of Long Island Sound. Off its open front porch lies a fleet of bobbing masts, and off its back, a genteel village that has changed little in the last hundred years. Martha Lyon "Sissy" Cargill spent her childhood in a big Greek Revival house across the street here, and whiled away her summers at the club. For Sissy, who

is now working in New York City as administrator of late-night programs for NBC, to have a village wedding with a yacht club reception meant both a sweet homecoming and a ceremonial send-off.

Thunderclouds and sea squalls being in the idiom of sailors, when the heavens opened to a downpour on Saturday afternoon, June 8, 1985, the crew of friends preparing the yacht club for the reception donned bright yellow raingear as casually as if they were on deck. Out on the lawn, they hung bunches of roses and peonies on a trellis arch, under which the wedding party and guests would pass. On the porch Butzi Moffitt, Sissy's godmother, arranged the flowers, picked that morning from roadsides and friends' gardens, in wicker baskets and picnic hampers for table decorations for the cocktail reception. Her buckets of bachelor buttons, delphinium, salvia, roses,

peonies, carnations, and cow parsnip—that wild flower similar to a colossal Queen Anne's lace—sparkled with raindrops. Her grapevine baskets of romantic herbs (rosemary for remembrance, rose for true love, sage for wisdom, lovage for strength), recycled from a bridal luncheon, were refreshed by this sudden bath. With years of experience working with flowers at the Metropolitan Museum, and with her painterly eye, Butzi moved by instinct, chatting happily to hold off panic as the wedding hour drew near. She had completed the four bridesmaids' bouquets, sprays of spring flowers held in baskets made of upside-down sun hats, an idea borrowed from *Portrait of Amelia Palmer,* a painting by the early-nineteenth-century American portraitist and miniaturist Charles Comwell Ingham. In order to win Sissy over from a theme of Venetian gondolier hats for the bridesmaids, Butzi had shown her Ingham's painting, which hangs in the American Wing of the museum, and then, as a clincher, pointed out that Amelia's father's name was Cortland Palmer, an ironic inversion of Sissy's favorite character in "All My Children," the soap opera in which she had once worked as an extra. Butzi had then designed the equally romantic bridesmaids' dresses: wraparound hoop skirts in a French provincial cotton with sculptured "turret" hemlines, paired with a frilly Laura Ashley sailor blouse, and worn with ballet slippers. An hour before the church ceremony was scheduled to begin,

while her daughter and son-in-law hung special nautical flags that spelled out Sissy and Kelsey in ship code from the rafters of the clubhouse, Butzi, quite wet, quite nervous, and more effervescent than ever, created a traditional white bride's bouquet of creamy white roses and baby's breath, which she wrapped with ribbons salvaged from Tiffany wedding presents. Then, as the cocktail buffet was laid inside the clubhouse, and a few tables arranged optimistically outside on the porch,

OPPOSITE: Butzi Moffitt orchestrated the decorations, which included table centerpieces fashioned from wicker baskets and a flower-garlanded arch. Guests of all ages had a wonderful time at this informal reception. ABOVE: A fife and drum lead the way to the reception.

PRECEDING PAGES, LEFT: Kelsey and Sissy kneel at the altar of Trinity Church. RIGHT: Rod and Maggie Moffitt Rahe hang flags spelling Sissy and Kelsey in ship's code.

she dashed off to change into wedding apparel.

Down a side street, at Trinity Church, another wedding was still in progress, it being June, and upstairs in the church parlor the bridesmaids were dressing and then adjourning to the hall to practice their processional walk: step, together, pause, step, together, pause. The scene, with the gathering of sisters, stepsisters, and sister-in-law zipping, arranging, admiring one another, all young, eager, and excited, brought to mind *Little Women*. Sissy's friend Teresa Bramble, then an executive with Revlon, did everyone's makeup. Sissy, wearing her mother's lace dress and a headpiece fashioned from her Juliet cap and veil, evoked dreamy looks and giggles from the bunch. "She looks like our fairy godmother," the youngest, Alison, said. "She should carry a wand with a star."

As four o'clock drew near, and guests swarmed in, the umbrella stand in the church vestibule downstairs filled beyond capacity. In the nave, the rows of eager faces waited for a sign that the ceremony was to begin. Children twisted and turned in their seats, craning young necks; a large contingency of girls in summer dresses peered back toward the door with big eyes. When Kelsey Biggers, the groom, entered to take his place at the head of the aisle, he beamed broadly. As bridesmaids processed in, they grinned and nodded to friends. Sissy and Kelsey greeted each other with a joy that suggested they had not met in ages, and then, during the ceremony, chatted so freely that they had to be shushed for the vows, which they offered to each other with great feeling, without ministerial assistance, holding hands. Two ministers, male and female, orchestrated the Episcopalian wedding service, alternating bass and soprano voices, and finishing it all with an embrace of their own.

Outside the church, where the lawn was soggy wet, the sidewalks shiny, and the sky gray, the rain had, in fact, precipitously ended, allowing the appearance, like a mirage, of a pair of colonial sailors with fife and drum. Playing jaunty old tunes, they led the way down a block of tidy old colonial houses to the sea and the yacht club. The procession—the sailors in their flat hats, striped shirts, and vests, the bride and groom in their own costumes, trailed by the wedding band in summer finery, all of them side-stepping big mirror puddles and frolicking—

was a vision from a storybook, and brought villagers to their windows and doorsteps.

Inside the yacht club, a lively band enticed guests to dance immediately. A friend of the bridal couple had acquired a supply of captain's hats, which she placed ceremoniously on important heads in the crowd. The music drifted out onto the porch, where a late-afternoon sun had broken through. Just before the wedding cake was cut, Sissy's family all sang "It's So Nice to Have a Party," a song that had become a tradition at important gatherings. As the now full-blown sun sank into the

Sound, the band adjourned to the dock to play "Anchors Aweigh," and Sissy and Kelsey made their getaway on brother Bill's sailboat, which, despite his last-minute attempts to repair its rudder, had to be towed off by the best man at the helm of the club launch.

"Sissy always wanted a real wedding," her mother remembers, "but she had a distaste for what she calls 'plastic' weddings, the formal and the stuffy. So we knew it would be offbeat, whatever its nature." Of the theme,

ABOVE: Sissy and Kelsey greet their guests on the porch of the club. OPPOSITE: Simple tables, garden flowers, and nautical chairs in the main room of the yacht club contributed to the atmosphere of this reception. The bride and groom found time to talk to all of their guests inside and on the veranda of the club overlooking the sailing boats.

Butzi Moffitt, the godmother who passes for best friend and helped plan the wedding, says, "We had been talking about this for years. Once we agreed on red, white, and blue, we decided to go for the American nautical idea full steam, rather than backing off."

Sissy Cargill's wedding was a family effort, which came together in a relaxed, spontaneous, unorthodox way that proved as efficacious for them as fastidious notebooks and coordinators are for others. Once the yacht club had been reserved, and its staff engaged to prepare a buffet of hot and cold hors d'oeuvres, other elements simply fell into place. Sissy's mother's wedding dress was recalled from an aunt's trunk in Minnesota (and lost in transit, to be recovered a month later in Memphis, Tennessee). The Laura Ashley blouses were acquired on a whim long before the skirts were even designed; Butzi had seen them in the store window and double-parked to make

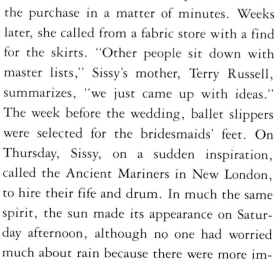

the purchase in a matter of minutes. Weeks later, she called from a fabric store with a find for the skirts. "Other people sit down with master lists," Sissy's mother, Terry Russell, summarizes, "we just came up with ideas." The week before the wedding, ballet slippers were selected for the bridesmaids' feet. On Thursday, Sissy, on a sudden inspiration, called the Ancient Mariners in New London, to hire their fife and drum. In much the same spirit, the sun made its appearance on Saturday afternoon, although no one had worried much about rain because there were more im-

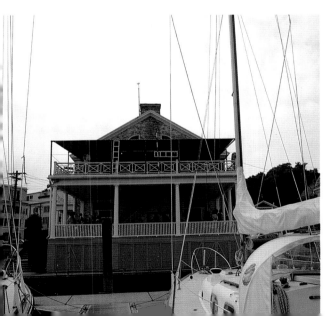

LEFT: A simple cluster of baby's breath and roses in the lace-mitted hand of the bride.
ABOVE: Painted in shaving soap the message is clear—Sissy and Kelsey are married.
OPPOSITE: The bride and groom embrace.

portant matters at the heart of the day.

There was a poignant sense of history in the Cargill wedding that came with its setting in the old village of Southport. In an earlier incarnation, the yacht club had housed warehouses for the prosperous onion trade of the area, and was at the center of village life then, as it is now, in other ways. And Trinity Church, built in 1725, had seen many weddings in its time. Houses on the narrow side streets of Southport seem to have a longtime relationship with each other, however pristine or grand some of them may be, and people always speak to each other in the road, preserving the old social fabric of a small town community. Near the end of her daughter's wedding, Mrs. Russell happened to look back toward the door to notice two little boys, whom she recognized as a friend's grandchildren, peering in at the event through a crack of light. Then, in a rush of memories, she thought of her own four children spying on all the local weddings. "Watching weddings is part of growing up in Southport," she said, "and now we have come full circle."

The Restaurant Wedding

Joyce Roquemore and Paul Hanly, Jr.

Choosing a restaurant for a wedding ultimately means choosing a style, a mood, and an ambiance as well as a menu. More than hotels, through which visitors pass rather anonymously, restaurants have distinct personalities, and, like clubs, they have a certain cachet. Restaurants are almost always smaller, more defined locations, however, dictating party size and yet providing intimacy. And their main attraction and raison d'être is a meal.

There are many kinds of restaurants, of course, ranging from a giant and informal steakhouse like Durgin Park in Boston, where diners sit family-style at massive harvest tables, or one of the cavernous Coney Island seafood establishments, to a sweet old-fash-ioned English-style tearoom. I remember a wedding reception in the wine cellar of a French restaurant (an elegant smaller wedding at which the guests enjoyed really talking to one another), and a spring affair in the city where a band for dancing was set up in the small townhouse garden. Some of the sites at which the rehearsal dinners for weddings in this book were staged could easily be converted into special reception sites—Larsen's Turkey Farm Restaurant near Califon, New Jersey, where Sharon Nelson and Harvey Siegel had their post-rehearsal meal, or the Woodshed Restaurant in New Hampshire, where the Cooks in effect expanded the barn-restaurant into a tent for al fresco dinner and dancing.

Back in the twenties and thirties, a familiar sight in Paris bistros was a zinc bar, solid, lustrous, and sculpted like a piece of statuary. Sadly these grand old centerpieces became casualties of World War II, when they were melted down by invading German soldiers, but one of the few remaining examples gave rise to a restaurant and bar called Le Petit Zinc, which became a favorite spot for a new generation of Parisians. Four years ago, Frenchman Philippe Bernard opened another Le Zinc on Duane Street in the Tribeca area of New York, and it, too, has become an elegant outpost for a devoted group of neighborhood artists, gallery owners, musicians, and actors. From its early days, Joyce Roquemore from Corpus Christi, Texas, worked nights as a maître d' there, and in the nature of bistros, she founded many good friendships among the staff and clientele, notably with Paul J. Hanly, Jr., a young lawyer who was a regular even before he focused on Joyce. Soon after Paul and Joyce decided to marry and had set the date as Sunday, March 31, 1985, they began to plan their wedding party at Le Zinc. The photographs are telling, for they capture the mellow atmosphere in a warm red room walled with leather banquettes and hung with provincial oil paintings and mirrors and show a swirl of friends dressed in chic, young, extravagant apparel: wide glossy lapels, snug feathery hats, deep drapes, old tuxes, elaborate shirts, hairdos from the forties. The scene conjured up café society as it might have been captured in French cinema. Just as the French famously treat their dogs as special children,

ABOVE: The smiling bride and groom. PRECEDING PAGES, LEFT: A reflected view of downtown New York City—Duane Street. RIGHT: The bride rushing from her car into the restaurant.

so Joyce's little white dog Nadie, who had been overlooked and then fetched from home by limousine, was the right presence.

Le Zinc seemed to be the perfect site—sophisticated, convivial, familial, and familiar.

But it was more, too. When Joyce, whose father is deceased, asked Paul who should give her away, his first response was Philippe. When Joyce chose her bridesmaids, she asked her sister, Jerryann Mills, and Sylvia Kadolsky, who was working as a waitress in the restaurant. And when she met Sylvia's friend Monika Eder, a young Parisian designer whose evening wear recalls the gowns of both the forties and the eighteenth century, she laid aside her thoughts about a tea-length antique gown.

At Thanksgiving, Joyce had seen the wedding bonnet worn by her future mother-in-law in the late thirties, a delicate latticework cap of champagne satin, which evolved as the inspiration for Monika's design, as well as its accompanying headpiece. "When I saw the dress I was thrilled because it had such a period look. My only revision was to poof out the hips a bit, to achieve the *panier* style, like Marie Antoinette's, rather than the bustle." The material was antique satin (*blanc cassé, un peu doré*), the skirt tulip-shaped, with a rather sexy rise in front, and a sweep of the floor behind, and the latticework reappeared provocatively on the bodice. Joyce kept the dress, Monika's first wedding design, a secret until the wedding.

From the beginning, Joyce and Paul conceived their wedding as a party. Joyce had choreographed other weddings at the restaurant, arranging tables and selecting menus, but, as she said, "planning my own wedding meant separating my feelings from the event itself." For the ceremony, she had considered a hotel, a church, or the apartment of her old

ABOVE: A silver wine bucket held the bridal bouquet of calla lilies after the ceremony.
BELOW: The bride with members of her family.

friend Keith Esterbrook, who ultimately gave her away—any one of which would have entailed the extra fuss of flowers and music for two locations. With the help of Paul's sister Margo, who had been married before, and the talents at the restaurant, Joyce organized menu, flowers, decoration, and dress herself, keeping in mind the intrinsic style and shape of Le Zinc, and ideas, good and bad, garnered from the other weddings they attended in the

prologue to their own. Paul, who loves the music of the Big Band era, engaged Ronny Whyte, whom he knew from his many evenings at the Carlyle and jazz clubs, and whose music (specialties: Gershwin and Porter) was intimately suited to the site and to easy mood dancing. David Salazar, a waiter at Le Zinc, who once designed the windows at Bergdorf Goodman, executed the decoration, which consisted of hundreds of yards and a small for-

BELOW: Philippe Bernard, owner of Le Zinc and a close friend of the bride. RIGHT: A bistro atmosphere was exactly what the bride wanted for her reception. BELOW FAR RIGHT: One of the chefs with a wedding flower tucked into his toque blanche.

tune of satin and silver lamé ribbon streamers, draped from the ceiling in arcs that suggested the billows of a tent. It was agreed that anything fussier would detract from the bistro charm of white tablecloths, heavy silverplate, votive candles, and small pots of flowers. For the ceremony, however, fluted white columns, holding large sprays of flowers, were added to demarcate the head of an invented aisle for the wedding procession.

On March 31, the weather was inclement, one of those last dark, wet, icy days of winter, so that stepping into Le Zinc was indeed entering a haven. At first, the scene was sweetly barroom, with Paul, Margo, honorary junior bridesmaid Katherine or "Cousie," and other relatives invited to the ceremony perched expectantly on barstools, waiting first for the judge, who was late, and then for Joyce, who was later. But when the white carpet was

rolled out before the bar, and the front door opened to bridesmaids and Joyce, it was a classic wedding. Framed by flowery columns, Joyce glided up the aisle to join Paul before the judge. The ceremony, short and civil, ended with cheers when Paul's embrace swept Joyce off the floor. A half-dozen Instamatics flashed, and the family closed in on Joyce to admire her dress. The dress, an exotic piece of costumery, was a centerpiece, even more than

RIGHT: Joyce's dog
Nadie was a guest of
honor. His presence
made the restaurant
even more French-like.

BELOW LEFT:
Joyce and her friend
Ed Marinaro dancing to
the music of Ronny
Whyte.

the bride's dress usually is. Set off by her bridesmaids in heavy, dark rust velvet ballgowns also designed by Monika, Joyce evoked shades of her Huguenot ancestors, and to some, Sarah Bernhardt.

Gradually, like a cocktail party, the restaurant filled with a new crush of one hundred friends invited for the reception. Joyce had selected all her favorite foods from the restaurant's repertoire—canapés of garnished,

flavored butters on toast (smoked salmon, crawfish, lemon and black sturgeon butters, pimiento butter with roasted pepper, dill butter with gravlax), duck livers wrapped in bacon, a connoisseur's spread of oysters mignonette. Later, a buffet table was laid with Le Zinc's noted terrines, standing prime ribs, the scalloped potatoes that have disappeared from the regular menu, and then sorbet and wedding cake—as Joyce concluded, "good party food."

Ceremony

"I take thee to my wedded husband [wife], to have and to hold from this day forward, for better for worse, for richer for poorer, in sickness and in health, to love and to cherish, till death us do part, according to God's holy ordinance; and thereto I give thee my troth."

These are the words that lie at the heart of the wedding tradition, that stir the mind and swell the heart, and bring tears to the eyes of even a casual acquaintance. The words have a simple beauty; the presence of the archaic in the intimate "thee," and the stolid "troth" or faith, creates a rich resonance that echoes on, at telling moments, down through the years of marriage, reminding us of the hopes and ideals expressed on this day.

Sometimes these words change, as they are modified or elaborated upon by couples whose sentiments demand other

phrasing. And these words change according to the many liturgies that represent the many religious traditions in the United States. Yet the ceremonies in which couples may choose to legalize and sanctify their marriage resemble each other more than they differ. The civil service is an unadorned secular version of the religious, a basic and abbreviated exchange of commitments. Most Christian services are similar with only minor variations. And as the Christian service grew out of that of the ancient Jews, a strong common thread binds them, too. The bride and groom stand before an altar, or before the Ark of the Covenant, surrounded by a best man and maid of honor and a circle of attendants. Music enhances important moments: the procession, the exchange of vows, and rings, the blessing, benediction, and the triumphant leavetaking.

Historically, a wedding ceremony has always been a public event, announcing a new relationship between two persons in whom society has an interest. According to the requirements of law, the only essential nuptial documentation, with a few state-specified exceptions, includes a marriage license, a blood test, and a ceremony at which a couple announces their intent before a recognized public official and witnesses who sign papers acknowledging the fact. The officials in whom authority is vested range from clerks and justices of the peace to a whole spectrum of legitimate and mail-order clergymen; witnesses, particularly in the movies, have been known to be milkmen, elevator operators, and strangers off the street. A friend of mine, celebrating her sixteenth anniversary, recently recounted her spur-of-the-moment marriage in a small town in Maine: The keeper of an inn fashioned from an old schoolhouse ushered them into a dining room, donned his justice-of-the-peace hat, and called in his wife and chef to witness the vows; afterward, he replaced that hat with a ski cap and ran upstairs to toll the schoolbell; later in the evening, in pajamas, he showed them to their honeymoon room. J.P.s, more often than not, are warm, colorful characters, who have sought their position out of delight in these official little dramas. In my hometown of Westport, the J.P. is a woman. On Martha's Vineyard, the J.P. is a well-known local politician who always dresses in a top hat and red suspenders for the occasion, and presides happily on beaches, docks, and the decks of swordfishing boats.

There is no difference in legal terms between a city-hall quickie and a two-hour nuptial mass, and little discrimination between the surge of joy that follows both, and yet the strains of the wedding march lead most people to conjure up the solemn ceremonies in Shakespeare and the beauty and pomp of royal weddings. Anthropologists remind us that we have a need for ritual to express basic emotions—this truth may explain the pleasure of crying at weddings—and brides say that "a special wedding will give me something to look back on all my life."

It used to be that wedding ceremonies were standardized tracts written by the state or church. Then came the sixties and seventies, the great epoch of improvisational, personal-

ABOVE: A huge floral arrangement specially designed by Susan Naff to match the majestic interior of a cathedral in New York City. PRECEDING PAGES, LEFT: The altarpiece at St. Francis Episcopal Church, where the Rev. Mayberry officiated at the wedding of Heather Bartling and Drake Sparkman III. Heather placed the peonies in silver wine cups the morning of the wedding. RIGHT: The facade of the Highland Park Presbyterian Church in Texas.

ized wedding ceremonies, preferably staged in a sun-dappled glen or on a serene hilltop to the accompaniment of folk songs and vegetarian feasts. Those weddings seem like period pieces now, and yet their raison d'être—to reclaim the event from institutionalized routine and to make something wondrous and memorable of it—was valid, and has made couples of the eighties thoughtful. "To write one's own vows is to think about marriage, what it is, what one wants it to be," a *Time* essay by Lance Morrow several years ago reminded us. "It is, at best, an act of self-awareness." As a result, few wedding ceremonies today are predictable affairs, and if they are, it is by choice.

Since the sixties, the prenuptial or antenuptial contract has had its impact, too, as a result of women's lib and the new domestic and economic realism, and, according to lawyers, if June is the month for weddings, May is the month for prenuptial agreements. Although the majority of contracts are written for second marriages, where children, property, and material possessions are a real consideration, Joyce Neiditz-Snow, a matrimonial lawyer in Cleveland, Ohio, has written clauses about such things as religion, job relocation, household duties, and family china. These arrangements are meant to safeguard against costly future conflicts and are in common, although not frequent, practice.

The first question confronting most brides is where the ceremony will take place. If there is an allegiance to a church or synagogue, or a longtime friendship with a minister or rabbi, the choice is obvious, and the bride and groom will meet several times with the clergyman to discuss the service, its meaning, components, and execution. If not, it can be discouraging, particularly in big cities, to hurry from church to church looking for an available date and a

Ernest Gordon performed the wedding ceremony of Meg Hester and Paul Giroux at the Bronx Botanical Gardens.

The Gothic cathedral of Notre Dame in Montreal—site of the Desmarais wedding.

A white-draped altar was specially constructed for Hilary Cushing's marriage at her parents' summer home on Long Island.

Joyce Roquemore and Paul Hanly, Jr., took their vows in the dining room of the restaurant Le Zinc in New York City.

Challises of gold and silver gleam on the wedding altar of a great cathedral.

Dana Temerlin's ceremony took place atop a platform erected in the parlor of a New York townhouse.

LEFT: Anne O'Herron and Jonathan Burleigh at the altar of St. Joseph's Catholic Church in Woods Hole, Massachusetts. RIGHT: Jacquelyn Van Den Berg was married at the South Salem Presbyterian Church in New York State.

sympathetic authority, and it may take time to find the appropriate space and personality. Meg Hester tells of a frustrating search, which ended with the choice of a distinguished clerical family friend, who presided at her wedding in her father's place of business, the New York Botanical Gardens, which, with its loft and glass, was indeed a holy place.

It is important that the place be sized to the guest list, for a full chapel is intimate and joyous, while a voluminous, partially filled nave

Les Petits Chanteurs du Mont-Royal sang at Sophie Desmarais's wedding in the cathedral of Notre Dame in Montreal.

is a bit sad. Given the dramatic significance of the ceremony, a beautiful church can make an unforgettable impression. The pristine interior of a colonial church, filled to capacity, will emphasize the unity of a group called upon as one to support vows. The Desmarais wedding in the Basilica of Notre Dame in Montreal was bathed in the beauty of the church, a small perfect drama being played out in a great abiding sacred place. A temple wedding was very affecting, in part because it was presided over by the bride's uncle, who spoke with emotion.

When a wedding ceremony takes place at home, or in a site outside a religious institution, there are other choices—an imposing hearth, a dramatic window, a grassy knoll, a sheltering tree. Where there is no obvious threshold, one has to be created. At Hilary Cushing's ceremony under a tent in the flat grassy backyard of her summer house, an ordinary table was draped with a white damask cloth which, with straight pins and tucks, was fashioned into a simple swagged altarpiece that was set with the candles and cross brought by her minister from the Church of Heavenly Rest. Joyce Roquemore created a setting for her civil ceremony in the restaurant Le Zinc with floral sprays set on columns. Mimi Dabrowski wove herself a processional aisle with metal garden stakes linked together with ribbons and flowers, and, at its head, placed standing wicker baskets with fall flowers.

Most etiquette books provide a series of carefully detailed diagrams to describe the proper choreography for the processional and recessional of the bridal party. The concept of bridesmaids and groomsmen harks back to the days of marriage by capture, when a covey of female friends surrounded the bride for protection, and a phalanx of strongmen attended the groom for support, and presumably both groups moved in gang formation. Custom has evolved into a stately march, led by pairs of groomsmen, followed by a single file of bridesmaids, the maid or matron of honor, a ringbearer, and then the flower girl sowing

the bridal path with rose petals; pause; change of musical tempo; and then crescendo with the bride on the arm of her father, moving up the aisle to meet her groom positioned with his best man at the altar. In Orthodox and Con-

Marion Barnes constructed a chuppah of garden trellis and masses of fresh flowers for the wedding of Allison Zucker and Jeffrey Perelman.

servative Jewish tradition, the groom, preceded by the best man and accompanied by both his parents, joins the middle of the processional march, three abreast, and the bride, too, walks in on the arms of her parents. In recent days, in many religions, it has become common for both the bride's mother and father to give her away. In the case of a deceased or absent father, a mother, brother, best friend, or indeed any carefully chosen designate may assume this role. For a second marriage, it is not necessary that the bride be ceremoniously given away, although she may wish a special friend or relative to accompany her down the aisle.

Floral decoration for the ceremony should be simple and subtle, for undue frivolity would detract from the beauty of the site, the ritual, the principals, and their dress. Sweet sprays of flowers and leaves tied to the ends of pews; a basket of autumn leaves at the entrance to a church; single lilies positioned along the aisle are all simple, expressive, complementary decorations. In the busy months of summer and fall, previous weddings may obviate the need for any individual adornment of a church or synagogue.

Meg Hester's ceremony was a short Presbyterian service. Dana Temerlin's was an amalgam of three possible Unitarian services, integrated with a special Jewish wine ceremony written by her groom. At her ceremony, Margot Olshan enjoyed the presence of a female justice of the peace, who matched her dress to that of the bridal party. Each of these ceremonies was a thoughtful choice, deliberated by both bride and groom, and, in the case of mixed religious backgrounds, carefully considered to be acceptable to and expressive of each party's beliefs. The large number of marriages between partners of different backgrounds in the U.S. today may be responsible for the care commonly invested in ceremony. One bride, a third-year law student, commented on the course of her decision. "My fiancé and I decided on a church ceremony, because we believed that God was going to help us with this. We talked with his priest, and learned that in the Catholic church, marriage is a sacrament. We investigated my own Presbyterianism, and found out that there marriage is a contract you make and have witnessed by the community. When we read the service, I loved the beautiful old words of its language (I was an English major), and we both came to think the idea of witnesses who help you keep your vows was important. Deciding who we wanted to be there to witness the ceremony filled us with great excitement."

Anne O'Herron and Jonathan Burleigh also forged an original and substantial ceremony as a result of Anne's Catholic and Jon's Protestant upbringing. It was printed in its entirety in the wedding program, and, according to the two clergymen who presided, stands as an example of "an historic ceremony." As Father Francis Virgulak, scriptural advisor to the bishop of Bridgeport, Connecticut, said to the Rev. Dr. Olin Robison, former president of Middlebury College, where Anne and Jon met, "there is a certain humor in the fact that we have sought in the Roman Catholic and Baptist ceremonies the material to cover all of Western Christian civilization and tradition." The wedding ceremony was indeed expansive, and included literary thought, traditional prayers, and a nuptial communion rite by Fa-

OPPOSITE: At a very special and personal outdoor celebration, Patrie Ball, Jeff Kontje, and their three children married each other. Five rings were exchanged among them.

ABOVE: Jeff, Patrie, and Patrie's sister.

ther Virgulak, nuptial blessings and reflections by Dr. Robison, and a final rite by both. As Dr. Robison said in his address to the couple, "We have discovered in our time that in a genuine partnership exists a possibility for a higher form of happiness." He concluded, "Be generous, take care to be loving, always ascribe a worthy motive to the other. Remember that marriage is not a sprint, but a marathon. And on dark days, remember this day and remember that family and friends love you very much."

Individual circumstances suggest individual ceremonies. Because the church was an important part of the life of Jacquelyn Van Den Berg and Stephen Myers, the church ceremony was the focus of their most thoughtful plans, and included Christian hymns sung by a brother and a friend, and a service by two clergymen.

Sandra Leo-Wolf had met her husband-to-be in the Christian Science Church in New Canaan, where he was a soloist, and their wedding was graced by a solo rendition of Mary Baker Eddy's hymn entitled "Love," a musical presentation by a friend who is a concert pianist, and readings from the Bible. After an interlude of hors d'oeuvres, the groom reduced the gathering to tears with his singing of "All the Things You Are" and "The Girl That I Marry."

For Patrie Ball and Jeff Kontje, who live on Martha's Vineyard, and were each embarking on a second marriage, an important part of their wedding ceremony centered on their three young children, because they realized that marriage was a new union for all of them. The wedding party, accompanied by a single flute playing Pachelbel, was led first by Nisa,

the Kontjes' one-and-a-half-year-old daughter, and Reade, Patrie's five-year-old daughter, who both carried baskets of rose petals, and then Jeff's five-year-old son, Eli, who was bearing a box of five delicate gold bands, each in its own velvet case. John Shule, minister of the Edgartown Federated Church, spoke of a faith that spreads across religions and ages, and related it to this marriage of one family, and then delivered the special passage he had written to bless the giving of the children's rings. For three wide-eyed children of tender ages, for a young couple who care deeply about their family, it was a very poignant moment.

As to the letter of liturgical law, many ministers, sympathetic to sincere and deeply felt desires of their charges, are willing to make room for personal expression. During the sixties, clergymen like the Rev. Bart Gould of

the Second Unitarian Church of Chicago and Rabbi Bruce Goldman were well known for their endorsement of personal and original vows. Today, Hugh Hildesley, the rector of the Church of the Heavenly Rest, who administered Hilary Cushing's wedding vows, says that very few couples ask to write their own vows. Although the Rev. Hildesley has performed joint ceremonies with rabbis, interlacing and interlocking important parts from two religions, he sees an enormous danger in being too personal. "You throw in all these elements and it becomes sentimental, whereas the beauty of the traditional service is that the standards have been formed over many years and have a dignity of their own. Creating a tradition, providing a sense of continuity is what liturgy is about." Nonetheless, he believes in dealing with family events in a manner that makes everyone comfortable: "If I leave something out (a reference to the Trinity, for example), God will understand."

Rabbi Jerome Davidson of Temple Beth-El, a Reform synagogue in Great Neck, Long Island, finds that young couples are bringing more intelligence and sensitivity to bear on their wedding ceremony. "It is not a return to tradition for its own sake, but an interest in learning and a desire to enrich their understanding." More frequently now, he says, couples ask for traditional elements such as an elaborate wedding contract or *ketubah*, which has no legal significance for most Reform Jews today, more for its old language and spiritual ideas than for the letter of its religious law, which is antique. Although Rabbi Davidson does not perform interfaith marriages, he is sympathetic to the desire for originality and

notes that perhaps 25 percent of wedding couples wish to make a personal statement, which he unites into the ceremony after the exchange of vows, saying simply, "Speak to one another your own words of commitment."

In his premarital session with the bride and groom, which is a dialogue meant to enlighten and to reassure, Rabbi Davidson explores both the sensitive and profound aspects of a relationship like marriage and the meaning of the various symbols in its service. Virtually all components of the wedding service in all religions—the veil, the flowers, the bridesmaids and the groomsmen, the throwing of rice, even the trail of tin cans on the getaway car—have roots in early and primitive practice and inspire many stories. The chuppah, for exam-

ABOVE: Beneath a leaf and flower-festooned chuppah, Sara Solis-Cohen and Peter Rabinowitz exchanged their wedding vows.
BELOW: The traditional cup of wine and wrapped crystal glass.

ple, the canopy of embroidered or silk flowers under which the nuptial vows are exchanged in Jewish tradition, symbolizes home and, in the days when a groom customarily lived with his bride's family until he could provide his own hearth, the promise of home. In ancient times, however, its message was superstitious, protecting the bride from evil spirits. In pure Hasidic tradition, the chuppah would be set out of doors, under the stars, for the couple's offspring are meant to be as numerous as the constellations in the sky. At the end of the service, when the groom breaks a glass (wrapped in a napkin), he is reenacting an ancient ritual, about whose origins there is much uncertainty. Although interpreted variously as a dispersion of evil spirits, a statement of the groom's sexuality, or a reminder of the destruction of the Temple of Israel, most people today accept it as a recognition of the joy and sorrow in the world. Rabbi Davidson notes that since the tradition is to say mazel tov and to applaud, its enduring message is happy. I like the folk interpretation that says the marriage will last as long as it takes to put the pieces of the glass together again.

There is a particular warmth that seems characteristic of Jewish weddings, and derives from the fact that it is a custom for the parents of the bride and groom, as well as the bridal party, which usually includes brothers and sisters, to stand together under the chuppah. At a recent wedding, which was Syrian Orthodox, there were grandparents, too, a great swelling expression of the deep sense of family commitment to the event. Other factors at other weddings make lasting impressions, too: the thoughtful and caring message of a minister or judge, special poems and readings. Judging from its many appearances at weddings I attended, one of the most popular biblical readings today is from First Corinthians 13 about the nature of love: "So faith, hope, love abide, these three; but the greatest of these is love."

Music conveys the mood, and sometimes, through specific hymns, the message of the

A joyous Heather Bartling is embraced by the groom, Drake Sparkman III.

ceremony. Particular thought should be given to the musical prelude, because it is a special pleasure for guests to spend the anticipatory moments before a service in the state of grace and reflection inspired by a small chamber concert, an organ recital, or a flute solo. And although guests rarely mind the frequent late appearance of bride and groom—it augments the drama—music also diminishes the pressure of an exact timetable. For the wedding

processional, the classic remains Wagner's bridal chorus from *Lohengrin*, known as "Here Comes the Bride" ever since its introduction in New York in Civil War days, and for the recessional, Mendelssohn's triumphant "Wedding March" from *A Midsummer Night's Dream*. Yet brides have also chosen suitable music by J. S. Bach and Mozart, François Couperin and César Franck, Handel's "Water Music" and "Royal Fireworks Music," Verdi's "Ave Maria" or Purcell's "Trumpet Voluntary" to accompany the grand moments of a service. Since Prince Charles and Lady Diana Spencer chose the "Trumpet Voluntary in D-flat" by Jeremiah Clarke, it, too, has become a "classic." There are stately, romantic, triumphant, and festive sounds for every soul, variegated even further by the choice of instrument—organ, harpsichord, violin, flute, orchestra, voice. For some brides, there are also popular or folk songs of such relevance that they become vehicles for fanfare in more informal services: Barbra Streisand's "The Way We Were" or the Beatles' "When I'm Sixty-Four." Rabbi Davidson was recently bemused by a bride's choice of "Chariots of Fire" for her processional, but remembered that the song is based upon a biblical verse relating to the flight of God's prophet and warrior at the time of Elijah.

The Crystal Palace Wedding

Meg Hester and Paul Giroux

It began as if according to the venerable upper-class New York ritual: an October engagement announcement in *The New York Times,* followed by an elegant party at the Knickerbocker Club in January to celebrate the forthcoming marriage of Meg Hester to Paul Giroux in early June. The Cosmopolitan Club and the Knickerbocker Club were alerted as possible candidates for the reception; Bill Harrington's orchestra was engaged for dance music; a fashionable city caterer was hired to provide a formal sit-down dinner for 175. Then practical considerations and personal aspirations began to come into play. The appro-

priate New York churches were booked. The Cosmopolitan Club was too specialized and the Knickerbocker Club too small to accommodate a large formal dancing reception. At this point, James Hester, father of the bride, and, since 1980, president of the New York Botanical Gardens in the Bronx, changed the nature of his daughter's wedding with his casual inquiry: "How about the Conservatory?"

The Conservatory in question was the Enid A. Haupt Conservatory, the turn-of-the-century Victorian centerpiece of the 252 acres of meadows, orchards, and flowers cultivated by the New York Botanical Gardens. It was inspired by the Crystal Palace, a magnificent structure in the Royal Botanical Gardens in London, created at a time when wealthy patrons were first beginning to travel to new

PRECEDING PAGES, LEFT: Guests assembled for postwedding cocktails on the terraces surrounding the Conservatory.
RIGHT: Meg Hester carried a bouquet of sterling star lilies, lilies of the valley, gardenias, stephanotis, and ivy.

lands in search of exotic plants to be housed in lofty and majestic greenhouses, which were often used to entertain guests. The Haupt Conservatory has as its most regal architectural element the central Palm Court, which rises up ninety feet to an airy ribbed dome, and is detailed with fanlights and Corinthian columns decorated with swags. From the Palm Court, the Conservatory branches out into two jointed wings, which contain five additional

galleries; before them lie wide "temperate" and "tropical" pools, planted appropriately; behind them lie broad terraces overlooking June rose gardens, bordered by trellised walkways.

As it happened, sometime before seven o'clock on the evening of June 9, 1984, balloon-festooned vans and buses, traveling from New York City and Princeton, New Jersey, discharged an elegant swirl of passengers before the long canopied entrance to the Conservatory. They gathered outside around the pools to sip lemonade, while the bridal party was assembling before the space devoted to Gardens of the Past. This garden would provide a processional aisle into the ceremony, which would take place in a cross-shaped gallery adorned at that moment with an extravagance of palladiums. There, taped baroque music played softly, as a harpist set up her golden harp beside a frilly gazebo, and gradually, the perfectly geometric rows of white chairs began to fill up on the bride's side and the groom's side. When the harpist played "Here Comes the Bride," Meg and her father, proceeded by two flower children, scattering paper rose petals from small white wicker baskets, and seven bridesmaids, made their entrance. Passing the sculpted topiary and the formal herb gardens, ducking through a central shady wooden walkway covered with giant-leafed ivy, they entered what seemed to be a natural chapel, defined by curving brick walks and bordered by huge specimen willow, ficus, camphor, and evergreen trees. With nature on display, a dark-blue sky above, and the late mellow sun refracted through the glass above, the scene seemed holy. Meg had asked Ernest Gordon, formerly the chaplain at Princeton University and a close friend, to preside over the ceremony. His rich voice, sculpted face, and deep-purple robe gave great resonance to the service. Meg, however, remembers a lovely blur. "I lost all feeling in my hands and feet in the middle of the ceremony," she recalls. "And Paul had this goofy expression on his face."

After the ceremony, guests moved out onto the wide back terraces for hors d'oeuvres and drinks. Appropriate to the second week in June, the senses filled with both the sight and the smell of pink and red roses in bloom. The scene had a classic English garden party beauty: there was visual play between the long natural vista and the exotic formal summer dress, between the romantic architecture and the pink bow-tied waitresses gliding through groups with silver trays of miniature shish kebabs and bite-sized beignets. As night fell,

and the outdoor scene faded from view, the Palm Court began to change character until it stood dramatically dominant in its illumination: a spaceship, an enchanted bubble, a glittering palace. The night was hot, and the stars clear, and because Meg and Paul had initiated the dancing early, young couples were already dancing on the terrace.

As the sun set, and the harpist played, the wedding party moved on to dinner inside the Palm Court, where a multitude of century-old palms rose up into the dome, and tile walkways wove between the tables. Guests ate leisurely, grateful for the cold refreshment on a blitzkrieg-hot night. Meg and Paul danced as long as they could, and at eleven took ritualistic leave, only to call the wedding party soon after their arrival at the Carlyle Hotel.

The site of the Conservatory was one of the

Meg and Paul knelt on the same cushion her grandparents used in their wedding ceremony.

memorable aspects of Meg Hester's wedding, for it combined many of the most sought-after elements in a wedding site: as a frilly glass high-tech structure in a resplendent park setting, it was both old-fashioned and contemporary. The Hesters benefited from the flora in residence at the Botanical Gardens, and had only to shift a few pots of palladiums and symphidium orchids to create a striking floral wedding design. They were rewarded, too, by the simple fact of the Conservatory as wedding site, which brought that rare and particular gratification that comes when professional and personal involvements converge.

To the observant eye, and to knowing family members, there was an intimate sense of tradition that animated the Hester wedding. Meg wore the heart-shaped locket set with pearls that her great-grandmother had worn for her wedding in 1882. Hidden under her gown was a flowery lace-and-ribbon garter, made by her grandmother for all the family weddings. On her feet were her aunt's wedding slippers—origin: Switzerland, the 1940s—which were adorned with a garland of fresh flowers. During the nuptial vows, Meg and Paul knelt on the betasseled satin cushion that had been an integral part of her grandparents' wedding ceremony. Meg's mother expresses her feelings about tradition by keeping meaningful pieces of past family history to contribute to the enrichment of the present. Modest in value yet irreplaceable today, these treasures added special charm and significance.

Through the years, as the wife of James Hester, who, before his post at the Botanical Gardens, was president of New York University, and, earlier, rector of the United Nations University in Tokyo, Janet Hester has had many opportunities to combine tradition with innovation in a way that reflects and inspires a

happy sociability. "Mom has always been a wonderful entertainer," Meg says, pleased and proud. "She thinks it's fun, and her positive attitude makes it all seem effortless." Meg had well-defined ideas of her own about her wedding, but, given the fact that she was finishing her master's degree in educational counseling at NYU and Paul was settling into a job in municipal investment at Salomon Brothers, she was happy to profit from her mother's time, talents, and energies, and to operate in a mother-daughter partnership. Meg was as sure about the nature of her wedding as she was about her future with Paul (after their second date, she dropped her other boyfriends, and he purchased the special Racqet Club tie he wore at his marriage). "I wanted a small black-tie wedding and dinner, and a fun band. I wanted my closest friends there, and all the people who have meant the most to me. I wanted everyone looking pretty and having the time of times."

Although she thought about wearing her mother's wedding dress, Meg also had a vision in her mind, which she realized at Anita Pagliaro, on Lexington Avenue. A couturier who had already provided evening dresses for her, Miss Pagliaro copied one of her favorites in pale pink moire, with leg-of-mutton sleeves, and pink-and-white-striped sashes, for the

bridesmaids. Meg's dress—today it is called Meg's Dress in the store—was a simple three-quarter-length gown of Belgian lace, with a round neck and three-quarter-length sleeves. Creamy off-white, it was a perfect match for her mother's triangular veil of Alençon lace, from Brussels, held in place by her mother's bridal wreath of tiny roses.

During the year before their own event, almost every weekend from May to September seemed to bring a friend's ceremony, and Meg and Paul made continual mental notes and then adjusted their own ideas accordingly. They masterminded an exceedingly efficient receiving line, to dispense quickly with that happy but often gridlocked formality, and upon its completion, they danced their first dance, so that other people could join in, which they did immediately. Although in the first swirl of the reception, Meg forgot about hors d'oeuvres, throughout the evening she persistently engaged in countermanding the notion that traditionally brides have a terrible

LEFT: Ernest Gordon, former dean of the Princeton Chapel, officiated at the ceremony with Meg and Paul, while guests and attendants stood in rapt attention. RIGHT: A newly married Mr. and Mrs. Paul Giroux emerge from the ivy-covered archway.

147

time, and says, with irrepressible girlish glee, "I had sooo much fun!"

When Janet Hester is questioned about her legendary organizational abilities, she responds modestly that Meg's wedding was easy to do with such a generous allotment of time. And she extracts two simple items from her files: a manila folder "with everything in it" (orders, correspondence, bills, receipts) and a schoolboy's notebook "in which to make lists, and then scratch items off." As early as October, she contacted Mary Cleaver, a serious and eclectic young caterer who runs The Cleaver Co. in Manhattan, and responded with interest and openness to all her suggestions. The decision was made immediately to have hot hors d'oeuvres and a cold dinner, which, as it happened, was a fortuitous and gracious choice. Grills, arranged at the end of the terrace to dispense tiny skewers of chicken satay and beef teriyaki to silver trays, added a pleasing note of informality to an elegant and distinguished formal gathering, and the light, cold supper suited the appetites of an unex-

ABOVE: Guests enjoy cocktails and hors d'oeuvres on the outdoor terrace. Skewered chicken with yogurt, mint, and ginger, corn bread with country ham and mustard butter, cheese fritters, and eggplant fritters were served.

pected tropical night and yet offered new and decorous tastes. The cold almond soup, called a white gazpacho, was garnished with white grapes and croutons; the main course of seafood salad, served with wild rice, combined shrimp, smoked mussels from Maine, scallops, herbs, and roasted red peppers; and the trays of giant strawberries with frothy and rummy zabaglione provided a light accompaniment to the wedding cake. The chocolate-almond cake, covered with a mocha buttercream and a white chocolate ganache, rose to six tiers (to serve 175 people) and was decorated with a fragrant gardenia on top.

In designing the table décor in the Palm Court, Miss Cleaver respected the inherent beauty of the space with all-white appointments—long white tablecloths, white fluted plates—and added only pink napkins and pink votive candles to each table, to match the bridesmaids' dresses. Fond of personal little gestures, in the same spirit she also made pink moire bow ties for the formally attired waitresses. Her choice of round tables of different

LEFT: The rose garden was in full bloom June 9. Guests in evening clothes strolled on the gravel paths and sipped champagne. ABOVE: Dinner was served on white clothed tables with centerpieces of white and green caladiums.

Meg and two of her attendants with nephew Campbell and cousin Jane.

sizes was a practical one, to accommodate 175 guests in a room divided by its walkways into different enclaves of space. And she utilized a service staff of twenty-four, in order to cover the large areas involved in presenting hors d'oeuvres, and to serve dinner French-style.

Probably the most complicated aspect of the Hester wedding's organization was providing transportation to a corner of the Bronx unfamiliar to all but Botanical Gardens and Bronx Zoo patrons. Mrs. Hester responded to the problem with easy aplomb, allowing a friend in Princeton to coordinate that contingent of guests with a mini-van (offered on a card enclosed with the wedding invitation); arranging a full-fledged bus, departing from the Metropolitan Museum (with another enclosure card); and finally, accepting the offer of vans for the relatives and bridal party from a friendly gardener at the Gardens. Undaunted by a breakdown in the South Bronx the night be-

ABOVE: The first course was cold almond soup. BELOW: The Crystal Palace at night.

fore, en route from the rehearsal to a dinner at the University Club, a trio of vans journeyed to the Gardens in true Gardens style; they looked happy-go-lucky, trailing clouds of white balloons, which popped, like champagne corks, in the heat. The breakdown was the Hester wedding's token disaster—there has to be at least one, for the stuff of later memories. The heat of the day, the blistering, shimmery, pale-eyed kind, which seemed to arrive unannounced out of darkest Africa, and set records in the city, turned out to be of little consequence. Mrs. Hester said, "It was hardest on the staff, who had to man grills and work feverishly." The caterer said, "It must have been hardest on the guests." Inside at dinner, the formal crowd sat uncomfortably for a few moments, and then a distinguished guest from Bangkok rose, removed his jacket, and said that in his circles, it was the proper thing to do.

Music

When Bill Harrington, the band-leader, is asked about weddings, he is likely to smile and then say something like, "Well, we have played with the minimum five musicians—fewer, too—and with as many as thirty-five. We have played in all our nineteen categories of music—fox trot, samba, cha-cha, rock, fifties, sixties, seventies, eighties. We have played going-away songs for couples leaving in fire engines, horse and buggies, gas balloons, helicopters, and rowboats. At one wedding, the bandstand, which was next to the dance floor, which had been laid over the swimming pool, caved in; it has become known as the wed-

ding where the band fell into the pool."

A bandleader like Harrington, who has played as many as five weddings a week since the late 1950s, when he left radio and TV for the full-time society music business, has unusual perspective on the diversity of weddings. From my own sampling of fifty-odd weddings, I have the calling cards of at least fifty musicians in my pocket. They range from the young violinist from Juilliard who plays on street corners for money to complete his studies, funky fledgling bands, chamber ensembles, weekend jazz groups, calypso bands, and country swing bands, to full twelve-piece orchestras and two dozen strings.

Music is an extremely important element at a wedding reception whatever its nature—background or feature, listening or dance, waltz or rock. It is part of the structure, like site and food. And although "music should just seem to happen," as entertainment people say, that very spontaneity requires thought and advance planning.

The top so-called society bands, who play all over the country, are generally thought to number six, including Peter Duchin, Bill Harrington, Meyer Davis, Lester Lanin, Mike Carney, and Bob Hardwick. All of them have been around long enough to have seen the rise and fall and rebirth of popular "society" and are in such demand that booking at least a year in advance may be necessary, particularly if a wedding is scheduled for the prime weekends in June or September, or if the presence of the famous bandleader himself is desired. Harrington, for example, may have fifteen bands under his name working on a given Saturday, but can only attend one event. Peter Duchin's Orchestra, which he says is the biggest musical office in the country, accepts 120 engagements a year, but Duchin limits himself to ten appearances, although from his own select group of musicians he forms different units that may play a thousand times a year. With ready musicians and with cancellations, it is possible to achieve a last-minute success, but unless you are the calm, free-wheeling sort, it is best to engage a popular band as soon as you

PRECEDING PAGES, LEFT: A talented pianist and one of Glorious Food's staff, Allen Anderson plays for everyone's enjoyment; Lester Lanin hats let guests know just who is playing. RIGHT: This bass player was part of the ensemble at the Temerlin yacht reception.

decide upon the day and site.

The size of a wedding and its site as well as its budget determine the number of musicians required, which builds up from the three basic pieces—piano, bass, and drums; the fourth player as a rule brings the sax (and also plays clarinet and flute), single-handedly providing the most versatile sound; the fifth, a trumpet, the sixth, violin. Today the bass player usually doubles as a rock-and-roll guitarist, and the pianist can provide an electronic keyboard, unless you have or wish to rent a piano. Yet within this practice, there are aesthetic variations. "Violins are always nice at weddings," Peter Duchin says, "for they have an old-fashioned texture. They can be quiet; they can play simply and grandly. You don't want to start swinging too soon; a wedding should evolve, not just pop up."

As an illustration of evolution, Duchin reconstructed an important wedding on Long Island that involved many contemporary media stars, and was given by the bride and groom, who had deferred to his musical ideas. Although few would have thought of classical music as expressive of the group, a string quartet accompanied the ceremony, which, together with an aisle of flowers and a summer night, created a very beautiful and unpredictably traditional service. Then Duchin played the music of Cole Porter and Gershwin, "because these people lived every day with rock-and-roll"; and only later into the night moved into heavy contemporary music. In summary he says, "It was the kind of wedding that was both imaginative and traditional; it was produced, and yet it was very simple."

Duchin asserts that the music of weddings has not changed dramatically in the last decades of social change, because by nature weddings call together an assortment of ages and personalities that always appreciates a wide range of music—"A lot of jazz, a lot of contemporary songs, and all the great old stuff." This mix, he asserts, is one of the reasons weddings are so much fun.

Most society bands can trace their roots back to the fifties—the heyday of debutante balls and cotillions; made their way through

ABOVE: The Duchin band was set up in a huge bandstand with theatrical lighting at this home. OPPOSITE: The inimitable profile of one of music's real stars—Peter Duchin.

the rebellious sixties and seventies with charity events; and take the social eighties in stride as a swing of the pendulum in an affluent world that tries on manners for fun. Many of the society bands, now in their second generation, remain faithful to their original sound; the Glenn Miller Band and the Tommy Dorsey Band can be trusted to produce the famil-

iar old strains, if not literally at least spiritually. Bill Lombardo, who grew up very much a part of his uncle Guy's musical career, has evolved a new, broader style he calls the American Music Machine, which emphasizes the swing of the thirties and forties, but encompasses songs and orchestrations of the twenties to the eighties. "The thirties and forties won't ever go out," he says, "but we have a different way of presenting them now, based on lush harmony." Like many bandleaders, he can produce jazz trios, woodwind ensembles, a single harpist, or a Top Forties group, and caters to all events; uniquely, he likes to feature his lead vocalists, called the Sweet Dreams Trio, who sing like the Andrews Sisters. "I have tried to create a sound that could be both feature and background," he explains, "wonderful a cappella versions of songs like 'Come Softly.'"

Lombardo confesses that fifteen years ago, he himself was married in painter pants, a Mexican linen shirt, and shoulder-length hair, on the top of a mountain in Marin County where he scratched the wedding names on a rock, although he adds, "I was a musician as opposed to a hippie." He speaks of the many different styles prevalent today, and the importance of providing a good time, and how involved he, too, becomes in that good time. Bill Harrington also has a democratic view of his responsibilities as a professional. Although his group is often referred to as a "blueblood band," an epithet that probably derives from his having played at the weddings of Tricia and Julie Nixon, as well as for the families Mellon, Grace, and Paley, the Duke and Duchess of Windsor, and, in the current context, Sophie Desmarais and Meg Hester, he says, " 'Society musicians' means we play for various societies. To me, 'society' has melded in the last ten to twenty years, and we have become well versed in all styles. We are a catering organization, not an act, and we often change the tempo to match the area in which we are playing. Cities dance differently. New York can't dance with Dallas. North Carolina likes to hear 'Stardust.' Washington is not as fast as Philadelphia, and Wilmington, Delaware, wants the fastest time in America. If a new husband doesn't dance well, we slow down the tempo; if he can't dance at all, we play a two-step. We have a different concept—we play for the people."

Experienced bandleaders have good advice to offer. Lombardo speaks of the problems of landscaping—the situation of a tent and the necessity to foresee needs for electricity and extension cords; he mentions that as most musicians play in union-determined four-hour segments, it is important to anticipate overtime, so that a band won't have to leave a swinging party abruptly for another scheduled commitment. Harrington, too, talks about siting and decries the "fliers" that tent men like to sell, small tents enclosing the musicians on three sides, saying they interfere with the sound. He tells me that acoustically, the best place for a band is opposite the entrance, as a side location produces short-wave blare.

Peter Duchin has counsel on the psychology behind an event. "Be sure that the bride and groom have something to say about the music, that their personalities are allowed to surface. Order music of a wide range and variety. Have as little speaking by the bandleader as possible, because it interferes with the natural progression; let it flow and let it happen." He continues more specifically: "I suggest that

The Whiffenpoofs came to this reception to sing for their classmates' wedding.

OPPOSITE: There are many different choices of musicians to hire, from individual soloists, such as a harpist or violinist, and small combos, to big-sound bands. The music can range from classical to jazz to pop to hard rock. The choice of musician and music should complement the style of the wedding.

These musicians used early instruments at the Mills's wedding.

graceful music start the reception, for it sets a tone and a mood, so that guests can talk to one another. Dancing comes later, with seating at tables. Unless otherwise dictated, I like the traditional musical ceremony: the bride and groom cutting the cake and then taking the floor for the first dance, because omitting it deprives the couple of a nice age-old ritual."

According to recent estimates, there are some two thousand society bands at large in America these days, many of whom are attached, preferentially, to hotels. Indeed, there are many, many choices available for wedding music, but a society band may not suit either the place or the mood of the event. Because Joyce Roquemore wanted an intimate, stylish sound to fill her small restaurant site, Ronny Whyte, a bandleader and piano player who is a regular at the Algonquin and the Carlyle, played the café society music her groom loves. Sissy Cargill liked the jazz she heard one night in a local Connecticut restaurant and proceeded to hire the group, whose brassy, informal music seemed perfectly suited to a yacht club wedding. Sharon Nelson and Harvey Siegel, too, acted on impulse and personal taste when they engaged Jan and Bob, local musicians discovered in a New Jersey restaurant, to play and sing an afternoon of love songs. With folk music like this, or country-western, or the country swing of Prime Rib on Martha's Vineyard, a dance floor can be eliminated in favor of grass and meadow, but when serious and continuous dancing is the intent, a dance floor or a stone terrace is essential unless guests are expected to take off their shoes. Dancing was so important to Debbie Cook that her family flew her favorite band up from the Bahamas as a special treat, and Debbie spent long hours beforehand taping her favorite new songs for them to learn.

George Furlan and Kathy GarDianos danced many ethnic dances at their reception.

Sammy Cahn sang new renditions of his most famous songs for Dana and Hayden Crawford.

Each bride has her own musical taste and priorities: great dance tunes for one, serene chamber music for another, a loud magnetic vocalist, or a sweet balladeer. While many people prefer a string quartet or chamber music to accompany cocktails and to provide a graceful transition between the ceremony and the meal, others feel that dance music breaks the ice and brings people together. Bill Harrington points out that dancing can enliven the long hours of the receiving line and the private photography session.

It is worthwhile, fun, and often economical to be inventive with the choice of musician, and to invest in the young groups discovered in restaurants and clubs, at parties and music schools. If the bride and groom are into New Wave, you need not be confined to established names, and with electronic music, there are many interesting sources. When I first used the funky young group of jazz musicians called Widespread Depression that I had heard at the local Georgetown Saloon, their sound was new, their success not yet evident. Vince Giardano and the Nighthawks, who played at Hilary Cushing's wedding, have not always been "the new darlings of old swing music." James Graseck was discovered playing his violin in the subway in Grand Central Station, and since he played at the Damerell reception—everything from schmaltz to Beethoven—he has appeared on "The Tonight Show." It took a spirit of adventure to approach him and a certain sangfroid to trust the reliability of a total stranger, and yet, in the end, the appearance added not only the fun of a new and exotic talent, but gave the guests a story to tell. For George Furlan, who married Kathy GarDianos in Central Park, the decision to engage a Brazilian funk rock street musician named Rinaldo, with his strong falsetto voice

and high-powered samba, was an original and rewarding one. In a gesture of thoughtfulness, George, knowing his guests to be an exotic mixture of Greek and Italian families and early Motown fans, also taped their favorite kind of music to play during the band's breaks.

For many weddings, the music proves to be the single most important ingredient, and it is important to choose it carefully. Consider hiring a small group of musicians—perhaps students, or promising young locals—to play soft lyric background for cocktails, a nice idea on its own and also an economical way to accommodate a dance band's four-hour minimum. For a young dancing crowd, get *good* dancing music, if necessary listening to the tapes most groups are happy to provide. Discuss the question of breaks, for continuous music, though more expensive, is a possibility; discuss tone, for you'll want quieter music in the beginning, building to flat-out rhythm later; discuss style (Top Forties is different from rock, and all rock can be as tedious as no rock in a mixed group) and special songs. Some brides, like Margot Olshan, insist on a circle dance like a hora or a tarantella to bring the crowd together. And place the musicians well; often a lovely string quartet is isolated in a *serene* corner of the great outdoors and its effect lost; troubadour strings may fix themselves near the bridal party and forget to wander. When the band begins to warm up, remember that your work is done and that the real party time of the wedding has arrived; then relax and go with the music.

OPPOSITE: Good music, happy guests, and space in which to dance—often these are the things that make a wedding reception memorable.

The
At-Home Wedding

A wedding at home is a very special drama. To send a child off into a new life from the lap of her childhood; to transform the backyard or living room in which she once romped into ceremonial ground; to see the teenage bedroom once hung with school memorabilia now filling with bridesmaids dressing, and the comfortable family kitchen crowded with the makings of a wedding feast is to experience the event in its deepest dimensions.

So many mothers and daughters feel strongly that home is the only place to be married. They dream of a wedding at home, and they design pretty yards outside in which the ceremony might take place. I have created a little arbor that Andy and I hope will one day hold my daughter Lexi's wedding ceremony. I see her walking up there by way of the brick path lined with apple trees in blossom, and afterward, celebrating in our new trellised garden entwined with climbing roses. We all talk about it and plan fancifully, and maybe it will come to be. It is ready anytime she is.

In these days of expressive and individualistic weddings, home offers the most personalized of sites. The possibilities are as diverse as the homes in which the weddings will take place: large or small, antique or avant garde, rustic or sleek. In my own home, which is an early nineteenth-century farmhouse in suburban Connecticut, I have hosted three very different family weddings in the past several years: the first for my sister Laura, an intimate, old-fashioned cocktail reception for fifty on New Year's Eve; for my brother George, a relaxed outdoor country luncheon for 175 in August; and for my brother Frank's second marriage, a sweet family party at Thanksgiving. Our house seemed to change, magnanimously, for each event, expanding, contracting, becoming spacious and then intimate, and inviting new ideas and decorations to suit its changing role.

Home—a house, an apartment, a backyard—has a warmth and an aura of its own, just from having been lived in. And a home wedding can take any form that seems expressive, comfortable, and pleasure-giving—a barbecue, a brunch, an elegant dinner party, a rock-and-roll bash. Size, of course, depends directly on the size of the home. Decoration, as a general rule, takes its cues from the style of the home, although for every rustic reception at a rustic house or Art Deco tent at a house filled with Lalique glass, there is probably an exception—someone who had the dream of creating a scene from *Arabian Nights* and the resources to make it happen. These days, tent men, interior designers, and florists take a wildly unrealistic extravaganza as an exciting challenge to their talents and are generally eager and undauntable. Rentals, too, encompass far more than a wide selection of

ABOVE: All of the flowers for the Sonnenblick wedding were designed by Charles Case. PRECEDING PAGES, LEFT: Emily Sonnenblick being escorted to her wedding by her father. RIGHT: A view from the parlor of the Sonnenblick home to the courtyard in which the ceremony took place.

tents, tables, and chairs; silver filigree table lamps, grills and smokers, grand pianos, flowering trees, chandeliers, tapestries all can be rented today. The more ambitious the plans, however, the more fastidious the organization has to be.

Some houses seem made to order for weddings: perhaps there is a long lawn for a tent, a terrace for drinks, even a lovely weeping willow in place for wedding photographs. Others require serious engineering efforts to become hospitable sites. From stories I have garnered, there seems to be no limit to the resources brought to bear on this occasion.

A large and ambitious home wedding can be a very expensive undertaking, for building gazebos and relandscaping backyards is more complicated than engaging a preordained space like a hotel or club. Rental supplies, too, in the case of large weddings, are costly, often surpassing the fees for food. Yet unless the guest list numbers four or five hundred, which necessarily calls for numerous rentals, a wedding that is indoors or informal and draws upon your own things and your own special physical situation can be lovely without the investment of fortunes. For most people, the big task of the day is putting home in pristine order. Receiving friends and relatives for one of the most important events of a lifetime is tantamount to opening up to a house tour. It is forced revitalization, often resulting not only in the repairing of the broken latches, the peeling paint, and the sagging sofa, but also in the planting of new gardens (for appearance and for cutting flowers), wallpapering of forgotten rooms, and refurbishing of bathrooms. Most people look back on this gigantic effort with pride and a sense of accomplishment.

The weddings in this chapter are specific to home: they were meant to take place here, and in the minds of the principals, there was no other place. Then, too, each home adapted easily to the dreams in mind and afforded perfect situations. In some cases, it was the site that was important, in others the food or the mood, but whatever the priority, home more than fulfilled the expectations. Home weddings appear in other chapters as well—summer houses, for example, are home, restaurants can be homes away from home, and rental spaces can feel like home. Home is, after all, a state of mind.

The rabbi blesses the wine during Emily and Kenneth's ceremony.

Emily Sonnenblick

and

Kenneth Offit

―――

A large, lavish wedding at home brings certain rewards. Indeed, one feels triumphant when home has been expanded to the dimensions necessary to stage a grand heroic party, and yet at heart remains a comfortable, familiar home.

For Emily Sonnenblick, home was an old stone house in Darien, Connecticut, set on five acres of land described by long lawns, Italian gardens, and the presence of swans, geese, and chipmunks. For her wedding to Dr. Kenneth Offit, a walled garden below the house was covered with a small white tent and set with flowers, creating a garden within a garden, a very special spot for the twelve-thirty ceremo-

ny. Beyond it in the yard, a voluminous white tent was set over a sweep of lawn for luncheon, serviced by a smaller kitchen and pantry tent. Here, too, was a show of flowers by Charles Case of Westport, notable for the individual beauty and variety of its blooms.

Many elements in this wedding had an aura of perfection. The bride, who is the daughter

of an eminent cardiologist, and who is herself a resident physician in radiology, was marrying a promising internist; she wore a dress from Bendel's that was as romantic as her landscape; the wedding gifts, displayed in the house, were exceptionally beautiful, the registered Limoges, crystal, and silver from Tiffany's, antique treasures from James Robinson. Yet the wedding had individuality, too, because Linda Sonnenblick, the mother of the bride, had a particular fancy for elegant food. And of all her carefully orchestrated decisions, it was ultimately the work of the caterer Glorious Food that seemed to distinguish the day.

The Glorious Food log of the day is telling,

LEFT: The procession of white-jacketed waiters serving each course of the luncheon French style. OPPOSITE: A collage of details from Emily Sonnenblick's wedding reception: the Glorious Food; the moments of private conversation; the beautifully set tables; the Patisserie Lanciani marzipan nut wedding cake.

for the organization was complete, the spirit lively, and the luncheon memorable. At 8:35 A.M. on Sunday, the account executive was on site, checking rentals, soon to be met by the setup crew under the direction of Jimmy, head of pantry and maintenance, indispensable and hard-working. At 10 A.M., twenty-three waiters arrived on site (one and a half per table) to begin setting tables. The choice of linens—white edged with lavender pearl stitching—turned out to be fortunate, for their cool aesthetics spiritually offset the heat that descended so aggressively that at 3:00 P.M. the thermometer registered 103 degrees outside and 120 degrees inside the tent. Ever so artful-

ly, napkins were fashioned into the Byzantine fold (when I inquired about the Byzantine fold, the answer was, inscrutably, "you know, the fold where you turn down the edge"), and beautiful calligraphy place cards were set in position. Eleven o'clock brought the captain Serge's review of all details with his staff, and the arrival of all food, mixers, ice, and cold Perrier-Jouët champagne. As chairs and dishes rattled, a waiter named Allen Anderson played wonderful jazz on the band's piano.

A reliable timetable is an important part of what one seeks in a caterer, and, admirably, the luncheon happened in as precise a manner as the advance preparation. Sharply at two-

ten, the waiters, dressed in tuxes and drenched from the heat, presented the first course of the meal, tricolor pasta salad primavera, in *marché* style, lining up and parading in with trays held high, and then, at table, in French style, serving guests from platters; at two-twenty-five, the second course, Silver Lake trout in a champagne sauce, served with haricots verts and tomatoes concassé, and a potato tart with truffles; at three, salad with cheese and bread. At three-thirty, the three-tiered wedding cake from Patisserie Lanciani in Manhattan emerged with due fanfare and an accompaniment of lemon sorbet with mint, coffee, and chocolate truffles. It was elegant clockwork.

LEFT: A simple hoop basket filled with spring flowers. OPPOSITE: The gracious living room where the wedding ceremony was performed.

A small, simple at-home wedding has a special beauty, for it means opening up one's hearth to an event in the most natural way. It need not be a production, necessitating the introduction of outside elements and props; instead, it can involve merely dressing up the immediate environment. Sandra Leo-Wolf, for example, had her wedding on Saturday, March 23, 1985, at the home of a dear and generous friend, and it took the form of a lovely formal luncheon for nineteen. The house was a large 1920s residence in New Canaan, Connecticut, as warm and rambling as an old

Sandra Leo-Wolf
and
Ralph Clarke

———

English inn, filled with the antiques and personal collectibles of the host; the lunch was the most elegant fare the bride and my catering staff could conceive. The day had evolved gradually in the thinking of Sandra, who was entering a second marriage, to Ralph Clarke: "I wanted it to be small, intimate, elegant, and perfect, and Ralph wanted what I wanted. At first, we thought we should invite our whole church, but when this house was donated with such love, we decided to have only close relatives and a large party later. I wanted our children to share in the joy of the event,

and somehow it was more appropriate that it be small. What was important was a feeling, and the beauty of the surroundings."

The ceremony took place before the fireplace in the living room, a large gracious room filled with beautiful art, antique damask-covered furniture, and a grand piano, and included readings, songs, and participation by everyone present. Afterward, the guests, all wearing special corsages, moved into the dinette for wedding punch and hors d'oeuvres under a big window with a view to the early spring outside, and then into the dining room for a seated, four-course wedding feast. The room, creamy beige with a blue-and-white Chinese rug and Federal cupboards displaying a collection of eighteenth-century blue-and-white china, had an intrinsic elegance that was respected by the decoration—Sandra's own repoussé silver candelabra on the sideboard, pale beige tablecloths and napkins bordered in blue, blue-and-white dishes, three sets of silverware, and hand-blown wineglasses. Menu cards and place cards had beautiful calligraphy by a woman Sandra had met over breakfast in a truck stop, and a pale pink wedding cake, decorated with roses and ranunculus, sat in prominence on a small round antique table. Everywhere in the house there were lavish bouquets of pastel flowers in elegant vases, Chinese bowls, and wicker baskets, promises of the spring to come, all coordinated to the colors of the house.

An American banjo clock c. 1815, with a commemorative eglomise panel, behind one of the spring flower arrangements asked for by the bride.

LEFT: Her son, Donald Neel, gave Sandra Leo-Wolf away. ABOVE: The bride and groom smiling broadly during the wedding luncheon. RIGHT: A lovely drapery frames the bridal wedding table.

CLOCKWISE FROM UPPER LEFT: Blue delphiniums bent under the weight of heavy raindrops; the bride's sister, one of the bridesmaids, holds her newborn baby; one of the many ornamental stone figures in the garden; Mrs. Childs requested that we make iced vodka bottles; drivers of the limousines stand under the portico of the Childs home; boughs of kousa dogwood in full bloom; a detail of the beautiful lace tablecloths used on the bridal tables; a place setting of hand-blown crystal at the dining tables; a friend of the family, a professional cake maker, fashioned an extraordinary cake for the newlyweds as well as an extra single layer for cutting; greenery-wrapped tent poles and lace-swathed tables; the elliptical pool around which canopies stretched for protection from the rain; scores of umbrellas protected family and friends.
OPPOSITE: The happy couple sits with all their attendants at a long, lace-draped table.

Shirley Childs

and

Christopher Kelly

When I think of home weddings, I think of the Childs family in New Canaan, Connecticut, for their home is an important, expressive, joyful place to parents, seven children, and assorted adopted children from around the world; their home weddings have reflected this, and stand as classics. Entering their large, rambling country house, with old post-office boxes at the door holding sorted mail for all; the two talking cockatoos and the fish tank in the kitchen; Mr. Childs's nearby office for work at home, the fine antiques, silver, and

171

porcelain appointing warm family rooms, immediately one senses their life-style. Outside, one finds Mr. Childs's greenhouse, where he propagates trees and seeds for his extensive gardens, a pool and tennis court, a compound with horses, a donkey, and chickens. More than an estate, it all constitutes simply a wonderful open family place, where everyone inevitably gathers (there are always many cars in the driveway) and where everyone loves to entertain.

In October 1983 daughter Constance had been married in a formal wedding ceremony performed by her cousin at St. Aloysius Roman Catholic Church. A candlelight reception for three hundred followed at home, under white tents winding through the gardens. Huge gatherings of late flowers from the garden, and glazed cotton linens in jewel-like tones of pink, mauve, lavender, melon, and apricot, two contrasting shades on each table, provided soft, rich color for the sit-down buffet dinner. The menu was elaborate—mousse of sole, salmon, and spinach in sorrel sauce, boned leg of lamb with herbs, smoked fillet of beef with horseradish cream, and elegant vegetable salads; the cake was by master baker friend Scott Wooley; the dancing long and lively; the mood as warm and spirited as the family celebrating.

When Mrs. Childs called me several months later, without a twinge of fatigue or even breathlessness, she said she wanted things to be different for the wedding of her daughter Shirley, the following June 30. The season would be different, suggesting a different color scheme; the guest list longer (450

people), requiring more extensive use of the property; and the decoration more elaborate, so that guests would not be bored. From the beginning, the immensity of the event required elaborate charts, floor plans, and decorative schemes. Mr. Deicke, of Deicke Tents, planned to use extensive canopies over walkways for the receivin line, eading down from the house to a main tent for dinner and dancing amid the gardens, to cover the tennis court below for the cocktail hour, and to place a tent by the pool house, for a raw-clam-and-oyster

bar. Inside the tents he suggested great swags of colored tulle across the ceiling, to create a softer atmosphere, and intricate lighting by Frost to emphasize it. The linens from Party Rental were shades of peach and pale blue, overlaid, for springtime, with a lilac print. And the menu was to be even more elaborate than before, and presented at oversized buffets, to prevent long queues.

It was a gigantic effort on everyone's part: the six tent men; the four lighting men; my thirty-nine bartenders-waiters, two captains, two chefs, and fourteen in-kitchen staff; eight

musicians; five policemen; Flora Stebbins Kendall Bryant, the bridal coordinator who organized the event; and Mrs. Childs, who was involved in every detail, at the end still busy finding beautiful vases to hold garden flowers, unearthing old lace cloths to decorate the bridal party tables, adding special soaps and perfumes to the pool house baths. When rain began to pour down the morning of the wedding and did not cease, Mrs. Childs remained unperturbed; she had survived a fire before her daughter Lore's wedding and her husband's heart attack on a boat at sea before Connie's. In any case, the two tent men who remained on duty for the inclement weather fortified the covers against seepage so well that no one even got his feet wet.

Mrs. Childs made sure that everyone entered the wedding reception through the house, because it was important to her to begin with the domestic homilies, the grace and hospitality of the home seat, and guests wandered freely through the rooms, used interior bathrooms, admired collectibles and mementos. (Other families with other priorities circumvent the house and hire port-o-johns.) To announce her intent, champagne and ice water were set up at the front door, and a bar arranged in the family room, also known as the Jungle Room, for its zebra upholstery. A pair of elephants, King Babar and Queen Celeste, dressed in bridal clothes and posed on an antique settee in the master bedroom, seemed to sum up the thoughtfulness, the caring, and the fun invested in the wedding.

OPPOSITE: A view of the interior of the huge tent, with foliage-wrapped poles and swags of colored tulle crisscrossing the immense space.

ABOVE: Babar and Celeste dressed in their wedding finery sat on an antique settee.

LEFT: A simple, delicate posy of pink tea roses and baby's breath.

173

Allison Zucker and Jeffrey Perelman

Food of course is the age-old companion of merrymaking, and often proves the heart and soul as well as the sustenance of an event. It is important to consider the appetites of a crowd in planning a wedding menu, for hearty eaters may be disappointed and subdued by wispy, delicate food, and the ascetic abashed at a spread worthy of *Goodbye Columbus*. Allison Zucker's wedding on Sunday, June 9, 1985, to Dr. Jeffrey Perelman in the garden of her large Normandy-style home in Greenwich, Connecticut, was by any measure a lovely affair, graced with a spectacular site overlooking the steeply terraced gardens leading to the pool, a ceremony under a flower-entwined chuppah in a quiet corner of the yard, a poignant violin solo by a friend studying at Juilliard, and a crowd so interlocked in

ABOVE: The Zuckers' pool, set in a terrace below the house, created a dramatic backdrop for the reception. RIGHT: Allison Zucker being led from the ceremony by her husband, Jeffrey Perelman. A white paper runner protected the long dresses from the green grass.

174

celebration that they constantly erupted with mazel tovs and embraces. Like a blessing, sunny skies appeared after so serious a threat of rain that the tent man had to act upon his option for inclement weather and make an emergency return visit to cover the al fresco dining area. Yet it was the appearance of silver trays of little blinis, wild rice pancakes, pâté à chou puffs, and the sight of the cheese table, tiered with a dozen cheeses and pâtés, that really brought the wedding to life. The feeling continued as the buffet tables began to fill with poached salmon, lemon chicken, fillet of beef with béarnaise sauce and horseradish, cold sesame noodles, wild rice, vegetable and fruit salads. The wedding cake, which I had decorated with swags and apricot-hued roses, and which I anxiously protected from encroaching humidity with maximum-force air conditioning, seemed more than ever the crowning touch to the day.

LEFT: A view looking from inside the tent, which was erected at the last minute because of threatening rain. ABOVE: A giant vine basket, entwined with ribbons and leaves, was the focal point for the cheese table. RIGHT: Guests seated and enjoying the buffet supper. OPPOSITE: A view over the stone wall into the supper tent.

Caroline Damerell and Carmine Santandrea

Caroline Damerell loves pink, so the invitation to her wedding reception was pink, the tent in the back was pink-and-white striped, and the wedding cake was pink, with pink mill roses. She also loves the big center hall colonial in a farmlike setting in North Stamford, Connecticut, that she and her groom, Carmine Santandrea, have been refurbishing over the last several years (with pink as the dominant color in the interior design). They knew they wanted their wedding to be fun, so

Caroline planned a small formal wedding ceremony and lunch for June 15, 1984, and a party at home for seventy-five dear friends the following afternoon.

The specifics of the long, relaxed celebration reflected both the couple's high style and commitment to easy country living. Caroline, who is English, and who had met Carmine on her way to a sojourn in California she never completed, has a very special, professional, well-defined taste. Carmine is an adventure-

LEFT: The floral designer at work. ABOVE: In the front hall of the farmhouse, a split oak basket filled with the bride's favorite flowers—peonies, stock, snap dragons, and roses—was placed on an English pine table.

some entrepreneur, who on impulse and instinct had hired a young violinist named James Graseck, who plays in the subways of New York, to entertain guests at the wedding. They both love to party and to entertain, and wanted a wonderful, relaxed country luncheon reception. The colorful menu featured lobster with red pepper sauce, fillet of beef salad, and an assortment of summer salads. Caroline wore a Victorian cotton-and-lace camisole with a petticoat skirt tied with a pink sash; Carmine, white Bermuda shorts with a Brooks Brothers shirt. Luncheon, long and lavish, in the midst of beautiful flowers—peonies, roses, fluffy pink blooms in bleached pine baskets—led to dancing (Caroline and Carmine had hired English Morris dancers to perform traditional country folk dances), walks through the woods, visits to the chickens, a casual and chic adventure at home that continued to unfold until nightfall.

ABOVE LEFT: Caroline and a friend smile at the music. ABOVE RIGHT: White dotted swiss overlays were placed atop cotton cloths. The plates were white bisque, and the stemware was handblown crystal. LEFT: A troupe of English Morris dancers and musicians performed during the reception.

LEFT: Centerpieces were simple: full clusters of early summer flowers arranged in glass bubble vases. BELOW: The bar looked elegant backlit by the sun.

Decoration

The decoration of a wedding is a personal statement. It begins with a vision, sometimes a picture from a book, sometimes a memory, more often a flight of the imagination. The vision is subjected to the pragmatic—budget and location and available craftsmen—and so shaped, begins to take concrete form, piece by piece, until one day the vision becomes real.

It used to be that for a wedding one rented a tent, added pretty tables, individual centerpieces, and, perhaps, some ribbons or baby's breath on the tent poles. This treatment produces lovely results and stands as classic. Yet these days, many brides seem to be more ambitious and are draping their tents in tulle, adding stands of topiary, renting ballroom chairs and Lalique vases, covering tables in checks and chintzes and brocades, and spotlighting the bandstand with colored gels. Wedding aesthetics are boundless, and the choices can be difficult.

Initially, you have to decide what kind of statement you want to make. Sometimes nature makes enough of a statement herself that one only wants to respect it, and, perhaps, point it up here and there with floral touches. For the wedding on their island on Golden Pond in New Hampshire, the Cook family added only a green-and-white-striped tent, to extend the ready-made dining area on their wide porch; a platform underfoot, to level the steep slope for dancing; and a few baskets of wild flowers, for there was little they could fabricate that could match the long view to the lake and the sun dapplings under the pine trees.

At the other extreme, the Desmarais family wanted to claim the grand but neutral space of the Museum of Fine Arts in Montreal for their own, and with the artistry of designer Jean-François Daigre and florist Eric van Horn utterly transformed the reception site with velvet-draped walls, sculpted Greek columns, hand-painted carpets, and tall Renaissance candelabra filled with orchids, lilies, roses, tulips, and ferns. The decorative thinking in play was so complete that the central motif of the classical evening, wreaths of magnolia leaves entwined around an ornate MS, for Michel and Sophie, reappeared hand-painted

on chair backs and cushions as well as on matchbooks.

The different approaches to wedding decoration might be categorized as simple respect, enhancement, transformation, and fantasy. For their wedding on their property in rural New Jersey, Sharon Nelson and Harvey Siegel chose to honor the site, graced with an old stone farmhouse, stone walls, and gently sloping meadows. They applied a light and con-

Carole Gordon used hundreds and hundreds of yards of draped and puffed white tulle to create fairy-tale entrances to the dining tent at this wedding.

PRECEDING PAGES, LEFT: Lake Siegel, lilacs in her hair, touching a basket cascade of lilacs. RIGHT: Some of my staff setting up tables and chairs for an evening wedding.

fident decorative hand, filling copper teakettles, bushel baskets, and an antique wheelbarrow with spring flowers. In Central Park, Kathy GarDianos, with the florist Jody Thompson Kennedy, designed a gardenlike

set of window boxes and flowering plants to make the Victorian Dairy even more of an enchanted cottage than it already was. In a more ambitious manner, and a different style, Carole and Shelly Gordon began with the Art Deco beauty of an exotic summer house and, both incorporating and inflating the existing design elements, transformed the yard into a fantastic and lavish scene reminiscent of a thirties Hollywood set.

My own fantasy is to cover my garden with tents, and drape their poles and ceilings with puffs of filmy tulle, like clouds, holding little twinkle lights, like stars. I would cover tables with an old floral chintz and white drawnwork cloths, and set them with ungilded bamboo ballroom chairs with very soft cushions in another pattern of chintz, and cabbage roses as centerpieces. The tents would be clear plastic, so that I could look up into the dark sky, and out into the surrounding walls of roses, fragrant and blooming. Beautiful music, from a small orchestra rather than a band, would accompany dinner.

The most basic structural element of wedding decoration is the tent, or often tents. These days, there is not really a standard tent, for as Wesley Deicke of Stamford, Connecticut, explains, he buys tents in sections, from a small ten-by-ten-foot section to a sixty-by-one-hundred-twenty-foot tennis court cover, constructs different shapes, and can offer 150 different forms, including scalloped, square, round, rectangular, and modular. Although white is currently the most popular color, he offers stripes and solids of pink, blue, green, yellow, red, and brown, and will custom-make almost anything. White is also the choice of photographers, for it doesn't distort natural light, whereas both pink and yellow, while soft and warm, cast a yellowish glow. Many people also buy or rent liners for their tents, which further extend the possibilities of the color palette. A family in Greenwich raised the sides of their tent an additional three feet, which created a more spacious, cathedral-like atmosphere. Another wedding called for five small fifteen-by-fifteen-foot tents, an inspired solution to the problem created by a landscape that sloped gradually down to a pond. Different foods were served in each tent, and guests wandered happy and active throughout the complex.

Mr. Deicke, who inherited a carnival business from his father at a time when circuses and carnivals were waning and the society business waxing, speaks with wonder of the demands of contemporary decoration, of running five hundred yards of canopy all over a yard, to the house and pool; of flooring and filling in swimming pools; of laying acres of Astroturf; of "decorating everything that stands still." When he is faced with slopes and different grade levels, his concerns are architectural: "It can be like building a house, but then I take it apart and transport it back to the warehouse." In the beginning, Mr. Deicke inquires about the size and nature of a wedding: stand up or sit down? receiving line? dancing? then he sets up an appointment to assess and measure land, determining site, any need for Astroturf in low or wet areas, or desires for more elaborate lighting than his standard track and spotlights. At least a month before the wedding, he confers with

Harvey Siegel's personal collection of antique copper teakettles inspired the wild flower bouquet centerpieces at his wedding to Sharon Nelson.

the other members of the work force, the caterer, decorators, or lighting men, to iron out any problems and avoid "last-minute surprises." The Tuesday or Wednesday preceding the event generally brings the setup, which, in the case of a single twenty-by-twenty-foot tent, will take four men only half an hour, although large or multipartite tents and extras like a dance floor, bandstand, or Astroturf, are much more time-consuming.

Mr. Deicke often works in concert with Brian Leahy, one of the partners at Frost Lighting in Manhattan, which also has offices in Chicago and Florida. Party lighting, or special temporary lighting, has developed into a veritable art form, and more and more frequently goes hand in hand with wedding decoration. While Leahy works in a wide variety of spaces, more than 35 percent of his calls these days come for weddings. In a typical tent treatment, which begins at a minimum cost of one thousand dollars, Leahy might introduce a source of ambient light like chandeliers or twinkle lights wrapped in a cloud of fabric; illuminate the buffet table, usually with down-lighting; down-light the centerpieces of dinner tables; and bathe the dance floor in a softer glow, achieved with spots with peach, pink, or lavender gels. Over the course of an event, he likes to change his light, beginning bright and clear over cocktails ("everyone wants to see everyone and everything"); growing warmer and dimmer over dinner; and then more intense for dancing, creating a romantic mood with some of the tricks he has picked up from the club scene. Although he adheres to decorative lights, and avoids using the trusses and big black lights of stage and disco, because they are conspicuous fixtures, his battery of equipment includes mirror balls, strobes, Leico, Parkhands, and smoke and fog machines, for special effects like shooting beams of light

Deicke Tents erected this massive white tent at the Cushing home on Long Island.

A perennial border surrounds the tent at the Solis-Cohen home near Philadelphia.

As night fell, votive candles were lit to illuminate Jacquie Van Den Berg's dancing tent.

On the shores of Long Island Sound amid the beach grasses, Joan Beranbaum set up two white tents.

On the island of Martha's Vineyard, a large pink and white tent protected guests from the noonday sun.

Caroline Damerell chose a pink and white striped tent for her wedding luncheon.

In Montclair, New Jersey, a large white tent was placed below the terraced rose gardens.

The Cooks had a huge rehearsal dinner under a striped tent at The Woodshed Restaurant.

Three large white tents at a Greenwich home. OPPOSITE: Ribbons woven through chicken wire were used to line this canopy.

through a cloudy dance floor.

Leahy loves lighting, and quietly waxes a contagious excitement while speaking of the aesthetic possibilities: chandeliers in many styles, holding globes, candles, shades, or swathed in fabric; coach lights; sponge-painted Japanese lanterns "floated" at different altitudes; lights in trees; columns or drums enclosing twinkle lights; lighted mylar banners; vanity lights in port-o-johns; landscape lighting; dropped ceilings—of colored fabric fanning out like a carnival with strings of tiny lights, or of black set with a night sky full of a thousand lights. Exclusive to Frost are balloons containing twinkle lights which can be hung individually at different heights, like surrealistic fixtures, or gathered into a bunch, which will illuminate a room with a soft glow.

Lighting evolves as the last decorative element in a wedding, the frosting on the cake. At first, Leahy visits a site to see the space—"I want to preserve the integrity of a room and respect the architectural elements"—and to evaluate existing light as well as electrical arrangements—with the needs of the caterer, video crew, and use of power packs and TV monitors, he often must bring in a generator. Then he meets with the wedding's work force—caterer, florist, decorator, band, video crew—to understand the scene being created as well as the lighting needs. The Monday before a wedding, he does the final fact-checking and coordination, and on Thursday, Friday, and Saturday, sets to work. If the wedding decoration is simple—just a tent and floral centerpieces—in a way his work is more difficult,

"for you don't want to see more unadorned tent." For the general party, three light sources is the rule, but eight or nine is more elegant, and Leahy's dream is to light many elements from many sources, very subtly and

The famous Christmas tree at the Pierre Hotel was a sparkling greeting for guests at the wedding of Emily Meyer and Joshua Sacks.

artfully: "I don't want people to say 'I love the lighting'; if they notice everything else, I know I did a good job."

Lighting demands serious consideration, particularly at a nighttime wedding, but many people have been known to overlook this dimension. The catering staff, too, needs good light in order to work well. There are lovely alternatives to supplant or supplement professional light, particularly appropriate to the intimate romantic atmosphere intrinsic to most weddings. Hilary Cushing rented small fringed silver filigree table lamps, which, in themselves, established the Gatsby mood she so desired. Hurricane lamps are country fare; torches are dramatic; tall fat devotional candles shed wonderful bright light; other candles have different effects in candelabra, brass candlesticks, and hobnail votive holders. And anyone can fashion luminarias by placing candles in paper bags full of sand; they send out a lovely glow that can be used to outline driveways, swimming pools, and garden paths.

The coordination of decoration is of the utmost importance. Many people coordinate their color scheme with the bridesmaids' dresses or the favorite color of the bride; others don't pay attention to this dictum, and there is no iron-clad rule that says they should. However, it *is* important to coordinate linens with the color of the tent and flowers. And even the choice of a container for the table centerpieces can make a difference, for a spare, modern-looking arrangement in an abstract vase would be at odds with a floral chintz. Remember that there is a great range of choices suiting every-

one's aesthetics, and that sometimes the use of a small item like Victorian or Art Deco vases can be the grace note that confirms and accentuates the style of a wedding. Don't hesitate to draw upon a personal collection of compotes, silver candy dishes, or yelloware bowls, for they will lend originality and personality to the decoration.

Flowers seem to become more beautiful, more varied, and more expressive every day. The new breed of creative and highly individualist florist, the exotic blooms that proliferate in their shops, and fresh aesthetics all give the choice of floral decoration new interest and depth. Wedding flowers can be plucked from the roadside or meadow, as Butzi Moffitt did, in part, for the red, white, and blue table decorations she made for Sissy Cargill's nautical wedding; they can be cut from home gardens purposefully planted for the affair; or they can be imported by the planeload from the rich fields of Holland and France. The Temerlins ordered thousands of lilies to fill a townhouse living room; for a June wedding, a mother of the bride brought hundreds of roses from Europe to supplement the local seasonal show with the exotic. Although most people don't have time to do it all themselves, they can seek out their favorite florist and contribute their own ideas with confidence.

Simple aesthetics should prevail for a wedding ceremony, particularly if it takes place in a church or synagogue. The Desmaraises tied single calla lilies with ribbon to the ends of pews; others have posted a candle and a sprig of baby's breath or ivy there, or as at the

Strings of round white lights create a spectacular tent-like illusion in this formal setting.

CLOCKWISE FROM TOP LEFT: Beneath a pink Bourbon climbing rose, a pink draped table (also opposite) dressed with Wedgwood Drabware, crystal, and a centerpiece of roses; a gigantic vine basket filled with fruits and berries; a table draped in ecru lace and set with Vermeil flatware, glass dishes, and a centerpiece of flowering herbs; atop a Famille Vert plate by Mottahedeh, a forest green napkin tied with a flowering chive; a thatched roof adds South Sea ambiance; astilbe and roses are the focal point of the Canton table; a poolside setting—a perfect place for a summer wedding lunch; a flowering herb bouquet and herbal centerpiece on a forest green table.

Cooks' outdoor service in the woods, a delicate gathering of pine boughs and tiny pine cones. For the chuppah, which used to be a relatively plain shelter under a ceiling created by a prayer shawl, many brides are now choosing to garland arches, gazebos, or rented trellises with garden flowers. The Zuckers found a shady, tranquil spot in their backyard for a chuppah entwined with foxgloves.

At home, a grouping of flowers near the entrance, in big urns or Victorian wicker baskets, bids welcome. Flowers also can camouflage unattractive elements like tent poles and flaps. Ropings of boxwood, smilax, or lemon leaves, or coverings of tulle, gauze, or ribbons, are popular and inexpensive ways to create a more romantic atmosphere. A further elaboration would add tiny lights to the poles. Other unnatural structures, like a platform or bandstand or even a tennis court fence, can be incorporated into the wedding landscape when they are set with baskets of roses or daisies or flowering plants or potted palms. The Gardellas, for example, rented fifty ficus trees to create a pretty wall of green behind the bandstand. A grand arrangement of flowers adds due moment to the buffet table, too, where everyone gathers attentively, although if the food is very impressive in appearance, the flowers may be superfluous. Sometimes I like to use food itself as decoration, masses of colorful vegetables or heads of flowering kale. And sometimes a

spectacular ice carving, silver or porcelain figurines, or a favorite sculpture adds the right note of importance. At holiday time, nothing surpasses a stand of Christmas trees, adorned with tiny lights.

Round tables are in general use for wedding feasts, for their shape is congenial and allows easy conversation among guests. Diameters range from thirty-six inches for four people to

ABOVE: At the Cook wedding simple pine boughs were tied onto the pews.
BELOW: Round beribboned clusters of baby's breath and roses on each pew of St. Joseph's Church in Wood's Hole, Massachusetts.

seventy-two inches for twelve. Chairs offer more stylish possibilities, and are available at rental places in great variety, from white, green, and black wooden folding chairs and clear lucite chairs, to gilded, white, natural, or black bamboo opera chairs.

In recent years, businesses with names like Table Toppers and Knights of the Round Table have devoted themselves exclusively to table linens. These firms, and the premier party agencies, offer a phenomenal assortment of linens for rent or custom manufacture. The swatch book from Party Rental in New Jersey shows checks, moires, chintzes, stripes, calicos, linens, madras, Oriental prints, lamés, taffetas, plaids, white piqué, dotted swiss, white eyelet, and velvets, and a spongy table liner to add softness—at least a hundred fabric selections. If a perishable fabric, other than the usual cotton or cotton blend, is selected—a silk or the moiré known as bengaline, for example—purchase is often required, because a stain renders it useless. Nonetheless, I've used bengaline many times, and found that it washes successfully, although, as with any linens, I avoid using colored candles on the tables. While pink and lavender are very popular colors now, many people are also venturing into bright chintzes and romantic prints, for they enliven the large neutral space of a tent. More fanciful ideas make the choice of flowers more complicated, and yet prove irresistible. Consider overlays of dotted swiss and lace, puffs of taffeta or gauze. Layers are luxurious, especially in a single color—white organza swagged with blue ribbon over a moiré underskirt over cotton—and evocative of a ballgown. At Christmas, consider using red velvet under lace, with centerpieces of individual croquembouches swirled with spun sugar. In choosing napkins, avoid small squares of a scratchy polyester, for the main virtue of a napkin, preferably large, soft, and damask, is its utility.

Party Rental has another book filled with pictures of an equally impressive assortment of the components for table settings: china, crystal, flatware, and serving plates. The dishes could be cobalt-rimmed white, Wedgwood frieze, versatile clear glass, or Art Deco black; crystal that is fluted, balloon-shaped, or cut in the Irish style. In making a selection, unless you are indulging in a fantasy, remember that the idea behind rentals is to duplicate or to extend the setting and the ambiance of home. Rentals often approximate or even exceed the cost of food for a wedding. For a smaller wedding, borrowing supplies is an attractive and more economical alternative. However, if you are using friends' antiques or precious dishes, include a housekeeper in your budget to wash

ABOVE: An English taxi, beribboned and strewn with flowers, made a charming exit for Anne O'Herron and Jonathan Burleigh. BELOW: A "Just Married" heart with ribbon streamers was a playful decoration on this getaway car.

and care for their valuables, so that you don't have to operate in fear. Borrowed goods don't necessarily have to be identical or even matching, for even with rentals, it can be interesting to combine patterns. When Butzi Moffit, Sissy Cargill's godmother, planned the marriage of one of her daughters at home, she borrowed favorite dishes from a dozen friends, set each table with an individual look, and, in so doing, created a rich, memorable tableau.

It is the large decorative elements of a wedding that cause sleepless nights. And yet it is often the trivial entries that signal the love and care invested in the event. However expendable at a time when expenses are inevitably mounting uncontrollably, the decoration of a bathroom with potpourri, hand towels, and samples of cologne and handcream, or of a cloakroom with flowers, are the personal touches that make the moment complete and memorable. A bar or simply a pitcher of fresh juice inside the house is a gesture of welcome. A homemade banner flying in the trees commemorates the day forever.

And don't forget to decorate the getaway car. In this epoch of white helicopters, hot-air balloons, and pink limousines, I still favor the family car trailing ribbons, tin cans, and old shoes.

The Summer House Wedding

Anne O'Herron and Jonathan Burleigh

It is the fairness of the weather, the bloom of the roses, and the romance of the summer solstice, along with its original consecration by Juno, Roman queen of heaven and goddess of femininity and marriage, that have made June *the* month for weddings. For many families, June also means leaving for the summer house, where the commitment to adventure, good health, and peace of mind is annually renewed. Filled as it is with memories of lazy childhoods, spontaneous fun, and family unity, the summer house is a poignant place for a wedding. Like summer itself, it seems to exert a certain influence that soothes nerves and stirs imaginations.

ABOVE: The large white tent erected for the wedding reception was set high on a bluff overlooking the sea.
RIGHT: Anne and Jon celebrate with the high-spirited bridesmaids.

194

ABOVE: Part of the wedding party on the high bluff overlooking
the Atlantic Ocean. BELOW: High in the peak of the main dining tent a worker secures a seam.

Anne O'Herron's summer house in Woods Hole, Massachusetts, is, in fact, a new house designed by her mother to supplant the cottage down the street they had lived in for many summers before. Set on a lane above Quissett Harbor, it is a very American nautical structure, a series of gabled clapboard squares assembled as if for a family portrait.

Behind the house, decks and stairs are bordered with ship's railings, and a second-story greenhouse projects toward the yard and sea like a gargantuan porthole. When an old-fashioned scalloped tent with a green stripe border, showing its seams like sails, was erected abutting the back of the house, the nautical theme seemed complete.

Significantly, it was a nor'easter that descended the morning of Saturday, June 29, 1985, and yet few people seemed to treat it as anything other than a natural phenomenon. Anne herself was happy and loose, at ten-thirty debating whether to wash her hair before or after her sister Sarah, her maid of honor, and showing early arrivals at the house her parents' Bachrach photograph album of their wedding, September 10, 1955, which, with minor alterations, she was about to duplicate. Her parents had been married at a large Catholic church in town and feted at the Woods Hole Country Club nearby, while Anne and Jonathan Burleigh had their rehearsal dinner at the club, and chose a smaller Catholic church for the ceremony and home for the reception. Anne was wearing her mother's dress, a white satin princess-line gown with cap sleeves and a scoop neck edged in lace, her mother's earrings, which matched her diamond-and-sapphire engagement ring, and like her mother, a single strand of pearls.

Looking at the photographs, one saw in mother and daughter the same big eyes and freckles and the same glow of vitality.

In Anne's bedroom, her maid of honor and four bridesmaids were dressing, posing and twirling for one another, and expressing pleasure at the choice of outfit: a white Laura Ashley sailor dress trimmed with red braid and a red tie, black patent leather ballet slippers, and boaters with streamers of red ribbon. Carrying dainty nosegays of snapdragons tied with long curls of white ribbon, they looked jaunty and sweet, old-fashioned and stylish all at once, costumed for fun and for romance. In a gesture of extreme thoughtfulness, Mrs. O'Herron had offered both the dresses and the groomsmen's pink-striped shirts and red-print ties as presents to the bridal party. "Annie has a closetful of dreadful-looking bridesmaids' dresses," she mused, "on which she has spent hundreds of dollars, even before the cost of travel and a wedding gift. This expense is a struggle for most young people begin-

ABOVE AND BELOW: Anne dresses for the ceremony with the help of her bridesmaids. Mrs. O'Herron was very pleased when Anne chose to wear the same dress she had worn for her wedding thirty years ago. A Bachrach portrait of Mr. and Mrs. O'Herron appears below.

ning new jobs, but it was easy for us to absorb; it would be nice if more people did it this way."

Outside in the rain, a crew of young workers were busily putting together the last details for the wedding lunch to follow a noon service. My catering staff was ensconced in the garage, where long service tables were an easy walk to buffet tables for a team of young white-tuxed waiters, hired from the local Landfall Restaurant. There was a long narrow canopy for the receiving line, which led from the front circle drive along the side of the house and through a buffet tent into a main arena behind, centered on two poles wrapped with red ribbon like peppermint sticks, and festooned in the upper reaches with baby's breath. Round tables covered with pastel chintz linens had been laid with white china and weathered wicker baskets of summer flowers, with several tables next to the dance floor set off importantly for the bridal party. The sides of the tent were rolled down and dripped with rain, giving the illusion of fog at sea, for the presence of the sea at the end of the yard could only be sensed. As the tent began to leak large plunking raindrops, buckets were positioned strategically.

Shirley O'Herron, Anne's mother, had first met with the tent man in January, when they had walked the property and realized that their space was too small and the Cape Cod grass too wild to host a tent. Consequently a stone wall was moved and set between upper and lower grades of the yard, and the area sodded and landscaped for the wedding. The wall, planted with roses, winding through the wedding scene and dividing dancing from dining, was picturesque in the midst of a big tent. "We may have created a monster," Mr. O'Herron had laughed about it, "but perhaps

Sarah will get married in time to enjoy it too."

In masterful pieces of timing, the ice truck and garbage trucks pulled out of the drive as the O'Herrons and party, under the shelter of very large umbrellas, climbed into an old London taxi and headed for the church. As they arrived at St. Joseph's, a Victorian church on a quiet side street in town, the clock struck noon. As the clergy processed in, the gathering sang "Love Divine, All Loves Excelling," a fervent swelling hymn that brought everyone together in voice as well as spirit. When they turned to see the father of the bride offer his arm with a fond and casual "Shall we go?" the harbor of Woods Hole could be glimpsed in the tall back windows.

The service that followed was original and personal, alternating traditional greetings, prayers, and rites. Two clergymen, Father Francis Virgulak of Bridgeport, Connecticut,

LEFT, TOP TO BOTTOM: Anne emerges from the car and is escorted by her father into St. Joseph's Church. A canopy was set up over the facade because of the inclement weather.
OPPOSITE RIGHT, TOP TO BOTTOM: Guests all signed the guest book as they came into the reception tent; familial embraces and warm smiles were seen all day long; the tables were covered in brightly colored, flowered chintz. Flowers were arranged in whitewashed baskets.
OPPOSITE FAR RIGHT, TOP TO BOTTOM: The bridesmaids' Laura Ashley sailor dresses and white boater hats with red trimmings were perfect for the setting; Anne and Jonathan cut the first slice of cake; Rafael and John, two of my service staff, came as party executives.

and Rev. Dr. Olin Robison, former president of Middlebury College, of which Anne and Jonathan are alumni, presented an ecumenical ceremony that was rich in literature, called often upon the gathering for participation, and spoke directly and profoundly to the bride and groom. Jon's boyish face shone with joy, and Anne's voice was deep and husky, either from tears, or from all the laughter of the night before. Emerging from the church, she cuffed her groom on the chin, kissed him several times, and said, "Hey, we're married!" And then, in a bright triumphant voice she called, "Hi, Mummy!"

Back at the house, rain continued to pour down; shoes, hairdos, and the wedding gown's hem grew soggy, and a handmade banner, hung outside between two pine trees, proclaiming ANNE O'HERRON AND JONATHAN BURLEIGH, JUNE 29, 1985, gusted in the wind. Spirits soared nonetheless. Catching the mood of the day, the waiters chatted with the guests like the old chums some of them were. From the dance floor, Anne called to the crowd to join her. Champagne flowed. The buffet table, groaning with whole poached salmons, lemon chicken, and exotic salads, provided second and then third helpings. The wedding cake and groom's cake were consumed without a trace left over. An intimate world was contained in a tent, and only dispersed toward dusk when the London taxi reappeared for the bride and groom's getaway.

Looking back a year on her daughter's wedding, Shirley O'Herron is still excited. "I suppose it was an inspiration to do it the way we did, but it seemed so natural, there at home, above the little harbor where we all sail. I even liked the inconsistency of the formal wedding dress, which Annie, despite our light-hearted theme, was determined to wear. The organiza-

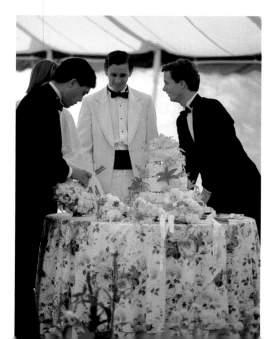

tion was easy, although that is my strength, for it was simply another party, a very gala party. My friends had warned me to brace myself for an emotional ordeal in which Annie and I would inevitably lock horns, but we think so much alike that whenever I had an idea, she was having the same thought." About the disasters common to weddings, she said, "Rain had become something of an obsession with me, because so many special events that week had been planned out-of-doors; a party for out-of-towners on a boat Thursday evening, with dinner en route to Martha's Vineyard (we had drinks on the boat and an indoor boat party at a clubhouse in town); my sister's lunch on the lawn on Friday, which saw one brief illusory moment of sun. I felt awful about the weather, but after the church ceremony, which was so moving, I never thought about rain again."

BELOW: An English taxi was used by the bride and groom as the getaway vehicle. Modest ribbons and neatly painted messages identified its purpose in an understated fashion.

LEFT: Dressed for departure for their honeymoon, the newlyweds Anne and Jonathan leave amid crowds of well-wishers and cascades of rice and rose petals. ABOVE: On the leather seat of the taxi, the best man left a bottle of Kriter champagne.

The
Rental Space Wedding

There are hotels. There are country inns. There are legion halls, granges, and historic homes of every era; barges, barns, public parks, and city landmarks, discothèques, and probably, should one have the desire and determination, battleships, airplane hangars, and vineyards. The wealth of rental spaces available for weddings these days is almost as great as the bride's imagination. Kathy GarDianos chose the Victorian Dairy in Central Park; Sophie Desmarais, the Museum of Fine Arts in Montreal; Dana Temerlin, a 120-foot charter yacht in New York harbor. In this chapter, a colonial home, a Tudor mansion, and a country inn fulfilled brides' visions for their day.

It used to be that the only popular alternative to a home wedding was a hotel wedding. Now it is one of many, but it is the classic choice. Hotels have romance, which has to do with their aura—all the personalities who have passed through their doors in the past, from European royalty to rock stars to Arab oil men—as well as with their purpose, which is to create a lavish home-away-from-home, comfortable, safe, and equipped with services such as one can only dream of domestically. To be married in a hotel is to join a glamorous and elegant continuum, to strike out for the grand style.

Pragmatically, hotels offer facilities that are complete, convenient, and tasteful, and a staff that is bent on service. When I married Andy twenty-five years ago, I had little money and little sophistication. I really didn't

know where to stage the wedding I was organizing myself, so I settled on the idea of a hotel, for hotels in most cities are magnetic places, and I scurried about visiting small elegant hotels I hoped would be hospitable. I chose the little Barberry Room in the Berkshire Hotel, made arrangements, agreed on the menu, and when we showed up on July 1, 1961, for our luncheon reception, they had done everything. There was a long table to accommodate the eighteen of us, delicious food (Cornish hens were the new rage), and a pretty cake. It was perfect for that moment, and just as important, the hotel staff was extremely nice to our little wedding party.

Hotels have the experience of thousands of weddings behind them, and they are knowledgeable and well seasoned. They have the resources to provide flowers, food, music, and decoration, as well as space. A hotel can accommodate a large number of guests in a way that would be virtually impossible elsewhere, all with the savoir-faire that makes numbers seem inconsequential, behind the concerns of budget.

For someone who seeks comprehensive coordination of a wedding, a hotel offers everything. With a hotel like the Plaza or the Pierre in New York City, which has caterers, cake makers, florists, decorators, bands, and even chocolatiers in their service, a bride has only to articulate her desires, define her budget, and make her choices. The only drawback is that because hotels have distinct personalities and defined ways of doing things, it can be difficult to impose your own personality on the occasion. Decorating possibilities are limited and certain styles, like an informal or country wedding, are inappropriate in a gilded ballroom. Nonetheless, many hotels will allow a bride to bring in a caterer of her choice, and

most are open to stylistic innovation.

In recent years, with the new interest in architecture and the decorative arts, and the sense of adventure prevalent in entertaining, many cities have seen their historic buildings opened for party rentals, both public monuments like the U.S. Customs House or the Dairy, and private properties like the Convent of the Sacred Heart of the Spanish-American Institute, all in New York City. Across the country, towns have been entrusted with the safekeeping of beautiful historic properties. It

PRECEDING PAGES, LEFT: Beth Gardella, champagne flute in hand, whisks past the camera on her way to the receiving line; RIGHT: A waiter at Meadowlands makes a last-minute check of the silverware. BELOW: One of four rooms in Meadowlands where dining tables are set up.

takes only a little investigating to unearth the possibilities for wedding sites on colonial ground in Massachusetts, in Spanish-American Texas, or in Newport, Rhode Island, where great architectural timepieces like the Colony House have been reclaimed and restored for public use. Beyond their physical distinction, such places are generally well maintained and delivered with sparkling windows and gleaming mantelpieces. Some offer the joys of opulent period interiors; others embrace gardens, sweeping lawns, and even extensive grounds. Those that have been restored with social functions in mind may come equipped with flatware, dishes, tables, and chairs. And in comparison to more commercial enterprises like hotels, they are relatively inexpensive choices. The popularity of some of these places makes it advisable to reserve them as far in advance as possible. With any rental property, it is also important to investigate the contractual arrangements and meet the staff, who, in some instances, can be proprietary, bureaucratic, and difficult enough to sour the wedding experience. Most places have specific restrictions on the use of interiors and exteriors. Even though a contract may seem patently clear, it is wise to review all clauses carefully in the early phases of planning, for seemingly minor details, like the time alloted for setup and cleanup, can be crucial to the success of an event. The standard allowance of five hours, for example, is unrealistic, and rather than finding yourself served with an exorbitant overtime fee, you should consider a per diem rather than an hourly rate. Four to five hours is needed for setup and at least two for cleanup for a reception for 200. Sometimes, a caterer, bringing experience and perspective to the situation, can act as a buffer for any unpleasantness that might occur.

LEFT: Beth and her attendants dressing for the wedding. BELOW LEFT: Simple but elegant napery and glass pedestals filled with late summer flowers. BELOW RIGHT: Accouterments for last-minute touch-ups of the bridal party.

Elizabeth Gardella

and

John O'Connor

Beth Gardella had a handful of alternatives to her chosen reception site at Meadowlands in Darien, Connecticut. One was home, a large, spirited, modern house, filled with light, objets d'art, and her mother's bright, expressive paintings, and set on a point of land above the water. Across the way sat the Darien harbor and the family marina where Beth and her sister charter yachts. Her mother's idea of hiring a barge to float the party below the house evoked concerns about weather, high tide, and the limited capacity of a seagoing vessel anywhere short of the *QE 2* (which, in fact, is

available for lease). The country club and the yacht club were possibilities, too, but Beth had envisioned an event that was large and lovely, 250 guests, a sit-down dinner, a band, and, in her fantasies, a lovely garden. In May, through the longtime esteemed bridal consultant Flora Stebbins Kendall Bryant, they secured Meadowlands, a community-run centerpiece of the town, and within days had established the shape of the wedding planned for Saturday, August 25, 1984.

Meadowlands is a gracious example of mid-nineteenth-century American architecture, Federal on its way to Victorian, and it is approached by a long circular drive. It holds a large reception hall, with piano, which hosted the receiving line and, later, Lester Lanin's

eight-piece band; a dining room, parlor, library, ballroom, and catering kitchen, where the buffet dinner was served, and a long, lovely yard bordered by gardens, for cocktails. Although house rules forbade the addition of canopies or furniture to the yard, bars on the screened back porch and good weather solved potential problems.

It seems that every wedding must have its disaster, as if to ground it in reality. Everything went as planned at the Gardella wedding until the last dramatic moment, when the stage was immaculately set and Beth was en route to her three-thirty marriage rites at St. Thomas the Apostle. Then the limousine lurched and the water from the champagne bucket splashed over her satin wedding dress.

As she snapped forward, her headpiece was crushed against the front seat, and the elastic in her puffy sleeves snapped and separated. As her father scrambled to the rescue, Beth saw that he had inadvertently sat on both the bridal bouquet and the skirt of her dress. The father of the bride ran across the street to the tailor, who turned out to be closed on Saturday. The family mopped the dress. And then Mrs. Bryant, like the omnipotent fairy godmother, stepped forward with her repair kit, and the wedding went forth, all beauty and joy abiding.

Lovely old homes like Meadowlands, with its high ceilings, fine floors, and historic appointments, offer not only a momentous sense of place, but also the spiritual warmth that

OPPOSITE, TOP: Beth having her hair braided by her sister Kathy. OPPOSITE, BELOW: Last-minute primping and lively conversation. ABOVE: The ceremony at St. Thomas the Apostle Church. BELOW: A smiling bridesmaid on her way to the church.

comes from having been lived in by generations of families. And although homes like this have inherent architectural interest, they can be decorated as extravagantly as desired. For the Gardella wedding, I chose generous gatherings of bright August flowers from my gardens for important corners of the house, with suggestions of blue and lavender to match the bridesmaids' dresses. The house, in all its spacious formality, seemed light-hearted. As guests wandered in the gardens, and the receiving line inched along through the reception hall; as the public rooms filled first with buffets of twentieth-century pleasures and then with Lester Lanin's famous sounds and hats, one would have said it had adapted well to the passage of time.

Margot Olshan and John Clapps

Only a few miles away in New Canaan, Connecticut, there is another magnificent property where I catered another wedding in another season. Like Meadowlands, Waveny House belongs to its town, which uses its 360-acre grounds for many different events. Its cow barn is used for art shows, its powerhouse for theater, and its twenty-two-room main house for social functions. Built in 1913 as a summer cottage for Jack Lapham, the house, which might be described as Gothic Tudor, is baronial and manorial and in all its fittings attests to a sumptuous aristocratic life of the past: richly carved paneled walls, vaulted ceilings, five massive stone and marble fireplaces, murals of the story of Camelot, tapestries, bay window seats, brick porches, formal terraces, and distant views. Each room is a story in itself, told on the labeled bells in the butler's pantry: the billiard room, the library, the Oriental sitting room, the dining room, the great hall, the solarium. Indeed, when one of the groom's aunts, who had traveled with a busload of other loving relatives from Wilkes-Barre, Pennsylvania, arrived at the house, she

OPPOSITE: The wedding party descended an oak-paneled staircase. ABOVE: A view of Waveny House from across the surrounding fields.

BELOW LEFT: Preparations prior to the reception. BELOW MIDDLE: Crisply clothed tables served as bars.

BELOW RIGHT: Tables, all set and decorated, were pushed together to make room for the ceremony in the great hall.

hesitated, and, with big inquiring eyes, asked if she was in the right place.

The bride, Margot Olshan, who is an artistic director of Wells, Rich, Green, where she first met John Clapps, her groom, and where her father is a partner, had been to Waveny for advertising parties, and liked its size and its proximity to her childhood home. Despite its grandeur, Waveny imposes a maximum of 180 guests, which corroborated her desire to avoid both a political company event (only four ad people attended) and a huge clamorous "zoo" affair (John has untold number of second and third cousins). As for its beauty, it was romantic, intimate, and important, all at once, and soon suggested the scene that unfolded on the evening of Saturday, April 6, 1985. The rooms off the great hall were filled with tables with pink cloths and adorned with lavish bouquets of spring flowers in pinks, purples, and reds, set on tables, mantelpieces, or in windows, to catch the last light. Bars were set up in adjacent areas, and the dark-paneled library reserved for the socializing of early arrivals. The great hall was filled with an assembly of white chairs facing the Gothic stone fireplace, bordered by marble urns holding dogwood and roses, and Bill Lombardo and his chamber

Margot and her father, Ken Olshan, descend the grand staircase of Waveny to the ceremony. The black tie-attired waiters, trays filled with champagne, await the end of the ceremony.

ensemble, and later his band, were tucked under an arch. The wedding party marched dramatically down the grand turned mahogany staircase, twined with wax flowers and pink bows: two bridesmaids in raspberry-and-pink satin gowns, then Margot in layers of appliquéd lace and short gloves. The medieval was present, but updated.

Margot's memories of the wedding, which

was performed by her old friend, Westport's Justice of the Peace Jan Marcus, are nostalgic, tempered by the realistic. "I had considered two dresses, one a very serious gown, older-looking, made of Chantilly lace, but when John, who is both old-fashioned and avant garde, began talking about a red tuxedo—he ultimately emerged in a pink one—I thought I had better not be too formal. I remember the bridesmaids arriving at Waveny in sunglasses, looking grumpy from the night before, and my younger brother Matt becoming very emotional. We all panicked about the staircase, because neither my father nor I is very agile. All our shoes were brand new, and suddenly, while dressing, we realized the potential for falls, found a cheese grater in the kitchen and grated the soles of our shoes out the bedroom windows. I saw joggers slogging by looking up at this strange spectacle. Descending, I had to hold my dress in one hand, and my bouquet in the other, and my father was to hold me by one hand, and the banister with the other. When he reached out, he saw that the railing had been camouflaged in beautiful flowers. My last words to him were, 'Forget the flowers,' although I had planned to say, 'I love you, Daddy.' After all the planning and all the

A stone balustrade outlines a brick-floored, curving terrace at the back of Waveny House.
The weather was perfect for a wedding.

arguments, everything felt right. I remember thinking that the light in the window was perfect and that John looked happy. I felt calm, and I remember looking around and saying to myself, 'This looks great, this works.'"

April 6, the day before Easter, was the only time Waveny was available for rental, and that restriction changed the nature of the wedding festivities. Mrs. Olshan worried about the timing for the sake of John's family, who is Catholic, and then realized it was also Passover. As it evolved, the family celebrated a seder on Friday night—John's first, as well as a first for the entire Olshan family, who had always gone to relatives for the celebration—and on Sunday, prepared an Easter breakfast, which, together with the rehearsal dinner at a local restaurant on Thursday, and the wedding, dinner, and dancing, created a four-day festival. On the morning of the wedding, at the Olshan house, Margot and her two younger brothers climbed onto their parents' bed, just as they used to do for Saturday-morning cartoons, and, fortified with leftovers from the seder dinner, watched a borrowed tape of the classic 1950 film *Father of the Bride* together, and cried.

Mimi Dabrowski
and
Thomas Thompson

It seems only a short while ago that the bed-and-breakfast began to crop up in quiet corners of the countryside; now, where once there were few, everywhere there are painted shingles outside old farmhouses, rural restaurants, and barns. Five years ago, on Martha's Vineyard, Beth Flanders decided to turn the early-nineteenth-century farmhouse on a family property called Bliss Pond Farm into the Captain Flanders Bed and Breakfast; two years ago, a sign of the times perhaps, she opened it for its first wedding, appropriately that of her friend Mimi Dabrowski, a long-time Vineyarder, who owns a shop called Silver and Gold in Vineyard Haven, the local temple of fine new and antique hand-crafted jewelry.

Although the island of Martha's Vineyard sits only five miles and a forty-five-minute ferry ride off Cape Cod, it is a world unto itself, with a landscape, a rhythm, and a style of its own; symptomatically islanders often refer to the journey to the mainland as "going to America." The topography of the island tells much about its life: the southern Atlantic coast, cut by the ocean into a fretwork of salt-water ponds that have been dammed up with barrier beaches; the natural harbors on the Sound, which hosted first the whaling and then the schooner era; the flat farmland and pine forests of the interior; the clay cliffs of "up-island"; the wild grapes hanging over roadsides everywhere. Islanders are a strong, honest, independent lot, determinedly idiosyncratic and self-sufficient, yet neighborly in

the old-fashioned way that recognizes independence, and finely tuned to the rhythms, the beauties, and the rigors of the natural world. Seasons are marked by the appropriate harvests of field and ocean; tides as well as the hour regulate days.

Anyone who knows Martha's Vineyard thinks that it is the perfect place to be married—quiet, familial, romantic, and offbeat, with salt air, golden meadows, and the ocean's roar. Mimi's wedding on September 22, 1984, to Thomas Thompson, a longtime "summer person" who has started a software business on the mainland, was an example of Vineyard style. Things were done the way Mimi and Tom live, with élan but without pretension. The site at the Captain Flanders Bed and Breakfast, up-island in Chilmark, set on a rise that overlooks a freshwater pond, stables, a chicken coop, an ancient windmill, and 100 acres of pasture cut into rural geometry by stone walls, was quintessentially Vineyard. The food for the long harvest lunch came from friends, the cake from the local cake lady; the flowers were picked fresh from island gardens. The band, Prime Rib from Boston, included two old roommates of Tom's, and played funky-lyric country swing music. Betty Ann Bryant, a friend and selectwoman in Chilmark and the newly elected Justice of the Peace, performed the ceremony written by Mimi and Tom, which included readings by her parents, and invited the participation of the guests.

In preparation for the wedding, Beth had mowed the fields (a giant bush hog tractor still sat in the wings), mended fences, and enlisted her friends to help make overdue repairs to the front door, porch, and barn. On Wednesday,

OPPOSITE: Simple ribbon markers outlined the "aisle" of the meadow church where Mimi and Tom were married. ABOVE: The balloon-festooned sign of the island inn that Mimi hired for her wedding and reception. BELOW: One of the quaint features of the captain's house—handpainted glass brought back from China.

her crew set up a large new ("not yet mildewed," Mimi had commented happily) yellow tent in the yard to the side of the farmhouse, conveniently sited between the back door and kitchen, and the front door, where Mimi would create a flowery walkway to the knoll above the pond where the wedding ceremony would take place. Friday, the groom's family settled into the inn, and the fridge began to fill with staples for the rehearsal dinner, beer and cider, fresh corn, and swordfish, from the docks down the road at Menemsha, for outdoor grilling.

By ten-thirty on the morning of the wedding, Mimi was alone out on the front meadow, filling old baskets with flowers, inventing her rustic aisle with white ribbon looped around garden poles and tied with ferns, bows, and alstroemeria, and then formalizing it with two standing wicker flower baskets. It was an intimate private time for her, both dreamy and reflective. Mimi's friend and matron of honor, Peggy Koski-Schweir, whose wedding a year before had been a major source of inspiration, and whose hand was apparent in virtually all the preparations, bustled about arranging tables and flowers, checking on linens and dishes, or the sun-tea brewing outside in tubs. A few ("just two, not corny") blue-and-white coverlets were spread under shade trees and set with bean pots of zinnias; a few chairs scattered about for elderly friends. On the far side of the tent, an old tin horse trough was filled with ice and champagne, and Chris Murphy, a local fisherman known for his shellfish, set up his new handmade molded white bar, which he stocked with clams from the early morning catch.

ABOVE: Guests dropped off their gifts for the couple in a sun-filled porch.
BELOW: A series of lively toasts by the bride and groom created a feeling of warmth and friendliness.

As the two o'clock wedding hour drew near, a parade of guests began to file through the kitchen, carrying platters, bowls, and baskets of their offerings, most of it home-grown, all of it homemade: tomatoes in many forms, roasted turkeys and baked hams, Mexican quiches, ratatouille, pasta salads, smoked Vineyard bluefish, Squibnocket Beach mussels vinaigrette. It added up to a carefully calibrated country feast rather than a potluck, for Mimi's caterer friend Kansas had not only organized specific contributions, but had also overseen their presentation, replacing stainless-steel bowls and roasting pans with lovely serving platters, rearranging and reslicing, and then decorating the food with flowers, and here and there the tomato flowers she seemed to carve effortlessly.

There was something so authentic about Mimi and Tom's wedding that it lasts in

memory as a classic. Some of this feeling was physical—the site flowing so well with the plans that one forgot about the house or the tent poles or the cars parked in the pasture. The view extended beyond to catch the band against a stone wall, the kegs of beer before the vegetable garden, young boys in ice-cube fights above the pond, young girls circling impatiently around the wedding cake. Chil-

dren climbed in trees; babies slept on the coverlets. Some of it was the mood, which was mellow from the start: 250 friends dressed in that casual Vineyard mode that combines costumery and chic for the sake of fun: men in fancy vests, women in thirties shawls, long full skirts, turbans. Mimi wore a forties-style dress with wide inset satin sleeves; Tom, a "nice gray suit" and silver tie that had the aura but not the formality of morning clothes. They all danced on the grass, some couples holding young children between them. About five o'clock, a group of local musicians arrived to join the band for a jam session. The overriding feeling about the couple's wedding was that it was *their* wedding, essentially simple, easy, and fun. The outside world could rightly find it stylish; on the Vineyard, it was merely personal, the result of camaraderie, cooperation, and love.

ABOVE: Dancing was lively and widespread. BELOW: Some of the food offerings brought by family and friends, and a very pretty cake made by a local island baker. An antique cake knife, heavily engraved, was used to cut the cake.

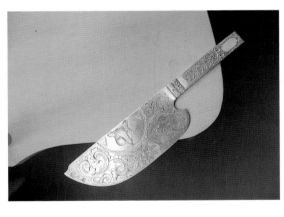

Wedding Menus

Whatever the fare—medieval wild boar and mead, or tiny Victorian potted-shrimp sandwiches and champagne punch—a wedding always has its proverbial feast, as one dictionary reads, "something that gives unusual or abundant pleasure." The "feast" honors those gathered, draws them together, provides the setting for the celebration and the substance to set spirits soaring.

Celebrating and feasting have gone hand in hand from the beginning of time. The annals of wedding food are rich, full of special cakes and breads, symbolic fruits and drinks, soups and roasts, chosen to renew tradition, to give abundant pleasure. This book describes the chosen food of many styles and seasons: elegant French dinners, sushi tables, southwestern picnics, kosher groaning boards, and cocktail hors d'oeuvres; brunch, lunch, and dinner; buffet-style, French, and family service. It tells of hotel, catered, and home-style preparations, and the differences between them, for by visiting more than fifty weddings,

I could see what worked well, where and why. In the whole spectrum of food at these weddings, there was great variety, personality, and often extravagance. With the new national passion for the culinary arts still growing, food has become one of the most important, and often most expensive elements of a wedding, and people seem more willing than ever to splurge on it.

The food at a wedding falls into a category of its own, ordained by both aesthetics and pragmatics. It is festive, to suit the day. It is personalized, to reflect the desires of the bride and groom, and usually the mood of the setting. It is varied enough to please the particular tastes of the guests. And, with appropriate exceptions, it is designed to be prepared in volume and in advance.

The ultimate menu choice should reflect these guidelines. Although a couple may dream of an elaborate Japanese banquet, that idea will have to be relegated to a small gathering, for the nature of Japanese food is individualized and involves last-minute preparations, and even a fine Japanese restaurant could not provide hors d'oeuvres for more than two hundred. Even though a delicate pastiche of exotic dishes from the realm of nouvelle cuisine might be appealing, it would be ill-suited to a meat-and-potatoes crowd. Likewise, despite current favor, Tex-Mex food is too strong and too informal for most wedding receptions, unless, like at the Jacominis' barbecue for Patricia Morrison and Ed Fleming, which took the form of an informal post-postnuptial picnic, the setting is a ranch and the dress so country casual as to render a spill inconsequential. Nonetheless, in certain circumstances, a very special menu may give a reception particular interest, as I learned when I catered a lunch for a vegetarian couple, and

found that the customary bland fare could be transformed into a colorful buffet of exotic pasta salads, grandiloquent vegetable melanges, and elegant frittatas, filled with surprising ingredients. The inclusion of ethnic Greek and Italian dishes in the GarDianos reception at the Dairy paid tribute to the families' backgrounds and added personal flair. And the whole spit-roasted lambs at a recent Armenian wedding honored both the farmhouse setting and the family heritage.

My staff and I catered approximately half the weddings in this book; others were prepared by hotels, other professionals, or a bevy of friends and relatives. Professional caterers are in common use at weddings—probably more than at any other event in our lives. But even when the food is provided by an energetic bride or mother of the bride, wedding food is generally *still* "catered" food in that it is in large part prepared in advance and brought to the site, needing only reheating or last-minute assembly of ready ingredients. Yet, as most of the following menus show, catered food can be creative, beautiful, and fresh-tasting.

The time of day, the place, and the style of a reception are the important factors in deciding upon the kind of wedding feast to offer. The choices are wide and promising. If the ceremony is taking place in the morning, say at eleven o'clock, one possibility is a brunch beginning with light hors d'oeuvres and Bloody Marys or champagne and peach nectar; then perhaps an offering of eggs Benedict on artichoke bottoms, spicy apple crêpes, an array of smoked fish and homemade breads. Another is a simple buffet luncheon, with fresh garden salads and an elegant poached fish, for example, or a served buffet luncheon with many courses to fill the sunny hours. Afternoon or early evening cocktails might bring a

festival of hors d'oeuvres, including warm oysters with beurre rouge and a well-laden cheese and fruit table, as evocative as a Bonnard still-life. More and more, first courses like these oysters or tomato and basil salad or tortellini on skewers are served as hors d'oeuvres, and have particular moment as well as easy preparation. A dinner reception can be buffet or sit-down, with possible extensions in dessert buffets, or, like the Desmaraises', a replenishing midnight supper.

If the place, or the background, style, and wishes of the bride and groom suggest special fare, be indulgent, for meaningful indulgence can make the difference between a routine and a memorable event. On Martha's Vineyard or Long Island or a beloved spot near the sea, consider a clambake, or at least a seafood bar or a bushel of littlenecks. In the country, choose a favorite meadow to stage a Victorian picnic, formal and elegant yet al fresco and, therefore, breezy and carefree. Wedding food has become more and more varied, a tribute to self-expression. Thus, Caroline Damerell planned a luncheon of lobsters in an informal country setting; Sharon Nelson and Harvey Siegel welcomed guests to their stone farmhouse with the assorted foods they love; and Mimi Dabrowski choreographed homemade contributions from all her friends on Martha's Vineyard.

Be dreamy and respond to inspiration, but don't overreach. The eminent Manhattan caterer Glorious Food provides a model, for they are always careful to serve realistic food that can be safely reserved or reheated in the caterers' mobile ovens; they rarely serve lamb, unless they have the necessary ovens, for it changes character in reheating, but choose chicken or beef or a cold main course, which holds up well. Bernard Mignot, the trained

restaurant chef who provided the elegant French dinner for Hilary Cushing's two hundred guests, quite miraculously managed an ambitious and single-handed effort, yet he had spacious and dependable Garland ovens to cook racks of lamb at the last minute, and other entrées of veal and duck in full readiness.

It is essential to investigate the facilities of the reception site at an early date. Consequently, in the process of deciding upon a menu, most caterers will wish to assess working conditions personally. Many rental spaces lack kitchen facilities, dictating a need to provide for ovens, work tables, and refrigeration. Tents, yards, and garages (emptied of their usual contents) can supply alternate spaces. On the other hand, other places, like Waveny Mansion and the Meadowlands in southern Connecticut, come equipped with excellent kitchens, spacious refrigerators, helpful equipment, like large coffee makers, and, in the case of Waveny, a stock of china and silver. The Burden Mansion in New York now accommodates so many parties that they have installed commercial stoves.

Working with a Caterer

These days, caterers operate in myriad ways in many styles and to many purposes: some provide only wedding cakes, others are willing to collaborate with friends or family on wedding food, and an increasing number will provide "full service party planning," which coordinates flowers, rentals, decoration, and even music with the food. It is important to hire the right caterer for your needs and style, and to establish a comfortable, trustful working relationship. Remember that hiring a caterer is much more than hiring a household

PRECEDING PAGE: A dress-up reception in the garden of a New York museum.

ABOVE: Glorious Food chefs surveying a tent setup before the guests arrive.

servant, and that using a caterer well means taking advantage of his or her particular skills, experience, and eye, as well as articulating your own ideas and desires.

The best way to find the right caterer is probably word of mouth from friends and successful hostesses of your acquaintance. Think, too, of the best party you have attended and find out who was responsible; take a caterer's card at a particularly enjoyable event; or investigate small new catering firms, which are likely to be at least as energetic, eager, and imaginative as older established concerns. Then make appointments—for a large and expensive party, two or three competitive bids

Rafael Rosario, my party executive, and I discuss last-minute changes in the tent decor of a wedding reception in Connecticut.

are useful for comparison of price, creativity, and menu.

In an interview, give a caterer a clear idea of your plans and ask for appropriate menu suggestions, mentioning specific requests, odd requirements, like an extra entrée for Aunt Millie, who eats only lean fish, or the children, who would be happiest with fried chicken. Ask about service: Does the caterer supply all the necessary help—bartenders and cleanup

as well as waiters? How much per hour? And is there a minimum? What does the help wear? Are travel time and expenses additional? Are gratuities included? Is there a service charge for hiring costs? Many caterers charge a 20 percent staffing charge, which helps deter insurance and hiring costs. Ask about rental of equipment: Does he provide this service? For a service charge? Who is responsible for breakage and loss? Discuss decoration and music if desired, and beverage suggestions, for although it is common practice for a client to provide the liquor, a caterer can offer valuable advice on quantity and selection. And, of course, clarify all the technicalities of deposits,

cancellation fees, payment of the final bill, and insist upon a written contract, which is for the protection of both parties, and, if carefully reviewed and approved, avoids unpleasant last-minute surprises.

At the first working consultation, the big decisions will be made and the contract signed. It is wise to include any other professionals in this and any ensuing meetings, for they will help one another with ideas and coordination. The rental people can expedite a caterer's decisions about presentation of food, a subject that involves the choice of trays, dishes, glasses, linens, and flatware. And a caterer may give the florist ideas for table or tent

On cool or rainy days, be sure the tents and canopies have plastic sides that can be removed or installed easily as needed.

decoration complementary to the food. It is an artistic team at work, and during the last week before a wedding, when well-laid plans begin to take form, it is truly exciting to witness a reception scene gathering life.

As a general rule, the wedding feast begins with the receiving line. Therefore, if the ceremony is taking place at a church, you know that the timing of the festivities should center on the moment guests arrive at the reception

site. If the place of the ceremony and reception is the same, you should be ready to pass champagne immediately after the ceremony, bidding welcome to the celebration, and also enlivening the process of receiving and being received. Sometimes a couple will invite more friends to the church than to the reception, in which case the receiving line should appropriately take place at the church. Sometimes a couple dispenses with the formality of a receiving line and commits itself to circulating energetically to greet all guests informally. And, sometimes, a receiving line is of such proportions that one has to plan carefully, both to support the members of the line and those waiting for its aftermath. The Carpenters, for example, with twelve hundred guests and a receiving line that lasted two and a half hours, were secure in the knowledge that their guests had three rooms of hors d'oeuvres to investigate; furthermore, they had forecast certain moments when all parties except the bride and groom could take a respite for refreshment. Whatever its length, these introductory moments are a time of greeting and transition, and I like to pass a few light hors d'oeuvres with champagne to enliven their course. Then comes a prologue of more plentiful and substantial hors d'oeuvres and the wedding feast.

The least expensive of possible receptions is still the cocktail party—perhaps a lavish spread of eleven or twelve hot and cold hors d'oeuvres—because it obviates the need for extensive rental supplies. While trays and glasses may well suffice, a cocktail setting can be further enhanced with groupings of small cocktail tables and an artistic display of the fare. Then, in order of mounting expense, there is a brunch, a buffet lunch, and a buffet dinner, for as the day grows, so do appetites. The most expensive choices are the multi-course sit-down lunch or dinner, for which there is almost no financial limit, given the inclusion of golden Beluga caviar on the hors d'oeuvres list, and lobster and foie gras on the menu. If one decides upon five or six courses, five or six plates per person and glasses for a progression of wines are *de rigeur*, and expenses mount. And if a meal is to be served French style, one must provide trays for each table for each course—perhaps fifty silver trays rented at five or six dollars apiece—and the numbers multiply into bigger numbers. Yet to many people the importance of a veritable wedding feast overrides cost; ultimately, it is their pleasure.

During an at-home wedding reception one's property is on view to guests, so it is best to have everything groomed and set.

At-Home Wedding Receptions

My particular pleasure is the at-home wedding, and I have now hosted three such affairs in my own family, each with its own style and warm character. At-home weddings are becoming more and more popular, although the "homemade" often demands greater efforts and extra care. Yet, in the case of an extended and energetic family, many hands may be called upon to participate, for the sake of communal joy and caring as much as for economy. Thus Babs Cook *wanted* to make her own French bread to accompany a caterer's dinner, for she knew it to be the best, and over the course of six months, she baked and froze dozens and dozens of baguettes. Thus many, many aunts, sisters, or friends bake the wedding cake, out of sheer love and a desire for a creative hand in the festivities. I know people who have prepared receptions for two hundred guests themselves, choreographing the menu so that its elements could be made, then frozen, and stored with neighbors until the moment they triumphantly pulled it all together. They were not caterers, but enthusiastic

cooks, whose determination and organization carried them through, step by step. As a support system, they hired professionals for service and cleanup.

More and more people seem to have the culinary expertise and the desire to create their own food for large parties, and yet ultimately many draw back from the undertaking out of fear. The sheer numbers seem terrifying, the necessary organization formidable. Yet, as with any large new project like wallpapering a room, careful planning and the mastery of a few techniques can lay the way for a great success. Personal rewards lie in the pleasure, the self-satisfaction, the sense of exhilaration that come with accomplishing something we think only professionals capable of doing.

Given a date, style, and place, the budget is the first task, and must take into consideration the menu, rental of any necessary equipment, liquor, and ice. The menu includes all ingredients of the feast, from hors d'oeuvres to cake, and everything from the skewers for the yakitori to the cherry tomatoes for garnishing the beef, cocktail napkins and fruits for the bar. Rental equipment might include trays, pitchers, glassware, linens, silverware, china, even an extra refrigerator for storing goods. As far as tableware goes, eclecticism is definitely in, and no one worries about matching sets of dishes. Although many rental agencies have lovely flatware, dishes, and glasses that may be compatible with your own, for a large wedding, it is probably simplest and most advisable to rent a uniform look, ordering well in advance.

The subject of beverages always seems to provoke anxiety, perhaps because there is nothing more distressing to a host or dampening to a crowd than to run out of them. The correct quantity is easy to calculate if you know that champagne or wine provides five glasses to the bottle, hard liquor, twenty-five drinks, a half keg of beer, 260 servings. It is important, however, to err on the side of generosity, and any reputable liquor merchant will accept returns. As a celebration, a wedding is a time to splurge, and ultimately, an additional several hundred dollars spent on a favorite champagne is unlikely to be consequential. I always think of the wise father who remembered his daughter's childhood dream of Perrier-Jouët with moonlight, and made this his gift of love. These days, with the prospering of California vineyards and French-American collaborations in that state, there are extraordinary domestic champagnes—Chandon and Domaine Mumm, for example—yet prices change from year to year, so that sometimes it can be cheaper to invest in French champagne. For many weddings, champagne alone is elegantly sufficient, with Perrier water, perhaps, on the side, but for a big full-hearted wedding, an open bar is a necessity, with a keg of beer or an assortment of interesting beers and ale in stock for young people. Take note of the renewed interest in mixed drinks, and consider the addition of a blender bar, or a special offering of fresh fruit piña coladas or strawberry daiquiris. Order ice to be delivered if large quantities are needed, or freeze and bag your own at home. In hot weather, count on one pound of ice cubes per person, less in winter months. If wine has to be cooled, have plastic tubs (or clean garbage pails, or galvanized tin washtubs, or copper boilers) ready. An extra refrigerator in the garage or basement is a great asset when beer, wine, sodas, and mixers must be kept cool.

The question of quantity is probably the most daunting aspect of food too. Having grown up in a large family where quantity as

Charles Case in Westport made fifteen different flower baskets for one wedding.

well as quality was the rule, at an early age I knew almost instinctively how much cheese thirty people would eat, or how large a roast beef to order for a dinner party of fourteen. Consequently, I have always approached the subject with a certain casualness, yet, in the course of my ten years of catering, I have also learned that there are simple rules based on simple mathematics that help make a party perfect.

Quantities, of course, differ according to the type of party: for a cocktail-party reception, ten to twelve different hors d'oeuvres with two or three of each per person and three or four drinks each is about right, but if an elaborate dinner is in the wings, a variety of five or six light hors d'oeuvres with three to five per person will suffice. At small dinners, with plate service, I portion-cook, a restaurant method in which each guest is allotted, say, a given number of asparagus stalks and a single steak. Although Bernard Mignot, with his restaurant training, portion-cooked at Hilary Cushing's wedding very successfully, at most weddings, one expects a guest to want, or at least to have available, a second serving. With

the aid of a cookbook, you can calculate the number of breasts of chicken to incorporate into a chicken salad for one hundred by simple multiplication, yet certain dishes, like salads, can seem unfathomable. It has been a revelation to me to realize that a handful of salad greens is indeed a single serving, and that a quart of vinaigrette will suffice for a salad dressing for seventy-five.

Reserve a section of your notebook for party information and lists; write down all ideas and prices; and keep good records of expenditures. I keep an envelope in my purse for all shopping receipts so that after the party I know exactly how much was spent. Create a menu that can be at least partially prepared long in advance. Make ahead and freeze what you can. Make comprehensive shopping lists, reading all recipes carefully, and checking your pantry for each staple required. Make day-to-day shopping lists too, for perishable items may have to be purchased only a day or two before the wedding. And schedule a dress rehearsal on major entrées for family or friends, so that you are confident about both the preparation and the taste.

My favorite at-home wedding is the sit-down buffet, for it can provide a sumptuous variety of food together with simple service and artistic display. A buffet is the obvious choice for a reception for fifty or more without an unlimited budget, and it enables you to create food that appeals to everyone, as the breadth of the menus in this chapter suggest. For me, a buffet begins with extensive hors d'oeuvres with cocktails or champagne, for the passing of five to ten different creations spurs chatter and movement and life, allows the wedding family time to attend to the receiving line and formal portraits, and addresses guests who may have traveled long hungry distances.

If the buffet is seated, it is gracious to set the tables with the first course (a salad, soup, or pretty seafood terrine), to establish a new sense of place, and eventually to stagger the buffet lines. As a waiter clears the course, he can direct individual tables to the buffet, avoiding congestion and queues, and also amplified announcements, which remind me of a bingo parlor. For ease of serving, I plan one entry to the buffet for every fifty guests, or for two hundred guests, two buffet tables with four entrances. Buffets connote self-service, but especially at weddings, servers should be posted to fill plates, in order to organize and apportion food graciously. In setting buffet tables, I am careful to intersperse vegetable dishes with meat platters, so that a guest doesn't unwittingly fill his plate with one kind of food before encountering others. When the buffet table has been consumed and completely cleared, the cake makes its appearance, and after due ceremony, and sometimes after an interlude of fruit and petits fours, it can be cut and set out on plates or served by waiters.

A sit-down meal necessitates methodical organization and service. Plate service, in which the meal is apportioned on plates in the kitchen and then carried out to guests, works well for a gathering of twenty or more people. French service, in which a heated plate is set before a guest prior to serving courses from passed trays, is more formal. While it is extremely nice in an elegant restaurant, the constant interruption of waiters can be intrusive, and unless it is very professional, even awkward, for people leaving the table to dance risk missing a course.

Service at a wedding should be very smooth and friendly without being obsequious. Waiters should be uniformly and nicely dressed in tux pants and formal shirts; sometimes a spe-

cial accessory like the silver-striped ties hand-made by George Furlan, or the carnations in the chefs' hats at Le Zinc, can add an important decorative note. Good waiters have the experience and savoir-faire to be calming presences; they know that the ice truck probably *will* materialize, that any spill can be disguised, any leaky tent amended with buckets, and as a part of the event, they will take pride in being helpful. Good waiters catch the mood of a wedding, and their high spirits are contagious.

Here is a variety of wedding menus, from hors d'oeuvres to sit-down dinners, barbecues to formal French affairs. Some are exact duplicates of weddings I have catered with great success; others are new combinations of ingredients that have worked well and that I hope to serve as an ensemble soon. All have been reduced to a basic amount that will serve ten to twelve people, which I knew would multiply easily for typical wedding crowds. There are menus listed here too, for the sake of documentation, inspiration, and imitation. Practically speaking, one could take my beef salad and add a few exotic ingredients, like the wild mushrooms or unusual herbs garnishing other dishes, and emerge with an original creation; or compile all the hors d'oeuvres detailed here and stage an amazing feast.

At the Siegel wedding delicate Ralph Lauren tablecloths in blue and white, napkins tied with satin ribbons, and pure and simple rented tableware contributed to the elegant country feeling.

Colorful Summer Buffet

Mrs. O'Herron's family has summered in Woods Hole for generations. Recently she and her husband completed their summer home on the family compound, a charming contemporary with extraordinary views of the ever-changing sea. When their daughter announced her marriage plans, there was no question as to where the ceremony and reception would take place, despite the fact that both the O'Herrons and the Burleighs live elsewhere most of the year.

Preparations took almost a year, for there was landscaping to be done and lots of long-distance planning to be attended to. Woods Hole has no large catering facility or rental company, so everything had to be "imported." I was called to cater the event and, in my own inimitable way, foresaw no problems transporting food and

cake for 235 guests four hours from Westport. I knew my staff would like the challenge of long distance, and indeed, it would be almost a vacation for them.

Both the bride and groom and their families were intensely interested in the food plans for the reception. They wanted a sophisticated, colorful, opulent "country" buffet. The menu, as a result, was extensive, and the two eighteen-foot-long buffets were amazingly beautiful. Bright summer salads, breads, and main courses were arranged amid garnishes of sweet pea vines, herbs, lemon leaves, kale, wild mushrooms, and brilliant garden flowers. The salmons were poached, skinned, and then garnished with flavored mayonnaises, which supported decorations of paper-thin slices of red onion, white Daikon radish, English cucumbers,

MENU

ASSORTED FAVORITE HORS D'OEUVRES

BUFFET

Lemon Chicken with Sautéed Lemon Slices

Whole Poached Salmon with Herb Mayonnaise
and Cucumber Sauce

Summer Beef Salad with Oriental Dressing

Seafood Salad

Summer Potato Salad with Walnut Dressing

Sliced Tomatoes with Green Basil Sauce

Rotelle with Olives and Wild Mushrooms

Cranberry-Orange Muffins · Carrot Muffins

DESSERT

Dessert Cheeses

Minted Melon Balls · Fresh Strawberries

Wedding Cake

and black-skinned white radishes. Each salad, the main courses, and the vegetables and pastas were dressed with specifically flavored mixtures so there would be a wide variety of tastes and textures. Unusual herbs—coriander, opal basil, lemon thyme, delicate chervil, and variegated sage—were used both as garnishes and flavorings, as were whole wild mushrooms, sun-dried tomatoes, and the carapaces of lobsters.

The families' favorite hors d'oeuvres were served while the receiving line greeted the guests. Sporadic showers kept most people under the tents, but because they were so spacious and extensive, wrapping the entire yard all the way to the edge of the land overlooking the sea, no one felt confined or crowded. The dancing began early and proved to be the most popular activity. Four lines of guests were served from the buffets. Additional breads and seconds of salads were passed on decorated trays through the tents, so that guests would not have to stand in line again, although many did come up again and again. The damp weather did not dampen anyone's appetite!

When it was time to serve the cake, a tiered, lily decorated confection, one buffet was turned into a dessert table and bowls of minted melon balls (honeydew, cantaloupe, and Persian melons), trays of cheeses (the bride's choice), and mounds of fresh ripe strawberries were placed atop freshly set linens.

PRECEDING PAGE: Brilliant patterned chintz, garden flowers, plain white china, and white cotton napkins set off the colorful buffet at the O'Herron wedding. RIGHT: Amanda O'Brien and I carry in whole decorated salmons for display on the buffet.

Lemon Chicken with Sautéed Lemon Slices

SEE RECIPE, PAGE 273.

Whole Poached Salmon with Herb Mayonnaise and Cucumber Sauce

SERVES 12 OR MORE

COURT BOUILLON

4 cups water
¼ cup dry vermouth
1 piece fresh lemon
1 small onion, peeled
1 bay leaf
1 teaspoon salt
3 whole black peppercorns

1 whole 8- to 9-pound salmon, skin, head, and tail left on, fins removed
  Cheesecloth
1 cup Herb Mayonnaise (recipe follows)
2 or 3 English cucumbers, unpeeled and sliced paper-thin (or substitute red onion, Daikon radish, or black-skinned radish)
  Cucumber Sauce (page 230)

GARNISH: Fresh herbs

In a large fish poacher, combine all court bouillon ingredients and simmer for 10 minutes. Lower the heat, but keep liquid hot.

Tightly wrap the whole salmon in several layers of cheesecloth and, using kitchen string, tie the fish at three or four places along its length. (This will help keep the poached fish from falling apart.) Measure the thickness of the whole fish to determine the proper cooking time, and carefully place the fish on the long rack of the fish poacher. Set the fish in the poacher (the bouillon should completely cover the fish; add more boiling water if necessary), and return to a boil. Re-

duce the heat to a low simmer, and cook the fish 10 minutes per inch of thickness of fish.

Very carefully remove the fish from the poaching liquid, and gently unwrap it. While still hot, remove the skin and fin cartilage from the salmon as neatly as possible. Let cool, then wrap in plastic wrap and chill.

To assemble, spread the entire surface of the cold skinned salmon with herb mayonnaise and cover with overlapping rows of paper-thin cucumber, red onion, or radish slices. (I use a small electric kitchen slicer to make these slices.) Refrigerate until ready to serve.

Garnish the salmon as desired and serve with cucumber sauce.

VARIATION: The salmon can also be served with Mustard-Fennel Sauce (page 243).

Herb Mayonnaise

MAKES APPROXIMATELY 2½ CUPS

BASIC HOMEMADE MAYONNAISE

2 eggs
¼ teaspoon dry mustard
¾ teaspoon salt
2 tablespoons freshly squeezed lemon juice
1 cup olive oil
1 cup vegetable or safflower oil
  Salt, to taste

½ pound fresh spinach leaves, washed and dried
2 tablespoons chopped shallots
¼ cup loosely packed watercress leaves (no stems)
¼ cup chopped fresh parsley
2 tablespoons coarsely chopped fresh tarragon leaves

To make the mayonnaise, mix the eggs, mustard, salt, and lemon juice in the bowl of a food processor. Add the olive oil, drop by drop, until the mixture begins to thicken. Add the remaining oil in a steady stream and process until smooth. Season to taste (you may also want to add more lemon juice) and refrigerate.

Bring a small pot of water to a boil, add the spinach, shallots, watercress, and herbs, and boil for 1 minute. Drain and immediately rinse with cold water to stop the cooking. Drain again and pat dry with a towel. Finely chop by hand or in a food processor and stir into the mayonnaise.

ABOVE LEFT: Glistening pieces of lemon chicken were mounded on a silver tray lined with lemon leaves and garnished with lamb's ears and lemon slices. BELOW: The salmon was decorated with paper-thin slices of white Daikon radish (*top*) and English seedless cucumbers (*bottom*) in a "scale" pattern.

Cucumber Sauce

MAKES APPROXIMATELY 2½ CUPS

- 2 large cucumbers, peeled and seeded
- 1 cup Homemade Mayonnaise (page 229)
- 1 cup sour cream
- 1 tablespoon Dijon-style mustard
- 1 tablespoon freshly squeezed lemon juice
- ½ teaspoon coarse salt
- ¼ teaspoon freshly ground black pepper
- ½ cup snipped fresh dill
- ¼ cup finely chopped fresh chives

Grate the cucumbers into a bowl. Add the remaining ingredients and mix well. Refrigerate until ready to serve.

Summer Beef Salad with Oriental Dressing

SERVES 12

- 2 tablespoons olive oil
- 2 tablespoons grapeseed oil (see Note, page 245)
- 1 4- to 5-pound filet of beef
- 5 sweet red peppers
- 1 bunch scallions
- ½ pound snow peas or sugar snap peas

ORIENTAL DRESSING

- 6 large shallots, peeled and minced
- 2 cups Madeira
  Juice and pulp of 6 oranges
- 1 tablespoon brown sugar
- 2 tablespoons peanut oil
- 2 tablespoons vegetable oil
- 2 tablespoons rice wine vinegar
- 1 tablespoon soy sauce
- 1 teaspoon grated gingerroot

GARNISH: 2 bunches watercress (optional)

Preheat the oven to 450°.

Combine the oils in a large heavy skillet and heat to a very high temperature; the oils should be almost smoking. Add the filet and brown well on all sides. The hot oils should sear in the juices. Remove the filet from the skillet and place on a baking sheet. Roast the meat in the oven for 12 to 20 minutes. Test frequently and do not let the meat overcook; it should be quite rare when done. Remove from the oven and let cool.

Seed the peppers and slice thinly or cut into wedges, as desired. Cover and refrigerate until ready to use.

Cut off the root of the scallions and julienne. Set aside. Remove the stem end from the snow peas, string them, and blanch in a large pot of boiling water for 30 seconds. Drain and immediately cool in ice water. Drain again and set aside.

To make the dressing, combine the shallots and Madeira in a saucepan and reduce to 1 cup. Stir in the orange juice and pulp and brown sugar and reduce to 1 cup. Combine the oils in a stainless steel bowl and whisk in the warm reduction. When well combined, whisk in the remaining dressing ingredients.

One hour before serving, cut the filet into ½-inch slices and toss in a large bowl with the peppers, scallions, snow peas, and dressing. Serve on a bed of watercress, if desired.

The summer beef salad was served from a silver tray lined with watercress.

Seafood Salad

SERVES 12

- 1 pound sea scallops
- 12 fresh cherrystone clams, scrubbed
- 12 fresh mussels, scrubbed and bearded
- 1 pound lump crab meat, picked over
- 2 cooked lobsters (about 1½ pounds each), cut into 6 pieces each and claws cracked
- 2 sweet peppers (red and/or yellow), seeded and diced

ORANGE VINAIGRETTE

MAKES ABOUT 2¼ CUPS

- ½ cup freshly squeezed orange juice
- ¼ cup white wine vinegar
- 2 tablespoons Dijon-style mustard
- 1½ cups olive oil
  Freshly ground black pepper, to taste
- 1 tablespoon finely chopped gingerroot
- 1 tablespoon chopped fresh dill (optional)
- 1 tablespoon chopped fresh tarragon (optional)

Steam the scallops, clams, and mussels separately in a bamboo or aluminum steamer over rapidly boiling water for 3 to 5 minutes, or just until the clams and mussels have opened and the scallops are done. Remove from the heat and combine with the crab meat, lobster, and peppers.

Whisk all vinaigrette ingredients together. Use just enough of the dressing to coat the seafood. Arrange on individual salad plates and serve.

Summer Potato Salad with Walnut Dressing

SERVES 10 TO 12

2   pounds baby zucchini (or smallest size available)
2   pounds haricots verts (or tender young green beans)
20 small red or yellow new potatoes
½   cup dry vermouth

WALNUT DRESSING

2   cups dry vermouth
1   red onion, finely minced
4   garlic cloves, peeled and sliced
2   tablespoons walnut oil
2   tablespoons vegetable oil
¼   cup heavy cream
¼   cup Crème Fraîche (page 291)
2   tablespoons Dijon-style mustard
1   teaspoon prepared horseradish
2   tablespoons finely chopped walnuts
2   tablespoons chopped fresh parsley
    Salt and freshly ground black pepper, to taste

Cut any brown stems off the zucchini and cut diagonally into ¼-inch slices. Steam over rapidly boiling water until barely tender, 2 to 3 minutes. Set aside.

Cut the ends off the haricots verts and steam over boiling water until just tender, 3 to 5 minutes. Set aside.

Wash the potatoes and place in a large pot; cover with cold water. Bring to a low boil, then reduce to a simmer (this will prevent the potatoes from falling apart). Cover and cook just until the potatoes are tender when pierced with a fork. Drain well and place in a bowl. Toss with the ½ cup of vermouth and let cool.

To make the dressing, combine the 2 cups vermouth, onion, and garlic in a saucepan, and reduce to ½ cup. Pour the mixture into a stainless steel bowl and whisk in the remaining ingredients.

To serve, quarter the cooled potatoes and place in a large bowl with the zucchini and haricots verts. Add the dressing (whisk again before pouring) and toss well. Serve at room temperature.

Sliced Tomatoes with Green Basil Sauce

SERVES 10 TO 12

8   large, ripe red or yellow tomatoes, cut into ⅜-inch slices
    Coarse salt and freshly ground black pepper, to taste
10 sprigs small-leaf basil or 10 large red basil leaves, torn with fingers into small pieces
    Chopped pignoli nuts
    Green Basil Sauce (recipe follows)

Arrange tomato slices decoratively on a platter, and salt and pepper to taste. Sprinkle basil and pignoli nuts over the slices.
Serve with green basil sauce.

Green Basil Sauce

MAKES APPROXIMATELY 2 CUPS

⅓   cup white wine vinegar or champagne vinegar
2   tablespoons Dijon-style mustard
½   cup tightly packed fresh basil leaves
1   large garlic clove
⅓   cup vegetable oil
1   cup sour cream
½   cup heavy cream
3   tablespoons minced fresh parsley
    Salt and freshly ground black pepper, to taste

Combine the vinegar, mustard, basil, and garlic in the bowl of a food processor and mix until completely smooth. With the machine running, drizzle in the oil, a little at a time, until the oil is well incorporated and the mixture is thick. Add the sour cream, heavy cream, and parsley, and purée until smooth. Season with salt and pepper and refrigerate.

Remove from the refrigerator about half an hour before serving.

ABOVE LEFT: The summer potato salad with its crunchy walnut dressing was served from a deep silver tray garnished with sweet pea vines. LEFT: Red ripe tomato slices served with green basil sauce and sprinkled with chopped pignoli nuts and opal basil are a sure favorite on any buffet.

RIGHT: A pasta salad is always delicious on a buffet, and this rotelle, garnished with purple sage and large shiitake mushrooms, is very well liked.

OPPOSITE LEFT TO RIGHT: Heart-shaped wicker baskets were filled with tiny cranberry-orange muffins; Corolle, Brie, St. André, and Camembert were arranged on silver trays; a glass bowl was filled with minted honeydew balls; others were filled with minted cantaloupe balls.

Rotelle with Olives and Wild Mushrooms

SERVES 10 TO 12

    1   10-ounce can jumbo
        California-style olives, pitted
  ⅓   cup red wine vinegar
    1   cup olive oil
    2   garlic cloves, peeled and
        crushed
    6   whole basil stems with leaves
    6   whole parsley stems with leaves
  ¼   pound lean bacon
  ¾   cup oil-packed sun-dried
        tomatoes
  1½ pounds rotelle
    1   cup freshly grated Parmesan
        Salt and freshly ground
        black pepper, to taste
  ½   pound shiitake mushrooms
    4   tablespoons (½ stick)
        unsalted butter
  ¼   cup chopped fresh parsley

The day before serving, drain the olives and cut into quarters. Make a marinade by combining the red wine vinegar, olive oil, and garlic. Place half the quartered olives in a glass bowl, layer the whole stems of basil and parsley on top, cover with the remaining olives, and pour on the marinade. Cover with plastic wrap and refrigerate overnight.

Cook the bacon until crisp, drain, and crumble when cool. Reserve the drippings. Set both aside.

Slice the sun-dried tomatoes into thin strips and set aside. Reserve the oil.

Cook the pasta in a large pot of boiling salted water until al dente. Drain and rinse with cold running water. Drain well. Place the pasta in a large bowl and toss with the reserved bacon drippings and sun-dried tomato oil, ½ cup of the grated Parmesan cheese, and salt and pepper to taste. Cover and refrigerate until an hour before serving.

Slice the mushrooms and sauté in melted butter until just slightly cooked, 1 or 2 minutes. Do not overcook. Set aside.

An hour before serving, drain the olives, reserving the marinade. Toss the mushrooms and olives into the pasta, adding a little of the olive marinade for flavor, if necessary. Sprinkle with the remaining Parmesan and parsley. Serve at room temperature.

Cranberry-Orange Muffins

MAKES SIXTY 1¼-INCH MUFFINS

    2   cups all-purpose flour
    1   cup sugar
  1½ teaspoons baking powder
    1   teaspoon salt
  ½   teaspoon baking soda
    4   tablespoons (½ stick) cold
        unsalted butter
    1   egg, beaten
        Grated rind of 1 orange
  ¾   cup freshly squeezed orange
        juice
  2½ cups fresh cranberries

Preheat the oven to 350°. Generously butter or spray with vegetable cooking spray the muffin cups or tins you will be using.

Sift the dry ingredients together into a large bowl. Using a pastry blender, two knives, or a food processor, cut in the cold butter until the mixture is crumbly. Add the egg, orange rind, and orange juice, and stir by hand just until evenly moistened. Fold in the cranberries.

Spoon the batter evenly into the prepared muffin cups and bake until done, approximately 20 minutes. Turn out onto a wire rack to cool.

Carrot Muffins

MAKES SIXTY 1¼-INCH MUFFINS

1½ cups all-purpose flour
½ teaspoon baking powder
1 teaspoon ground cinnamon
1 teaspoon freshly grated nutmeg
½ teaspoon salt
½ teaspoon baking soda
⅔ cup vegetable oil
1 cup sugar
2 eggs, beaten
1 cup grated carrots
¾ cup chopped walnuts

Preheat the oven to 350°. Generously butter or spray with vegetable cooking spray the muffin cups or tins you will be using.

Sift together the dry ingredients and set aside.

Combine the oil, sugar, and eggs in a large bowl, and mix by hand until blended. Gradually add the dry ingredients and mix well; stir in the grated carrots and chopped nuts.

Spoon the batter into the prepared muffin cups and bake 20 minutes, or until a toothpick inserted in the center comes out clean. Turn out onto a wire rack to cool.

Dessert Cheeses

When Anne O'Herron and I sat down to discuss her menu, she had very specific ideas about which cheeses she wanted served. Cheese selection *is* personal, but some guidelines are necessary; it is very important not to choose smelly cheeses or cheeses that soften into pools of cream in a few moments.

There are so many excellent varieties of cheeses available that the creation of a cheese table or dessert cheese is fun. One could design a display of all-French cheeses, for example, using goat cheeses, double and triple crèmes, Camemberts, and a couple of herb or pepper Bries. Many Italian cheeses are being imported now—choose toma, smoked and fresh mozzarellas, gorgonzola, a layered marscapone, and one or two of the flavored tortas. Another idea would be a splendid array of English cheeses—Cheddars, veined Cheshires, Gloucestershires, Caerphilly, and Stilton. Whatever you decide, pick cheeses of unusual shapes and sizes, keeping variety and quantity in mind.

The display can be garnished with fruits, flowers, or foliage (grape leaves are appropriate, as are kale, lettuce, or herbs), or just assorted breads and crackers.

Minted Melon Balls

SERVES 10 TO 12

2 ripe but firm honeydew melons
2 ripe but firm cantaloupes
⅔ cup Cointreau (optional)
⅔ cup chopped fresh mint leaves

Cut the melons in half and scoop out the seeds with a wooden spoon. Using a melon ball scoop, cut as many balls as possible from each half, keeping the balls uniform in size and whole. Place the melon balls in a bowl, add the liqueur, if desired, stir well, and refrigerate until ready to use. Sprinkle with mint immediately before serving.

Seasonal Wedding Lunch

Seasonality has a lot to do with planning a perfect menu. Although one can find almost everything all year round nowadays, it is still appropriate and lovely to serve lamb in the spring and duck in the autumn. Recipes for salads using these meats are included in this menu. The simple hors d'oeuvres can be made at any time of the year, but all three go very well in either spring or fall and the ingredients are easily found.

Because there is only one course for this meal, the hors d'oeuvres can serve as an appetizer or first course. Both salads are hearty enough to stand alone, but a soup or simple fish mousse could be added as a first course.

Potato slices topped with caviar and crème fraîche are one of our most popular hors d'oeuvres. I often use whole or halves of red bliss potatoes, but here I chose to use Idaho baking potatoes. Boiled gently until tender, they are then sliced evenly and served warm. Puffy pâte à choux filled with a rich onion jam and quartered figs wrapped with good-quality prosciutto ham were the other hors d'oeuvres.

The lamb salad is a delectable and easy main course. A small leg or rack of lamb is marinated in wine, olive oil, and herbs, roasted until rare, and sliced from the bone. The lamb is mixed, while still warm, with lamb's lettuce, sugar snap peas, red peppers, and fennel, and dressed with a balsamic vinaigrette.

For the duck salad, breasts of Moulard ducks are marinated in gin and fresh thyme and then sautéed or grilled. They are sliced while still warm and mixed with arugula and red-leaf lettuce, haricots verts, exotic mushrooms, and quartered cherry tomatoes. The dressing is mixed at the last moment, a mixture of oils, vinegar, cream, and mustard.

MENU

HORS D'OEUVRES
Potato Slices with Caviar and Crème Fraîche

Deviled Eggs

Pâte à Choux with Onion Jam

Prosciutto-Wrapped Figs

MAIN COURSE
Lamb or Duck Salad

DESSERT
Wedding Cake

Potato Slices with Caviar and Crème Fraîche

MAKES 48 HORS D'OEUVRES

8 medium California waxy
　potatoes
8 ounces red salmon or
　whitefish caviar
½ cup Crème Fraîche (page 291),
　whipped stiff, or sour cream

Wash the potatoes and place them in a large kettle of water. Bring to a boil, reduce the heat, and boil gently just until the potatoes are tender. Do not overcook or let the skins of the potatoes crack. Drain and let cool.

When the potatoes are cool enough to handle, cut them a bit thicker than ¼ inch thick, and spoon a small amount (½ teaspoon) of caviar onto the center of each. Pipe or spoon a bit of crème fraîche or sour cream onto each potato and serve.

VARIATION: Instead of caviar, the potatoes can be topped with Tapenade (recipe follows).

PRECEDING PAGE: Warm slices of lamb are mixed at the last moment with the other ingredients for this main course salad.
BELOW: An old Irish glass tray holds the potato slices.

Tapenade

MAKES 1 CUP

½ cup oil-cured Mediterranean
　or Greek olives, drained and
　pitted
4 to 6 oil-packed anchovy
　fillets (or to taste), drained
1 to 2 tablespoons freshly
　squeezed and strained
　lemon juice
1 teaspoon dry mustard
　Freshly ground black
　pepper, to taste
　Approximately ¼ cup
　olive oil

Place all the ingredients, except the oil, in the bowl of a food processor and process until the mixture forms a paste. Scrape down the sides of the bowl and slowly add the olive oil in a steady stream until the mixture is creamy. Correct the seasonings if necessary and refrigerate, covered, until ready to use.

The tapenade can be flavored by placing any of the following in the food processor with the other ingredients: 1 small crushed garlic clove; 1 tablespoon finely chopped parsley; ¼ teaspoon ground bay leaf; ¼ teaspoon dried thyme; 3 tablespoons drained tuna; 1 hard-cooked egg; and/or 1 teaspoon Cognac.

Deviled Eggs

MAKES 48 HORS D'OEUVRES

24 hard-cooked eggs
½ cup Homemade Mayonnaise
　(page 229)
¼ cup green basil leaves,
　blanched for 30 seconds and
　drained (see Note)
1 tablespoon freshly grated
　Parmesan cheese
　Salt and freshly ground
　black pepper, to taste

Peel the eggs and cut each in half lengthwise or crosswise (for variation). Carefully remove the yolks and arrange the whites on a platter or tray. (The tray can be covered with a thick bed of parsley, dill, or other greens to keep the eggs from rolling.)

In the bowl of an electric mixer or a food processor, blend the egg yolks, mayonnaise, blanched basil leaves, and cheese until smooth. Season with salt and pepper.

Put the egg yolk mixture into a pastry bag fitted with a decorative tip and pipe it carefully and very neatly into the egg halves. Cover with plastic wrap and refrigerate until ready to serve, up to 3 hours.

NOTE: The basil leaves should be blanched to retain their bright green color; without blanching they may bruise and turn dark.

VARIATIONS: Other flavor and color combinations can be made by omitting the basil and Parmesan cheese and adding and blending the following in the food processor: 1 sautéed roasted sweet red pepper (see Note, page 277) and a dash of cayenne; 1 peeled and seeded tomato, 1 tablespoon of tomato paste, and ½ teaspoon curry powder; 4 anchovy fillets with 8 finely minced black olives.

Pâte à Choux with Onion Jam

MAKES 40 HORS D'OEUVRES

PÂTE À CHOUX
1 cup water
8 tablespoons (1 stick)
　unsalted butter, cut into
　small pieces
¼ teaspoon salt
½ teaspoon sugar
1 cup all-purpose flour
4 large eggs

GLAZE: 1 egg beaten with
1 teaspoon water

ONION JAM
MAKES 1½ QUARTS

8 tablespoons (1 stick)
　unsalted butter
20 medium onions (7 to 8
　pounds), peeled and sliced thin
2 bottles dry red wine
1 cup crème de cassis
¼ cup sugar, or to taste
　Salt and freshly ground
　black pepper, to taste

An oval copper tray, lined with a French cotton lace doily, holds the pâte à choux puffs.
Creamy white ranunculus make a lovely bouquet tied with champagne-colored ribbons.

To make the puffs, combine the water and butter in a small, heavy saucepan and bring to a boil. When the butter has melted, stir in the salt and sugar. Remove from the heat and add the flour, stirring until smooth.

Place the saucepan over high heat and cook, stirring continuously, until a smooth mass forms and the bottom of the pan is coated with a thin film (this indicates that the flour is cooked).

Transfer the mixture to a mixing bowl and let it cool slightly. Add the eggs, one at a time, beating the batter until very smooth. (At this point, the dough can rest, covered, at room temperature for an hour or two.)

Preheat the oven to 425°. Lightly butter two baking sheets, or line them with parchment paper, and set aside.

Place the pâte in a pastry bag fitted with a plain round ½-inch tip, and pipe onto the baking sheets, forming mounds 1 inch in diameter and ¾ inch high. Lightly brush with the egg glaze, smoothing the top of each. Bake for 10 minutes, reduce the oven to 375°, and continue baking until the puffs are golden brown, about 20 minutes more. Lower the oven to 325° and bake until the puffs are firm and the inside is not doughy or sticky, about 8 to 10 minutes. Cool the puffs on a wire rack. The puffs can be used immediately or frozen in airtight containers for future use.

To make the onion jam, melt the butter in a large skillet and sauté the onions, covered, over low heat for about 20 minutes, until they are wilted but not browned. Add one bottle of red wine, raise the heat, and simmer until there is no liquid (or very little) left. Add the second bottle of wine and cook the mixture down once again. Stir in the cassis (add just enough to turn the onions a deep burgundy color) and correct the tartness with as much sugar as necessary (this will depend not only on your taste but also on the onions used). Simmer the mixture until all liquid has been cooked away. Season with salt and pepper.

To assemble, cut the tops off the warm pâte à choux puffs (cold or frozen puffs should be recrisped in a 325° oven) and fill with a teaspoon of warm onion jam. Serve immediately.

VARIATION: Pâte à choux puffs can also be stuffed with Crab Meat Filling (recipe follows).

Crab Meat Filling

MAKES ENOUGH FOR 60
HORS D'OEUVRES

4 ounces cream cheese, at
   room temperature
4 ounces Montrachet or other
   goat cheese, at room
   temperature
½ sweet red pepper, seeded
   and finely chopped
½ sweet green pepper, seeded
   and finely chopped
2 scallions, finely chopped
   (white and green parts)
4 ounces frozen snow crab
   meat, thawed and well
   drained
   Dash of Tabasco sauce
   Salt and freshly ground
   black pepper, to taste

Combine all the ingredients.

NOTE: Crab Meat Filling is also delicious stuffed into blanched snow peas.

Prosciutto-Wrapped Figs

SEE RECIPE VARIATION, PAGE 267.

Quartered figs, wrapped with prosciutto, are arranged on a fabric-and-glass-lined tray.

Lamb Salad

SERVES 10 TO 12

2 small baby racks of lamb
(about 3½ pounds)

MARINADE

1 bottle dry white wine
1 cup olive oil
4 sprigs fresh rosemary
6 sprigs fresh thyme
2 large yellow onions, peeled
and sliced
6 garlic cloves, peeled and
crushed

½ pound sugar snap peas
2 medium fennel bulbs
¼ cup olive oil
2 roasted sweet red peppers
(see Note, page 277), cored,
seeded, and sliced

VINAIGRETTE

½ cup balsamic vinegar
2 shallots, peeled and minced
¾ cup olive oil
¼ cup very rich lamb stock
Salt and freshly ground
black pepper, to taste

3 bunches mâche (lamb's
lettuce)

Place the lamb in a pan just large
enough to hold it. Combine all the marinade
ingredients and pour over the lamb. Marinate, covered, overnight in the refrigerator.

The next day, remove the lamb from
the marinade, place on a rack to drain, and
bring to room temperature.

Preheat the oven to 425°. Sprinkle
the onions from the marinade over the lamb.
Allowing 15 minutes per pound, cook the
lamb to an internal temperature of 150° (medium). Remove from the oven and set aside.

In a pot of boiling water, blanch the
sugar snap peas for 1 minute. Drain and
plunge immediately into ice water to stop
them from cooking further. Drain well.

An arrangement of black-eyed susans and
zinnias from the garden makes a lovely autumnal centerpiece.

Cut the end off the fennel bulbs and
separate into sections. Cut crosswise into
¼-inch slices and sauté in the olive oil until
lightly browned and softened. Drain on paper
towels and set aside.

While still warm, carve the lamb
into small pieces (about 1½ inches square)
and place in a large serving bowl. Add the sugar snap peas, fennel, and roasted red peppers, and toss lightly.

To make the vinaigrette, place the
vinegar in a small saucepan and add the
minced shallots and lamb stock. Reduce the
liquid by half and remove from the heat.
Whisk in the olive oil and season to taste.

Add the mâche to the other ingredients and pour the warm vinaigrette over the
salad. Toss well and serve immediately.

Duck Salad

SERVES 12

6 Moulard duck breasts (1 to
1¼ pounds each), boned,
skin left on (see Note)

MARINADE

1½ to 2 cups gin
2 tablespoons fresh thyme
leaves
1 shallot, finely minced
1 garlic clove, finely minced
1 teaspoon coarse salt
Freshly ground black
pepper, to taste

DRESSING

¾ cup olive oil
¾ cup vegetable oil
½ cup red wine vinegar
4 teaspoons heavy cream
4 teaspoons Dijon-style
mustard
4 whole garlic cloves
2 shallots, finely minced
4 dashes of Tabasco sauce

1 pint ripe red cherry
tomatoes
1 pound blanched haricots
verts (page 299)
4 tablespoons (½ stick)
unsalted butter
½ pound fresh shiitake
mushrooms, sliced
½ pound fresh chanterelle
mushrooms, sliced
1 shallot, finely minced
2 sprigs fresh thyme
One handful salad greens
per person (we used arugula
and red-leaf lettuce)

Two days before serving, place the
duck breasts in a large shallow dish. Whisk
together all marinade ingredients and pour
over the duck. Cover and refrigerate for 48
hours, turning occasionally.

One day before serving, combine all
ingredients for the dressing and refrigerate.

On the day of the party, quarter the
cherry tomatoes and toss lightly with just
enough dressing to coat. Marinate in the refrigerator for at least 6 hours.

Let the haricots verts cool slightly after cooking; toss with a few tablespoons of dressing. Chill.

To prepare the duck, remove the breasts from the marinade and pat dry. Using a sharp knife, score the skin of each in a neat crisscross pattern. Place the breasts, skin side down, in a large skillet, and cook over medium heat until all the fat is rendered; how long this will take depends on how fatty the ducks you use are. Turn the duck and cook to desired doneness, approximately 4 minutes (the duck should be served pink). Remove from the pan, drain on paper towels, and let cool to room temperature.

Melt approximately 2 tablespoons butter in a sauté pan and add half the shallot, one sprig of thyme, and the shiitake mushrooms (use just enough butter to prevent the mushrooms from burning while they cook). Quickly sauté just until the mushrooms soften, a minute or so. Remove from the pan and drain on paper towels. Repeat with the remaining butter, shallot, thyme, and chanterelles.

To assemble the salad on individual plates, arrange the greens around three quarters of the plate. Cut the duck breasts crosswise into ¼-inch slices and fan several on the uncovered portion. Surround the duck with the mushrooms, tomatoes, and haricots verts (dividing each equally among the plates). Remove the garlic cloves from the dressing, and spoon a small amount on the greens, tomatoes, mushrooms, and haricots verts. Serve immediately.

N O T E : Moulard ducks are a cross between mallard and Peking ducks; their meat is more flavorful, darker, and less fatty than that of most other ducks. If they are not available, other types of duck can be used for this salad, although I would suggest using one whole native American duck breast per serving.

Glistening slices of sautéed duck breast are set amid garden lettuces, haricots verts, cherry tomatoes, and sautéed mushrooms.

Garden Party in Pink

Caroline Damerell and Carmine Santandrea travel a great deal in Europe and the United States, and eat varied, sophisticated foods. They wanted their wedding menu to reflect their fondness for fresh, colorful regional foods and eclectic ethnic cuisines.

Because they live in Connecticut and sail every weekend, they asked for clams and lobsters. Because it was summer, they asked for lots of fresh vegetables. And because Caroline loves pink, all the desserts were some shade of her favorite color. Even the wine was pink! The chocolate petits fours were for Carmine.

The hors d'oeuvres were all very pretty and delicate, from the raw littleneck clams with a shallot-flavored cocktail sauce to the carefully sliced anise-flavored salmon gravlax, to the heart-shaped toasts with herbed cheese topping. The hors d'oeuvres were served simply, garnished with sprigs of herbs.

The buffet was displayed on a sixteen-foot-long table. (This table was later used as the dessert buffet, and a new pale pink cloth was placed over the original white buffet cloth.) Silver trays and baskets were used as the serving dishes. Salads were mounded on the silver trays and garnished with greenery—curly kale, radicchio, watercress, ferns, and tansy. More branches of herbs and fronds of ferns were used to decorate the table itself. The platters of lobster halves were garnished with whole, plump pink pears that had been poached in red wine. The red pepper sauce was gently pink, and the strawberry butter was pink as well.

The finale of the meal was the Rose Cake, a lemon pound cake interior with an Italian meringue exterior, lavishly swathed in old roses. A silver-footed compote was filled to brimming with more roses. Caroline gasped with pleasure at the sight of so many of her favorite flowers.

Menu

HORS D'OEUVRES

Raw Clam Bar with Shallot-Flavored Cocktail Sauce

Gravlax on Black Bread with Mustard-Fennel Sauce

Heart Toasts with Herb Cheese

Smoked Salmon Mousse on Cucumber Hearts

BUFFET

Poached Lobster Halves with Red Pepper Sauce

Peasant Salad · Filet of Beef Salad

Sesame Noodles with Tree-Ear Mushrooms and Cucumbers

Endive, Beet, and Orange Salad

Homemade French Bread with Pink Strawberry Butter

DESSERT

Fraises des Bois Sorbet · Long-Stemmed Strawberries

Chocolate Petit Fours · Wedding Cake

LEFT: A well-flavored sauce of fennel and mustard added a delicate flavoring to the gravlax. BELOW LEFT: A long rectangular tray, filled with ice, was the serving station for littleneck clams. A decoratively carved cantaloupe contained the cocktail sauce.

Raw Clam Bar with Shallot-Flavored Cocktail Sauce

SEE PAGE 263.

PRECEDING PAGE: Caroline wanted everything pink—her flowers and her cake reflected her wishes. A footed silver compote was filled to brimming with old roses, and the small cake was covered with rose buds.

Shallot-Flavored Cocktail Sauce

MAKES 1 QUART

5 shallots, peeled and finely minced
⅔ cup balsamic vinegar
3½ cups ketchup
¼ teaspoon cayenne pepper
Freshly ground black pepper, to taste

Combine the shallots with the vinegar in a saucepan and cook until tender. Remove the shallots with a slotted spoon and set aside. Reduce the vinegar to ⅓ cup.

Add the shallots and vinegar reduction to the ketchup, season with pepper, and chill until ready to use.

Gravlax on Black Bread with Mustard-Fennel Sauce

MAKES 50 HORS D'OEUVRES

1 4- to 5-pound piece of
    salmon, cut in half and very
    carefully boned, skin left on
¼ cup coarse salt
¼ cup sugar
2 tablespoons peppercorns
    (preferably white), crushed
    or coarsely ground
½ cup olive oil
2 large bunches of fennel tops

2 loaves thinly sliced black
    bread

MUSTARD-FENNEL SAUCE
MAKES APPROXIMATELY ½ CUP

4 tablespoons Dijon-style
    mustard
1 teaspoon dry mustard
3 tablespoons sugar
2 tablespoons white vinegar
⅓ cup light vegetable oil
1 small bunch of fennel tops,
    finely chopped

To cure the salmon, put half the
salmon, skin side down, in a glass dish. Combine the salt, sugar, and pepper, and sprinkle
on the fish, covering the whole side. Spoon
the oil over the fish. Spread the fennel over
the seasonings. Put the other half of the salmon over the fennel, skin side up. Cover with
plastic wrap. Put a smaller dish on top of the
salmon and weight down with a heavy object.
Refrigerate for 3 to 4 days. Turn the salmon
every day.

To make the mustard sauce, combine
the mustards, sugar, and vinegar in the bowl
of a food processor. Add the oil drop by drop
until the mixture is thick. Stir in the fennel.
Refrigerate until ready to use, up to 4 weeks.

To serve, remove the fish from the
marinade. Wipe clean and pat dry. Slice each
side on the diagonal, much as you would
smoked salmon. Serve on half-slices of black
bread, topped with the mustard-fennel sauce.

Heart Toasts with Herb Cheese

MAKES 30 TO 40 HORS D'OEUVRES

HERB CHEESE
MAKES APPROXIMATELY 1¼ CUPS

½ cup Crème Fraîche
    (page 291)
4 ounces cream cheese, at
    room temperature
1 teaspoon chopped fresh
    thyme
1 tablespoon chopped fresh
    parsley
    Dash of cayenne pepper
1 teaspoon freshly squeezed
    lemon juice

10 very thin slices Pain de Mie
    (page 264) or good store-
    bought white bread, sliced
    very thin

To make the herb cheese, whip the
crème fraîche with an electric mixer until
fluffy and set aside. In a separate bowl, whip
the cream cheese with the remaining ingredients until light and fluffy. Fold in the
whipped crème fraîche and refrigerate until
ready to use.

Preheat the oven to 300°.

Cut the bread using a heart-shaped
cookie or biscuit cutter small enough to yield
3 or 4 hearts per slice. Put the cutouts on a
baking sheet and bake until dry but not colored, about 10 minutes, turning after 5 minutes so the edges do not curl. Remove from
the oven and let cool on a wire rack.

Using a pastry bag fitted with a
decorative tip, pipe a bit of the herb cheese
onto each toast.

NOTE: More chopped herbs and/or half a
clove of garlic, crushed, can be added to the
herb cheese mixture if you prefer a stronger
flavor. You can also vary the herbs, using dill,
chervil, chives, etc.

VARIATION: Herb cheese can be used to
fill blanched snow peas. Use ½ teaspoon for
split snow peas and 1 teaspoon for open ones.

Smoked Salmon Mousse on Cucumber Hearts

MAKES 40 HORS D'OEUVRES

8 ounces cream cheese, at
    room temperature
2 ounces smoked salmon
    Few drops of freshly
    squeezed lemon juice
    Pinch of hot paprika or
    cayenne pepper
2 to 3 tablespoons heavy
    cream
    Freshly ground white
    pepper, to taste

2 seedless English cucumbers

In the bowl of a food processor, combine the cream cheese, smoked salmon, lemon
juice, paprika or cayenne, cream, and white
pepper, and blend until smooth. Chill for at
least 30 minutes.

To prepare the cucumbers, wash and
cut each into slices a little less than ¼ inch
thick. Using a heart-shaped cookie or biscuit
cutter slightly smaller in diameter than the
cucumber slices, cut them into hearts. The
cucumbers can now be placed on a towel-lined
baking sheet, covered with plastic wrap, and
refrigerated for up to 3 hours.

No more than 30 minutes before
serving, remove the mousse from the refrigerator and soften it with a wooden spoon. Using a pastry bag fitted with a decorative tip,
pipe the mousse onto the cucumber hearts.

Thin cucumber hearts with a piped topping
of smoked salmon mousse.

LEFT: Pink wine-poached pears were an unusual garnish for the lobster halves.
OPPOSITE RIGHT: Peasant salad.
OPPOSITE FAR RIGHT: Filet of beef salad.

Poached Lobster Halves with Red Pepper Sauce

SERVES 12

2 bottles dry white wine
2 garlic cloves
1 bay leaf
1 sprig of fresh parsley
6 1¼-pound lobsters

RED PEPPER SAUCE
MAKES 2½ CUPS

2 eggs
¼ teaspoon dry mustard
¾ teaspoon salt
2 tablespoons freshly
   squeezed lemon juice
1 cup olive oil
1 cup safflower or vegetable
   oil
6 roasted peppers, seeded and
   finely diced (see Note, page 277)
3 teaspoons ground pink
   peppercorns
3 tablespoons Cognac
   Salt to taste

GARNISH: 6 Red Wine-Poached Pears

Combine the wine, garlic, bay leaf, and parsley in a 10-gallon pot of water, and bring to a rolling boil. Plunge the lobsters head first into the boiling liquid and cook for 10 minutes. Add additional boiling water to the kettle if necessary to cover the lobsters completely; there must be sufficient water in the pot to cook the lobsters evenly.

When the lobsters have cooked and turned bright red, remove them from the pot and let them cool. Refrigerate.

To make the sauce, mix the eggs, mustard, salt, and lemon juice in the bowl of a food processor. Add the olive oil, drop by drop, until the mixture begins to thicken. Add the remaining olive oil and the vegetable oil in a steady stream and mix until smooth. Add half of the diced red peppers and purée until smooth. Remove the mixture from the food processor and place in a large mixing bowl. Fold in the remaining diced pepper, the pink peppercorns, and the Cognac; season to taste. Refrigerate until ready to serve.

When the lobsters are thoroughly chilled, cut each in half lengthwise with a very sharp knife. Serve with the sauce. Garnish the platter with wine-poached pears.

RED WINE-POACHED PEARS
MAKES 6

4 cups dry red wine
1 cup sugar
   Peel of 1 lemon
1 vanilla bean
1 cinnamon stick
1 star anise
6 ripe but firm Comice or
   Packham pears, carefully
   peeled, with stems left on

Combine all of the ingredients, except the pears, in a large saucepan. Bring the mixture to a boil and cook for 5 minutes. Add the pears, lower the heat, and cook for 20 to 30 minutes, until the pears are tender. If necessary, turn the pears very gently by rotating the stems with your fingertips so that they cook evenly. Remove the pears to a bowl, bring the poaching liquid to a rapid boil, and reduce by half. Pour the syrup over the pears and refrigerate, covered, for at least 6 hours, preferably overnight. Drain before using.

Peasant Salad

SERVES 12

20 small new red potatoes, unpeeled
10 spears fresh asparagus
3 zucchini
3 ounces sun-dried tomatoes, thinly sliced (reserve oil for dressing)
4 sweet green peppers, seeded and julienned
½ red onion, thinly sliced
¼ pound pitted black olives, drained and halved

DRESSING

1 egg yolk
3 tablespoons Crème Fraîche (page 291)
3 tablespoons freshly squeezed lemon juice
1 teaspoon salt
1 small garlic clove, minced
Dash of Tabasco sauce
3 tablespoons freshly grated Parmesan cheese
1 tablespoon chopped fresh dill
2 tablespoons chopped fresh parsley
1 cup oil (use the oil reserved from the sun-dried tomatoes, adding olive oil to make the full amount)

Cut the potatoes in half and steam over boiling water just until tender. Do not overcook or they will become mushy. Remove from the steamer and let cool.

Cut off the ends of the asparagus and slice each stalk diagonally into ½-inch lengths. Blanch the asparagus in a pot of rapidly boiling water until tender. Drain and plunge into ice water to stop the asparagus from cooking and help retain the bright color. Drain well.

Slice the zucchini diagonally ¼ inch thick and steam over boiling water until tender. Set aside to cool.

Combine the sun-dried tomatoes, peppers, onion, and olives with the cooled vegetables in a large bowl and set aside.

To make the dressing, place all ingredients, except the oil, in a bowl and mix well. Gradually whisk in the oil until well blended. Use just enough dressing to coat the vegetables. Serve at room temperature.

Filet of Beef Salad

SERVES 12

2 tablespoons olive oil
2 tablespoons grapeseed oil (see Note)
1 4-pound filet of beef
5 sweet red peppers
5 sweet yellow peppers
½ pound snow peas
6 carrots

DRESSING

4 tablespoons red wine vinegar
1 small garlic clove
1 teaspoon sugar
¼ teaspoon chopped fresh rosemary
1 cup pimiento oil (see Note, page 294)
Salt and freshly ground black pepper, to taste

2 bunches of watercress, washed and dried

Preheat the oven to 450°.

Combine the olive and grapeseed oils in a large heavy skillet and heat to a very high temperature; the oils should be almost smoking. Add the filet and brown well on all sides. Remove the filet from the skillet and place on a baking sheet. Roast the meat in the oven for 12 to 20 minutes, until rare to medium-rare. Do not overcook. Remove from the oven and let cool.

Seed the red and yellow peppers and slice thinly. Wrap in plastic and refrigerate until ready to use.

Remove the stem end and string the snow peas. Blanch in a pot of rapidly boiling water for no more than 30 seconds. Do not overcook; the snow peas should be crunchy. Drain and plunge immediately into ice water. Drain well and refrigerate.

Peel the carrots and cut them on the diagonal into 1½-inch slices. Blanch in a pot of rapidly boiling water until barely tender, no more than 1 minute. Drain and plunge immediately into ice water; drain well and refrigerate.

To make the dressing, combine the vinegar, garlic, sugar, and rosemary; gradually whisk in the oil until blended. Season with salt and pepper to taste and set aside.

Immediately before serving, cut the cooled filet into ¼-inch slices and toss in a large bowl with the peppers, snow peas, carrots, and dressing. Arrange the salad on a bed of watercress and serve.

NOTE: Grapeseed oil, available in gourmet shops and specialty markets, is good for browning because it can be heated to a very high temperature without burning.

Sesame Noodles with Tree-Ear Mushrooms and Cucumbers

SERVES 10 TO 12

2 medium cucumbers
⅓ cup dried tree-ear mushrooms, softened in 1 cup boiling water
½ cup rice wine vinegar
1½ tablespoons sesame paste
4 tablespoons smooth-style peanut butter
2 tablespoons honey mustard
⅓ cup light soy sauce
1½ tablespoons chili oil (or to taste)
½ cup Oriental sesame oil
⅓ cup vegetable oil
 Juice of 1 large orange
 Salt and freshly ground black pepper, to taste
2 pounds Oriental egg noodles or buckwheat pasta
⅓ cup light or dark sesame seeds

Peel and halve the cucumbers lengthwise, and, using a melon baller, scoop out and discard the seeds. Cut the cucumber halves into ¼-inch slices. Drain the mushrooms.

In a mixing bowl, blend the vinegar, sesame paste, peanut butter, honey mustard, and soy sauce together until smooth. Combine the oils and slowly whisk them into the mixing bowl. Add the orange juice and salt and pepper and set aside.

To toast the sesame seeds, place them in a hot frying pan and toss gently over high heat until light golden.

Cook the noodles in a large kettle of boiling water until al dente. Drain in a colander and rinse with cold water to stop the cooking. Drain well.

In a large bowl, toss the drained noodles, cucumbers, tree-ears, and sesame dressing to coat completely. Chill at least 30 minutes. Serve the salad topped with the toasted sesame seeds.

VARIATIONS: Snow peas, sweet red, green, or yellow peppers, blanched carrots, or any other fresh or dried mushrooms, domestic or wild, could be substituted for the cucumbers and tree-ears.

Endive, Beet, and Orange Salad

SERVES 24

DRESSING

1 cup orange juice
1 cup dry vermouth
1 teaspoon sugar
1 tablespoon balsamic vinegar
¼ teaspoon ground cumin
 Pinch of ground cinnamon
 Salt and freshly ground black pepper, to taste
½ cup safflower oil

24 small fresh beets
6 oranges
6 heads of Belgian endive, julienned
¼ cup dried currants, soaked overnight in vodka
¼ cup coarsely chopped toasted walnuts (see Note)

To make the dressing, combine the orange juice, vermouth, and sugar in a saucepan, and boil until reduced to 4 tablespoons. Pour the reduction into a small mixing bowl

OPPOSITE FAR LEFT: Tree-ear mushrooms and crescents of cucumbers were the unusual additions to the sesame noodles. OPPOSITE MIDDLE: Each place setting was pristine and beautiful. Centerpieces were simple and elegant arrangements of peonies, ivy, and fragrant stock. OPPOSITE LEFT: Julienned orange rind made with a zester is a colorful decoration for this salad. RIGHT: In keeping with the pink theme, even the butter was tinted with strawberries.

and whisk in the vinegar, cumin, cinnamon, and salt and pepper. Gradually whisk in the oil until thoroughly blended. Set aside.

Cut off the tops of the beets, leaving 1 inch of the stem, and wash them. Place the beets in a large pot, cover with cold water, and bring to a boil. Cook, covered, until the beets are very tender, 30 to 40 minutes. Drain the beets and let cool. When the beets are cool enough to handle, slip them out of their skins and cut them into quarters. Place in a large bowl and set aside.

With a sharp vegetable peeler, remove the rind of 1 orange and cut it into thin julienne. (Reserve the orange.) Blanch the rind in a pot of boiling water until tender, 3 to 4 minutes. Drain and let cool. Using a sharp knife, peel the remaining oranges, carefully removing all of the bitter white pith and membranes. Carefully section all the oranges.

Combine the orange sections, julienned orange rind, and endive with the quartered beets. Drain the currants, and add them and the chopped walnuts to the other ingredients. Pour on the dressing (whisk again before using) and toss to coat all ingredients evenly. Serve immediately.

NOTE: To toast the walnuts, place on a baking sheet in a preheated 350° oven for 8 to 10 minutes, until golden brown.

Homemade French Bread with Pink Strawberry Butter

MAKES 6 BAGUETTES OR 36 LITTLE ROLLS (PISTOLETS)

    1   ounce fresh yeast cake or 2
        packages active dry yeast
    2¾ cups lukewarm water
    7   cups unbleached all-purpose
        flour
    4¼ teaspoons salt

Soften the yeast in ¼ cup of the lukewarm water.

Mix the flour and salt in a large bowl. Add the remaining water and mix well. Add the yeast mixture and blend well.

Turn onto a floured board and knead until the dough is smooth and elastic. If you have a heavy-duty mixer with a dough hook, this whole procedure will take only 4 to 5 minutes.

Put the dough in a large bowl, cover, and let rise until doubled in bulk. Punch the dough down and let it rise a second time until doubled. Punch down again, and turn onto a floured board.

To form baguettes, divide the dough into 6 equal pieces and roll into long thin loaves using the palms of your hands. Place the loaves into buttered French bread pans and cover with plastic wrap or a warm damp cloth, and let rise for 30 minutes, or until doubled in bulk. Make 3 or 4 cuts in each baguette with a sharp knife or razor blade.

Bake in a preheated 400° oven for 25 minutes. To obtain a fine crust, spray the loaves with water 3 or 4 times during baking. The loaves are done when golden brown and crisp. Serve with Pink Strawberry Butter (page 248).

VARIATION: To make pistolets, after the second rising divide the dough into 36 equal pieces, cutting with a pastry cutter. Form into round rolls by pinching the dough, drawing up the loose perimeter, never touching the floured bottom of the piece. Place the rolls, pinched side down, on buttered cookie sheets, leaving 3 inches between the rolls. Let rise and bake as for baguettes, slashing the tops before putting into the oven.

Pink Strawberry Butter

MAKES 2 CUPS

1 pound (4 sticks) unsalted
  butter, at room temperature
½ cup strawberry jam

Using an electric mixer or food processor, mix the butter with the jam until well blended. Refrigerate up to 2 days, or freeze.

VARIATIONS: Substitute damson plum, blueberry, or raspberry jam or orange marmalade for the strawberry jam.

Fraises des Bois Sorbet

MAKES 1½ QUARTS; SERVES 12

2 pints fresh fraises des bois
  (see Note)
1½ cups sugar
2 tablespoons freshly
  squeezed lemon juice
2 cups cold water
1 tablespoon framboise
  (optional)

If necessary, immerse the fraises in a bowl of cold water to rinse off any dirt. Drain well and place on paper or kitchen towels to dry completely. Remove any stems or hulls.

Put the fraises in a large bowl, sprinkle with sugar and lemon juice, and stir gently to coat all the berries. Let stand, stirring occasionally, until the sugar is completely dissolved and the berries are soft.

Purée the sugared fraises in a food processor. Stir in the cold water and framboise, if desired. Put the mixture in an ice-cream machine, and freeze according to the manufacturer's directions. This is best made the day of serving.

NOTE: Strawberries can be used if fraises des bois are not available, but the flavor of the wild berries cannot be duplicated.

Chocolate Petit Fours

MAKES 36

½ cup dried currants
½ cup Scotch whiskey
14 ounces semisweet chocolate
¼ cup water
½ pound (2 sticks) unsalted
  butter, cut into small pieces
6 eggs, separated
1⅓ cups sugar
9 tablespoons cake flour
1⅓ cups finely ground blanched
  almonds
  Pinch of salt

CHOCOLATE GANACHE
1 cup heavy cream
8 ounces semisweet chocolate,
  chopped into very small
  pieces

GARNISH: Candied roses
and/or violets

Soak the currants in the whiskey overnight.

Preheat the oven to 350°. Carefully butter and flour 36 small (1¼ inch) muffin cups.

In the top of a double boiler, melt the chocolate with the water. Stir in the butter, a piece at a time, until the mixture is smooth. Transfer to a large shallow mixing bowl.

Beat the egg yolks with the sugar until thick and pale in color. Stir into the chocolate mixture by hand. Add the flour, almonds, and currants and whiskey, and mix together very gently.

Beat the egg whites with the salt until stiff but not dry. Fold into the chocolate mixture by thirds, being careful not to deflate the egg whites. Spoon the batter into the prepared muffin tins and gently smooth the tops. Bake approximately 20 minutes, or just until done. (The cakes should still be moist in the center and just beginning to pull away from the pan.) Let rest in the pan for 10 minutes before turning out onto a wire rack to cool.

To make the ganache, bring the cream to a boil over low heat (stirring often so that it doesn't burn) and remove from the heat. Add the chocolate and stir vigorously until smooth and completely melted. If the ganache is too thin, let it cool slightly over ice water to a spreadable consistency.

Turn the cakes upside down so that the smaller bottom becomes the top, and gently coat the top and sides of each with the chocolate. Top with a candied rose or violet and let cool completely before serving.

NOTE: The petit fours should be made at least 1 day before serving, or they may be made several days in advance, wrapped, refrigerated, and iced the day they are served.

LEFT: The cake was accompanied by a serving of fraises des bois sorbet. These tiny strawberries are also known as woodland berries. OPPOSITE: In contrast to the very tiny fraises, giant long-stemmed berries were also passed with the cake.

Reception in a Country Barn

It was the bride's father's ethnic background that influenced this family's choice of wedding food. Combined with the fact that the reception was to be an informal, friendly gathering at the weekend farm, the Middle Eastern menu of grilled whole lambs, pilaf of rice, and eggplant was an excellent, delicious, and unusual offering.

I catered this reception and worked closely with the bride's mother on the recipes. She had several favorites that we adapted to our menu, and the result was a colorful, outdoorsy event that epitomized the young couple's love of nature and of good, plain food and colorful, fresh ingredients.

My gardener Celso Lima and I dug the barbecue "pit"

MENU

HORS D'OEUVRES
Date Nut Bread with Cream Cheese and Green Tomato Chutney
Vegetable Fritters · Mushrooms Stuffed with Spinach and Prosciutto
Wild Rice Pancakes with Red Pepper Jelly
Dried Pears with Bleu de Bresse

FIRST COURSE
Golden Carrot Soup

BUFFET
Rice Pilaf with Whole Almonds and Raisins · Eggplant Clafouti
Grilled Leg of Lamb with Herbs and Spices
Grilled Tomatoes · Grilled Peppers
Wild Green Salad with Tart Lemon Dressing
Whole Wheat-Raisin French Rolls

DESSERT
Wedding Cake

the day before the wedding. It was a rectangle three feet by seven feet by one foot deep. Celso cut green trees from the woods for the upright supports and spits. He removed the bark from the spits so that none of its strong flavor would be imparted to the tender young lambs. We lined the fire pit with clean, smooth granite rocks. The fire was set on top of the rocks using hickory and apple logs from the woodpile. I lit the fire at 10 A.M. the day of the wedding. The reception dinner was to be served at 5 P.M. It took two hours to get the fire perfect—glowing red coals and very hot rocks were what we placed the three baby lambs over. They were turned every twenty minutes to ensure even cooking, and after

four and a half hours they were roasted to perfection. In addition, we grilled eight legs of lamb on Big John grills that were fired with mesquite and hickory and charcoal. They required less time, about 40 to 50 minutes to grill.

We used the same Big John grills to cook the peppers and to grill the whole tomatoes. Guests were very interested in the grilling pit, and many came to watch.

The barn was a long distance from the kitchen in the main house, so we "constructed" a catering kitchen in the stone garage, which was very near to the barn. We used proofing cabinets as warming ovens for the pilaf and the eggplant clafouti and the homemade whole wheat-raisin rolls.

We prepared the hors d'oeuvres from this same "kitchen." They were chosen because of the variety of flavors they repre-

PRECEDING PAGE: An expansive country barn was the site of this reception. ABOVE: The buffet table was decorated with an autumnal still life of sunflowers, squashes and pumpkins, flowering kales, daisies, and leaves. OPPO-SITE: An oval Shaker tray, garnished with a large sunflower, holds date nut bread hors d'oeuvres.

sented, and because of the unusual combinations.

The carrot soup was ladled into the shallow bowls before the guests were seated. It was served cold, garnished with generous dollops of crème fraîche.

There were two twelve-foot buffets covered with plain white linen cloths. All the food was served from copper trays and wooden carving boards. The succulent lamb was expertly carved by my housekeeper Necy and her sister Edna, who come from Brazil, where such outdoor barbecues are extremely popular. Flowering kales, red, yellow, and green peppers, and other bright vegetables, squashes, and flowers decorated the simple buffets.

Whole baby lambs can be special ordered from Greek or Middle Eastern butchers or from a farmer who raises his own lamb.

Date Nut Bread with Cream Cheese and Green Tomato Chutney

MAKES 40 HORS D'OEUVRES

GREEN TOMATO CHUTNEY
MAKES APPROXIMATELY 3 CUPS

4 cups peeled and chopped
  green tomatoes
⅔ cup chopped onion
¼ cup sweet yellow pepper,
  seeded and chopped
1 small garlic clove, minced
1 cup packed light brown sugar
⅔ cup cider vinegar
2 tablespoons peeled and
  minced gingerroot
1 teaspoon salt
1 tablespoon mustard seeds
¼ teaspoon ground turmeric
1½ teaspoons grated lemon rind
1 cup golden raisins

DATE NUT BREAD
MAKES 1 LARGE LOAF

2 cups unbleached flour
2 teaspoons baking powder
1 teaspoon salt
½ cup packed dark brown
  sugar
1 egg
1 cup milk
½ teaspoon vanilla
2 tablespoons (¼ stick)
  unsalted butter, melted and
  cooled slightly
1 cup coarsely chopped pitted
  dried dates
½ cup chopped walnuts

8 ounces cream cheese,
  softened and whipped

To make the green tomato chutney, place all ingredients in a large enamel or stainless-steel pot, and bring to a boil. Reduce the heat and simmer until the mixture is very thick, 1½ to 2 hours. Let cool slightly. Ladle into jars and refrigerate until ready to use. (The chutney can also be put into hot, sterilized jars and sealed for longer keeping.)

Preheat the oven to 350°. Butter a 9 × 5 × 3-inch loaf pan and set aside.

In a large bowl, sift together the flour, baking powder, and salt. Stir in the brown sugar.

Place the egg in a mixing bowl and beat until light and fluffy. Stir in the milk, vanilla, and melted butter, mixing until blended. Stir this mixture into the sifted dry ingredients, mixing thoroughly. Fold in the chopped dates and nuts.

Spoon the batter into the prepared pan and bake about 40 minutes, or until the bread begins to pull away from the sides of the pan and the center is done when tested. Let cool in the pan.

To serve, slice the bread and cut each slice lengthwise into halves. Place the whipped cream cheese in a pastry bag fitted with a decorative tip (we used a leaf tip) and pipe it on top of the bread. Spoon on a small amount of green tomato chutney and serve.

VARIATION: To make simple nut bread, omit the dates and increase the amount of chopped nuts to 1 cup.

Vegetable Fritters

SEE RECIPE VARIATION, PAGE 285.

Mushrooms Stuffed with Spinach and Prosciutto

MAKES 24 HORS D'OEUVRES

1 tablespoon unsalted butter
1 shallot, finely minced
1½ cups cooked, chopped spinach, well drained
¼ cup chopped fresh parsley
2 cups fresh whole-milk ricotta cheese
6 slices prosciutto, finely chopped
¼ teaspoon freshly grated nutmeg
Salt and freshly ground black pepper, to taste
24 medium to large mushroom caps, cleaned
Approximately ¼ cup freshly grated Parmesan cheese

Preheat the oven to 350°.

Melt the butter in a saucepan and sauté the shallot until soft. Put the shallot in a mixing bowl and stir in the spinach, parsley, ricotta, prosciutto, nutmeg, and salt and pepper.

Set the mushroom caps on a baking sheet and fill each with a bit of the stuffing. Sprinkle with a little Parmesan cheese, and bake just until heated through, about 20 minutes. Serve immediately.

Wild Rice Pancakes with Red Pepper Jelly

MAKES 36 HORS D'OUEVRES

½ cup wild rice
1 cup water
4 tablespoons (½ stick) unsalted butter
2 tablespoons grated onion
1 cup all-purpose flour
2 tablespoons baking powder
1 teaspoon salt
3 eggs, lightly beaten
Approximately 1¼ cups milk

1 6-ounce jar red pepper jelly

Combine the wild rice and water in a saucepan and bring to a boil. Reduce the heat and simmer, covered, until the rice is tender, 35 to 40 minutes. Drain well.

Melt the butter in a skillet and sauté the onion until tender but not browned. Remove from the heat and let cool slightly.

Sift the flour, baking powder, and salt into a mixing bowl. Add the sautéed onion and butter, eggs, and milk, and stir until well blended. (The batter should be smooth and slightly thicker than crêpe batter; if necessary, add more milk to reach the proper consistency.) Stir in the wild rice.

Spoon 2 tablespoons of batter onto a hot buttered skillet and cook until the pancakes are brown on one side; turn and cook about 2 minutes longer. Keep finished pancakes hot in a warmed oven until all the batter has been used. Serve immediately with a dollop of red pepper jelly.

VARIATIONS: Sauté ½ pound chopped wild or domestic mushrooms with the onion and add to the batter.

Wild rice pancakes can also be topped with whipped Crème Fraîche (page 291).

Dried Pears with Bleu de Bresse

MAKES 40 HORS D'OEUVRES

BLEU DE BRESSE TOPPING

MAKES APPROXIMATELY 1 CUP

4 ounces Bleu de Bresse cheese, at room temperature (any good blue cheese can be used)
4 ounces cream cheese, at room temperature
2 tablespoons heavy cream

40 dried pear halves

GARNISH: Sprigs of fresh thyme

Put all topping ingredients in a mixing bowl or the bowl of a food processor, and whip until smooth. (Use a bit more heavy cream to smooth the mixture if necessary.) Refrigerate until ready to use.

Let the mixture soften a bit before placing it in a pastry bag fitted with a large leaf tip and piping onto the dried fruit. Garnish with a small sprig of thyme and serve.

NOTE: The Bleu de Bresse topping can be frozen in an airtight container for up to 1 week. Thaw to room temperature and rewhip before using.

VARIATIONS: Fresh or dried apricots or peaches can also be used as a base for this topping, as well as halves of small fresh Seckel pears.

Golden Carrot Soup

SERVES 12

- 8 tablespoons (1 stick) unsalted butter
- 3 pounds sweet small carrots, peeled and sliced
- 3 sweet red peppers, seeded and sliced
- 3 medium onions, sliced
- 6 cups chicken stock, preferably homemade
  Juice of 2 oranges
- 1½ cups heavy cream
  Grated rind of 1 orange
- 2 to 3 tablespoons Grand Marnier (optional)

GARNISH: Crème Fraîche (page 291)

Melt the butter in a large heavy saucepan, and sauté the carrots, peppers, and onions, covered, for about 7 minutes. Add the chicken stock and orange juice and bring the mixture to a boil. Reduce the heat and simmer, covered, until vegetables are very tender, 20 to 25 minutes. Set aside to cool.

Purée the cooled mixture in the bowl of a food processor until very smooth. Add the cream, orange rind, and Grand Marnier, if desired, and heat through. Do not boil. Garnish with a dollop of crème fraîche and serve immediately.

NOTE: If the carrots are not very sweet, add 2 teaspoons sugar to the sautéed vegetables after they have cooked for 7 minutes and cook 1 minute longer before adding the chicken stock and orange juice.

OPPOSITE FAR LEFT: Stuffed mushroom caps served from a wooden tray.
OPPOSITE ABOVE: Tender wild rice pancakes, topped with a dollop of red pepper jelly.
OPPOSITE LEFT: Dried pears topped with a piping of Bleu de Bresse. RIGHT: The first course of golden carrot soup topped with crème fraîche.

Rice Pilaf with Whole Almonds and Raisins

SERVES 10 TO 12

8 tablespoons (1 stick) unsalted butter
1 medium onion, peeled and chopped
4 cups long-grain rice
7½ cups boiling chicken stock (preferably homemade)
½ cup hot coconut milk (see Note, page 265)
Salt and freshly ground black pepper, to taste
1 cup whole toasted almonds (see Note)
¾ cup dark raisins

Melt the butter in a heavy saucepan. Sauté the onion until soft but not browned. Add the rice and cook just until the rice turns golden and transparent. Pour in the hot liquids, cover the saucepan tightly, and cook over very low heat until the rice is tender and all the liquid has been absorbed, 20 to 25 minutes. Season to taste with salt and pepper and let the covered pan sit in a warm place for 10 to 15 minutes. Just before serving, stir in the toasted almonds and raisins.

NOTE: To toast the almonds, place whole blanched almonds in a single layer on a baking sheet and bake in a preheated 350° oven until lightly browned, 10 to 15 minutes.

Eggplant Clafouti

SERVES 10

Vegetable oil
2 whole eggs, lightly beaten
2 egg yolks, lightly beaten
1 cup heavy cream
1 cup milk
¾ cup fresh whole-milk ricotta cheese
Pinch of freshly grated nutmeg
Salt and freshly ground white pepper, to taste
4 long, thin Japanese eggplants
6 deep purple Italian eggplants
Olive oil for sautéing
1 cup whole fresh basil leaves
½ cup freshly grated Parmesan cheese

Lightly oil a 1½-quart casserole or ovenproof dish and set aside.

Whisk together the eggs, egg yolks, cream, milk, ricotta, and nutmeg until well blended. Season to taste with salt and white pepper and set aside.

Wash the eggplant. Cut the Japanese eggplant lengthwise into very thin (⅛ inch) slices, and the Italian variety crosswise into ¼-inch slices. Separately place the eggplant into two colanders, sprinkle with a bit of salt, and let drain for at least 30 minutes. Rinse salt from eggplant and pat dry with paper towel.

Heat a thin layer of olive oil in a large skillet. When it is very hot, add a layer of eggplant and sauté until browned, turning the eggplant to cook it evenly. Drain on racks while you continue to sauté all the eggplant. (If you add more oil, heat it well before adding more eggplant.)

Preheat the oven to 350°.

Place a layer of sautéed Japanese eggplant in the bottom of the baking dish. Cover with a layer of whole basil leaves; place a layer of sautéed Italian eggplant on top of the basil. Continue layering in this manner until all the eggplant and basil are used. Pour the custard over it, and bake until the custard is set, about 30 minutes. Sprinkle with Parmesan cheese and serve immediately.

Grilled Leg of Lamb with Herbs and Spices

SERVES 10 TO 12

1 7- to 8-pound leg of lamb
4 garlic cloves, peeled and halved
½ cup olive oil
2 tablespoons fresh rosemary leaves, or 1 tablespoon dried rosemary
1 tablespoon ground cumin
1½ teaspoons coarsely ground black pepper
Salt to taste

Rub the entire leg of lamb with the cut sides of garlic, and coat it liberally with the olive oil. Pat the rosemary, cumin, and black pepper evenly over the surface, and sprinkle with salt.

Grill the lamb over hot coals, turning it frequently, for about 40 to 50 minutes. Check for doneness by cutting into the thickest part of the meat and return to the grill, if necessary, testing frequently. For medium-rare, the lamb should be pale pink in the center. Slice into slivers and serve.

VARIATION: Whole baby lambs (35 to 40 pounds) can be grilled this way also; they should cook on spits for approximately 4 to 5 hours; check for doneness with a meat thermometer inserted into the thickest part of the leg, which should register 150°.

OPPOSITE FAR LEFT: The rice pilaf is enhanced with roasted almonds and plump raisins. OPPOSITE LEFT: Eggplant clafouti was baked directly in this clear glass oval dish.

ABOVE: Edna Martins is at ease grilling on the Big John. Here she cooks the red tomatoes while the legs of lamb complete their grilling. LEFT: Whole baby lambs cook over hot coals.

Grilled Tomatoes

SERVES 12

12 ripe red tomatoes
¼ cup chopped fresh dill
½ cup olive oil
1 cup fresh bread crumbs
   (optional)
   Salt and freshly ground
   black pepper, to taste

Halve the tomatoes and sprinkle the cut side of each lightly with the chopped dill. Drizzle with a bit of olive oil and sprinkle with bread crumbs, if desired. Season to taste. Grill over hot coals for 4 to 5 minutes or put under a hot broiler for 5 to 7 minutes; the tomatoes should be warm but still firm.

VARIATION: Bake stuffed tomatoes on a bed of yellow pepper strips at 400° for 10 minutes or until just tender.

Grilled Peppers

MAKES 10 TO 12 SKEWERS

5 sweet green, red, and yellow
   peppers (use a combination
   of colors), seeded and cut
   into 1-inch wedges
8 tablespoons (1 stick)
   unsalted butter, melted
   Salt and freshly ground
   black pepper, to taste

Place 2 to 3 pieces of pepper on each 10-inch bamboo skewer (see Note, page 265). Grill over hot coals for 5 to 7 minutes, turning often and basting frequently with melted butter. Season to taste and serve immediately.

Wild Green Salad with Tart Lemon Dressing

One large handful of greens
per person, washed and
dried (Endive, escarole,
chicory, and dandelion
would go well with this
menu.)

TART LEMON DRESSING
MAKES APPROXIMATELY 1¼ CUPS

¼ cup freshly squeezed and
   strained lemon juice
1 egg yolk
¾ cup safflower oil
¼ cup olive oil
   Salt and freshly ground
   black pepper, to taste

Put the salad greens in a large bowl. Keep refrigerated, covered, until ready to serve.

To make the dressing, combine the lemon juice and egg yolk in the bowl of a food processor, and blend well. With the machine running, add the oils in a slow, steady stream. Scrape down the sides of the bowl and season to taste. Refrigerate until ready to use.

Immediately before serving, toss the greens with just enough dressing to coat. Serve from the bowl or arrange on individual salad plates.

Whole Wheat-Raisin French Rolls

MAKES 30 LARGE ROLLS OR 6
BAGUETTES

2½ cups warm water
1 2-ounce fresh cake yeast
2 tablespoons sugar
1 tablespoon salt
3 tablespoons cider vinegar
3 cups whole wheat flour
4 to 5 cups unbleached white
   flour
1 cup dark raisins
1 cup chopped walnuts
   (optional)
3 tablespoons walnut oil
2 egg whites, lightly beaten

Dissolve the yeast in the warm water with the sugar and let it stand until the yeast begins to "work." Add the salt and vinegar and stir until dissolved. Stir in the whole wheat flour. Add the white flour, 1 cup at a time, until the dough is manageable. Turn out onto a lightly floured board and knead by hand, adding only as much flour as necessary to make a smooth and elastic dough, about 10 to 15 minutes, or knead using the dough hook of an electric mixer. Knead in the raisins and walnuts, if desired, and shape into a round.

Rub the walnut oil over the entire surface of the dough and place in a bowl. Let rise, covered with plastic wrap, in a warm place until doubled in size, about 1½ to 2 hours.

Punch the dough down and let rise for another hour.

Divide the dough into thirty pieces, cutting with a pastry cutter. Form into round rolls by pinching the dough, drawing up the loose perimeter, never touching the floured bottom of the piece. Place the rolls, pinched side down, on buttered cookie sheets, leaving 3 inches between the rolls. Allow to rise, covered with plastic wrap or a warm damp cloth, until doubled in bulk. Slash tops of rolls with a sharp knife, brush with beaten egg whites, and bake in a preheated 400° oven until puffed and golden brown, about 18 to 20 minutes. To obtain a fine crust, spray rolls with water at least three times during the baking.

VARIATION: To make baguettes, after the second rising divide the dough into 6 equal pieces. Pat each into an oval, press down the middle of each with the edge of your hand, and fold the dough in half. Seal the edge with the heel of your hand, pressing hard to expel any air bubbles. Roll each oval into an even, cylindrical shape. Again, press down the middle with the edge of your hand, fold over, and seal edges and roll as if modeling clay. Place the baguettes into buttered French bread pans. Cover lightly with plastic wrap or a warm damp cloth and let rise until doubled in size. Uncover the loaves, and slash the top of each lengthwise with a sharp razor or knife, 3 or 4 cuts in each loaf. Bake the baguettes in a preheated 400° oven until golden brown and crispy, about 25 minutes. To obtain a fine crust, spray the loaves with water three or four times during the baking.

ABOVE: A stone-walled enclosure made a natural barbecue area for the reception. The buffet tables formed a divider that separated the guests from the "cooking" area. LEFT: Peppers cook on the grill. RIGHT: Baked tomatoes on a bed of yellow peppers.

Finger Food for a Crowd

~

MENU

HORS D'OEUVRES

Fresh Fruit, Vegetable, and Cheese Table

Raw Bar with Steamed Mussels

Heart Toasts with Salmon Roe Caviar and Sour Cream

Gravlax on Black Bread with Mustard-Fennel Sauce

Grilled Swordfish on Skewers

Grilled Eggplant and Squash on Skewers

Coconut Seviche · Pissaladière Niçoise

Prosciutto-Wrapped Melon

Homemade Sausage in Puff Pastry

Almond-Stuffed Dates Wrapped in Bacon

Carpaccio on French Bread

DESSERT

Wedding Cake

There is an immense amount of preparation in the creation of finger food for so large a number of guests as were entertained by the Childs family at the wedding of their daughter Shirley. The selection was large, ten hors d'oeuvres in all, plus a very big display of fruits and cheeses and breads. There were two extraordinary raw bars, with masses of clams, oysters, shrimp, and mussels. Rectangular "trays" carved from blocks of ice and huge ice-sculpted dolphins were specially made for the seafood bars, and these were much admired by the guests, most of whom loved the opulence of so much shellfish. Guests milled around these tables as well as near the four sixteen-foot-long bars of drinks, sipping and sampling. Iced vodkas were star attractions on the beverage bars. Tuxedoed waiters passed the

other hors d'oeuvres on trays of silver and glass, garnished with fresh flowers, beribboned posies, and clusters of herbs.

One of the garages, with a canopied front and tented walkways connecting it with the main reception tents, acted as our catering kitchen. Grilling was done on three Big John grills, which are five-foot-long grills on pipe legs. Three tall proofing cupboards, which are heated with Sterno, warmed the hors d'oeuvres that needed heating.

There were thirteen people manning the kitchen and grills, constructing hors d'oeuvres, and decorating the outgoing trays. As trays were returned, one person would wash and dry each tray before it was refilled with another finger food.

The food was served for more than three hours, during which time more than ten thousand individual hors d'oeuvres were served, three bushels of clams, four bushels of oysters, and almost two bushels of mussels. Fifty-one pounds of cheese were consumed from one large cheese table, along with innumerable fruits and slices of bread and crackers.

More than fifty-five trays were used to serve these various hors d'oeuvres. More than twenty cases of French champagne were consumed along with full bars of other wines and liquors. Guests were hungry and ate extremely well and long.

PRECEDING PAGE: This elaborately composed cheese, fruit, and vegetable display is arranged within a huge, specially constructed vine basket, garnished with leaves and flowers.

How to Assemble a Raw Bar

The usual components of a raw bar can include any or all of the following: clams on the half shell, oysters on the half shell, steamed mussels on the half shell, boiled crawfish, boiled shrimp (peeled or unpeeled), sea urchins, king crab claws, rock crab claws from Maine, or stone crab claws from Florida and crawfish from Louisiana. Allow 2 to 3 pieces of each shellfish variety per person. When determining how much seafood to buy, remember that:

1 bushel of littleneck clams holds approximately 225 to 250 clams

1 bushel of mussels (small to medium) holds approximately 500 mussels

1 bushel of oysters holds anywhere from 200 to 275 oysters

10 jumbo shrimp to the pound

18 large shrimp to the pound

35 small shrimp to the pound

King crab claws should be served chopped into pieces and cracked

Rock crab claws are purchased cooked and ready to eat

Stone crab claws, also purchased cooked, should be carefully cracked

In addition, you will need the following to assemble the bar:

A large shallow tray, fitted with a rubber tube drain

Lots of ice cubes and crushed ice

OPPOSITE AND ABOVE: Glorious Food catering is famous for its shell-shaped, carved-ice raw bar. A true work of art, it makes an extraordinary presentation.

Seaweed or decorative leaves and ferns for decoration

Lemon wedges or halves, preferably wrapped in cheesecloth

Bowls or shells to hold the sauces

Small spoons for serving the sauces

Baskets lined with leaves or ferns for discarded shells

For a large raw bar, hire two experienced workers to open the shellfish. Provide them with gloves, appropriate knives, wooden boards, and rinsing water. All the shellfish should be scrubbed clean and be kept very well iced until serving time.

The tray can be filled with ice, garnished, and filled with shellfish right before guests arrive. As the shellfish is eaten, it should be replenished with freshly opened clams and oysters, etc.

Raw Bar with Steamed Mussels

TOMATO-RED ONION SAUCE

MAKES APPROXIMATELY 1 QUART, ENOUGH FOR 50 PIECES OF SHELLFISH

8 ripe red tomatoes, peeled, seeded, and chopped
½ cup chopped fresh coriander
2 medium red onions, peeled and finely chopped
1 sweet red pepper, seeded and finely chopped
¼ cup balsamic vinegar
Salt and freshly ground black pepper, to taste

4 tablespoons (½ stick) unsalted butter
4 shallots, minced
2 cups dry white wine
3 tablespoons finely chopped parsley

Allow 3 or 4 raw shellfish per person (a combination of clams and oysters)
Fresh lemon wedges
3 to 4 steamed mussels per person (see Note)

Combine all ingredients for the tomato-red onion sauce and refrigerate until ready to use.

Arrange each mussel on one shell and keep chilled until ready to serve at the raw bar with the clams and oysters, lemon wedges, and tomato sauce.

NOTE: To steam the mussels, melt the butter in a deep, covered kettle and sauté the shallots. Add the wine and parsley and bring to a boil. Add scrubbed mussels (up to 4 quarts per large pot), cover, and cook for 4 minutes, shaking the pot frequently to cook the mussels evenly. Uncover the pot to see if the mussels have opened; if not, cover again and continue to check every minute. As soon as all (or most) of the mussels are opened, remove them from the kettle and let cool.

ABOVE: This wedding had a certain formality, and all the hors d'oeuvres (here, heart toasts with caviar and sour cream) were served from silver trays. BELOW: An oval silver tray filled with black bread rectangles topped with delicate salmon gravlax.

Heart Toasts with Salmon Roe Caviar and Sour Cream

MAKES 24 TO 30 HORS D'OEUVRES

8 thin slices Pain de Mie (below), or good store-bought white bread, sliced very thin
3½ ounces salmon roe caviar
¼ cup sour cream

Preheat the oven to 300°.

Cut the bread using a heart-shaped cookie or biscuit cutter small enough to yield 3 or 4 hearts per slice. Put the hearts on a baking sheet and bake until dry but not colored, about 10 minutes, turning after 5 minutes so that the edges do not curl. Remove from the oven and let cool on a wire rack.

To serve, spoon approximately ½ teaspoon of caviar onto each heart and top with a bit of sour cream (the sour cream can either be piped or spooned onto the heart toast).

VARIATIONS: Black caviar can also be used and whipped Crème Fraîche (page 291) substituted for the sour cream.

PAIN DE MIE
MAKES 2 LOAVES

1 2-ounce fresh cake yeast or 3 packages active dry yeast
½ cup warm water
5 teaspoons salt
4 cups warm milk
10 cups unbleached all-purpose flour
12 tablespoons (1½ sticks) unsalted butter, at room temperature

Dissolve the yeast in the warm water. Dissolve the salt in the warm milk. Be sure the temperature of the liquids does not exceed 100° or the yeast may not proof.

Combine the liquids in a large dough bowl or in a large mixer with a dough hook. Add the flour, 2 to 3 cups at a time, mixing with a wooden spoon or dough hook until a sticky dough is formed. Turn out on a floured board, continuing to add flour and kneading until all 10 cups of flour have been incorporated and the dough is somewhat smooth or continue mixing dough in mixer with dough hook until flour is incorporated. Add the butter, a tablespoon at a time, kneading until smooth. The dough will be slightly sticky.

Put the dough in a large bowl, cover with plastic wrap or a towel, and let it rise until almost tripled in bulk, about 2 to 3 hours. Punch down, knead for several minutes, and let rise a second time until doubled in bulk, about 1 more hour. Punch down and turn out on a floured board. Divide the dough in half (or two-thirds and one-third, depending upon the size of your pans). Flatten the dough into rectangle shapes the length of the pans; fold into thirds and put in two buttered pain de mie or 9 × 5 × 3-inch loaf pans. Press the dough carefully into the corners of the pans so air bubbles are broken. Cover the pans with sliding tops, if you are using traditional pain de mie pans, or with buttered cookie sheets and a heavy weight, and let rise until the dough fills two thirds of the pan.

Preheat the oven to 450°.

Bake for 30 to 40 minutes. Reduce the oven temperature to 375° and continue baking until the loaves are done, another 15 to 20 minutes. The bread should have risen to the tops of the pans, crusts should be golden brown, and sides slightly shrunk away from pan. When turned out, the loaves should sound hollow when tapped. If in doubt about doneness, return them to the oven and bake 5 to 10 minutes longer.

Turn out onto wire racks to cool, and wrap very well when cool. Pain de mie is best cut the second day. To keep it longer than 3 days, freeze well-wrapped bread.

To cut, slice with an electric slicer, if available, or with a serrated bread knife, into slices ⅛ inch to ¼ inch thick.

Gravlax on Black Bread with Mustard-Fennel Sauce

SEE RECIPE, PAGE 243.

Succulent grilled squares of swordfish served from bamboo skewers.

Diagonal slices of eggplant and summer squashes, another well-liked skewered food.

Fresh, tiny bay scallops are essential when making seviche.

Grilled Swordfish
on Skewers

MAKES 20 SKEWERS

½ cup peanut oil
3 tablespoons light soy sauce
1 tablespoon grated
  gingerroot
1 pound fresh swordfish, cut
  into ¾-inch cubes

Mix together the oil, soy sauce, and ginger, whisking to combine. Pour the marinade over the swordfish cubes, and marinate for 3 to 4 hours in the refrigerator.

Put 2 cubes of swordfish onto each 6-inch bamboo skewer (see Note) and grill over hot coals for 1 or 2 minutes, turning once. Serve immediately.

NOTE: Soak bamboo skewers in water for an hour before using, to prevent burning while grilling.

Grilled Eggplant and
Squash on Skewers

MAKES 10 TO 12 SKEWERS

½ cup olive oil
1 tablespoon chopped fresh
  coriander or parsley
1 garlic clove, finely minced
¼ teaspoon freshly ground
  black pepper
1 long light purple Japanese
  eggplant
1 large zucchini

Combine the olive oil, coriander or parsley, garlic, and pepper, whisking well. Set aside.

Cut the vegetables diagonally into ½-inch slices. Put one piece of each onto a 6-inch bamboo skewer (see Note), running the skewer through the diameter of each so they will hold while cooking, and alternating the bend of each slice (one should turn upwards, the other down). Grill over hot coals for 6 to 7 minutes, basting 2 or 3 times with the olive oil mixture, until the vegetable slices are tender. Serve immediately.

Coconut Seviche

MAKES 30 TO 40 SKEWERS

1 pound bay scallops
½ cup freshly squeezed lime
  juice
½ cup unsweetened coconut
  milk (see Note)
½ cup fresh grated coconut (or
  any unsweetened packaged
  brand)

Combine the scallops, lime juice, and coconut milk and refrigerate overnight, stirring occasionally.

Drain the scallops and place 2 or 3 on each 10-inch bamboo skewer (see Note). Sprinkle with or roll each skewer in the coconut, and grill over hot coals for 10 to 15 seconds. Serve immediately.

NOTE: To make coconut milk, combine ½ cup milk with ½ cup shredded fresh coconut. Bring to a boil and remove from heat. Strain the liquid; discard the coconut.

Pissaladière Niçoise

MAKES 84 HORS D'OEUVRES

PASTRY

9 tablespoons (1⅛ sticks)
  cold, unsalted butter, cut
  into small pieces
  Approximately 3½ cups all-
  purpose flour
2 teaspoons salt
1 fresh yeast cake
6 tablespoons lukewarm water
3 eggs, at room temperature,
  beaten

FILLING

3 pounds onions, peeled and
  coarsely chopped
¼ cup olive oil
8 ripe red tomatoes, peeled,
  seeded, and chopped
2 garlic cloves, peeled and
  crushed
  Salt and freshly ground
  black pepper, to taste

¼ pound Niçoise olives, pitted
  and sliced
10 anchovy fillets, drained and
  cut into thin strips
1 sweet red or green pepper,
  seeded, cored, and diced
½ cup chopped fresh oregano
  leaves or ¼ cup dried
  oregano

To make the pastry, cut the butter into the flour and salt until it resembles coarse meal.

Proof the yeast in the lukewarm water. Stir into the beaten eggs and set aside.

Make a well in the center of the flour mixture, and pour in the egg-yeast mixture. Stir together, then knead until the dough is smooth and no longer sticky. (You may have to add more flour to reach the proper consistency.) Shape the dough into a ball, put in a floured bowl, and let rise, covered, in a warm, draft-free place until doubled in volume, about 1 hour.

Waiters in white linen jackets offer elegant service at the buffet.

To make the filling, cook the onions in the olive oil over very low heat until soft and golden, about 45 minutes; do not let them brown. Add the tomatoes and garlic, raise heat, and cook until the water from the tomatoes has evaporated. Season with salt and pepper, remove from the heat, and let cool.

Butter an 11 × 17-inch baking sheet with sides, and set aside.

Pat down the dough, and knead until smooth. Press the dough into the pan, pushing it evenly into the edges and up the sides. Spoon the filling evenly over the pastry, and decoratively place the olives, anchovies, and peppers on top. Sprinkle with the chopped oregano. Preheat the oven to 400°.

Let the pissaladière rise for 15 minutes. Bake for 20 minutes, then reduce the heat to 350° and bake until the crust is puffed and evenly browned, about 20 minutes more. Slice and serve hot or at room temperature.

Prosciutto-Wrapped Melon

MAKES 32 SERVINGS

½ pound very thinly sliced prosciutto
1 ripe cantaloupe or honeydew melon

Cut each slice of prosciutto lengthwise into 3 strips.

Cut the melon in half lengthwise and scoop out the seeds with a wooden spoon, taking care not to bruise the flesh. Cut the melon into quarters; cut each section again into quarters. Using a sharp paring knife, remove the skin from each wedge, and cut each wedge in half. Wrap one strip of prosciutto around each piece of melon; the prosciutto should adhere to itself. Serve immediately.

VARIATIONS: Many other foods can be wrapped with prosciutto: papayas, mangoes, fresh figs, or blanched asparagus. Each should be cut into small, manageable pieces, and the fruits should be seeded.

Homemade Sausage in Puff Pastry

MAKES 90 HORS D'OEUVRES

1 pound Puff Pastry (page 286)
1 pound lean ground pork
¼ teaspoon ground allspice
¼ teaspoon ground cloves
2 tablespoons chopped fresh herbs (thyme, sage, and marjoram would be excellent)
½ teaspoon salt
¼ teaspoon freshly ground black pepper

Roll the puff pastry into a rectangle 15½ × 9 inches and cut the rectangle into three strips, each 3 inches wide.

To make the sausage meat, combine the pork, spices, herbs, salt, and pepper in a bowl. Divide the meat into thirds and roll each into a "snake" the length of the pastry. Place each roll of sausage along one edge of a pastry strip. Roll the pastry around the sausage and wet the edges with ice water and press to seal tightly. Chill the rolls for at least 1 hour.

Preheat the oven to 400°.

Cut the sausage rolls into ½-inch slices and put them on parchment-covered baking sheets. Bake until the pastry is puffed and golden brown, about 12 minutes. Serve warm, or reheat immediately before serving.

NOTE: The sausage rolls can be sliced and frozen before they are cooked. To bake, preheat the oven to 400° and cook as above.

TOP: Astilbe and thyme are simple garnish for a silver tray of pissaladière squares. MIDDLE: Lavender chive blossoms and sage leaves garnish this tray of prosciutto and melon. BOTTOM: Pink thyme lines this round silver tray of puff pastry sausage rolls.

Almond-Stuffed Dates Wrapped in Bacon

MAKES 60 HORS D'OEUVRES

1 pound whole pitted dates
4 ounces whole blanched almonds
1¼ pounds thinly sliced lean bacon, cut into thirds

Stuff each date with an almond, wrap with a piece of bacon, and secure with a round wooden toothpick.

Preheat the oven to 400°.

Put the dates on a foil-lined baking sheet and bake until the bacon is crisp, 12 to 15 minutes. Drain on a wire rack or on paper towels, and serve warm.

VARIATIONS: Wrap small sea scallops, water chestnuts, chicken livers, or oysters with bacon and broil until the bacon is crisp, approximately 6 minutes, turning once. Serve immediately.

NOTE: The stuffed and wrapped dates can also be frozen and baked, unthawed.

Carpaccio on French Bread

MAKES 30 HORS D'OEUVRES

CARPACCIO SAUCE
MAKES ¾ CUP

2 tablespoons white vinegar
6 cornichons
1 cup chopped fresh parsley
1 garlic clove
1 anchovy fillet
¼ cup capers, drained
2 tablespoons chopped onion
2½ tablespoons Dijon-style mustard
6 tablespoons olive oil

HERB BUTTER
MAKES ½ CUP

1 tablespoon finely chopped fresh parsley
1 tablespoon finely chopped fresh dill, chervil, or tarragon
8 tablespoons (1 stick) unsalted butter, at room temperature

1 Homemade French Bread baguette (page 247), warmed
½ pound very lean top round, sliced no more than ¹⁄₁₆ inch thick

LEFT: Flat-leaved Italian parsley decorates this tray of bacon-wrapped dates. RIGHT: Thin rounds of homemade French bread are covered with carpaccio; lunaria garnishes the tray. OPPOSITE: Bottles of iced vodka were carried to the bar on paper-napkin-covered trays.

To make the sauce, place all ingredients, except the oil, in the bowl of a food processor and chop coarsely. With the machine running, add the oil, drop by drop, until the mixture is creamy; do not overmix. Refrigerate, tightly covered, until ready to use.

To make herb butter, mix the chopped herbs and softened butter, by hand or in the bowl of a food processor, until well blended. Refrigerate, covered, until ready to use.

To serve, spread one side of the bread with a small amount of herb butter. Place a small piece of meat on top of the bread, covering the surface completely and "rippling" the meat if necessary. Spoon some sauce over the meat and serve.

VARIATION: Use red pepper butter instead of herb butter: combine half of a seeded roasted red pepper (see Note, page 277) and 1 stick of softened butter in the bowl of a food processor and purée until the mixture is smooth and the pepper finely chopped.

Small Sit-Down Lunch or Supper

※

A small sit-down lunch or supper of several courses is lovely and leisurely and a real treat for guests. This particular menu lends itself to last-minute preparation and careful serving. Each plate should be created in the kitchen or pantry and served plated to the guests. No hors d'oeuvres are served because the meal is substantial, and a lunch or supper does not require hors d'oeuvres.

The first course of sliced yellow tomatoes, buffalo mozzarella, and opal basil is a well-liked combination. If you are unable to find the yellow tomatoes, substitute ripe red plum tomatoes, sliced lengthwise.

The pasta course of homemade red and yellow pepper pasta, is served with a fresh red tomato sauce.

MENU

FIRST COURSE
Sliced Tomatoes with Mozzarella and Basil

PASTA COURSE
Red and Yellow Pepper Pasta
with Fresh Tomato Sauce

MAIN COURSE
Pistolets
Lemon Chicken with Herb-Sautéed Lemon Slices
Summer Salad with Lime-Champagne Vinaigrette

DESSERT
Wedding Cake

The lemon chicken is superb and simple to make. Most lemon chicken recipes call for sautéing or frying. In this recipe, the chicken is marinated in a mixture of lemon, crème fraîche, and herbs, then oven-poached and sauced. Herb-sautéed lemon slices are a tasty garnish.

We have always been known for our use of flowers as garnishes, but recently I have also become an advocate of edible flowers in salads and beverages. The nasturtium is the most popular edible flower, and this summer salad of unusual greens is colorfully garnished with this spicy, tender flower. Violas, violets, chive and allium blossoms, borage flowers, and rose petals can also be used as edible parts of salads.

Sliced Tomatoes with Mozzarella and Basil

SERVES 10 TO 12

8 large ripe red or yellow tomatoes, sliced ⅜ inch thick
1 pound fresh or smoked mozzarella, sliced ¼ inch thick
10 sprigs small-leaf basil or 10 large red basil leaves, torn into small pieces
6 tablespoons extra virgin olive oil
   Coarse salt and freshly ground black pepper, to taste

Alternate slices of tomatoes and mozzarella on a platter. Sprinkle with basil, drizzle with olive oil, and season with salt and pepper.

Red and Yellow Pepper Pasta with Fresh Tomato Sauce

SERVES 10 TO 12

3 sweet red peppers, seeded
3 sweet yellow peppers, seeded
2 large egg yolks
   Pinch of salt
   Pinch of cayenne pepper
6 to 8 cups all-purpose flour
   Yellow cornmeal for dusting

FRESH TOMATO SAUCE

1 cup balsamic vinegar
¼ cup fresh rosemary leaves
1 cup heavy cream
   Pinch of cayenne pepper
8 large ripe red tomatoes, peeled, seeded, and chopped
   Salt and freshly ground black pepper, to taste

   Freshly grated Parmesan cheese

   GARNISH: Fresh rosemary sprigs

PRECEDING PAGE: Pistol-handled flatware, simple rimmed plates, and summer flowers make an elegant setting for a colorful second course of homemade red and yellow pasta. LEFT: The first course of golden yellow tomato slices and mozzarella garnished with red opal basil.

To make the pasta, purée the red peppers in the bowl of a food processor. Add 1 egg yolk, a pinch of salt and cayenne pepper, and process until the mixture is smooth and there are no large pieces of red pepper. Add 1½ cups flour and mix well. Continue adding flour, ½ cup at a time, and processing until the dough becomes stiff and smooth. It will eventually hold together and form a ball, pulling away cleanly from the sides of the bowl; you will use 3 to 4 cups flour. Remove the dough, kneading in a bit more flour if it sticks to your hands. Shape into a ball and place under an overturned bowl to keep it from drying out.

Divide the dough into ½-cup amounts, and pass each piece through the widest setting of a pasta machine. Reduce the setting by one notch and pass it through again. Repeat until the desired thickness of dough is reached. Dry the broad pasta for a few minutes on a pasta drying rack.

Set the machine on fettuccine width and pass the broad noodles through it. Dust each batch with a bit of cornmeal to prevent the strips from sticking together. Cover the pasta, or place it in a plastic bag, so that it remains fresh and moist, and refrigerate until ready to use.

Repeat this process with the yellow peppers to make the yellow pepper pasta.

To make the sauce, combine the vinegar and fresh rosemary in a small saucepan and reduce by half. Remove from the heat and whisk in the cream and a pinch of cayenne pepper. Stir in the tomatoes and season to taste. Keep the sauce warm while you cook the pasta.

Bring two large pots of lightly salted water to a boil and cook the two types of pasta separately for 2 to 3 minutes, just until al dente. Drain well.

To serve, arrange portions of the cooked pasta on individual salad plates, and spoon a small amount of the sauce on top. Sprinkle with freshly grated Parmesan cheese and garnish with sprigs of fresh rosemary. Serve immediately.

Pistolets

SEE RECIPE VARIATION, PAGE 247.

Lemon Chicken with Herb-Sautéed Lemon Slices

SERVES 10 TO 12

6 chicken breasts, skinned, boned, halved lengthwise and halved again

MARINADE

½ cup dry white wine
 Grated rind of 2 lemons
½ cup freshly squeezed lemon juice
¼ cup Crème Fraîche (page 291)
2 tablespoons vegetable oil
¼ cup coarsely chopped fresh herbs (thyme, parsley, rosemary, etc.)
½ teaspoon coarsely ground black pepper

HERB BUTTER

8 tablespoons (1 stick) unsalted butter, melted with 1 tablespoon chopped fresh herbs (parsley, dill, thyme, etc.)

CREAM SAUCE

½ cup heavy cream
½ cup Crème Fraîche (page 291)
2 tablespoons Cognac
1 tablespoon brown sugar
 Salt and freshly ground black pepper, to taste

GARNISH: Slices of lemon ¼-inch thick sautéed in additional herb butter

Cut each half chicken breast in half again lengthwise so that you have two neat strips. Arrange the strips in a single layer in a glass or stainless steel casserole.

Combine all marinade ingredients in a small bowl, whisking to blend, and pour over the chicken. Cover with plastic wrap and refrigerate overnight, preferably for 24 hours.

Remove the chicken from the marinade, pat dry, and place in a single layer on a baking sheet. Let the chicken return to room temperature. Preheat the oven to 375°.

The tempting main course of lemon chicken, garden salad, and pistolet.

When the chicken has reached room temperature, bake until done but still tender, 15 to 20 minutes, brushing occasionally with the melted herb butter. Remove from the oven and let cool to room temperature.

To make the sauce, place the cream, crème fraîche, Cognac, and brown sugar in a saucepan, and reduce to the consistency of thick cream. Season to taste and let cool.

Arrange the chicken on a serving platter and spoon the sauce over it. Garnish with sautéed lemon slices and serve.

Summer Salad with Lime-Champagne Vinaigrette

SERVES 10 TO 12

Radicchio
Nasturtium blossoms
Chives
Baby spinach
Borage flowers

LIME-CHAMPAGNE VINAIGRETTE

MAKES APPROXIMATELY 1½ CUPS

¼ cup champagne vinegar
1 tablespoon Dijon-style mustard
1 cup vegetable oil, preferably safflower or sunflower
¼ cup light olive oil
1 tablespoon freshly squeezed lime juice
 Finely grated zest of 1 lime
 Salt and freshly ground black pepper, to taste

Wash and dry the greens and put in a large bowl. Keep refrigerated, covered, until ready to serve.

Whisk together all the ingredients for the dressing and refrigerate until ready to use.

Immediately before serving, toss the greens with just enough dressing to coat.

Very Special Chicken Dinner

Many of my catering clients, when interviewed about their wedding reception plans, specify immediately "No chicken!" Asked why, their reply generally has to do with not wanting to appear "cheap" or ordinary. However, with most of us eating more carefully nowadays, and with less red meat being consumed, beautifully prepared chicken menus are becoming popular or are at least being considered.

This menu is simple but elegant. There is only one hors d'oeuvre served with cocktails—delicate hearts of puff pastry filled with creamy wild mushrooms. Guests then sit down to a first course of red pepper-parsnip soup.

The main course consists of plump whole boned chicken breasts that are filled with an herbed bread stuffing, which was carefully placed under the

skin of each breast. This method works well with a variety of fillings (a spinach/chèvre variation is also given). The breasts can be stuffed the day before the party and baked or roasted several hours prior to serving. Though best served hot from the oven, they can be reheated successfully or served at room temperature, or even served cold, sliced. The yellow pepper custard is excellent and can be made in individual ramekins or in larger casseroles and spooned to each guest. The beet-carrot-radicchio sauté, served in individual leaves of radicchio, is extremely colorful and delicious. It is flavored and garnished with fresh rosemary.

The tables were set with white antique linens and the bride's collection of Canton and Meissen plates, which set off the whiteness of the tables and flowers and also the decorative food.

MENU

HORS D'OEUVRES
Wild Mushroom Heart Puffs

FIRST COURSE
Red Pepper-Parsnip Soup

MAIN COURSE
Beet-Carrot-Radicchio Sauté · Yellow Pepper Custard
Old-Fashioned Bread-Stuffed Chicken Breasts

DESSERT
Wedding Cake

Wild Mushroom Heart Puffs

MAKES 5 DOZEN HORS D'OEUVRES

⅔ pound Puff Pastry (page 286)

GLAZE: 1 egg yolk beaten with 1 tablespoon cream

4 large fresh chanterelle mushrooms, chopped
4 large fresh shiitake mushrooms, chopped
Approximately 2 tablespoons unsalted butter
¼ cup Armagnac, Cognac, or brandy
1 to 1¼ cups Crème Fraîche (page 291)

Roll out the pastry into a rectangle no more than ⅛ inch thick. Cut pastry into 1½-inch hearts with a heart-shaped cookie cutter. For other shapes, use a zigzag. Place the cutouts 1½ inches apart on parchment-lined baking sheets and refrigerate for at least 30 minutes.

Preheat the oven to 400°.

Using a ⅝-inch round biscuit cutter, make an indentation in the center of each cut-out (do not cut through the pastry). Brush lightly with the egg glaze and bake for 12 to 15 minutes, until puffed and golden. Remove from the oven and let cool on wire racks.

When the puffs have cooled, use a sharp paring knife to cut through the indentations. Pull out the centers with your fingertips and discard.

Make the chanterelle and shiitake fillings separately but following the same procedure: Melt approximately 2 teaspoons butter in a skillet and add approximately 1 tablespoon Armagnac, Cognac, or brandy (you may need a bit more butter for sautéing the shiitakes as they tend to absorb more). Sauté the mushrooms only a minute. Whisk in approximately ½ cup crème fraîche and another tablespoon of Armagnac (or to taste); add more crème fraîche if necessary to obtain a thick but manageable consistency. Remove the filling from the heat but keep warm.

To serve, spoon ½ teaspoon of warm mushroom filling into the cavity of each puff and serve immediately.

PRECEDING PAGE: A pressed-glass flower container, full of narcissus, white lilacs, and baby carnations.

ABOVE: A hobnail opalescent glass plate holds heart-shaped puffs filled with wild mushrooms.

Red Pepper-Parsnip Soup

SERVES 10 TO 12

- 5 sweet red peppers
- 6 tablespoons (¾ stick) unsalted butter
- 3 shallots, peeled and minced
- 2 garlic cloves, peeled and minced
- 2 ripe pears, peeled, seeded, and cut into chunks
- 2 pounds parsnips, peeled and cut into chunks
- 3 quarts chicken stock, preferably homemade
  Salt and freshly ground black pepper, to taste

GARNISH: Approximately ½ cup **Crème Fraîche (page 291)**
Fresh cilantro leaves

Seed, core, and thinly slice 3 red peppers and set aside. Roast the other 2 according to the Note, below, and slice thinly.

Melt the butter in a large heavy saucepan. Sauté the unroasted red peppers, shallots, garlic, and pears over low heat for about 10 minutes, until tender but not browned. Add the parsnips and chicken stock, bring to a boil, and simmer until the parsnips are very tender, about 35 to 40 minutes. Let cool slightly.

Purée the mixture (2 to 3 cups at a time, or as much as your machine will hold) in a food processor or blender until smooth, adding two thirds of the roasted peppers. Season with salt and pepper. Return to the saucepan and reheat.

To serve, place several small dollops of crème fraîche on top of the soup, and, using a kitchen knife, swirl it through the soup. Garnish with a strip of the reserved roasted pepper and a cilantro leaf. This soup may also be served at room temperature.

NOTE: The red peppers can be roasted either under a very hot broiler or directly over a gas flame (if using a broiler, make sure it is preheated). To roast, rotate the peppers with tongs until completely blackened. Place them in a paper bag or wrap in paper towels to "sweat" for 5 to 10 minutes. Rub off the charred skin and remove the seeds.

Red pepper-parsnip soup topped with swirls of crème fraîche is a bright and cheerful first course.

Beet-Carrot-Radicchio Sauté

SERVES 12

5 medium beets, unpeeled
1½ pounds baby carrots
2 small heads radicchio
3 tablespoons unsalted butter
2 tablespoons balsamic
    vinegar
1 tablespoon chopped fresh
    rosemary

GARNISH: Sprigs of fresh
rosemary

Preheat the oven to 350°. Cut off all but 1 inch of the beet tops and wrap the beets in aluminum foil. Bake for approximately 1 hour, until the beets are tender. Let the beets cool, then slip them from their skins. Grate or julienne and set aside.

Peel the carrots and blanche them in a pot of rapidly boiling water for approximately 7 minutes, until tender. Drain well and set aside.

Remove and reserve 12 large outer leaves of radicchio. Cut the remaining radicchio into a fine chiffonade and set aside.

Combine the butter, vinegar, and chopped rosemary in a large skillet, and heat to melt the butter. Stir the mixture, add the carrots, and sauté for about 5 minutes, until heated through. Remove to a large serving bowl and keep warm. Add the grated beets to the skillet and warm through. Add the beets to the warm carrots, then add the radicchio chiffonade and toss gently but thoroughly.

Put the reserved whole radicchio leaves on individual salad plates, spoon equal amounts of the vegetable mixture into the leaves, letting it "spill" out, garnish with a sprig of fresh rosemary, and serve.

The main course of chicken, yellow pepper custard, and sautéed beets, carrots, and radicchio was served from patterned Meissen plates.

The filling for the stuffed chicken breasts is gently spooned under the loosened skin.

Yellow Pepper Custard

SERVES 12

2 egg yolks, lightly beaten
2 whole eggs, lightly beaten
1 cup heavy cream
1 cup milk
½ cup crumbled chèvre
  Freshly grated nutmeg, to
  taste
  Salt and freshly ground
  white pepper, to taste
5 roasted sweet yellow
  peppers (see Note, page
  277), cored and thinly sliced

Preheat the oven to 350°. Lightly oil 12 ramekins or small fluted porcelain tartlet pans and set aside.

Whisk together the egg yolks, eggs, cream, milk, chèvre, and nutmeg until well combined. Season with salt and white pepper.

Put pepper slices into the bottom of the ramekins and cover with the custard mixture. Bake in a hot water bath in the oven for approximately 30 minutes, or until the custard is set. Serve warm.

Old-Fashioned Bread-Stuffed Chicken Breasts

SERVES 12

2 medium onions, peeled and
  finely chopped
2 garlic cloves, minced
8 tablespoons (1 stick)
  unsalted butter
4 cups bread cubes (about ¼
  inch) cut from Pain de Mie
  (page 264) or brioche
1 tablespoon chopped fresh
  green herbs (parsley, chives,
  dill, tarragon, chervil)
  Salt and freshly ground
  black pepper, to taste
6 whole chicken breasts,
  halved and boned, skin left
  on
1 cup Herb Butter (page 273),
  melted

Preheat the oven to 350°. Butter a baking dish large enough to hold the chicken breasts in one layer.

Sauté the onions and garlic in the butter until soft; do not brown. Add the bread cubes; toss well until all the butter is absorbed by the bread and the bread is evenly coated. Stir in the chopped herbs and season well with salt and pepper.

Place each breast half skin side up on a board and trim away any excess fat. Gently loosen the skin from one side of the breast and stuff approximately ⅓ cup of bread filling under the skin. Tuck the skin and meat underneath, forming an even, round shape. Put the stuffed breasts in the prepared baking dish, brush with a bit of melted herb butter, and roast until golden brown, 35 to 40 minutes. Baste occasionally while baking with more herb butter. (Do not overcook or the meat will dry out.) Remove from the oven and serve hot or warm.

VARIATIONS: Chicken breasts can also be stuffed with a Chèvre, Spinach, Wild Mushrooms, and Herb Stuffing (recipe follows); or glazed with a bit of melted red pepper jelly before baking.

Chèvre, Spinach, Wild Mushrooms, and Herb Stuffing

SUFFICIENT FOR 12 CHICKEN
BREAST HALVES

2 tablespoons unsalted butter
1 medium onion, finely
  chopped
¼ pound wild mushrooms,
  thinly sliced
1 10-ounce package frozen
  chopped spinach, thawed
  and drained
8 ounces chèvre, at room
  temperature
½ cup ricotta cheese, at room
  temperature
1 egg, lightly beaten
¼ cup chopped fresh parsley
1 tablespoon *each* fresh
  thyme, chervil, and oregano
  leaves
  Salt and freshly ground
  black pepper, to taste

Preheat the oven to 350° and prepare a pan as in the preceding recipe. Melt half the butter in a medium skillet and sauté the onion until soft; remove from the skillet. Melt the remaining butter and sauté the mushrooms a minute or two. Set aside.

Combine the spinach, chèvre, ricotta, egg, and herbs, and mix well. Stir in the sautéed onion and mushrooms. Season to taste.

Follow the instructions for stuffing the breasts as in the preceding recipe. Put the stuffed chicken breasts in the prepared pan and bake 30 to 35 minutes, or just until the juices run clear when the chicken is pierced with a fork; do not overcook or the chicken will be dry. Serve hot, cold, or at room temperature, sliced or whole.

Cocktails and Cake

This young couple wanted the epitome of the sophisticated New York cocktail party for their wedding reception. The space was elegant—a lovely Romanesque cathedral in New York. The music—contemporary jazz. The guests—Wall Street, Hollywood, Fairfield County. The time—late afternoon. The weather—perfect New York— warm, clear, gentle breezes.

We catered this affair with an assortment of delicate, smallish hors d'oeuvres. We served them on silver platters, intricate baskets, and huge china platters. We wanted the appearance of the food to be romantic as well as sophisticated, so we covered some trays with lace doilies (washable, reusable), others with soft mounds of fresh green thyme. Pearl balls were served on lemon leaf-covered trays garnished with lavender iris. Stuffed snow peas were garnished with the flowers from snow pea vines.

Two bars were set up, one outside near a dozen small cocktail tables, which were shaded by ancient trees and cathedral shadows, the other indoors in one of the main reception rooms. The musicians were at home indoors, where their music could be enjoyed without competition from New York traffic.

The champagne and all the hors d'oeuvres were passed on trays by waiters attired in black tie. The cake was made by a friend of the bride's mother and was displayed indoors amid beautiful flowers on a large round table.

The reception, enlivened by dancing and toasts, lasted approximately three hours, very much in keeping with the cocktail-party theme. Guests left happy, while it was still light.

MENU

HORS D'OEUVRES

Yeast Blini with Sour Cream and Black Caviar

Tarragon Chicken Salad on Nut Bread

Smoked Turkey on Currant Scones

Snow Peas Stuffed with Pimiento Cheese

Chinese Pearl Balls

Smoked Salmon Mousse on Cucumber Hearts

Carrot Lace Fritters

Tartlets with Melted Brie and Herbs

Puff Pastry Cheese Straws

Roquefort Grapes

Ham on Cranberry-Orange Muffins

DESSERT

Wedding Cake

PRECEDING PAGE: A stately wedding cake with its basketweave frosting and decoration of white roses and freesias.

LEFT: Garden phlox made a lovely garnish for the cucumber hearts.

OPPOSITE PAGE, TOP ROW, LEFT TO RIGHT: Puff pastry cheese straws were served from white wicker trays lined with a small dresser doily and decorated with a posy of herbs; the Roquefort grapes looked like eggs in a fluffy nest when served from a tray completely covered with pink creeping thyme, which was flowering at the time we cut it; carrot lace fritters looked even lacier served atop a mound of alfalfa sprouts.

CENTER ROW, LEFT TO RIGHT: Blini topped with caviar and a squiggle of sour cream. Small wooden heart boxes served as tiny flower holders; freesia, flowering thyme, and a delicate crochet-work dresser scarf cover this tray of cheese tartlets; rice-coated pearl balls were carefully placed atop individual lemon leaves. The tray was garnished with Higo iris.

BOTTOM ROW, LEFT TO RIGHT: A crochet doily covered another tray, which was filled with heart-shaped scones; pink astilbe and chives added interest to this lace-covered tray of nut bread slices topped with chicken salad; sweet peas garnished a tray of stuffed snow pea pods.

Yeast Blini with Sour Cream and Black Caviar

MAKES 40 HORS D'OEUVRES

BLINI

1 package active dry yeast
½ cup warm water
1 cup milk
1½ cups all-purpose flour
3 eggs, separated
½ teaspoon salt
Pinch of sugar
6 tablespoons (¾ stick) unsalted butter, melted, plus additional for cooking

3½ ounces black caviar
1 cup thick sour cream

To make the blini, first proof the yeast in the warm water for 15 minutes.

Combine the yeast mixture, milk, flour, egg yolks, salt, sugar, and 6 table-spoons melted butter in the bowl of a food processor or blender. Process at high speed for 40 seconds; turn off the machine, scrape down the sides, and blend for few seconds more. Pour the batter into a large bowl (it will double in volume so the bowl must accommodate this), cover, and set in a warm place for 1½ to 2 hours. (If the dough rises much longer than this, the blini may taste overfermented.)

Immediately before cooking the blini, beat the egg whites until stiff and fold them into the batter. Drop the batter by tea-spoonfuls onto a hot buttered skillet or griddle, and cook until lightly browned. Turn and briefly cook the other side. Keep the blini on a warm platter until all the batter is used, then place on a serving tray or platter. Put a few grains of caviar on top of each blini, and then a small amount of sour cream. Serve immediately.

Tarragon Chicken Salad on Nut Bread

MAKES 40 HORS D'OEUVRES

2 whole chicken breasts
3 tablespoons sour cream
3 tablespoons Homemade Mayonnaise (page 229)
1 tablespoon fresh tarragon leaves, chopped, or ½ teaspoon dried tarragon
½ cup finely chopped celery
¼ cup chopped pecans
Salt and freshly ground black pepper, to taste

Nut Bread (see Variation, page 253)

GARNISH: Fresh herbs (thyme, oregano, etc.)

Poach the chicken breasts in simmer-ing water to cover until done, 25 to 30 min-utes. Do not overcook. Remove the chicken from the poaching liquid and cool completely.

Remove the skin and bones from the chicken breasts and cut or tear the meat into small pieces, and put it in a mixing bowl.

Mix the sour cream and mayonnaise together and stir into the chicken, a little at a time, just until the mixture is creamy. Gently stir in the tarragon, celery, and nuts, and sea-son with salt and pepper.

To serve, thinly slice the nut bread and cut each slice in half (or into thirds de-pending on the loaf size). Spoon a small amount of chicken salad onto the bread, gar-nish as desired with fresh herbs, and serve.

VARIATIONS: Add ½ cup finely chopped apple, 1 tablespoon mild curry powder, or ¼ cup rum-soaked dried currants to the chicken salad.

The chicken salad can be served on other types of bread or on biscuits, as well as on cucumber slices.

Smoked Turkey on Currant Scones

MAKES 40 HORS D'OEUVRES

CURRANT SCONES

4½ cups sifted all-purpose flour
2 teaspoons baking powder
½ teaspoon baking soda
2 tablespoons sugar
Pinch of salt
½ pound (2 sticks) unsalted butter, cut into small pieces
1 cup dried currants, soaked overnight in 3 tablespoons brandy
1 to 1¼ cups heavy cream

GLAZE: 1 egg beaten with ¼ cup light cream

½ pound thinly sliced smoked turkey or turkey breast
½ cup grape jelly, cranberry relish, or red currant jelly

Sift the dry ingredients into a large mixing bowl. Using a pastry blender or two kitchen knives, cut in the butter until the mixture resembles coarse meal. (This can also be done in a food processor, using half the flour mixture, and adding the processed mix-ture to the remaining flour before adding the currants and cream.) Stir in the drained currants.

Mixing lightly with your fingers, add just enough heavy cream to hold the mix-ture together. Wrap in plastic wrap and chill approximately 30 minutes or overnight.

Preheat the oven to 375°. Lightly butter a large baking sheet.

Roll out the dough ½ inch thick, and, using a biscuit or cookie cutter, cut the dough into various shapes: 1½-inch hearts, scalloped rounds, or plain rounds. Place on the prepared baking sheet, brush the tops lightly with the glaze, and bake until golden brown and puffed, 13 to 15 minutes. Let cool on a wire rack.

To serve, put a small amount of smoked turkey on a split scone that has been spread with a small amount of jelly or relish.

VARIATIONS: Scones can also be made without currants, or by substituting ¼ cup caraway seeds, ¼ cup poppy seeds, ¼ cup finely chopped fresh dill, or ¼ cup minced candied orange peel for the currants.

Smoked turkey can be served on any kind of tiny muffin. Baked or smoked ham would also be a delicious filling for scones or muffins.

Snow Peas Stuffed with Pimiento Cheese

MAKES 36 HORS D'OEUVRES

36 tender young snow peas
 8 ounces cream cheese
 1 sweet red pepper, roasted and peeled
 1 small red chili pepper, seeded and chopped very fine
    Salt and freshly ground black pepper, to taste

Remove the stem end from the snow peas, string them, and blanch in a large pot of rapidly boiling water for 30 seconds. Plunge them immediately into cold water to stop the cooking and preserve their green color. Set aside.

In the bowl of a food processor fitted with a metal blade, purée the roasted red pepper and red chili pepper. Pour off any liquid, keeping the purée in the bowl. Add the softened cream cheese and process until smooth and creamy. Season with salt and black pepper, and chill until ready to use.

With a small sharp knife, slit open the straight seam of each snow pea and pipe the softened pimiento cheese into each one, using a small tip pastry tube.

Chinese Pearl Balls

MAKES 36 HORS D'OEUVRES

¾ cup sweet or glutinous rice
 6 dried brown Chinese mushrooms
 1 pound lean pork, finely ground
 1 egg, lightly beaten
 1 tablespoon soy sauce
½ teaspoon sugar
 2 teaspoons finely minced gingerroot
 8 water chestnuts, finely chopped
 2 scallions, finely chopped

Soak the rice in water to cover for 4 hours. Drain, pat dry, and set aside.

Soak the mushrooms in ½ cup warm water for 1 hour. Drain and discard the stems. Chop the caps finely.

Mix together all ingredients, except the rice; blend well. (Your hands are best for this job.) Shape into 1-inch balls.

Spread the rice on a baking sheet and roll the pearl balls, one at a time, in it, coating each completely. Set them on a baking sheet lined with wax paper and refrigerate for up to 4 hours. (The pearl balls may also be frozen at this point.)

Set a steamer in a pan or wok and add enough water to come to within 1 inch of the bottom of the steamer. Bring the water to a boil, put the balls on a steamer rack, and cover and steam for 30 minutes. Serve immediately.

NOTE: If the balls have been frozen, defrost to room temperature and steam as above.

Smoked Salmon Mousse on Cucumber Hearts

SEE RECIPE, PAGE 243.

Carrot Lace Fritters

MAKES 30 HORS D'OEUVRES

BATTER

 2 tablespoons flour
 3 eggs, lightly beaten
    Salt and freshly ground black pepper, to taste

 2 cups coarsely grated carrots
 2 teaspoons grated gingerroot
½ teaspoon chopped fresh tarragon
    Vegetable oil for frying

GARNISH: Alfalfa sprouts

Mix the batter ingredients together in a medium bowl until smooth. Add the grated carrots, ginger, and chopped tarragon and combine thoroughly.

Heat a small amount of vegetable oil (about ⅛ inch) in a heavy skillet, and drop the batter in the hot oil by tablespoons, frying until golden, about 2 to 3 minutes on each side. Drain well on paper towels and serve hot on small nests of alfalfa sprouts.

NOTE: We have discovered that the slicer-shredder attachment for the Kitchen Aid works very well for grating the vegetables.

VARIATIONS: To make other vegetable fritters, add the following to the batter: 2 cups coarsely grated zucchini, 2 finely chopped shallots, and 2 tablespoons chopped fresh parsley; or 2 cups grated parsnips, 2 finely chopped scallions, and ½ teaspoon freshly grated nutmeg; or 2 cups grated white turnip, 1 small onion, chopped, 1 peeled and grated carrot, 1 tablespoon chopped coriander, and a pinch of ground cinnamon.

Tartlets with Melted Brie and Herbs

MAKES TWENTY-FOUR 1- TO
1½-INCH TARTLETS

PÂTE BRISÉE
2½ cups all-purpose flour
1 teaspoon salt
½ pound (2 sticks) cold
  unsalted butter, cut into
  small pieces
¼ to ½ cup ice water

½ pound Brie, cut into small
  pieces
4 to 6 sprigs fresh herbs
  (tarragon, parsley, thyme,
  etc.)

To make the tartlet shells, place the flour and salt in the bowl of a food processor. Add the pieces of butter and process approximately 10 seconds, or just until the mixture resembles coarse meal. Add just enough water, a drop at a time, until the dough holds together without being wet or sticky; this should take only 10 to 15 seconds. Turn the dough out onto a large piece of plastic wrap, and, grasping the ends of the plastic wrap with your hands and making a fist, press the dough into a flat circle. Wrap well in the plastic and chill at least an hour.

To form the tartlets you will need twice as many tartlet pans as the number of tartlets you plan to make. Lightly butter or spray with vegetable oil the insides of half the pans.

On a lightly floured board, roll out the pastry to a thickness of no more than ⅛ inch, moving the pastry around continually and turning it over once or twice to prevent it from sticking. Put half the tartlet pans on the rolled-out pastry and, with a sharp knife, cut the pastry into pieces slightly larger than the pans. Place the pastry in the prepared pans, pressing firmly, and cut off the excess pastry with your thumbs. Press an unbuttered pan into each pastry-lined one (this will act as a weight to keep the pastry from puffing up while baking). Set the tartlets on a baking sheet and chill for at least 30 minutes.

Preheat the oven to 375°.

To bake the tartlet shells, place an-

other baking sheet on top of the tartlets (this will act as an additional weight), and bake until the pastry begins to color around the edges, 10 to 12 minutes. Remove the baking sheet and liner tartlet pans, and bake just until the pastry dries out and turns a light golden color. Remove the shells from the pans and cool completely on a wire rack.

Preheat the oven to 350°. To assemble the tartlets, place a small piece or two of Brie in each tartlet shell and top with an herb leaf. Bake just until the cheese melts. Serve immediately.

VARIATION: These tartlets can also be filled with custard and baked. Pour a small amount of custard (made by whisking together 1½ cups heavy cream, 3 eggs, a pinch of ground nutmeg, and salt and pepper to taste) into each cheese-filled tartlet shell, top with herbs, and bake in a preheated 350° oven until the custard is set, approximately 10 to 15 minutes. Serve warm.

NOTE: Unbaked tartlet shells can be refrigerated, well-wrapped, for up to 1 day, or they can be frozen. Baked tartlet shells can be cushioned with wax paper and stored in a tightly covered container for up to 2 days, or frozen and recrisped in a 350° oven.

Puff Pastry Cheese Straws

MAKES 10 DOZEN 10-INCH STRAWS

1 pound Puff Pastry (recipe follows)
½ cup finely grated Parmesan
  or Gruyère cheese

Divide the pastry into three parts and cover and refrigerate 2 portions. Roll out the remaining pastry into a rectangle 10 inches wide and no more than ⅛ inch thick. Sprinkle a third of the cheese over the pastry and firmly press it into the dough with a rolling pin. Using a very sharp knife (or a zigzag pastry wheel), cut the pastry into strips ½ inch wide. Carefully twist the strips and place them on a parchment-lined or water-sprayed

baking sheet and refrigerate until all the pastry is rolled out and cut.

Preheat the oven to 400°.

Bake the straws until puffed and lightly golden, about 8 to 10 minutes. Let cool and serve.

NOTE: If the cheese straws are not to be used immediately, they should be frozen. Reheat without defrosting in a 350° oven until crisp.

VARIATION: Puff pastry straws can be made by omitting the cheese and rolling ½ cup poppy seeds, ½ cup light sesame seeds, or a light sprinkling of cayenne pepper into the pastry before it is cut.

Puff Pastry

MAKES APPROXIMATELY
2½ POUNDS

1 pound all-purpose flour,
  very accurately weighed
1 pound (4 sticks) cold
  unsalted butter, cut into
  small pieces
1 teaspoon salt
1 cup heavy cream (or ½ cup
  heavy cream mixed with ½
  cup ice water)

In the bowl of a food processor or using the flat paddle of an electric mixer, mix ½ cup flour with the butter until very smooth. Shape the mixture into a square 1-inch thick, wrap well in plastic wrap, and chill at least 30 minutes.

Combine the salt with the remaining flour in a large mixing bowl and add the cream (or the cream-and-water mixture). Mix the dough well by hand or with an electric mixer; the dough will not be completely smooth but it should not be sticky. Shape this dough into a flat 1½-inch-thick square, wrap in plastic wrap, and chill.

Remove the flour dough from the refrigerator. Cut a + into the top of the square and roll the dough into a cross. Place the butter in the center of the cross, fold the ends up to completely encase the butter and seal the edges. Wrap well in plastic wrap and chill for at least 30 minutes so that the dough and the butter are the same temperature.

Remove the dough from the refrigerator and roll it out into a large rectangle approximately ½ inch thick. Fold the dough into thirds, matching the edges as carefully as possible and brushing off any excess flour. It is very important that the butter be distributed evenly between the layers of flour and cream/water so that the pastry will puff evenly when baked. Wrap the dough and chill for at least 30 minutes. This completes one "turn."

Repeat this entire process five more times; classic puff pastry gets six turns. Use as little flour as possible when rolling out the dough and always brush off any excess. (I use a 4-inch brush.) Remember to let the dough rest for at least 30 minutes in the refrigerator between turns; the cooling process can be speeded up in the freezer.

By the sixth and final turn, the dough should be very smooth with no lumps of butter visible. Wrap the pastry in plastic wrap and refrigerate until ready to use (up to 2 days), or freeze for future use. (I usually divide the dough into 1-pound pieces for freezing.)

Roquefort Grapes

MAKES 50 HORS D'OEUVRES

10 ounces raw pistachio or macadamia nuts, or toasted pecans, almonds, or walnuts
8 ounces cream cheese, at room temperature
4 ounces Roquefort cheese, at room temperature
2 tablespoons heavy cream
1 pound seedless red or green grapes, washed and dried

Chop the nuts coarsely by hand or in the bowl of a food processor.

Combine the cream cheese, Roquefort, and cream, and beat until smooth using an electric mixer or food processor. Gently stir in the grapes by hand. Roll the coated grapes in the chopped nuts, place on a tray lined with wax paper, and chill until ready to serve.

NOTE: Any unused cheese mixture can be frozen for later use.

A deep wicker tray lined with a piece of French lace, garnished with a border of thyme flowers, was used to serve tiny filled muffins.

Ham on Cranberry-Orange Muffins

MAKES 30 HORS D'OEUVRES

30 Cranberry-Orange Muffins (page 232)
¼ cup grainy mustard
½ pound baked, smoked, or country ham (recipe follows), sliced thin

Cut each muffin in half crosswise and spread with a bit of mustard. Cut the ham into small pieces and put a small amount on each muffin.

VARIATIONS: Slivers of ham can also be served on Angel Biscuits (page 316), Currant Scones (page 284), Carrot Muffins (page 233), etc.

How to Bake a Country Ham

I have found the overnight method for baking a country ham to be the easiest. Start by soaking the ham (use the southern variety, such as a Smithfield) for 8 to 10 hours in cold water to lose some of the saltiness. Rinse well and scrape off any mold or green rind.

Wrap the ham well in aluminum foil and place on a baking sheet. At 7 P.M., preheat the oven to 500°. Place the wrapped ham in the oven and bake for 30 minutes. Turn off the oven but do not open the door. At 10 P.M., turn the oven back on to 500°. Bake the ham for another 15 minutes. Turn off the oven but do not open the door. Leave the ham in the closed oven overnight.

Remove the ham from the oven and serve hot, warm, or at room temperature. This ham must be cut into very, very thin slivers; it is quite salty and cannot be consumed in large quantities.

Country ham, once baked, can be frozen. Slivers can be removed from the frozen ham as you need them. Keep the ham very well wrapped in the freezer.

VARIATION: The ham can also be glazed after baking. Trim the ham of all but ¼ inch of the fatty coating. Score the fat, cutting it with a sharp knife into a fine diamond pattern.

Mix 1 cup of firmly packed dark brown sugar with ½ cup sherry and one small jar of hot pepper jelly. Spoon a portion of this mixture over the ham and bake in a 350° oven for 15 minutes. Baste two or three times more, baking until the coating is glistening—up to 45 minutes. Serve as directed above.

Wedding Buffet for Friends

The Gardellas toyed with the idea of "just cocktails" for their daughter's wedding reception, but then decided that a gathering of their large family and many friends called for great music, dancing, and a full meal.

The old Colonial house they rented for the reception is equipped with an excellent catering kitchen, several small dining rooms, and one large ballroom. A spacious hallway joins the smaller rooms to the ballroom, and we set the long, twenty-four-foot buffet tables there.

The bride wanted the reception line to be at the reception rather than at the church, so those who were waiting could begin partying with champagne and hors d'oeuvres while they stood in line to greet the newlyweds. Hors d'oeuvres were served for another hour while guests talked, danced, and wandered through the gardens.

The buffets were covered with peach cloths and were decorated lavishly with garlands of flowering kale, miniature fruits, savoy cabbages, and red cabbages. The buffet offerings were displayed either on silver or glass trays or in large glass or silver bowls. Sprigs of herbs and flowers decorated the serving dishes, and all the food looked extremely colorful and delicious. We served all the hors d'oeuvres on glass trays—rounds, squares, and ovals—and garnished them with light-colored blossoms.

There were three bars offering an assortment of mixed drinks, wines, and champagne and a tea punch. Toasts and the cake were accompanied by champagne.

MENU

HORS D'OEUVRES

Cherry Tomatoes Filled with Hearts of Palm and Spring Onions

Smoked Trout Mousse on Cucumber Hearts

Dill Crêpes with Crème Fraîche

Fresh Pear Slices with Bleu de Bresse

Chicken Liver Pâté on Heart Toasts

BUFFET

Salmon Mousse with Cucumber Sauce

Smoked Filet of Beef with Horseradish Sauce

Pecan-Breaded Chicken

Mélange of Seasonal Vegetables · Fusilli Primavera

Homemade French Bread

Sliced Tomatoes with Mozzarella and Basil

DESSERT

Tea Punch or Spiced Tea Punch

Wedding Cake

Cherry Tomatoes Filled with Hearts of Palm and Spring Onions

MAKES 30 HORS D'OEUVRES

30 red firm cherry tomatoes
(about 1 pint)

FILLING

8 ounces canned hearts of
palm, drained
Juice of ½ lemon
2 tablespoons tarragon
vinegar
3 tablespoons olive oil
6 spring onions, finely
chopped
2 tablespoons chopped fresh
dill
2 tablespoons chopped Italian
parsley
Freshly ground black
pepper, to taste
Fresh herbs or salad greens

Wash and dry the cherry tomatoes and remove any stems. With a sharp serrated knife, cut off the round bottom of each tomato, remove the seeds and pulp with a small melon ball scoop, and put the tomatoes, cut side down, on paper towels or a wire rack to drain. Refrigerate until ready to serve.

To make the filling, place the hearts of palm in the bowl of a food processor and chop coarsely.

Combine the lemon juice, vinegar, and olive oil in a medium mixing bowl, and stir in the chopped spring onions and hearts of palm. Add the dill and parsley, stir to combine, and season to taste.

To serve, use a small spoon to fill the tomatoes with the mixture, and place the tomatoes on a bed of herbs or salad greens, which will keep the tomatoes from rolling.

PRECEDING PAGE, CLOCKWISE FROM UPPER LEFT: Hollowed cherry tomatoes, filled with a savory filling, sit amid a garnish of miniature ivy and pink asters; a tray of cucumber hearts garnished with baby gladiolus and rose leaves; salmon mousse from the buffet garnished with paper-thin cucumber slices; piped stars of chicken liver pâté are served on heart-shaped melba toasts; thin slices of fresh Bosc pears are topped with a piped leaf of creamy Bleu de Bresse cheese; rolled, filled dill crêpes are mounded in a fan on a round glass tray.

Smoked Trout Mousse on Cucumber Hearts

MAKES 50 TO 60 HORS D'OEUVRES

SMOKED TROUT MOUSSE

8 ounces smoked trout
¼ cup heavy cream
Salt and freshly ground
black pepper, to taste
Freshly squeezed lemon
juice, to taste
1 to 2 tablespoons fresh or
drained bottled grated
horseradish
2 8-ounce packages cream
cheese, at room temperature
2 seedless English cucumbers

Remove the skin and bones of the smoked trout and put the flesh into the bowl of a food processor. Chop the trout very fine. With the machine still running, add the cream in a steady stream. Add salt and pepper, lemon juice, and horseradish.

Transfer the trout mixture to a bowl and add the cream cheese. Blend until well combined and smooth. Using a rubber spatula, press the mixture through a fine sieve to remove any lumps. Refrigerate until ready to use.

To prepare the cucumbers, wash and cut each into slices a little less than ¼ inch thick. Using a heart-shaped cookie or biscuit cutter slightly smaller in diameter than the cucumber slices, cut them into hearts. (If they are not to be used immediately, put the cucumber hearts on a towel-lined baking sheet, cover with plastic wrap, and refrigerate for no more than 3 hours.)

To serve, pipe approximately 1 tablespoon of mousse onto the center of each heart with a pastry bag fitted with a decorative tip.

Dill Crêpes with Crème Fraîche

MAKES 40 HORS D'OEUVRES

1¼ cups sifted all-purpose flour
4 eggs
1 cup milk
1¼ cups cold water
3 tablespoons unsalted butter,
melted
½ teaspoon salt
6 tablespoons finely chopped
fresh dill
1 cup Crème Fraîche (page 291)

GARNISH: 1-inch lengths
of fresh chives

To make the crêpes, combine the flour, eggs, milk, water, melted butter, and salt in a blender or food processor and mix at high speed for 30 seconds. Scrape down the sides of the bowl and blend 30 seconds longer. Pour the batter into a mixing bowl, stir in the dill, and refrigerate for at least 1 hour.

Spoon 2 tablespoons of batter onto a hot buttered griddle or crêpe pan and cook over medium-high heat until the surface is bubbly. Flip the crêpe and cook until golden brown, about 30 seconds. Remove from the heat and stack until ready to use. (If the crêpes will not be used for several hours, wrap them and keep them at room temperature. They can also be wrapped in plastic wrap and frozen for longer storage, and thawed at room temperature or in a microwave oven.)

To serve, pipe or spoon a small amount of crème fraîche onto the center of each crêpe, garnish with a chive, and roll it (either cornucopia-style or cylindrically), or fold the crêpe into quarters.

VARIATIONS: Other types of crêpes can be made using this basic recipe. For plain crêpes, omit the chopped dill. To make scallion crêpes, substitute 2 tablespoons melted unsalted butter and 1 tablespoon Oriental sesame oil for the 3 tablespoons melted butter, and add 6 tablespoons slivered scallions to the blended batter. Refrigerate and cook as directed.

Crêpes can also be made in a larger 5-inch size by spooning ¼ cup of batter onto the hot griddle.

Filling variations for crêpes are many. Try sour cream and caviar, pencil asparagus and mustard sauce, or pear conserve and whipped cream.

CRÈME FRAÎCHE
MAKES 2 CUPS

2 cups heavy cream
2 tablespoons buttermilk or sour cream

Heat the cream over low heat to exactly 100°. Add the buttermilk or sour cream and mix well. Put in a covered jar and let sit at room temperature for 6 to 8 hours. Refrigerate at least 24 hours before serving. The crème fraîche will become thick like sour cream. It can be kept refrigerated in a tightly covered jar for 2 to 3 weeks.

Fresh Pear Slices with Bleu de Bresse

SEE RECIPE VARIATION, PAGE 254.

Chicken Liver Pâté on Heart Toasts

MAKES APPROXIMATELY 1 CUP, ENOUGH FOR 50 HORS D'OEUVRES

½ pound chicken livers, cleaned
½ cup brandy
1 tablespoon minced shallots
1 tablespoon unsalted butter
½ teaspoon chopped fresh sage or ¼ teaspoon dried sage
Salt and freshly ground black pepper, to taste
4 tablespoons (½ stick) unsalted butter, at room temperature

Heart Toasts (page 264)

GARNISH: Cornichons

To make the pâté, soak the chicken livers in the brandy for 3 to 4 hours in a cool place; do not refrigerate. Drain the chicken livers, reserving the brandy.

Sauté the shallots in the 1 tablespoon of butter until wilted. Add the chicken livers, sage, and salt and pepper. Sauté until the chicken livers are done, approximately 5 minutes. Transfer the mixture to the bowl of a food processor, add the softened 4 tablespoons butter, and process until smooth and thoroughly combined. Add the reserved brandy and process another 30 seconds. Transfer to a shallow bowl, cover, and refrigerate for at least 24 hours.

To serve, spread each heart toast with a small amount of pâté. Garnish with thin crosswise slices of cornichon and serve.

VARIATIONS: The pâté may also be spread on toasted rounds of French bread or apples that have been cored, halved, and sliced.

Salmon Mousse with Cucumber Sauce

SERVES 10 TO 12

Court Bouillon (page 229)

MOUSSE

2 pounds fresh salmon
2 tablespoons unflavored gelatin
¼ cup fresh lemon juice
⅓ cup Homemade Mayonnaise (page 229)
½ cup sour cream
½ teaspoon freshly grated nutmeg
1 teaspoon salt
¼ teaspoon freshly ground black pepper
¾ cup heavy cream

GARNISH: Cucumber slices

Cucumber Sauce (page 230)

Combine all court bouillon ingredients in a pot and simmer for 10 minutes.

Place the salmon in the court bouillon and bring to a boil. Reduce the heat and simmer, covered, for 10 to 15 minutes, or until the salmon flakes easily with a fork. Remove from the heat and let the salmon cool in the liquid. Remove the salmon, strain the court bouillon, and reserve.

Remove the skin and bones from the salmon. Break the salmon into small pieces and place in a bowl with ½ cup of the bouillon.

Soften the gelatin in the lemon juice and set aside.

In a medium saucepan, bring 1 cup strained bouillon to a boil. Remove from the heat, add the gelatin mixture, and stir until dissolved. Set aside to cool.

Combine the salmon, gelatin mixture, mayonnaise, sour cream, nutmeg, salt, and pepper in a large bowl, mixing gently but thoroughly. Beat the cream until stiff and fold into the salmon mixture.

Oil a 6-cup ring mold, loaf pan, or fish-shaped mold. Carefully fill to the top with the mousse, cover with plastic wrap, and refrigerate for 3 to 4 hours, until set.

Unmold the mousse onto a serving tray and garnish. Serve with Cucumber Sauce.

Smoked Filet of Beef with Horseradish Sauce

SERVES 10 TO 12

1 4- to 5-pound trimmed filet of beef
½ cup olive oil
¼ cup coarsely ground black pepper

HORSERADISH SAUCE 1

MAKES APPROXIMATELY 2 CUPS

¼ cup well-drained prepared horseradish
1½ cups sour cream
2 tablespoons Dijon-style mustard
1 tablespoon whole-grain mustard
2 tablespoons finely chopped onion (optional)

HORSERADISH SAUCE 2

MAKES APPROXIMATELY 2 CUPS

½ cup well-drained prepared horseradish
1¼ cups sour cream
¼ cup unsweetened applesauce
2 tablespoons grated tart apple (optional)

Rub the filet with olive oil and press the pepper into it. Smoke in a commercial smoker, according to the manufacturer's directions, or over mesquite in a smokehouse (approximately 1 hour or until cooked to your taste).

To make either horseradish sauce, whisk together the horseradish, sour cream, and mustards or applesauce until well blended. Fold in the onion or grated apple, if desired, and refrigerate until ready to use.

To serve, cut the filet into ½-inch slices, and serve, warm or at room temperature, with horseradish sauce.

Pecan-Breaded Chicken

SERVES 12

½ pound (2 sticks) unsalted butter
½ cup Dijon-style mustard
6 chicken breasts, skinned, boned, halved lengthwise, and halved again lengthwise. Each breast will yield 4 long pieces.
1 pound coarsely ground pecans
¾ cup safflower oil
2 cups sour cream
Salt and freshly ground black pepper, to taste
24 pecan halves, lightly sautéed in butter

In a small saucepan, melt 2 sticks of the butter over medium heat. Remove from the heat and whisk in ⅓ cup of the mustard.

Place the chicken between sheets of wax paper and flatten slightly with a meat pounder. Dip each piece into the butter-mustard mixture and roll in the ground pecans, which have been spread out on another sheet of wax paper. Coat the chicken heavily with the nuts; pat any extra on with your hands.

Melt the remaining butter in a large skillet and add the oil. When hot, sauté the chicken until browned, about 3 minutes on each side, cooking as many pieces as possible at one time without crowding.

As the chicken is done, remove it to a baking dish and keep warm in a preheated 200° oven. (The chicken can also be refrigerated at this point and reheated later in a 350° oven.) Continue sautéing until all the chicken is done.

Pour off butter and oil from the pan and discard any burnt pecans. Deglaze the pan with the sour cream, scraping up all the browned particles. Whisk in the remaining mustard and season to taste.

To serve, spoon a little sauce over each piece of chicken and garnish with a pecan half.

OPPOSITE: A plate with several offerings from the buffet: pecan chicken, seasonal vegetables, and freshly baked pistolets.
ABOVE: Just-cooked pecan chicken pieces, with sauce made from the cooking juices and nuts in the pan.
RIGHT: Another plate from the buffet.

Mélange of Seasonal Vegetables

SERVES 12

½ pound snow peas, stem ends removed
1 pound broad beans, cut into 2-inch pieces
½ pound baby okra, stem ends removed
1 pound baby zucchini
2 scallions, cut into 2-inch pieces
½ cup pecan or walnut halves
2 tablespoons (¼ stick) unsalted butter
Salt and freshly ground black pepper, to taste

Steam each vegetable separately, until tender. Toss with the pecans, butter, and salt and pepper. Serve hot.

The fusilli primavera, garnished with basil.

Fusilli Primavera

SERVES 10 TO 12

VINAIGRETTE

⅓ cup red currant vinegar (or other fruit vinegar)
1 teaspoon sugar
1 tablespoon Dijon-style mustard
¾ cup olive oil
¼ cup pimiento oil (see Note)
2 tablespoons chopped purple basil
Salt and freshly ground black pepper, to taste

2 pounds fusilli
1 or 2 tablespoons pimiento oil
½ pound haricots verts or young green beans
½ pound sugar snap peas or snow peas
2 roasted sweet red peppers (see Note, page 277), peeled, seeded, and sliced
1 medium red onion, peeled and thinly sliced crosswise
1 pint ripe red cherry tomatoes, stemmed and halved
Freshly grated Parmesan cheese

GARNISH: Fresh cut small-leaf basil (*basilico fino*)

To make the vinaigrette, combine the vinegar, sugar, and mustard, stirring to dissolve the sugar. Combine the oils, and gradually whisk them into the vinegar mixture. Stir in the basil, season to taste, and set aside.

Cook the fusilli in a large pot of boiling water just until al dente. Drain and rinse in cold water. Drain again and toss with enough pimiento oil to prevent the noodles from sticking together. Set aside.

Trim the ends of the green beans, string the peas, and steam over boiling water just until tender but still crisp, 30 seconds to 1 minute. Remove from the heat and immerse in ice water. Drain well.

Combine the pasta and all the vegetables in a large bowl, and toss with the rewhisked vinaigrette, using just enough to coat the noodles. Sprinkle with Parmesan cheese, garnish with basil, and serve chilled or at room temperature.

NOTE: Pimiento oil is a mild vegetable or safflower oil to which dried chili peppers have been added for flavor. It can be found at gourmet shops or made at home.

Homemade French Bread

SEE RECIPE, PAGE 247.

Sliced Tomatoes with Mozzarella and Basil

SEE RECIPE, PAGE 272.

ABOVE: Concentric circles of fresh ripe tomatoes and thinly sliced mozzarella garnished with opal basil. OPPOSITE: Spiced tea punch was served from a large silver punch bowl into champagne flutes.

Tea Punch

SERVES 10 TO 12

4 cups brewed aromatic tea
  (such as Earl Grey, Darjeeling,
  or Assam), chilled
4 cups apple juice, chilled
2 cups unsweetened pineapple
  juice, chilled
  Club soda to taste (optional)

GARNISH: Orange slices,
lemon slices, fresh mint

Combine the tea, apple and pineapple juices, and refrigerate until ready to serve.
Add the club soda, if desired, fruit slices, and mint immediately before serving. Serve iced from a large punch bowl.

VARIATION: For a more spirited punch, add a bottle of dry red wine.

Spiced Tea Punch

SERVES 10 TO 12

1 cup sugar
2 cups cold water
1 tablespoon whole cloves
1 stick cinnamon
2 tablespoons fragrant tea
  leaves (such as Rose Pouchong,
  Jasmine, or Fort Mason)
6 cups boiling water
  Juice of 2 lemons
  Juice of 2 oranges
1 cup unsweetened pineapple juice

GARNISH: Fresh orange
or lemon slices, fresh mint
or strawberries

Combine the sugar, cold water, cloves, and cinnamon and bring to a simmer.
In a separate pot, pour the boiling water over the tea and let steep for 3 minutes. Strain the tea and combine with the fruit juices. Add to the spice mixture and simmer for 5 to 10 minutes. Serve hot from a silver bowl, or let cool and serve iced from a crystal or glass punch bowl.

Spring Wedding Lunch

Harvey Siegel and Sharon Nelson knew exactly what they wanted served at their spring wedding luncheon. When we met for our catering consultation, they had a list prepared of their very favorite foods and said, "Please try to include all of these things in our menu," not realizing that they had composed a virtually complete menu. All I had to do was suggest a few hors d'oeuvres and appropriate dressings for the salad and asparagus.

The tables were set in a stone-walled garden adjacent to the stone farmhouse. A spacious country kitchen, replete with Garland restaurant range and plenty of refrigeration, opened right onto the garden, making our cooking, serving, and cleanup chores extremely simple.

We set the tables with long white cloths over which we draped blue-and-white overcloths designed by Ralph Lauren. Napkins were of the same pattern (Charlotte). Old blue-and-white dishes were mixed with rental white plates, and the centerpieces were wild flowers arranged in Harvey's collection of antique copper teakettles. A very special romantic feeling was evoked by this combination of delicate colors and old collectibles. The buffet was served from a weathered country table. We used old wooden trays and bowls, wooden spoons and forks, and other country baskets and copper for the display of food.

The hors d'oeuvres were numerous and varied so there was no need for a first course. We arranged these finger foods on copper heart trays and oval Shaker trays garnished with spring flowers and green foliage.

The main course was rack of lamb. We bought the smallest racks we could find and trimmed them completely of fat, leaving the rib bones long. The bones were "Frenched" and the chine bone was well trimmed. Thick slices of onions were

---

MENU

ASSORTED HORS D'OEUVRES

FIRST COURSE
Vegetable Crudités with Zucchini-Coriander Dip

Spring Salad with Hazelnut Vinaigrette

MAIN COURSE
Rack of Lamb

Pencil-Thin Green Beans (Haricots Verts)

Roasted Onion Slices

Spring Asparagus with Cornichon Beurre Blanc

Individual Pommes Anna

Homemade French Bread

DESSERT
Sweet Bing Cherries

Wedding Cake

roasted in butter and olive oil in a single layer until they were golden brown and tender. The individual pommes Anna were made in 3-inch plain tart molds and baked until they were very crisp and brown. Both fat green and white asparagus were steamed until they were tender. A warm beurre blanc, flavored with French cornichons, was served with the asparagus. I think that was Harvey's favorite part of the meal.

A family friend made the wedding cake. She baked the layers at home and made the frosting the morning of the wedding at the farmhouse. While we prepared for the wedding feast, she decorated the cake, confident in her skill as decorator and baker, and casual and relaxed in her attitude toward what is to most a formidable task. The result was a beautiful cake, of lovely flavor.

PRECEDING PAGE: One of my bartenders waiting for the wedding to begin.
RIGHT: The Siegels chose rack of lamb, their favorite cut, for the wedding lunch. The lamb, haricots verts, and roasted onion slices created a perfect pattern on the antique Royal Doulton "Chrysanthemum" plates. BELOW: Harvey had collected a lot of kitchen antiques, including this treenware trencher in which we served the salad.

Vegetable Crudités with Zucchini-Coriander Dip

MAKES 2¼ CUPS

1¾ cup Crème Fraîche (page 291)
2 tablespoons light olive oil
1 to 2 tablespoons white wine vinegar
2 medium garlic cloves, minced
2 small firm zucchini, washed, trimmed, and finely grated
3 tablespoons chopped fresh coriander leaves
Salt and freshly ground white pepper, to taste

Whisk together the crème fraîche, oil, vinegar, and garlic until smooth. Stir in the remaining ingredients and refrigerate, covered, for at least 2 hours.
Serve dip with a variety of vegetable crudités, such as carrots, broccoli flowerets, asparagus, or radishes, blanched quickly to maximize their flavor and color.

Spring Salad with Hazelnut Vinaigrette

SERVES 12

HAZELNUT VINAIGRETTE
MAKES APPROXIMATELY 1¼ CUPS

⅔ cup safflower oil
¼ cup olive oil
2 tablespoons hazelnut oil
1 tablespoon light cream
Dash of Tabasco or pinch of cayenne pepper
1 garlic clove, smashed
1 teaspoon Dijon-style mustard
2 tablespoons freshly squeezed lemon juice
Salt and freshly ground black pepper to taste
A combination of spring salad greens, like mâche, ruby lettuce, arugula, and endive

GARNISH:
Chopped toasted hazelnuts
Coriander flowers

Whisk together all the ingredients for the vinaigrette. Arrange the lettuces in a large bowl or on individual plates. Just before serving, remove the garlic clove from the vinaigrette and drizzle over the greens. Top with garnish, if desired.

Rack of Lamb

SERVES 12

4 1¼- to 1½-pound racks of lamb (allow one-third rack or 2 to 3 chops per person)
2½ cups chopped fresh parsley
2 tablespoons Dijon-style mustard
Approximately ¾ cup olive oil
Salt and freshly ground black pepper, to taste

Preheat the oven to 425°.
Carefully trim the racks of lamb, cracking between each chop and removing any chine bone (or have the butcher do it), leaving the rib bones as long as possible. Leave ⅛ inch of fat on the outside of each rack.
Combine the parsley, mustard, olive oil, and salt and pepper, and rub most of the mixture on the fat side of the lamb up to the rib bones. Place the racks in a roasting pan and cook for 20 minutes. If the rib bones are browning too much or too quickly, wrap them with foil. Remove from the oven, pat on the remaining parsley mixture, and return to the oven for 3 to 5 minutes; the lamb should be served pink (160° on a meat thermometer). Carve into individual chops and serve immediately.

Pencil-Thin Green Beans (Haricots Verts)

SERVES 12

1½ pounds haricots verts, stem end cut off
4 tablespoons (½ stick) unsalted butter, melted (optional)
Salt and freshly ground black pepper, to taste

Blanch the haricots verts in a large pot of boiling water or steam over boiling water just until tender, 2 to 3 minutes. Drain well and place in a large serving bowl. Pour the melted butter over the haricot verts, if desired, toss well, season with salt and pepper, and serve immediately.

VARIATIONS: Haricots verts can also be served hot or cold with Mustard-Fennel Sauce (page 243).

Roasted Onion Slices

SERVES 12

6 large yellow onions (sweet Vidalia onions are delicious)
3 tablespoons unsalted butter
¼ cup olive oil
Salt and freshly ground black pepper, to taste

Preheat the oven to 400°. Butter a cookie sheet.
Peel and slice the onions crosswise into ¼-inch-thick slices. Arrange the slices in one layer on the cookie sheet, brush with olive oil, and sprinkle lightly with salt and pepper.
Roast in a hot oven until the onion slices are golden brown (about 20 to 30 minutes).

Spring Asparagus with Cornichon Beurre Blanc

Allow 4 to 6 fat asparagus stalks per person

CORNICHON BEURRE BLANC
MAKES APPROXIMATELY 1 CUP,
ENOUGH FOR 12 SERVINGS

- ¼ cup minced shallots
- 1 cup dry white wine
- 1 teaspoon salt
- 2 tablespoons tarragon vinegar
- ½ pound (2 sticks) unsalted butter, at room temperature, cut into small pieces
- 2 to 3 cornichons, finely diced

To prepare the asparagus, cut off the tough end of each stalk so that all are approximately the same length. Peel the stalks and place them on a rack. Steam over rapidly boiling water until tender, 5 to 6 minutes. Keep warm while you prepare the sauce.

In a small saucepan, combine the shallots, wine, salt, and vinegar. Bring to a boil and cook until the liquid has been reduced to about ¼ cup. Remove the pan from the heat and cool slightly. The liquid must be just warm enough to incorporate the butter but not hot enough to liquefy it. Whisk in the butter, a piece at a time, until the mixture is well blended and creamy. If the mixture becomes too cool and the butter will not incorporate, return the pan to low heat for a moment or two. Do not melt the butter.

When all butter is incorporated and the mixture is smooth, whisk in the cornichons. Serve immediately over the asparagus.

VARIATION: The asparagus can also be served with Mustard-Fennel Sauce (page 243).

LEFT: White and green asparagus, sure signs of springtime, were served with a cornichon beurre blanc sauce. OPPOSITE: Four-inch pie tins were used to cook the individual pommes Anna, and we served them in antique English square dishes.

Individual Pommes Anna

SERVES 12

6 to 8 large baking potatoes,
  peeled and very thinly
  sliced, soaked in ice water,
  then well drained and dried
  on a cotton towel
  Approximately 3 cups
  clarified butter (see Note)
2 teaspoons salt
  Freshly ground black
  pepper, to taste
12 sprigs fresh thyme, stripped
  of leaves

Preheat the oven to 400°.

Using a fourth of the clarified butter, pour it into 10 small ramekins, timbale molds, or tiny pie plates, dividing it equally among them. Arrange fresh thyme sprigs in bottom of each dish. Place one layer of potato slices on top of thyme, arranging them in a concentric circle and overlapping the slices. Continue to layer the potato slices in this manner until they are all used, dribbling each layer with a bit more clarified butter and sprinkling on a little salt and pepper and thyme leaves. Bake until golden brown and soft, 20 to 25 minutes. (Press the potatoes with a spoon or spatula once or twice while baking to keep them flat.)

Remove from the oven and pour off any excess butter. Invert the baking dishes onto a platter and unmold. Serve hot.

NOTE: Clarified butter should be used here since it burns less easily than regular butter. To make it, simply melt the butter in a saucepan over low heat and skim off any foam. Strain the butter through cheesecloth and discard any watery residue at the bottom of the pan. For 3 cups of clarified butter, you will need 2¼ pounds (9 sticks) of unsalted butter.

VARIATION: When layering the potatoes, sprinkle them with chopped fresh herbs (parsley, tarragon, dill, chervil, etc.).

Homemade French Bread

SEE RECIPE, PAGE 247.

ABOVE: An old pine knife box was used to display the early crop of bing cherries and a floral arrangement of wood hyacinths and chive blossoms. OPPOSITE: Sharon's orange-almond wedding cake was made for her by one of her best friends. It was frosted with Italian buttercream and decorated with stripes and swags. The floral decoration consisted of white lilacs, verbena, and ivy.

High-Style Wedding Lunch

Of all the menus in this chapter, this is the most elegant, the most akin to what one would find offered in a fine restaurant as lunch or dinner fare. It is not a menu for mass production, but rather a combination of dishes that can be prepared in small quantities for small groups.

Guests were seated at designated places at formally set tables. The bride used a combination of rental linens and family dishes, flatware, and crystal. White wooden chairs were rented for all the tables.

Posies tied with satin ribbons decorated the hors d'oeuvres trays. We used copper trays for the five hors d'oeuvres, which were quite small and light because they preceded lunch. Gen-

MENU

HORS D OEUVRES
Cucumber Hearts with Chèvre and Sun-Dried Tomatoes
Phyllo Triangles with Curried Chicken Filling
Carrot Lace Fritters
Marinated Shrimp with Snow Peas
Homemade Chicken Liver Pâté on French Bread Rounds

FIRST COURSE
Minted Pea Soup

ENTRÉE
Veal Scallops with Hazelnut Sauce
Wild Rice and Wheatberry Mélange with Shiitake Mushrooms
Carrot-Raspberry Purée
Watercress, Haricots Verts, and Pears in Tarragon Vinaigrette

DESSERT
Chocolate Heart Cookies · Fresh Strawberries
Wedding Cake

erally I encourage people to serve fewer cocktails and hors d'oeuvres before a luncheon because guests are not as hungry as they are later in the day. Also, I stress the importance of not serving lunch too late, which can make guests uncomfortable and cranky.

Guests were first served hot minted pea soup in shallow bowls. The soup was garnished with lemon peel, crème fraîche, and parsley. The entrée of veal scallops was especially sophisticated with its topping of hazelnut sauce. The wedding cake, fanciful chocolate heart cookies, and fresh strawberries were an appropriate ending to this carefully planned and luxurious meal.

Cucumber Hearts with Chèvre and Sun-Dried Tomatoes

MAKES 40 HORS D'OEUVRES

CHÈVRE TOPPING
MAKES APPROXIMATELY 1 CUP

- 3 to 3½ ounces chèvre, at room temperature
- 3 ounces cream cheese, at room temperature
- 2 tablespoons heavy cream

- 2 seedless English cucumbers

  GARNISH: Tiny slivers of sun-dried tomatoes

Place the chèvre, cream cheese, and cream in a large mixing bowl or in the bowl of a food processor and blend until well combined and very smooth. Add a bit more heavy cream if necessary. Chill.

To prepare the cucumbers, wash and cut each into slices a little less than ¼ inch thick. Using a heart-shaped cookie or biscuit cutter slightly smaller in diameter than the cucumber slices, cut them into hearts. The cucumbers can now be placed on a towel-lined baking sheet, covered with plastic wrap, and refrigerated for up to 3 hours.

Let the chèvre topping soften a bit before placing it in a pastry bag fitted with a decorative tip, and piping a bit onto each cucumber heart. Garnish with a sliver of sun-dried tomato and serve.

VARIATIONS: Instead of chèvre and sun-dried tomatoes, you can also pipe Smoked Salmon Mousse (page 243) or Herb Cheese (page 243) onto the cucumber hearts.

ABOVE: Galax leaves are a perfect base for buttery phyllo triangles. BELOW LEFT: Heart-shaped cucumbers were served from a copper tray garnished with bells of Ireland. BELOW RIGHT: Lacy and colorful carrot fritters were served from a square copper tray lined with opal basil leaves. OPPOSITE: Snow pea-wrapped shrimp.

Phyllo Triangles with Curried Chicken Filling

MAKES 48 HORS D'OEUVRES

CURRIED CHICKEN FILLING
- 2 whole chicken breasts
- 2 tablespoons unsalted butter
- 2½ tablespoons all-purpose flour
- 1 teaspoon curry powder
- ½ teaspoon ground turmeric
- 1 cup milk
- ½ teaspoon salt
- ½ cup chopped toasted almonds or chopped toasted walnuts
- ¼ cup golden raisins
  Grated rind of 1 orange
- 1 tablespoon chopped dill

- 1 pound phyllo pastry
- 1 pound (4 sticks) unsalted butter, melted and cooled

306

Preheat the oven to 375°. Place each chicken breast on a piece of lightly buttered aluminum foil, seal to make a pouch, and bake until done, approximately 45 minutes. Unwrap the chicken and let cool. Remove the skin and bones, and cut the meat into small pieces. Set aside.

Melt the butter in a small saucepan, add the flour, curry powder, and turmeric, and cook over low heat for 2 minutes. Add the milk, whisk to blend, and continue to cook over low heat until the mixture has thickened, about 7 minutes. Remove from heat. Season with salt, and stir in the nuts, raisins, orange rind, dill, and chicken. Let cool completely.

Preheat the oven to 400°. Lightly butter a baking sheet and set aside.

To assemble the triangles, place 1 sheet of phyllo on a flat work surface and brush lightly with a bit of the cooled melted butter. Top with 2 more sheets, buttering each. Cut the sheets in half lengthwise, then cut each half crosswise into 6 equal parts. Place 1 heaping teaspoon of cooled filling onto the end of each strip and form a triangle by folding the right-hand corner to the opposite side, as you would fold a flag. Continue folding until the entire strip is used. Repeat with each strip.

Place the folded triangles on the prepared baking sheet and brush the top of each with melted butter. Bake for 12 minutes, until golden brown, and serve warm.

NOTE: Unbaked filled triangles can be refrigerated for up to 2 days or frozen immediately for future use. Do not thaw before baking.

Carrot Lace Fritters

SEE RECIPE, PAGE 285.

Marinated Shrimp with Snow Peas

MAKES 30 HORS D'OEUVRES

1½ pounds large shrimp
(approximately 30), peeled
and deveined

MARINADE

2 tablespoons sweet rice wine
vinegar

⅓ cup Oriental sesame oil

1 large garlic clove, peeled
and crushed

1 teaspoon finely minced fresh
gingerroot
Salt and freshly ground
black pepper, to taste

Approximately 15 snow peas

Bring a large pot of water to a boil. Add the shrimp and cook just until pink, 2 to 3 minutes. Do not overcook. Drain the shrimp and immerse them in cold water to cool; drain again. Place the shrimp in a glass or stainless steel bowl.

Whisk the marinade ingredients together and pour over the shrimp. Stir to coat well, cover, and refrigerate for 1 or 2 days, stirring at least twice a day.

No more than a few hours before serving, string the snow peas and blanch in boiling water for 30 seconds. Immerse immediately in ice water to chill. Drain well. Using a sharp paring knife, split the snow peas lengthwise so that you have 30 separated halves. Wrap one half around each drained shrimp and fasten with a round toothpick. Serve chilled or at room temperature.

Homemade Chicken Liver Pâté on French Bread Rounds

SEE RECIPE VARIATION, PAGE 291.

Minted Pea Soup

SERVES 12

- 4 tablespoons (½ stick) unsalted butter
- 2 tablespoons minced shallots
- 3 leeks, white part only, cleaned and sliced crosswise
- 2 tablespoons chopped fresh parsley
- ¼ cup chopped fresh mint
- 2 tart apples, peeled, cored, and diced
- 1 cup sweet sherry
- 1 head Boston lettuce
- 5 cups chicken stock, preferably homemade
- 1 white potato, peeled and diced
- 4 cups fresh sweet peas or frozen petits pois
- 2 cups heavy cream
  Salt and freshly ground white pepper, to taste

GARNISH: Crème Fraîche (page 291)
Thin strips of lemon peel

Melt the butter in a large kettle and sauté the shallots, leeks, parsley, and half the mint just until soft; do not brown. Add the diced apples and cook until tender, approximately 7 minutes. Add the sherry and bring to a boil. Cut the Boston lettuce into thin strips, or a chiffonade, and place in the kettle along with the chicken stock and potato. Return to a boil, reduce the heat, and simmer for 20 minutes, or until the potato is very tender.

Bring a large pot of water to a boil and blanch the peas for 1 minute. Drain and refresh them in ice water. (This helps the peas retain their color.) Drain well. Add to the soup with the remaining mint.

Purée in a food processor until very smooth and stir in the cream.

Just before serving, gently reheat the soup but do not let it boil. Garnish each serving with a dollop of crème fraîche and a strip of lemon peel.

ABOVE: The mint pea soup was a beautiful shade of green. It was garnished with crème fraîche, lemon peel, and fresh parsley. BELOW: The veal scallop lunch was arranged in the kitchen and served to each guest on a warmed plate. OPPOSITE: The beautiful salad, a course by itself, elicited a lot of compliments.

Veal Scallops with Hazelnut Sauce

SERVES 12

- 2 cups hazelnuts
- ¾ pound (3 sticks) unsalted butter
- 4 cups heavy cream
- 1 tablespoon Worcestershire sauce
- 1 teaspoon Dijon-style mustard
  Dash of cayenne pepper
- 24 medium veal scallops (approximately 3 pounds, see Note)
  Flour for dredging
  Salt and freshly ground white pepper, to taste

Roast the hazelnuts by placing them on a cookie sheet in a 350° oven for 15 minutes. Turn onto a clean cotton towel and rub the skin off with the towel. Set aside 24 hazelnuts and finely grind the remainder in the bowl of a food processor.

Bring half the butter (1½ sticks) to room temperature and place in the bowl of a food processor. Process the butter and add two thirds of the ground hazelnuts to make a paste. Remove the mixture from the food processor, wrap well in plastic wrap, and chill well.

Shortly before serving, combine the cream, Worcestershire sauce, mustard, and cayenne in a saucepan, and reduce the mixture by one third. Remove from the heat and whisk in small pieces of the chilled hazelnut butter. When the butter is completely incorporated, keep the sauce warm by setting it, covered, over a pan of hot water. Do not heat the sauce directly or the butter will melt.

Heat the remaining ¾ cup butter in a large skillet. Lightly dredge the veal scallops in flour, season with salt and pepper, and sauté until done, 3 to 4 minutes on each side.

To serve, spoon a small amount of warm sauce onto each plate and place 2 sautéed veal scallops on top. Spoon more sauce over the scallops (you should use approximately 3 tablespoons of sauce for each serving), sprinkle with the reserved ground hazelnuts, and garnish with 2 of the roasted hazelnuts.

N O T E : Veal scallops are best sliced from the leg, very thin and of uniform size. Pounded scallops tend to shrink more during cooking than thinly sliced scallops.

Wild Rice and Wheatberry Mélange with Shiitake Mushrooms

SERVES 10

1 cup wild rice
1 cup wheatberries
4 tablespoons (½ stick) unsalted butter
½ pound fresh shiitake mushrooms
¾ cup dried currants, soaked overnight in vodka
4 scallions, chopped (white and green parts)
¼ cup hot chicken stock
Salt and freshly ground black pepper, to taste

Place the wild rice and 4 cups of water in a large pot and cook until the rice is tender, approximately 45 minutes. Drain the rice well and set aside to cool.

Cook the wheatberries in the same way, and set aside to cool.

Melt the butter in a skillet and sauté the mushrooms just until they have begun to wilt. Remove from the heat.

To serve, combine the wild rice, wheatberries, mushrooms, drained currants, and scallions in a large skillet. Add the hot chicken stock, cover, and cook over low heat until the mixture is hot, approximately 10 minutes. Season with salt and pepper and serve immediately.

Carrot-Raspberry Purée

SERVES 10 TO 12

2½ pounds carrots
6 tablespoons (¾ stick) unsalted butter
Salt, to taste
4 tablespoons sherry vinegar
2 tablespoons crème de cassis
1½ cup frozen raspberries, thawed, drained, and juice reserved

Peel the carrots and cut them into 2-inch pieces. Place them in a heavy saucepan with just enough water to keep them from burning, and add 5 tablespoons butter. Cook the carrots, covered, over low heat until very tender, approximately 30 minutes.

Remove the carrots from the saucepan, reserving the liquid, and place them in the bowl of a food processor. Purée the carrots, adding only enough reserved liquid to obtain a smooth, even consistency. Place the purée in the top of a double boiler or over a pot of boiling water to keep it warm. Season with salt, to taste.

Combine the vinegar, cassis, and 1 tablespoon of the reserved raspberry juice in a small saucepan and reduce by half. Add the remaining tablespoon butter and the raspberries, and immediately remove from the heat. Gently swirl the raspberries into the warm carrot purée and serve.

Watercress, Haricots Verts, and Pears in Tarragon Vinaigrette

SERVES 10 TO 12

TARRAGON VINAIGRETTE
MAKES ½ CUP

1 teaspoon Dijon-style mustard
3 tablespoons tarragon vinegar
1 tablespoon chopped fresh tarragon
1 teaspoon minced shallots
2 tablespoons walnut oil
6 tablespoons olive oil

2½ pounds haricots verts, blanched and cooled
3 ripe unblemished Comice or Bartlett pears
3 bunches watercress, washed, dried, and large stems removed
½ cup chopped lightly toasted walnuts (optional)

Make the vinaigrette by mixing together the mustard, vinegar, tarragon, and shallots. Gradually whisk in the oils until blended. Set aside.

One hour before serving, toss the haricots verts with approximately one third of the vinaigrette. Set aside at room temperature.

Just before serving, peel, core and quarter the pears. Cut each quarter into thin slices (¼-inch thick), and toss with half of the remaining vinaigrette.

Toss the watercress with the remaining vinaigrette and arrange the watercress, haricots verts, and pear slices on individual salad plates. Sprinkle with chopped walnuts, if desired, and serve immediately.

N O T E : Crumbled Roquefort cheese can be added for additional interest.

ABOVE: The top layer of the Italian cream wedding cake, garnished with fresh roses and ferns. RIGHT: Large chocolate sugar cookies were glazed on the diagonal with very pale pink icing. Satin ribbons, orchid sprays, and galax leaves were decoration.

Chocolate Heart Cookies

MAKES FORTY 3-INCH COOKIES

- ¾ pound (3 sticks) unsalted butter
- 1¾ cups sugar
- 2 eggs, lightly beaten
- 3 cups all-purpose flour
- 1½ cups imported cocoa
- ¼ teaspoon salt
- ⅓ teaspoon freshly ground black pepper
- Pinch of cayenne pepper
- 1 teaspoon ground cinnamon

ICING

- Approximately 1 cup sifted confectioners' sugar
- 1 egg white
- ¼ teaspoon freshly squeezed lemon juice

Cream the butter and sugar together in a large bowl until light and fluffy. Add the eggs and beat well.

Sift the dry ingredients together and stir by hand into the butter mixture until thoroughly incorporated. (You may need to add more flour if the dough seems too soft.) Divide the dough into three flat rounds, wrap in plastic wrap, and chill for at least 1 hour.

Preheat the oven to 375°. Lightly butter a baking sheet, or cover it with parchment paper.

On a well-floured board, roll out the dough to a thickness of slightly more than ⅛ inch. Cut the dough into 3-inch hearts, and place on the prepared baking sheet. Bake for 8 to 10 minutes, just until the cookies are crisp but not darkened. Let cool on wire racks.

To make the icing, mix the sugar, egg white, and lemon juice in a bowl until very smooth and creamy. It should be the consistency of heavy cream; add more confectioners' sugar if necessary. When the cookies have cooled completely, dip one half into the icing, gently shake off the excess, and place on a rack until the icing hardens. Store in an airtight container or freeze.

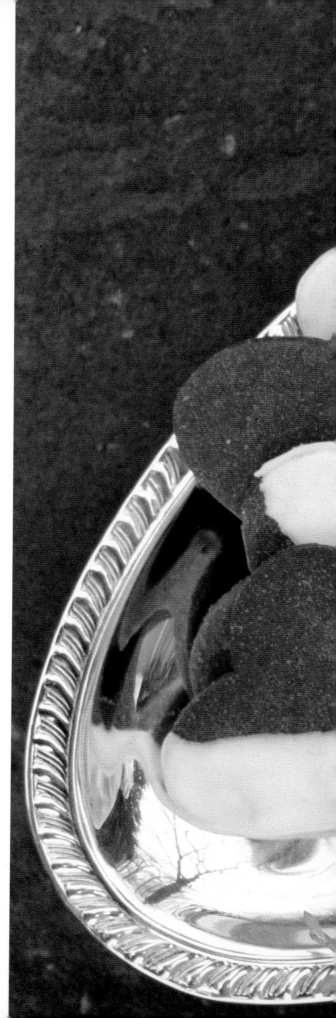

Formal Winter Pork Dinner

Only in the past few years has pork been considered an appropriate meat for a formal dinner menu. However, it is an excellent and delicious choice for a catered dinner because, of all the meats and poultry used for party occasions, only pork and chicken can be cooked in advance and reheated with little or no damage to taste and texture. This particular menu has been served at several large and small weddings and has always met with success.

The hors d'oeuvres served with this menu are varied, hearty winter fare. The nuts have been prepared with three different coatings—spicy, sugary, and curried. They should be served with champagne or champagne cocktails. The puff pastry cheese straws, or the variations we like to make with poppy seeds or cayenne, also go excellently with champagne. The savory palmiers—really puff pas-try with a pesto mixture rolled into it—the Beggar's purses filled with caviar and crème fraîche, and the deviled eggs and country ham biscuits are more substantial and can be served with mixed drinks. There are six hors d'oeuvres served with this menu, about the correct number for a wedding reception that precedes a sit-down or buffet dinner.

No first course is necessary, but if one wished, a clear consommé with julienned vegetables or a watercress purée soup or something else light could be served. The root vegetables Anna can be assembled and baked before the dinner and reheated.

The pork can be roasted until just done, then kept wrapped at room temperature for reheating. The sauce can be made in advance, also, and reheated, and the carrots may be steamed or parboiled and finished right before serving.

MENU

HORS D'OEUVRES

Spiced, Curried, and Sugared Nuts

Puff Pastry Cheese Straws · Savory Palmiers

Red Pepper Beggar's Purses · Deviled Eggs

Angel Biscuits with Country Ham

DINNER

Roast Loin of Pork with Prunes

Steamed Baby Carrots

Root Vegetables Anna

DESSERT

Wedding Cake

Spiced, Curried, and Sugared Nuts

SPICED NUTS
SERVES 10

4 cups shelled whole pecans, walnuts, or blanched almonds
4 cups sugar
1 teaspoon salt
2 tablespoons paprika
1 teaspoon cayenne pepper
1 teaspoon ground cumin
  Peanut oil for frying

Poach the nuts in a large pot of boiling water for 1 minute. Remove the nuts with a strainer, shaking off as much water as possible, and toss them immediately with the remaining ingredients in a large bowl.

Fill a deep heavy saucepan to a depth of approximately 3 inches with the peanut oil and heat to 340° to 350°. (An electric deep fryer is good for this job as it will maintain the proper temperature and the basket allows you to remove all the nuts at the same time.) Fry the nuts in the oil until they begin to turn golden brown; remove them with the strainer and toss a second time in the sugar and spices. Remove, shake off the excess, and let cool on a wire rack. The nuts will turn crispy as they cool. Serve nuts at room temperature. Store in an airtight container in a cool place for up to 2 weeks.

Three varieties of homemade spiced nuts were arranged in a deep-sided wicker basket.

ABOVE: Puff pastry cheese straws were served from a silver tray.

PRECEDING PAGE: The main course was served on pink Depression glass plates.

CURRIED NUTS
SERVES 10

4 cups shelled whole pecans, walnuts, or blanched almonds
4 cups sugar
1 teaspoon salt
2 tablespoons curry powder
1 teaspoon ground turmeric
1 teaspoon ground cumin
  Peanut oil for frying

Follow the directions for Spiced Nuts.

SUGARED NUTS
SERVES 10

4 cups shelled whole pecans, walnuts, or blanched almonds
4 cups sugar
1 teaspoon salt
2 tablespoons ground cinnamon
1 teaspoon freshly grated nutmeg
1 teaspoon ground ginger
  Peanut oil for frying

Follow the directions for Spiced Nuts.

Puff Pastry Cheese Straws

SEE RECIPE, PAGE 286.

Savory Palmiers

MAKES 36 HORS D'OEUVRES

PESTO FILLING

2 tablespoons pignoli nuts
1 garlic clove, peeled
¼ teaspoon coarse salt
⅛ teaspoon freshly ground black pepper
1 cup fresh basil leaves, blanched for 30 seconds, drained, and dried (see Note, page 236)
¼ cup freshly grated Parmesan cheese
¼ cup freshly grated Romano cheese
  Approximately ½ cup extra virgin olive oil

1 pound Puff Pastry (page 286)
1 cup freshly grated Parmesan cheese

In the bowl of a food processor, combine the pignolis, garlic, salt, pepper, basil, Parmesan and Romano cheeses, and 2 tablespoons olive oil, and process until finely

Rows of savory palmiers were served from a fabric and glass-lined wicker tray.

ground. Add the remaining oil in a steady stream and process until smooth and creamy.

Roll out the pastry into a rectangle approximately 8 inches wide and no less than ⅛ inch thick; cut the edges so that they are even. Sprinkle the cheese evenly over the rectangle and press it into the pastry with a rolling pin. Spread the pesto filling evenly over the cheese and roll each long end of the pastry to the center of the rectangle, making sure the pastry is tight and even. Chill well.

Cut the log crosswise into ⅜-inch slices, and place them 3 inches apart on parchment-lined baking sheets. Chill for at least 1 hour.

Preheat the oven to 450°.

Bake the palmiers until puffed and lightly golden, 6 to 7 minutes. Remove from the oven, quickly turn them over, and return them to the oven and bake for another 4 to 5 minutes. Let cool completely on wire racks.

NOTE: Baked palmiers can be refrigerated for 2 to 3 days in an airtight container or frozen. To recrisp, place them, unthawed, in a preheated 350° oven for 5 minutes.

VARIATION: Instead of pesto sauce, red pepper purée and a sprinkling of cayenne pepper can be spread on the puff pastry. Roll and bake as directed.

A Philippine mahogany basket was used to serve the beggar's purses.

The ingredients for making the beggar's purses—red pepper crêpes, caviar, sour cream, and chives.

Red Pepper Beggar's Purses

MAKES 40 HORS D'OEUVRES

CRÊPES

1 tablespoon olive oil
1 sweet red pepper, seeded and chopped
1 cup sifted all-purpose flour
4 eggs
1 cup milk
1¼ cups cold water
3 tablespoons unsalted butter, melted
½ teaspoon salt

FILLINGS

½ cup sour cream mixed with 7 ounces red caviar or fine black caviar (Sevruga) or
4 ounces chèvre mixed with ¼ cup crème fraîche and 1 teaspoon chopped scallion

1 large bunch fresh long chives

Heat the oil in a skillet and sauté the red pepper until tender. Place the sautéed pepper in a blender or food processor and purée. Add the flour, eggs, milk, water, melted butter, and salt, and mix at high speed for 30 seconds. Scrape down the sides and blend 30 seconds more. Pour the batter into a mixing bowl and refrigerate for at least 1 hour, preferably overnight.

To make the crêpes, spoon 2 tablespoons of the batter onto a hot buttered griddle or skillet. (Each crêpe should be about 3½ inches in diameter.) Cook over medium-high heat until the surface is bubbly. Flip the crêpes and cook until golden brown, about 30 seconds. Remove from the heat and stack until ready to use, covered with a damp cloth.

To serve the beggar's purses spoon a small amount of the desired filling (approximately 1 tablespoon) onto the center of each crêpe, gather up the edges of the crêpe as evenly as possible, and tie the bundle closed with one long chive.

NOTE: The crêpes may be made several hours before using and kept well wrapped at room temperature. They may also be made further in advance, frozen, and thawed at room temperature or in a microwave just before filling.

315

Deviled Eggs

SEE RECIPE, PAGE 236.

ABOVE: Angel biscuits with a filling of country ham slivers sit atop a glass-lined fabric-
covered wicker basket. RIGHT: A silver tray
lined with fresh dill makes a perfect bed for the
deviled eggs and prevents them from rolling.

Angel Biscuits
with Country Ham

MAKES FORTY-EIGHT 1½-INCH
BISCUITS

  2 packages active dry yeast
¼ cup warm water
  5 cups all-purpose flour
  1 tablespoon baking powder
  1 teaspoon baking soda
2½ tablespoons sugar
  1 teaspoon salt
½ pound (2 sticks) unsalted
    butter, cut into small pieces
  2 cups buttermilk
  8 tablespoons (1 stick)
    unsalted butter, melted and
    cooled
    Herb Butter (page 268)
    Country Ham (page 287)

Preheat the oven to 450°. Butter a baking sheet or line it with parchment paper and set aside.

Dissolve the yeast in the warm water and let proof.

Sift the flour, baking powder, baking soda, sugar, and salt together into a large bowl. Cut in the butter until the mixture resembles coarse meal. Stir in the yeast and buttermilk. Turn out onto a floured board and knead the dough until it is smooth and no longer sticky. Roll out the dough to a thickness of ½ inch, and cut out 1½-inch rounds with a biscuit cutter (you could also use a sharp knife to cut 1½-inch squares). Set the biscuits 2 inches apart on the baking sheet, brush the tops with melted butter, and bake until lightly golden (they should not brown), 10 to 12 minutes.

Slice warm and spread with herb-flavored butter, and fill with slivers of country ham.

VARIATION: Angel biscuits are also delicious filled with gravlax, smoked salmon, or smoked turkey.

Roast Loin of Pork with Prunes

SERVES 10

1 cup pitted prunes
1¼ cups Armagnac or Calvados
2 2½- to 3-pound boneless loins of pork, neatly tied, with almost all fat removed
4 to 6 garlic cloves, peeled and halved
4 teaspoons coarse salt
2 teaspoons freshly ground black pepper
8 bay leaves, crumbled
Approximately ½ cup olive oil for browning
4 tablespoons (½ stick) unsalted butter
½ pound fresh chanterelle mushrooms, halved lengthwise
2 tart green apples, peeled, cored, and cut into thin strips

Macerate the prunes in ⅔ cup Armagnac or Calvados overnight.

At least 1 hour before roasting, rub the loins of pork with the cut garlic, salt, pepper, and bay leaves, and let stand at room temperature for up to an hour, or longer in the refrigerator. (However, remove the pork from the refrigerator an hour before roasting.)

Preheat the oven to 375°. With aluminum foil, line a roasting pan just large enough to hold the pork. Rub as much of the marinade as possible off of the pork loins.

Heat the olive oil in a heavy skillet and brown the pork; this should take 6 or 7 minutes. Place the browned meat in the prepared roasting pan and pour the remaining Armagnac or Calvados over it. Flame the brandy with a lighted match and let it burn until all the alcohol evaporates. Place the pork in the upper third of the oven and roast for approximately 40 minutes; the internal temperature should register 160° on a meat thermometer. Remove from the oven while you prepare the sauce.

Melt the butter in a small skillet and sauté the mushrooms for 3 minutes. Add the apple slices and cook 2 minutes longer. Add the prunes and their macerating liquid, and cook for 3 to 4 minutes.

Slice the pork ¼ inch thick, and serve with the sauce spooned over each serving.

Steamed Baby Carrots

6 baby carrots with tops per person
Melted unsalted butter (optional)
Salt and freshly ground black pepper, to taste (optional)

Carefully peel the carrots, and cut off all but 1 inch of the green tops. Steam over rapidly boiling water until tender, 3 to 5 minutes. Remove from the steamer and serve immediately, tossed with melted butter and seasoned, if desired.

Root Vegetables Anna

SERVES 12

4 medium sweet potatoes
6 yellow waxy potatoes
1 medium butternut squash
1½ cups clarified butter (page 301)
Salt and freshly ground black pepper, to taste
Fresh thyme, to taste

Peel both types of potatoes and thinly slice. Peel the butternut squash, remove the seeds, and slice it as thinly as possible. Place the sliced vegetables in separate containers of ice water for at least 30 minutes.

Preheat the oven to 400°. Drain the vegetables and pat dry.

Pour one quarter of the clarified butter into a 9-inch ovenproof dish, pie plate, or iron skillet. Starting with the sweet potatoes, arrange the slices in concentric circles, overlapping them to cover the entire pan bottom. Drizzle with a bit of clarified butter, and season to taste with salt, pepper, and thyme. Repeat with a layer of waxy potatoes, then a layer of squash. Repeat these 3 layers until all the vegetables are used. Bake until the vegetables are golden brown and soft, approximately 35 to 50 minutes. Press the vegetable slices with a spoon or spatula once or twice while baking to keep them flat.

Remove the dish from the oven and pour off any excess butter. Cut the vegetables into wedges, as you would a pie, and serve.

Light Wedding Lunch in a Meadow

If I were getting married today, I would probably choose a menu very similar to this. It can be served indoors or out, in a formal or informal setting, to a small intimate group or to a medium-size wedding party of thirty to fifty guests.

The two hors d'oeuvres are especially tasty with champagne. They can be freshly made and served from silver trays or baskets. In this instance, the turquoise-painted basket was filled to brimming with bright green creeping thyme (it grows under my quince trees). The cayenne wafers were arranged on the thyme. The gravlax-filled angel biscuits were served from a silver tray that was decoratively lined with deeply cut leaves of red flowering kale.

This particular wedding luncheon was held in the middle of an open field. The round table was set for ten guests. A white undercloth was covered with an off-white lace cloth. Green lacquered chairs, white linen napkins, crystal glassware and dishes, and vermeil flatware were rented. The centerpiece was created from garden-cut herbs and arranged in a footed silver compote. Even in bright sunlight, this centerpiece stayed fresh, fragrant, and unwilted.

The first course was a delicate soup made from beets and cucumbers. It was served cold, in clear glass bowls, and garnished with finely chopped spring onions and chives. The main course was a full, plated salad of home-smoked chicken, wild mushrooms, and baby summer vegetables served atop a bed of varied lettuces. Crispy French pistolets with unsalted butter were served as an accompaniment to the salad.

A light, lemony wedding cake was served as dessert.

MENU

HORS D'OEUVRES
Cayenne Shortbread · Angel Biscuits with Gravlax

FIRST COURSE
Pink Cucumber Soup

MAIN COURSE
Smoked Chicken Salad · Homemade French Rolls

DESSERT
Wedding Cake

Basket trays were specially painted, then lined with herbs for serving hors d'oeuvres.

Deeply cut leaves of flowering purple kale lined this silver tray.

Cayenne Shortbread

MAKES APPROXIMATELY 6 DOZEN
WAFERS

- 1 teaspoon cayenne pepper
- 1 teaspoon salt
- 2½ cups all-purpose flour
- ½ pound Cheddar or Gruyère cheese, grated
- ½ pound (2 sticks) unsalted butter, at room temperature
- 1 cup chopped pecans

Sift together the cayenne pepper, salt, and flour and set aside.

Using an electric mixer, cream together the cheese and butter until well blended. Gradually add the dry ingredients; if the dough becomes too thick, use a wooden spoon to stir it. Add the chopped pecans. Divide the dough in half and shape into logs approximately 1½ inches in diameter and 9 inches long. Wrap well in plastic and chill for at least 1 hour or freeze (see Note).

Preheat the oven to 350°. Generously butter several baking sheets, or line them with parchment paper.

Using a sharp knife, cut the logs into ¼-inch slices and place the wafers on the prepared baking sheets. Bake just until slightly colored, approximately 15 to 20 minutes. Remove from the baking sheets and let cool on wire racks. Store in an airtight container.

NOTE: The dough may be frozen and baked just before serving.

Angel Biscuits with Gravlax

SEE RECIPE VARIATION, PAGE 317.

PRECEDING PAGE: This very small wedding lunch was served at a solitary table in a beautiful field seemingly in the middle of nowhere. (In fact, it is in Westport, Connecticut.) RIGHT: The soup, a delicious concoction, was garnished with pieces of chive blossom.

Pink Cucumber Soup

SERVES 10 TO 12

6 cucumbers
1 tablespoon coarse salt
4 to 6 fresh beets (depending
  on size)
1 tablespoon unsalted butter
1 tablespoon safflower oil
4 tart green apples, peeled,
  cored, and diced
2 medium onions, peeled and
  chopped
1 cup dry vermouth
½ cup medium-dry
  (Amontillado) sherry
1 head Boston lettuce
6 cups chicken stock,
  preferably homemade
  Salt and freshly ground
  white pepper, to taste
2 cups sour cream

GARNISH: Chopped fresh
chives or fresh mint leaves

Peel the cucumbers and halve them
lengthwise. Using a melon baller, remove the
seeds and discard. Grate the cucumbers into a
colander, sprinkle with the salt, and let drain
for at least 30 minutes. Put the drained cucumbers into a large piece of cheesecloth,
bring up the ends, and twist the cheesecloth
gently to squeeze out the excess liquid. Set
aside.

Preheat the oven to 350°.

Wash the beets and cut off the tops.
Wrap them in aluminum foil and bake until
tender, approximately 30 minutes. Let cool;
peel and dice the beets. Set aside.

Combine the butter and safflower oil
in a large saucepan. Sauté the diced apples and
onions until soft, about 10 minutes, but do
not let them brown. Add the vermouth and
sherry and bring to a boil.

Cut the lettuce into thin strips, or
chiffonade, and add to the mixture along with
the diced beets, cucumbers, and chicken
stock. Season to taste and set aside to cool.

When the soup is cool, purée in a
food processor until very smooth. Blend in the
sour cream and refrigerate.

Serve the soup chilled with a sprinkling of chopped fresh chives or a fresh mint
leaf on top.

Smoked Chicken Salad

SERVES 12

MARINADE

1 large yellow onion, peeled
and sliced

2 garlic cloves, peeled and sliced

½ cup chopped fresh parsley

½ cup olive oil
Juice and zest of 2 oranges

¼ cup dry vermouth
Salt and freshly ground
black pepper to taste

3 sprigs tarragon

4 whole chicken breasts

VINAIGRETTE

⅔ cup safflower oil

⅔ cup light olive oil

⅔ cup rice wine vinegar

2 tablespoons Dijon-style
mustard
Salt and freshly ground
pepper, to taste

¾ pound sugar snap peas,
stems removed

6 tablespoons (¾ stick)
unsalted butter

½ pound shiitake mushrooms

¼ teaspoon saffron threads

2 sweet yellow peppers,
seeded and thinly sliced

1 pound red or green baby
okra

2 heads red-leaf lettuce

GARNISH: Fresh red and
green basil

Combine all marinade ingredients and place in a large bowl or pan along with the chicken breasts. Marinate, covered, in the refrigerator at least 10 hours.

To smoke the chicken, remove it from the marinade and place on a smoker rack. Smoke in a water smoker or covered kettle grill according to manufacturer's instructions until the flesh shows no pink and the juices run clear when the chicken is pierced, 45 to 60 minutes. Remove from the smoker and let cool. Halve the breasts and carefully remove the meat in one piece. Cut into ⅛-inch-thick slices and set aside.

LEFT: A basket filled with freshly cut thyme, sage, rosemary, lamb's ears, mint, parsley, allium, and basil. ABOVE: The main course of smoked chicken salad.

Whisk all vinaigrette ingredients together and set aside.

In a large pot of boiling salted water, blanch the sugar snap peas for 1 minute. Plunge immediately into ice water to stop the cooking and drain well.

Over medium-high heat, melt half the butter in a sauté pan and sauté the mushrooms with the saffron until lightly browned, 3 to 4 minutes. Set aside.

Melt the remaining butter and sauté the sliced peppers for 3 to 4 minutes, until just barely tender. Set aside.

In a large pot of boiling water, boil the okra until tender, 4 to 5 minutes. Drain well and place it in a large bowl with the other vegetables; add ¾ cup of the vinaigrette and toss lightly. (Make sure the okra is warm so it will retain some color and not become glutinous.)

Line a serving bowl or individual plates with large, perfect lettuce leaves and add the vegetables. Carefully arrange the slices of smoked chicken on top and dress with a bit of the remaining vinaigrette. Garnish with fresh basil leaves.

Homemade French Rolls

SEE RECIPE, PAGE 247.

Wedding Cakes

The centerpiece of any wedding feast, ritualistic, traditional, fanciful, and real, is the wedding cake. It rolls in on its own little mobile stage, or waits prominently on a special round table or even on a Doric column. Drums roll; photographers scurry; an ornate cutting utensil gleams (a pretty knife, an heirloom spatula, occasionally a golden sword); the bride and groom blush and carve and share the first slice of cake, sweetly, romantically, and usually Marx Brothers style. It is a nice tradition, and everyone always smiles and cheers, for it is the climax of the festivities, after which guests relax and dance and prepare for the ceremonial send-off, the rice, tin cans, and emotional good-byes.

It has always been so, back when the early Romans made simple barley cakes to offer to Jupiter (crumbled over the bride's head as a fertility rite), and in the Middle Ages, when small sweet buns were brought by the guests themselves and stacked in a tower before the bridal couple, who tried to kiss over the mound in

the hope of many children and lifelong prosperity. But it is only in the last several hundred years that an elaborate, many-tiered fantasy like our traditional wedding cake has been the custom, and only recently that the white bride's cake has given way to chocolate, hazelnut, carrot, lemon, and orange confections, constructed in a multitude of shapes, and decorated with unimaginable whimsies.

The baking of wedding cakes today brings to mind the great Antonin Carême's pronouncement in the seventeenth century that the fine arts numbered five: sculpture, painting, poetry, music, and architecture, whose main branch was confection. As in Carême's day, when master pastry chefs were known to invest a year in creating a masterpiece like Notre Dame cathedral in sugar, there is again a passionate artistry in the profession, encouraged by a new appreciation of the results. And the zeal seems contagious; when I illustrated how to make my favorite basketweave wedding cake step-by-step in *Entertaining*, I never imagined that years later, I would go to weddings where the sister or aunt or mother of the bride would shyly approach me to mention proudly that she had made the basketweave cake on display, or that I would receive hundreds of letters enclosing pictures of similarly inspired creations. Now I have enlarged my repertoire, for I've received requests for carrot cakes, spice cakes, and orange cakes, and I have discovered wonderful new tastes, like an ethereal Italian cream cake, made with buttermilk or heavy cream. The state of the art grows richer by the moment, as weddings become more expressive.

The choice of wedding cake seems to typify contemporary wedding behavior, which is directed by a combination of "once-in-a-lifetime" and "this-must-be-right-for-me."

Cakes vary greatly in cost, which is usually determined by the number of portions provided, and can range from one to seven dollars per serving. Yet in the end, price seems to play a secondary role to design. Many brides have a preconceived idea of the perfect wedding cake, distilled from photographs, friends' weddings, or pure imagination. Some find its cosmetics more important than its edibility, for it is, in fact, a frivolity as much as a dessert. Some have dramatic images in mind—eight-foot towers caging a pair of doves, or an all-white cake festooned with cherubs and lace. (There are precedents: Queen Victoria's wedding cake, which weighed three hundred pounds, was crowned with an ice sculpture of Britannia, and surrounded by cupids; and a Texas couple recently had their likenesses recreated within a gilded frame.) Some wish to respect their heritage with a traditional French croquembouche or Swedish fomekaken.

Today, fewer brides seem to order a groom's cake, traditionally a fruitcake, dark and substantial, although Anne O'Herron added a carrot cake for Jon, and the Carpenters served many chocolate mousse cakes to accompany the spectacular bride's cake made by the renowned Ida Mae. A fruitcake like the groom's cake was, in fact, the typical wedding cake until the introduction of finely ground flour and baking powder in America in the eighteenth century, when the white wedding cake became "the bride's cake" and the dark, "the groom's."

Most brides like to contribute something individualistic to the wedding cake—a few making it themselves, with the support of mothers and talented friends; more of them choosing the shape, flavor, color scheme (coordinated to the wedding party or the flowers in the surrounding gardens) or the decoration (favorite flavors, animals, memorabilia). It is

all possible today, even in the extreme. Until not too long ago, small figures of a bride and groom customarily crowned the cake, but now almost any decorative memento might appear at the top—tiny tennis rackets, a couple of wedding mice, a sailboat, a horse and carriage (as at the Cook wedding), police badges (for star of *Dragnet* Jack Webb), a tree seedling (which, in Bermuda, is later planted by the couple). Many bakers consult at length with the prospective couple, in order to understand their mission. As a breed, they seem to be less cranky than chefs, for their art is less invention than perfection, and they take less umbrage in their eccentricities. Bakers like to make wedding cakes, not only because it implicates them in a happy occasion, but because it also calls for the precision and creativity with which they flourish. As Maurice Bonté, the master chef of Bonté in Manhattan, said in his charming way, "*Vous savez*—you know, making cakes is a business, but sometimes it is just a pleasure to make pretty things."

If one were to stage an exhibit of contemporary wedding cakes, it would suggest in range and personality the rich panorama of styles visible in the art world today, the baroque, the naïve, the pop, the postmodern, Art Deco, Expressionism. Tucked away in small towns

PRECEDING PAGES, LEFT: The orange-almond cake, with fraises des bois and white chocolate curls, made for Sissy Cargill's wedding. RIGHT: Patrie Kontje cuts her cake under the watchful gazes of her children and little friends. OPPOSITE: At this farmhouse wedding the food was ethnic and informal, but the cake remained traditional, even though it was served from a huge square basket.

and suburbs, there is inevitably a cake man or cake lady, a Jane Stacey or an Ida Mae, creating his or her own kind of masterpiece. To illustrate the wealth of possibilities confronting a bride today, as well as the aesthetics and techniques in vogue, I asked an interesting sampling of bakers each to create a special cake for this book, and to talk about the sensibilities of their work.

Ida Mae

Ida Mae and her "Cakes of Distinction" are a tradition in the South that rivals hush puppies and burritos in importance, and at least one of her creations—a fourteen-foot masterpiece that was covered with hundreds of sugar flowers and tiny lights, crowned with Swiss porcelain likenesses of the bride and groom, and had to be transported in a moving van—has become the stuff of legend around Dallas. Out from the kitchen, located in the tiny town of Jacksboro, Texas, founded three decades ago by grandmotherly Ida Mae Stark, and now run by Becky Sikes Crump, trucks also roll as far away as Louisiana, Georgia, Tennessee, and Boston, as the word about Ida Mae cakes spreads. Home base, however, is Dallas, and Becky Crump says she could set up a cake at the Dallas Country Club in her sleep. An Ida Mae cake is something of a local treasure, and has graced the parties of Lady Bird Johnson, Robert Strauss, and many Hunts.

I saw my first Ida Mae cake at the wedding of Barbara Carpenter and Spencer Kendrick in Dallas in 1984. It was a five-tier, eight-foot-tall, lemon-scented bride's cake for two thousand, completely encrusted with hundreds of tiny white sugar flowers, and holding a dramatic flower topknot. These sugar flowers, concocted of gum tragacanth and sugar and

shaped with a sculptor's skill into all the blooms of the garden ("fluties" or trumpetlike flowers resembling morning glories or hibiscus are a specialty still made weekly by Ida Mae herself), are the trademark of an Ida Mae cake, and call to mind the finest eighteenth- and nineteenth-century Meissen porcelain. Such decoration is customized, and, working from fabric swatches, the bakery staff can re-

Typical of the Ida Mae traditional cake, this towering edifice is truly an extraordinary example of cake decoration at its finest.

produce the colors of a bridesmaid's dress or the reception table dressing. It has created a cake decorated with flowers ranging from the rich American Beauty rose at the base to the palest pink at top; a dark ecru cake covered with creamy gardenias; and, for Victoria Principal last year, an extravagance of lilies. For

other design details, Ida Mae first drew her inspiration from antique lace and old sterling silver patterns.

Most brides seem to request Ida Mae's standard white cake, flavored lightly with citrus, although a spice, chocolate, and carrot cake are in the basic repertoire too. One source of pride in the kitchen is that cakes last for weeks because they do not contain butter or eggs or milk. What transforms the taste of a rather plain cake is the addition of sweet rich fillings, usually spiked with liqueurs. But it is the look rather than the delicacy of an Ida Mae cake that is the cause for its glory, and that brings 365 people a year in contact with Jacksboro, Texas.

Since the succession of Mrs. Crump three years ago, the business of cakes has become more streamlined, and although the shop is not open to the public, literature (illustrations of cakes and prices of about two dollars a serving) is available, and Mrs. Crump happily travels about to consult on decisions. Often a staff member accompanies a cake's delivery, for its setup can be a feat of engineering. Under the frilly tiers are sturdy metal stands designed by Ida Mae's geologist-engineer husband, and inside are steel pipes, guaranteeing stability and effortless cutting. But in the case of a recent spring wedding creation, which consisted of a main cake surrounding a maypole and leading by ribbons to four satellite cakes suspended from the ceiling, sophisticated assembly was in order. Becky Crump's actor-husband Jim is *her* engineer, and he solved the challenges of the maypole cake with plumbing supplies. He also built her new shop and delivers cakes across the countryside. "Last year we went to Hollywood for the first time," Mrs. Crump said eagerly. "Now we sure would like to do New York."

A smiling M. Bonté in front of his shop in New York. The cake in the window is garnished with Bonté's signature— pulled sugar bows and ribbons.

Maurice Bonté

In a city in which a bakery appears in the streetscape every other block, and the number of French bakeries rivals that in most European capitals, Bonté has a secure and special place. It is a simple, straightforward shop on Third Avenue and Seventy-fourth Street in Manhattan, in which the décor pays homage to the patisserie on display. At the cash register is Suzy Bonté, from Brittany, and behind the counter and by the ovens is Maurice Bonté, from Normandy. They married shortly after they met in America in the 1960s, and opened the store together in 1974. Maurice Bonté has been baking cakes since he was thirteen, when he began to train with his father, who baked cakes in Trouville.

Whereas the traditional wedding cake in France remains a croquembouche, that pyramid of little cream puffs held together with caramel and graced with spun sugar, in his decade in New York, Monsieur Bonté has evolved four delicious many-tiered wedding

cakes that remain true to the aesthetics of classical French pastry and yet are distinguished by an original and elegant beauty. The croquembouche is fragile, badly suited to humidity, and would do poorly tucked under a pillow, Monsieur Bonté offered as an explanation for its frequent absence at American weddings; besides, Americans love chocolate and Grand Marnier, the flavors of his two most popular cakes.

I first knew Bonté as the source of the best croissant in New York; then I tasted their cassis cake, created of layers of white genoise sponge cake soaked in black currant liqueur, filled with black currant preserves, and frosted with a white buttercream or marzipan icing; most recently, I became aware of Monsieur Bonté's mastery of the art of decorating with pulled sugar—sugar colored in a possible rainbow of hues, cooked until glassy hard, and then fashioned into frills, notably the lavish bows that have become the Bonté signature.

Monsieur Bonté has acquired a devoted following for his mocha cake (white genoise with mocha buttercream), and his chocolate cake

too (chocolate genoise filled with raspberry preserves and covered with ganache), but my particular favorite now is his Grand Marnier cake (genoise soaked in the orange-scented liqueur and filled with Grand Marnier buttercream and orange marmalade), which he decorates with a swag-festooned marzipan coating and great wonderful bows of red and white pulled sugar. Although Monsieur Bonté loves to make his bows ("time consuming, but something special of my own, like a personal touch"), and sometimes adds a lineup of smaller bows around the base of a cake, he responds to requests to decorate with fresh or frosting flowers too.

There is an aura of perfection to a Bonté cake, derived from its elegant simplicity and its rich, delicate taste. When I said that I felt like I was in the presence of *the* classic French cake, Monsieur Bonté demurred, however, explaining that in France, cake layers are flat, and that if his father were to see his, he would say they were too fat. "But Americans like fat cakes," he said happily. "And classical is many things. Classical is especially quality."

Sylvia Weinstock

Sylvia Weinstock is known as the Cake Lady in Manhattan and environs, where she supplies hotels like the Pierre and the Plaza, and individual cake cognoscenti with her ornate, romantic, and imperial creations. Like many bakers of wedding cakes today, she began professional life as something else—in her case as a pianist and artist—but then one day found herself quite consumed with a desire to make cakes. She learned the basic techniques of the art from classes with French pastry chefs, worked a while with her friend William Greenberg, whose bakery is a landmark on the Upper East Side, and then began to adapt her knowledge of French traditions to the American taste. Almost a decade ago, she and her husband bought and renovated a beautiful four-story Federal house on Church Street in the financial district, and within it carved out a home, an office, and a professional work space where she holds forth.

Her cakes include a lemon curd cake, a sponge cake, an orange pound cake, a chocolate cake, and a hazelnut torte; they are unusually high-sided to provide exhibition space for her fanciful sugar dough flowers and they assume a variety of shapes, formal and country, depending on her inspiration and that of the bride. Mrs. Weinstock makes a point of talking at length to the bride, for she believes the choice of wedding cake is a once-in-a-lifetime decision, and she wants to create an appropriate fantasy. She concerns herself with what the

This small but lavish one-layer cake, 5 inches tall, was created by Sylvia Weinstock. It was frosted with buttercream and then covered with an amazing variety of Sylvia's handmade sugar dough flowers.

bride will be wearing and what the décor of the wedding will be, and duplicates lace and flowers in her designs. She loves formal and romantic cakes, and she thinks that every cake should look as if it were specially ordered and that it should be one of the most fabulous elements of each wedding.

Mrs. Weinstock made a basketweave cake for this book, rounded at the top, woven with buttercream and pastry cream on the sides, and then studded with a garden of fantasy flowers. To me, it suggests nineteenth-century English porcelain. It has both a realism and a grandeur, even a regalness, and yet it is memorably edible.

Jane Stacey

Jane Stacey is the model of the determined young pastry chef, well trained in the classical basics, open to new inspirations, all the while evolving an expressive style of her own. She worked in my kitchen as a pastry chef for two years, turning out beautiful cakes and tarts, but was inwardly consumed with her own ideas. Now she is forging a career of her own, with great individualism and ability. What has always been special about Jane's cakes is that they offer a simple, elegant facade, and a rich complicated interior. They are classical yet whimsical, and always delicious.

For this chapter Jane created a beautiful and unusual four-tier white cake, already proven a great success at many weddings. It combines the dacquoise, one of the glories in the French heritage, and a traditional light bride's cake, and emerges looking like a period piece from the Belle Epoque. Its construction involves a delicate process of interfacing layers of hazelnut genoise with layers of hazelnut dacquoise, all filled with bittersweet chocolate ganache

and Swiss meringue buttercream, and then coated with white chocolate Swiss meringue buttercream and decorated with white chocolate curls. All this pastry terminology indicates a complex and time-consuming effort, delivered in the cause of art for art's sake, and an unforgettable pleasure for the palate.

Larry Rosenberg

While he was the director of the Roth Institute of Cake Decoration, operating out of H. Roth's thirty-five-year-old emporium of pastry supplies and kitchenware in Manhattan, Larry Rosenberg taught a little bit of everything, including a bilingual Spanish-American course in cakes to an upper-Upper East Side neighborhood community, many of whom came from the West Indies, and wanted to make black fruitcakes with marzipan and royal icing for their wedding cakes. Now he is a freelance baker, with a multitude of other enterprises up his sleeve (he has published a book on cake decorating, teaches at the New York Restaurant School, and has finished a video on icing roses), and his enthusiasm for cakes in general and his diverse repertoire convey the guiding spirit of the profession today.

"I like to cook. I like to work with fresh flowers. Sometimes I get a sample of the flowers in a bridal bouquet and make icing flowers to match, so that they can be kept as a memento, like the statue of the bride and groom. Sometimes I put wristlets of icing flowers on the columns I place between tiers, so that they can be given away to caring guests. I love to make wedding cakes. They are a challenge for me and very satisfying, because customers invest more thought in them. I want a cake that looks different, and American taste is so open-minded these days that I am not locked into a tradition or a traditional look. People who don't like icing flowers go in for fondants or whipped cream. It is very exciting, and for this one big event, people appreciate quality. Commercial bakers can't really compete, because they use mixes and plastic flowers."

To mention just two of his wedding cakes, Mr. Rosenberg makes a chocolate cake with a chocolate mousse filling and a new rendition of strawberry shortcake, with a stately cream frosting and a garnish of many perfect strawberries. For me, he made a wonderfully original-looking carrot cake, rising three tiers, frosted with a cream cheese and sweet butter icing, encrusted on its sides with ground walnuts, and decorated with silver shot dragées, baby's breath, and roses. It had a beautiful mellow autumnal look, and a presence all its own.

Rose Levy Beranbaum

Rose Levy Beranbaum is known around New York City as Cordon Rose. She has a loyal entourage, who await her articles in *Cook's* magazine or *Bon Appétit*, and who take her first book, *Romantic and Classic Cakes*, to bed with them to plot and fantasize about elegant creations. (A second book, called *The Cordon Rose Cake Book*, is in the works.) A longtime teacher of baking classes, based on impeccable technique and whimsical invention, Rose made her newest confection for this book, called a Golden Glory Wedding (Cheese)cake, a twenty-four-pound, three-tier, apricot-studded cheesecake, frosted with white chocolate, and decorated with spun sugar and wide gold lamé ribbon from Paris.

"Romantic" and "classic" describe Rose's style well, for while she favors classical lines over the baroque, she also dreams of the moments when she can weave fresh wild violets

into a cloud of spun sugar, for example, as she did with the cheesecake, which was created for her niece Joan Beranbaum's springtime wedding. Although it is everyone's favorite eating, a cheesecake, Rose points out, was a risky choice for a wedding cake, because its moist, heavy tiers are unlikely candidates for suspension. Yet the rigid white chocolate cream-cheese frosting, and an inner support provided by straws, gave the cake great stability, even during hours of display outdoors. Uncharacteristically, even in these days of eminently edible wedding cakes, it was completely consumed. Rose prides herself on using only the best ingredients in her cakes, in this case, Tobler's Narcisse white chocolate, Philadelphia cream cheese, unsulfured dried California apricots, and Barack Palinka, an apricot eau de vie from Austria. It is a unique creation, for while most cheesecakes are creamy in the center, this one emerges creamy throughout, because it has been coddled like a custard in a waterbath. It is sweet, yet it is also tart, with the taste of lemon and little pockets of apricot purée steeped in apricot brandy.

———

I continue to make wedding cakes out of the sheer pleasure of invention. It is individual expression, and I never tire of decorating cakes because I try to alter each one, taking inspiration from a dress (Hilary Cushing's pleated cake came to me after seeing her wonderful Mary McFadden study in pleats), an old piece of lace, flowers, or classical elements of design. For years, I did variation upon variation of the basketweave cake, using many different pastry tips. Although it is still one of my favorites, I have been experimenting more, using the leaf tip to create swags and ribbons and

pleats on cakes. Although I still like the Italian meringue buttercream best as a frosting, I have been diverted by the Swiss meringue white chocolate icing, which is also very good. I still prefer a fresh flower decoration, especially one calling for old roses of which I now have two hundred different varieties in my garden. Specifically, I like a swag-decorated cake reminiscent of a small piece of theater, and I like to decorate it with old-fashioned tea roses in shades of apricot, champagne, and Cognac. But I also can't resist trying the new. Despite the problems humidity can sometimes pose, I've added a croquembouche to my repertoire, and now that I feel more sure of myself with pastry bags and tips, I'd love to create a Majolica cake, incorporating the fanciful colors of that nineteenth-century pottery.

It is an exercise in precision and order to create a wedding cake, as all the preceding bakers know. First, you make the various-sized layers, which will then be frosted and gently laid on supports, to create the final wonder. The assembly is difficult, in fact rather scary, for there is no room for mistakes. Although there is always extra frosting to correct or disguise any small distress incurred in transport, a cake cannot be recast, for the wedding is on. And until it is securely established on its special table, a multitude of mishaps threaten. Fortunately, only once has the worst happened to one of my cakes, as a result of a wild ride in an un-air-conditioned car.

I like to make cakes that look unique, as if they somehow just happened. I like cakes that are irresistibly edible, inside and out. And I like to run out to the garden before the wedding to gather a bucket of the freshest, most beautiful flowers conforming to the decorative scheme of the event, and then, minutes before presentation, adorn the cake according to the tone of the day. Often, while I am completing a cake at a wedding, working away on an adjacent lawn or in a garage service space, I find many pairs of eyes watching intently. They belong to guests who have been drawn in by their interest in the drama of the wedding cake, and they stand wide-eyed and appreciative as I align the tiers, and begin to fill them with the sprigs of boxwood or the bunches of tiny alpine strawberries. When the act is complete, they release a deep sigh of satisfaction and then move off, looking dreamy and a little misty-eyed.

LEFT: A wall of wedding cake ornaments in Larry Rosenberg's kitchen. The variety and ethnicity of the choices are wonderful.
RIGHT: In a pinch, even the back of a station wagon can be used to assemble a wedding cake.

Jane Stacey's Hazelnut Genoise and Dacquoise Wedding Cake

MAKES 4 LAYERS—
3×6 INCHES, 3×10 INCHES,
3×12 INCHES, AND 3×14 INCHES

All the elements of this cake can easily be made in advance of the wedding reception. The cake can be double-wrapped in plastic and frozen for up to one week. The buttercream icing can also be refrigerated or frozen for up to two weeks. To thaw the icing, cake, and dacquoise, simply set out, wrapped, and bring to room temperature. Whip icing with the paddle of an electric beater. It may "break" initially, but keep beating and it should become creamy and fluffy.

HAZELNUT GENOISE

48 eggs, lightly beaten
8 cups sugar
6 cups sifted cake flour
3 cups toasted, skinned, and ground hazelnuts
12 tablespoons (1½ sticks) brown butter (see Note)
4 teaspoons vanilla extract

HAZELNUT DACQUOISE

4½ cups sugar
¾ cup cornstarch
1½ cups toasted, skinned, and ground hazelnuts
18 egg whites
1 tablespoon vanilla extract
¾ teaspoon cream of tartar

A portrait of the finished cake atop the serving pedestal. More white chocolate curls were arranged around the base.

SWISS MERINGUE BUTTERCREAM (FOR MOCHA FILLING AND WHITE CHOCOLATE ICING)

4 cups egg whites
   (approximately 30)
8 cups sugar
5 pounds (20 sticks) unsalted
   butter, cut into 2-tablespoon-
   size pieces
½ cup instant coffee dissolved
   in 2 tablespoons hot brewed
   coffee
½ cup Cognac
2 pounds white chocolate,
   melted and slightly cooled

CHOCOLATE GANACHE

2 pounds bittersweet
   chocolate
3 cups heavy cream
1 pound (4 sticks) unsalted
   butter, at room temperature,
   cut into small pieces

WHITE CHOCOLATE CURLS

10 ounces white chocolate
   (page 363)

Preheat the oven to 350°. Generously butter and flour the cake pans and then line with parchment paper.

To make the genoise, place the eggs and sugar in a large bowl and set over a pan of simmering water (the bowl should not touch the water). Whisk the mixture occasionally until it becomes warm and the sugar begins to dissolve. Transfer one fourth of the mixture to the bowl of an electric mixer. Using the electric mixer, beat at high speed until the mixture is very thick and pale yellow and forms a ribbon when dropped from a spatula. (This will have to be done in batches since most standard mixers will hold only 12 eggs.)

If the egg/sugar mixture has been mixed in a deep bowl, transfer it to a wide shallow one; the greater surface area will keep the batter from deflating too much.

Quickly but gently sift the flour over the mixture and fold in just until blended; follow with the ground hazelnuts. Finally fold in the brown butter and vanilla just until all ingredients are incorporated. Immediately pour the batter into the prepared pans, filling them two-thirds to three-quarters full, and bake for approximately 25 minutes, or until the cakes test done with a skewer, spring back when lightly touched in the center, and begin to pull away from the sides of the pans. Let cool slightly before removing the cakes from the pans to cool completely on wire racks.

To make the dacquoise, lower the oven temperature to 300°. Trace the bottoms of the pans onto parchment paper, cut out the circles, and set aside. Combine 1½ cups of the sugar, the cornstarch, and ground hazelnuts in a bowl; set aside.

Using an electric mixer, beat the egg whites, vanilla, and cream of tartar on medium speed until soft peaks form. (Again, remember that a standard mixer will hold only 12 egg whites.) Add remaining 4 cups of sugar, a tablespoon at a time, until stiff peaks form. Sprinkle one third of the sugar-hazelnut mixture over the meringue and fold in by hand. Repeat this two more times with the remaining sugar-hazelnut mixture. Place this mixture in a pastry bag fitted with a plain tip no larger than ½ inch in diameter. Beginning at the center pipe concentric circles onto the parchment, using the traced circles as your guide.

Bake for 40 to 45 minutes, or until the dacquoise is dry and brittle to the touch. Turn off the oven and leave the dacquoise in the oven until it reaches room temperature, approximately 1 hour.

To make the buttercream for both the filling and icing, combine the egg whites and sugar in a large mixing bowl and place over simmering water (the bowl should not touch the water), whisking occasionally until the mixture is warm and the sugar has dissolved. Remove from heat and, using an electric mixer, beat on high speed until stiff peaks form. Continue beating on medium speed until the meringue reaches room temperature. Still on medium speed, add the butter, a piece at a time, until all the butter is well blended. Scrape down the sides and bottom of the bowl from time to time.

Remove one third of the buttercream, add the coffee mixture and Cognac, and beat until thoroughly blended. Set aside.

This is the mocha buttercream filling.

Beat the remaining buttercream at high speed for a minute or two. Add the melted white chocolate and continue beating at high speed until evenly blended, again scraping down the sides of the bowl from time to time. Refrigerate until ready to use. This is the icing for the cake.

To make the chocolate ganache, chop the chocolate into small, matchstick-size pieces and place in a large stainless steel or heat-resistant bowl. Bring the cream to a rising boil and pour, all at once, over the chopped chocolate. Stir until the chocolate is melted and completely smooth with no lumps. Quickly stir in one or two pieces of the softened butter at a time, until completely dissolved. Set aside to thicken to a spreadable consistency.

To make the chocolate curls, follow the directions on page 363.

To assemble and decorate the tiers, first cut the hazelnut genoise layers into fourths crosswise. Spread mocha buttercream in between two of the thin layers of genoise, top with chocolate ganache, the dacquoise layer, more ganache, and then the remaining two thin genoise layers with mocha buttercream in between. These five thin layers make one 3-inch-thick tier of wedding cake. Continue to layer and stack the other tiers.

Chill the tiers well on cardboard supports cut exactly to size.

Frost the exterior of each tier with the white chocolate buttercream, smoothing the icing with a warm knife or spatula. (Warm the spatula by dipping it into hot water.)

Cut six chopsticks exactly to the height of each tier, insert in each tier as support for the next tier, and set one tier on top of the other. Apply a final, very smooth coat of buttercream over the entire cake, sides and top. With a very small round tip, decorate with the buttercream as illustrated.

Right before serving, garnish with white chocolate curls.

NOTE: To make the brown butter, simply melt unsalted butter in a sauté pan until it becomes a nutty brown color.

1. Jane begins stacking the five thin layers that will make up each of the four large tiers of her cake. A cardboard round, cut exactly to size, is placed beneath each of the tiers.

4. The white chocolate buttercream icing is put on very, very smoothly. For a glossy finish, Jane lightly sprays a mist of water over and smoothes out any imperfections.

2. Jane spreads the mocha buttercream filling between the genoise layers.

5. Jane applies her very simple, characteristic decoration with a small round tip.

3. The bottom tier being frosted with the white chocolate Swiss meringue buttercream.

6. Jane inserts three sharp bamboo skewers in each tier, then cuts them off to the height of that tier. (Straws and chopsticks will not work with this cake because of the very stiff, crunchy dacquoise layer sandwiched between the layers of ganache.)

7. The final two tiers being placed atop the bottom. Jane is careful to center them exactly. Her eye is very practiced and she needs no measuring.

8. Jane artfully garnishes the cake with the creamy white chocolate curls, placing them around each tier, on the top, and around the base.

9 & 10. *Left:* The completed cake, in the kitchen. It is on a slightly larger cardboard base so that it can be moved without disturbing the icing. *Right:* A detail of the neoclassic decoration: small dots and squiggles and white chocolate curls.

1. Larry carefully brushes
the crumbs off each layer
of unfrosted cake.

2. A thick layer of creamy
icing is spread over the
top and sides of each
layer.

3. Finely chopped
walnuts are pressed into
the icing-covered sides of
the cake. The tops are left
white.

4. Larry applies a shell
edge to the top and
bottom of each layer using
a large star tip. The cake
is ready for stacking.

5. Larry assembled his
cake on store-bought
plastic bases and tops,
which were specially
fitted with columns to
give an airy appearance to
the cake.

6. Larry puts the columns
in place, then adds silver
dragées around the edge
of each layer.

7. The layers are placed
atop the columns.

8. Larry begins to garnish
the cake with flowers.

The finished cake, garnished with miniature carnations, baby's breath, alstroemeria, and white satin bows.

Larry Rosenberg's Carrot Cake

MAKES 3 LAYERS—
3×6 INCHES, 3×8 INCHES,
AND 3×10 INCHES

This is the perfect cake for the bride who wants a homey, delicious, moist, atypical wedding cake. Carrot cake seems to be everyone's favorite, and because it is so easy to make it is a good choice for all but the most formal weddings. Both the cake and the icing recipes can be halved or reduced as desired. The cake can also be made in advance and frozen, without the icing, well wrapped in plastic for up to two weeks.

Chopped walnuts, which are pressed into the sides of the cake, are optional. The silver shot dragées dress up this cake beautifully.

9 cups sifted cake flour
2 tablespoons baking powder
2 tablespoons baking soda
1 tablespoon ground cinnamon
1½ teaspoons salt
6 cups sugar
4½ cups vegetable oil
12 large eggs, lightly beaten (or use jumbo eggs for an even moister cake)
6 cups grated carrots
1½ cups golden raisins
1½ cups dark raisins

ICING

3 8-ounce packages cream cheese, softened
6 cups confectioners' sugar, sifted
1½ cups (3 sticks) unsalted butter
3 cups solid shortening
1 tablespoon "clear" vanilla (available at fine baking stores)

2 cups finely chopped walnuts, optional
1 ounce silver shot dragées (optional)

Preheat the oven to 375°. Butter and flour the cake pans, then line with parchment paper (this prevents the raisins from burning).

Sift together the cake flour, baking powder, baking soda, cinnamon, and salt. Set aside.

In a large mixing bowl, beat the sugar, oil, and eggs until light and fluffy. Stir in the grated carrots. Add the sifted dry ingredients and stir together by hand, adding the raisins last.

Pour into the prepared pans and reduce oven temperature to 350°. Bake for approximately 1 hour, or until the cakes test done (they should still be slightly moist in the center). Let cool on wire racks before removing from the pans.

To make the icing, combine all ingredients in the bowl of an electric mixer and beat at low speed for 3 minutes. Scrape down the sides of the bowl and beat at high speed for 5 minutes.

Spread the icing smoothly over the top and sides of the layers, and press finely chopped walnuts into the sides. Stack the layers and decorate as desired with the silver shot dragées and fresh flowers.

Rose Levy Beranbaum's Golden Glory Wedding Cake

MAKES 3 LAYERS—
3×6 INCHES, 3×9 INCHES,
AND 3×12 INCHES

Most cheesecakes are creamiest in the center, but this one is creamy throughout because it is treated like a delicate custard, coddled in a water bath. It is tart with lemon and little pockets of apricot purée and perfumed with apricot brandy. If you don't have seamless cake pans, springform pans will do, but be sure to surround them with two layers of heavy-duty aluminum foil to keep the water from seeping in.

The ivory frosting is exceptionally mellow and creamy, ideal for frosting a wedding cake. The white chocolate adds texture, sweetness, and an undefinable flavor. And the addition of spun sugar, also known as "angels' hair," is well worth the effort.

APRICOT TOPPING

1 cup sieved apricot lekvar
   (see Note)
2 tablespoons Barack Palinka
   (see Note) or apricot brandy

APRICOT FILLING

1¾ pounds (approximately 4½
   cups packed) dried
   California apricots (The
   unsulfured variety found at
   most health food stores have
   a better flavor than
   commercially dried
   apricots.)
4 cups water
1 cup superfine sugar
3 tablespoons freshly
   squeezed, strained lemon
   juice

CRUMB CRUST

9 ounces (approximately 2¼
   cups) lemon cookie crumbs

CREAM CHEESE BATTER

10 8-ounce packages cream
   cheese, at room temperature
   (Philadelphia Brand preferred)
5 cups sugar
15 large eggs
⅓ cup cornstarch (optional)
⅔ cup freshly squeezed lemon
   juice, strained
2½ tablespoons vanilla extract
1¼ teaspoons salt
15 cups (7½ pints) sour cream

WHITE CHOCOLATE-CREAM CHEESE FROSTING

4 8-ounce packages cream
   cheese, at room temperature
   (Philadelphia Brand preferred)
1½ pounds white chocolate,
   melted (preferably Tobler's
   Narcisse, but any brand is
   all right as long as it contains
   cocoa butter)
1 pound (4 sticks) unsalted
   butter, at room temperature
¼ cup freshly squeezed,
   strained lemon juice

SPUN SUGAR

½ cup sugar
⅓ cup light corn syrup
1 teaspoon grated beeswax
   (optional, but highly
   recommended as beeswax
   has a high smoking point
   and will keep the strands
   flexible for a long time)

To make the apricot topping, process the apricot lekvar in the bowl of a food processor. Warm it slightly to soften, and put it through a fine sieve. While warm, combine it with the Barack Palinka or apricot brandy and set aside. Stored in an airtight container, this topping may be prepared weeks in advance and refrigerated, or kept at room temperature for a week.

To make the apricot filling, place the apricots and water in a saucepan and let stand, covered, for at least 2 hours. Bring to a boil and simmer, covered, for 20 minutes, or until the apricots are soft. Add more water as necessary. Transfer the apricots and any remaining liquid to the bowl of a food processor and purée (you should have 3 to 3¼ cups purée). Add the sugar and lemon juice; you should

have 4 cups. The filling can be prepared two days in advance and refrigerated, or frozen for up to three months.

Preheat the oven to 350°. Butter the cake pans and line with parchment paper. You will also need three pans slightly larger than these for the water bath and three rounds of cardboard cut to the sizes of the cake pans.

Sprinkle the lemon cookie crumbs into the bottoms of the buttered pans (1¼ cups for the 12-inch, ⅔ cup for the 9-inch, and ⅓ cup for the 6-inch pan) and pat them evenly and gently into place. Set aside.

To make the cream cheese filling, cream together the cheese and sugar in the large bowl of an electric mixer at medium speed until very smooth, about 3 minutes. Add the eggs, one at a time, beating until smooth after each addition. Beat in the optional cornstarch (which will prevent a slight watering-out later, but the texture will not be quite as silky and smooth). Add the lemon juice, vanilla extract, and salt, and beat just until all ingredients are well blended; do not overbeat. Blend in the sour cream.

Fill each of the prepared pans one-third full. Spoon small dollops of the apricot filling onto the cream cheese filling. Pour more cream cheese filling into each pan to a capacity of two-thirds, and repeat with the remaining apricot purée. (You should use a total of 2¼ cups purée for the 12-inch pan, 1 cup for the 9-inch pan, and ½ cup for the 6-inch pan.) Top with the remaining cream cheese mixture and, using a small spatula, swirl the apricot purée through the cream cheese, carefully avoiding the cookie crumb crust. The cake pans should be almost filled to the top with batter.

Set each pan into a larger pan into which you have poured 1 inch of hot water and bake for 50 minutes, rotating the cakes halfway through the cooking time. Turn off the oven but do not open the door and let the cakes cool for 1 hour. Remove to a wire rack and let cool to room temperature. Wrap well with plastic wrap and refrigerate for up to three days.

To unmold the cakes, run a thin metal spatula around the side of each cake. Place the pan on a heated burner for 10 to 20 seconds, moving the pan back and forth. Place a flat platter or baking sheet on top of the pan and quickly invert. If the cake does not unmold, reinvert and return the pan to

The finished cake, decorated with a cloud of spun sugar at the base and fresh violets.

the burner for a few more seconds. Do not panic—the cake will unmold eventually. Peel off the parchment paper and invert onto cardboard rounds (the top of the cake should remain the top).

To make the frosting, beat the cream cheese until smooth and creamy. Add the melted white chocolate and beat until smooth. Beat in the butter and lemon juice. Use at once or refrigerate for up to two days. Warm to room temperature and beat until creamy before using.

With a flexible metal frosting spatula, spread the frosting on the tops and sides of each layer, smoothing well. Chill thoroughly at this point. Insert plastic straws cut the exact length of the thickness of each layer into each layer (except the top) as the supports. Arrange the layers atop one another, being careful to center them.

With a small spatula spread the apricot topping around the tops of each layer, as illustrated. This must be done extremely carefully and neatly.

Create a decorative shell edge of frosting for each layer with a star tip.

Decorate the cake as desired, with

fresh violets, a cloud of spun sugar, or ribbon.

Before making the spun sugar, completely cover the floor near your worktable or countertop with newspaper. Tape additional newspaper to the edge of the counter to protect cabinets. Oil the handle of a long wooden broomstick and tape it to the countertop so that the handle extends beyond the edge (or use a plastic or plexiglass dowel).

Stir the sugar and corn syrup together in a small saucepan and bring the mixture to a boil over medium heat. (An unlined copper pan is preferred; if one is not available, make sure you have a marble slab or pan of cold water handy to set the pan in so that the temperature stabilizes and doesn't rise any more. Above 270°, spun sugar will look brassy instead of golden.) Increase the heat and boil until the liquid turns pale amber at 260°. Remove the saucepan from the heat and let cool for 2 to 3 minutes; add the beeswax. If the mixture is too hot it will fall in droplets instead of strings, it will not spin, and the wax will smoke. The optional wax (which is edible) coats the strands of spun sugar, making them easier to work with.

Standing on a stool so that you are

above the wooden spoon handle, hold two forks side by side in one hand. Dip them into the sugar and vigorously wave the forks back and forth above the handle, allowing the strands to fall in long, thin threads. Waving must be continuous or droplets will form. It is normal to have a few small droplets, which are known as angels' tears.

Wrap the strands around the base and sides of the frosted cake; it is best to do this immediately after spinning because the strands tend to become brittle and hard to shape after too long. Do not attempt to make spun sugar in hot and/or humid weather as it will collapse. (If you wish to make the spun sugar ahead, wrap the spun sugar around an oiled, inverted cake pan the size of the finished cake. When the sugar hardens, carefully lift it off and wrap well with plastic wrap or store in an airtight container in a cool, dry area for an hour or two.

NOTE: Apricot lekvar is a rich apricot butter available in Hungarian specialty food stores. Barack Palinka is an apricot-flavored eau de vie from Austria.

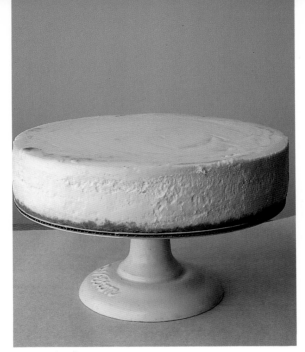

1. Rounds of cardboard cut exactly to size are placed under each layer, and the layer is brushed free of crumbs.

2. Each layer is coated with a smooth, perfect coating of frosting and then chilled. Rose always uses a turntable for decorating.

3. Rose's decorative foil cardboard, which she places on top of a wooden round to support the cake.

4. Rose uses French metal measuring rounds to center each layer perfectly. Cardboard rounds could also be used, or the layers can simply be stacked by eye.

5. Sturdy plastic straws are cut exactly to the size of the thickness of each layer. These supports are absolutely essential when stacking the layers of a wedding cake because they prevent the layers from sinking into one another.

6. Straws are positioned ½ inch in from the perimeter of each layer.

7. Carefully stacking the next layer.

8. Apricot glaze is carefully spooned around the top of each layer, then smoothed with a small spatula.

9. Gold gauze ribbon is cut to size, using the cake pans as a guide.

10. The ribbon is applied around the perimeter of each layer.

11. Using a star tip, Rose creates a decorative shell edge of frosting around each layer.

12. The spun sugar strands being formed. Rose uses a plexiglass dowel and her own multitonged tool. (You can make an excellent spun sugar tool by snipping off the round portion of a stainless steel whisk with wire clippers.)

My Favorite Wedding Cake Recipes

For all of the cake recipes that follow I have given the amount of batter in cups that the recipe yields to make it easy to determine how many times the recipe must be made. I line all the pans with parchment and insert paper collars so that the pans can be filled a little more than three-quarters full with no risk of the batter overflowing, and at the same time, ensuring straight, even-sided layers.

Wedding cakes, especially the very rich cakes—my Chocolate-Almond and Orange-Almond, for instance, or Rose Beranbaum's Golden Glory Cheesecake—should be served in small pieces. The "approximate" number of servings indicated by the chart on page 346 will generally provide for seconds for some of the guests. The topmost layer is usually reserved for the bride and groom and preserved, well wrapped, in the freezer for the first wedding anniversary.

I usually make a larger cake than necessary so that it looks more lavish and opulent. Leftovers can always be given away or frozen.

The evening before a wedding day is generally the best time for me to decorate the wedding cake. I often work late into the night making batches of frosting and creating new and different patterns. Cool temperatures and good lighting are imperative.

When baking the wedding cake, it is important not to try to make too much batter at one time. I find that each electric mixer has an optimum capacity. The Kitchen Aid 5-quart model can beat fifteen egg whites, but the 4½-quart model can only do twelve. To fill the largest pans it may be necessary to make two or three batches of cake batter separately.

It is a good idea to measure the capacity of your cake pans before you start to bake. Use water to measure the capacity, filling to the brim. Any good-quality aluminum or tin pans will do. They should have sides of at least 2 inches. For deeper single layers, use 3-inch-deep pans.

When choosing cake pans, determine the approximate number of servings desired, then select pans that will stack gracefully and yield a cake with beautiful proportions and enough height. For example, I wanted a tall, narrow cake for Hilary Cushing's wedding, so the pans I chose decreased in size by 2 inches from layer to layer. The heart cake pans come in a set of four, and the pans decrease by an average of 3 inches. Three-inch-deep pans work very well for the Rich Yellow Cake, the Wedding Spice Cake, and the Sour Lemon Cake. The heavier cakes, such as the Chocolate-Almond, the Orange-Almond, and the Whipped Cream Cake, cook better in 2-inch pans. For thicker layers, I sometimes make two of each 2-inch layer, and stack them on top of each other with a small amount of filling between.

Golden Rules for Wedding Cakes

1. Always use cake flour (the plain, non-self-rising type), sifting it before measuring and then sifting two or three more times with the other dry ingredients.
2. Always use room temperature large eggs.
3. Always use unsalted butter.
4. Always butter and flour your cake pans, then line with buttered and floured parchment paper. If you cannot find parchment paper, use a good-quality wax paper.
5. For nice, even sides, form a collar of parchment paper for each pan.
6. Fill cake pans two-thirds to three-quarters full of batter.
7. Remember that different-size pans will require different baking times. Check the cake layers several times during baking for doneness.
8. To test for doneness insert a skewer or toothpick in the center, which should come out clean (except for some chocolate cakes which should still be moist in the center). The sides of the cake should also be pulling away from the pan when the cake layer is done.
9. If the center does not seem to be cooking, reduce the oven temperature and extend the cooking time. Be careful not to burn or brown the cake layers.
10. Always cool cakes in pans for at least 10 minutes before removing, then let cool thoroughly on wire racks, right side up, removing parchment paper from cake.
11. Make sure all the layers are the same height. Uneven layers result in an uneven, crooked-looking cake. If the cake has risen higher in the center, trim off the unevenness with a sharp serrated bread knife.
12. To freeze the cakes, cool thoroughly, wrap very well in plastic wrap, and freeze on cake cardboards. Be very careful not to bend or damage the individual layers.
13. Always frost the cake the day before the wedding and refrigerate it so the icing will be thoroughly chilled. Decorate the cake with flowers, spun sugar, etc., as close to serving time as possible.

Round Cake Pans	Capacity of Pan to Brim	Approximate Servings
IN INCHES	IN CUPS	GENEROUS SLICES
2 × 6	4	6
2 × 8	5	8
2 × 9	6	10
2 × 10	8	12
2 × 11	10	16
2 × 12	11½	20
2 × 14	16	30
2 × 17	26	40
3 × 6	6	8
3 × 8	10	12
3 × 9	13	14
3 × 10	16	16
3 × 12	20	22
3 × 14	32	36

Heart Cake Pans	Capacity of Pan to Brim	Approximate Servings
2 × 6	2½	6
2 × 9	7	10
2 × 12	11	16
2 × 14	17	25

How to Decorate and Assemble a Wedding Cake

1. Make all layers of the cake in advance. Trim layers and brush each so there are no crumbs. Layers can be made two days in advance and refrigerated, or earlier and frozen. Wrap extremely well in single layers, using plastic wrap. When ready to frost the cake, thaw all layers in their wrapping. If the cakes are slightly cold, the icing will set better.

2. Cut cardboard rounds the same size exactly as each layer of cake.

3. Have an empty refrigerator ready so layers can be chilled while you are decorating. This is especially important in warm weather. In any event, the cake will need a very large space in the refrigerator where it can be kept until serving time. The following cakes, with their meringue buttercreams, do not sit well out of refrigeration.

4. Make the icing one batch at a time. The first batch will be for the undercoating and successive batches will be used for the actual decoration.

5. Undercoat each layer with an even, thin layer of white (or chocolate) icing. Refrigerate each layer after coating.

6. Decorate one layer at a time. Decorate first the sides and tops and then the edges. Use the tips indicated for the specific decorations.

7. To stack the layers atop one another, cut wooden chopsticks or heavy plastic straws ½ inch longer than the thickness of each layer (if spaces are desired, or the exact size if no spaces are wanted). Insert seven or eight chopsticks ½ inch in from the perimeter of each layer so the next layer will sit atop the supports. The small space between the layers prevents the icing from being damaged and also provides a place to insert the flowers without sticking them into the cake. To make sure the layers do not move once they are stacked, put a long bamboo skewer down through the middle of the entire cake. This locks the layers together.

8. To move the cake from one location to another, either carry the layers separately, on large trays, and assemble the cake where it is going to be served, or completely assemble it, refrigerate it until it is very cold, then place in a large packing box. I cut one side of the box down and slide the cake into the box. The side can be taped back in place and the top of the box secured with tape. If the weather is very hot, you can line a shipping carton with 1-inch-thick sheets of Styrofoam and use this insulated box to carry and store the cake until it is to be served.

9. Always take a repair kit to the place where the cake is to be served to fix any disturbed frosting and decoration. Garnish the cake with flowers right before it is to be put on view. Flowers should be kept in water up until the time the cake is to be decorated.

The tools of a cake decorator—soft, clean brushes, many sizes of spatulas, a large variety of tips, adapters, and pastry bags.

The cake was iced with buttercream slightly tinted with rose coloring and garnished with roses and ferns.

Italian Cream Wedding Cake

MAKES 1 ROUND LAYER—
2×11 INCHES
APPROXIMATELY 6½ CUPS BATTER

The Leo-Wolf wedding reception was very small, so by necessity the cake, too, had to be small. We baked three layers of an Italian cream cake, a dense, moist, delicious white cake made with buttermilk (or heavy cream).

> 5 extra-large eggs, separated, at room temperature
> 2 cups sugar
> ¼ pound (1 stick) unsalted butter, at room temperature
> ½ cup solid vegetable shortening, at room temperature
> 1 teaspoon vanilla extract
> 1 teaspoon baking soda
> 1 cup buttermilk, at room temperature
> 1 teaspoon salt
> 2 cups sifted cake flour

Preheat the oven to 325°. Butter and flour the cake pan, then line with parchment paper.

Using an electric mixer, beat the egg whites until soft peaks form. Gradually beat in ½ cup sugar until the mixture thickens to a meringuelike consistency. Set aside.

In a separate bowl, cream the remaining sugar, butter, vegetable shortening, and vanilla. Add the egg yolks, one at a time, until the batter is thick and well blended.

Stir the baking soda into the buttermilk and set aside.

Sift the salt together with the flour, and add to the butter mixture alternately with the buttermilk, beginning and ending with the flour. Fold the egg whites into the batter. Spoon the batter into the prepared pan, filling it two-thirds full and bake approximately 55 minutes, or until the cake has pulled away from the sides of the pan and tests done in the center. Cool cake in pan for 10 minutes; remove the cake from the pan and let cool completely.

Wedding Spice Cake

MAKES 1 ROUND LAYER—
2 × 12 INCHES
APPROXIMATELY 8½ CUPS BATTER

Jacquie Van Den Berg loves spice cake, and so I adapted my favorite recipe for her wedding cake. I made five large layers, baked in 2-inch-deep pans. The cake is light, yet it is firm enough for a wedding cake when baked in 2-inch layers. If the cake is well chilled, it cuts beautifully into nice, neat slices.

¾ pound (3 sticks) unsalted butter
3 cups sugar
6 eggs, separated
4 cups sifted cake flour
2 teaspoons baking powder
2 teaspoons baking soda
2 teaspoons freshly grated nutmeg
2 teaspoons ground cinnamon
1 teaspoon ground cloves
1 teaspoon salt
1¾ cups buttermilk

Preheat the oven to 350°. Butter and flour the cake pan, then line with parchment.

Using an electric mixer, cream the butter until soft. Gradually beat in the sugar, mixing until light and fluffy. Add the egg yolks and beat well.

Sift together the cake flour and the remaining dry ingredients. Resift the dry ingredients into the sugar-butter mixture by thirds, alternating with the buttermilk. Beat until smooth after each addition.

Beat the egg whites until stiff but not dry and gently fold into the batter. (This should be done in a wide, shallow bowl; the greater surface area will help to prevent the egg whites from deflating too much.)

Pour the batter into the prepared pan. Bake until the cake is done in the center and has begun to shrink away from the sides of the pan, approximately 55 minutes. Let cool on a wire rack.

The cake was decorated in a basketweave pattern and garnished with tiny pink roses and lemon leaves.

349

1. Each layer must be trimmed
to uniform thickness.

2. Every loose crumb is brushed
from the surface of the cake.

3. A smooth undercoating of
frosting is applied to each layer.

4. A horizontal zigzag tip is
used to make the vertical sides.

5. A small rose tip
is used to create a swag.

6. A small star tip is used
to create a shell pattern.

7. Bows are applied with the
same rose tip used in step 5.

8. Six wooden chopsticks
act as supports for each layer.

9. The chopsticks are cut
¼ inch longer than the
thickness of each layer.

10. Inserting the
chopsticks layer by layer
as the cake is stacked.

11. The fourth layer is
lifted onto its supports
with a large spatula.

12. More chopsticks are
inserted.

13. Starting the decora-
tion of the top layer,
using a horizontal
zigzag tip.

14. Adding swags with
a small rose tip.

15. The decoration of the
top of the cake must
be elaborate and perfect.

16. Adding the final
bows and swags with
the Italian buttercream.

Chocolate-Almond Wedding Cake

**MAKES 1 ROUND LAYER—
2×12 INCHES
APPROXIMATELY 8½ CUPS BATTER**

Margot Olshan always wanted a chocolate wedding cake, and we suggested this chocolate-almond confection—a dense, slightly underbaked cake that is moist in the center, and very, very rich. I baked five 2-inch layers, which were trimmed to even size and undercoated with Italian meringue buttercream. The elaborate frosting was then piped on, using a variety of plain, star, leaf, and rose tips. The layers were placed one atop the other, leaving a ½-inch space between each so the frosting decoration would not be disturbed.

- 1 pound (4 sticks) unsalted butter, at room temperature
- 2¾ cups sugar
- 12 eggs, separated
- 1 pound semisweet chocolate, melted and slightly cooled
- 3 cups sifted cake flour
- 1 teaspoon almond extract
- 1½ cups very finely ground blanched almonds
  Pinch of salt

Preheat the oven to 350°. Butter the cake pan, line it with parchment paper, and butter and flour the paper.

Cream the butter and 2½ cups of the sugar until fluffy. Add the egg yolks, one at a time, beating well after each addition, and continue to beat until the mixture is thick and pale yellow.

Stir in the melted chocolate just until incorporated. Stir in the flour, almond extract, and almonds, again mixing just until incorporated.

In a separate bowl, beat the egg whites to soft peaks. Add the salt and remaining ¼ cup sugar and beat until the mixture reaches a meringuelike consistency. Fold this mixture gently into the chocolate mixture.

Spoon the batter into the prepared

pan and bake for approximately 25 to 30 minutes, or just until the edges are set. The center may appear slightly underdone, but the cake will be rich and moist if baked this way.

Cool the cake on a wire rack for 10 minutes; remove it from the pan and let cool completely.

Ecru satin ribbons were cut and placed around the layers to create an elegant appearance.

Tiny rosebuds and roses were used to decorate each layer of the cake, and more roses completely lined my huge silver tray.

Whipped Cream Cake

MAKES 1 ROUND LAYER—
2×9 INCHES
APPROXIMATELY 5 CUPS BATTER

Caroline Damerell wanted everything "barely" pink for her wedding to Carmine Santandrea. As a wedding gift, I created my "Rose Cake" and floral arrangements, using blooms from my rose gardens. The cake was quite small, four 2-inch-thick layers of whipped cream cake, a white cake of unusual richness and excellent texture. The icing was tinted slightly with red food coloring, and it was applied in vertical stripes with ruffled edges and swags.

- 2 cups sifted cake flour
- ½ teaspoon salt
- 3 teaspoons baking powder
- 3 egg whites
- 1 cup (½ pint) heavy cream
- 1½ cups sugar
- ½ cup cold water
- 1 teaspoon vanilla extract
- ½ teaspoon almond extract

Preheat oven to 350°. Butter and flour the pan, then line with parchment paper.

Sift the flour, salt, and baking powder together three times, and set aside.

Beat the egg whites until stiff but not dry.

Whip cream until stiff and fold into eggs. Add sugar gradually and mix well, folding in with a rubber spatula.

Add dry ingredients alternately with water in small amounts, mixing well. Add extracts and blend well.

Pour batter into pan and bake for about 40 to 50 minutes. If the center is still soft, reduce the oven temperature to 325° and bake until the center is set.

Let cool in the pan for about 10 minutes, then remove to a wire rack and cool thoroughly.

Pound Cake

MAKES 1 ROUND LAYER—
3×9 INCHES
APPROXIMATELY 7½ CUPS BATTER

I call this cake, made for the Gardella wedding, my "Leaf Cake." The interior is a golden pound cake, heavy, rich, delicious, and long-lasting. The layers can be baked four or five days before the wedding, and, if kept refrigerated, they actually improve in flavor. The seven layers were heavily undercoated with the Italian meringue buttercream, then decorated with a variety of different leaf tips so that the entire surface was covered with leaves of icing.

    4 cups sifted cake flour
    1 teaspoon salt
    4 teaspoons baking powder
    ¾ pound (3 sticks) unsalted
        butter, at room temperature
 2¾ cups sugar
    8 eggs, at room temperature
    1 cup milk, at room
        temperature
    2 teaspoons vanilla extract
    1 teaspoon grated lemon rind

Preheat the oven to 325°. Butter and flour the cake pan, then line with parchment.

Sift the flour with the salt and baking powder two times and set aside.

With an electric mixer, cream the butter until fluffy. Add the sugar gradually, beating until light and fluffy.

Add the eggs, one at a time, beating well after each addition. Add the flour mixture to the butter mixture, alternating with the milk and vanilla. Stir only until thoroughly blended.

Gently fold in the lemon rind.

Pour batter into prepared pan and bake for about 1½ hours. Let cake cool in pan for about 10 minutes; then remove to a wire rack to cool thoroughly.

Cut boxwood was inserted in between the layers of the cake, and the base was garnished with roses and more boxwood.

Sour Lemon Cake

MAKES 1 ROUND LAYER—
3×9 INCHES
APPROXIMATELY 7 CUPS BATTER

I made this cake for Emily Arth, the bride on the cover of the book. The cake itself is very dense, really a lemon-zest-flavored pound cake. We baked the six layers in 3-inch deep pans (the largest layer was 16 inches in diameter) and had to adjust the oven temperature downward often, so that the layers would cook through without burning.

I call this cake my "Stripes and Dotted Swiss" cake. The frosting was applied first as an undercoat, then in vertical stripes using a zigzag horizontal tip, ½ inch wide. Small dots were applied with a small round tip between the stripes, and the edges were finished off with the same zigzag tip.

    5 eggs
    2 cups sugar
    3 cups sifted cake flour
    4 teaspoons baking powder
 ½ teaspoon salt
    Grated rind of 2 lemons
    1 tablespoon lemon juice
    1 tablespoon vanilla extract
    2 cups (1 pint) heavy cream

Preheat the oven to 325°. Butter and flour a 9-inch springform pan.

Beat the eggs with an electric mixer until thick and pale yellow. Gradually beat in the sugar.

Mix the flour with the baking powder, salt, and lemon rind. Set aside. Mix vanilla and lemon juice with the heavy cream.

Alternately add the flour and cream mixtures to the eggs, beginning and ending with flour. Pour the batter into the prepared pan and bake for 1 hour and 40 minutes, or until the cake feels firm to the touch and is dry when tested in the center with a toothpick. Cool the cake in the pan for 10 minutes, then cool thoroughly on a wire rack.

Emily's cake was garnished with lace flowers in pastel shades, a few stephanotis blossoms, and individual flowerets from hyacinths.

354

Rich Yellow Cake

MAKES 1 ROUND LAYER—
2×10 INCHES
APPROXIMATELY 5 CUPS BATTER

Hilary Cushing is very fond of rich yellow layer cake, so I made her cake from this recipe. The cake is rich, moist, not crumbly, flavorful, and very golden in color. It stacks well and slices well too. Six layers were baked, each only slightly smaller in diameter than the one below it. The frosting was applied first in an undercoat and then in "pleats" with a horizontal plain tip, in overlapping vertical layers.

> 4 cups sifted cake flour
> 4 teaspoons baking powder
> ¼ teaspoon salt
> ½ pound (2 sticks) unsalted butter, at room temperature
> 1¾ cups sugar
> 6 egg yolks, well beaten, at room temperature
> 2 teaspoons vanilla extract
> 1½ cups milk, at room temperature

Preheat the oven to 375°. Butter and flour cake pan, then line with parchment paper.

Sift flour with baking powder and salt and set aside.

Cream butter until fluffy. Add the sugar gradually and beat until light and fluffy. Beat in egg yolks and add vanilla.

Add the flour mixture to the butter mixture, alternating with milk. Stir the batter until smooth.

Pour the batter into prepared cake pan and bake for about 45 minutes. (Note that this cake rises very well so only fill the pan two-thirds full.) Cool the cake in the pan for 10 minutes, then cool thoroughly on a wire rack.

ABOVE AND ABOVE LEFT: I garnished Hilary Cushing's cake with a spectacular variety of old roses from my garden, as well as with fluffy white sweet peas.

Orange-Almond Cake

MAKES 1 ROUND LAYER—
2×11 INCHES
APPROXIMATELY 6½ CUPS BATTER

This cake, which I made for Allison Zucker's wedding, I call my "Rose Swag Cake." The frosting decoration is quite simple to execute, yet flamboyant looking. A smooth undercoating was applied to each of the five layers and then a swag was applied with a wide rose tip. The same tip was used to create the ruffled edging.

The interior of this cake was the orange-almond cake, a French cake made with fresh orange juice, grated orange rind, and egg whites for leavening. It is a dense, rich, melt-in-the-mouth cake, and a favorite of brides.

  1 cup plus 3 tablespoons sugar
  6 eggs, separated
    Grated rind of 2 oranges
  ⅔ cup freshly squeezed,
    strained orange juice
  ½ teaspoon almond extract
  1½ cups finely ground blanched
    almonds
  1½ cups sifted cake flour
    Pinch of salt
  ½ pound (2 sticks) unsalted
    butter, melted and cooled

Preheat the oven to 350°. Butter and flour the cake pan, line it with parchment paper, and butter and flour the paper.

With an electric mixer, beat 1 cup sugar with the egg yolks until the mixture is thick and pale yellow. Beat in the orange rind and juice and almond extract. Quickly stir in the ground almonds; then beat in the flour.

In a separate bowl, beat the egg whites to soft peaks. Add the salt and remaining 3 tablespoons sugar and beat until stiff but not dry.

Quickly fold the melted butter into the batter, a bit at a time, until incorporated. Gently fold the beaten egg whites into the batter, taking care not to deflate them. Immediately spoon the batter into the prepared pan and bake for 35 minutes, or until the center tests done. Cool on a wire rack for 10 minutes; remove the cake from the pan and cool completely.

I used old roses from my garden, in shades of apricot, to decorate Allison's cake.

Grand Marnier-Italian Meringue Buttercream

MAKES 6 CUPS

This remains my favorite frosting and the one I have used for all of the preceding cakes. It has a creamy texture, almost like whipped cream, and the delicate flavors of rich butter and Grand Marnier (Cointreau is good also), and vanilla make this frosting special. It is imperative to follow the directions carefully, however, and to use very high quality, unsalted, unwhipped butter. Make one batch at a time, use it up, and begin the next. This recipe cannot be doubled or tripled and cannot be made in advance. A 4- or 5-tier cake will require two to three batches; one for the undercoat and the others for the decorative frosting. The frosting really does not freeze well, nor does it sit well.

2 cups sugar
⅔ cup water
6 egg whites
   Pinch of salt
¼ teaspoon cream of tartar
1¼ pounds (5 sticks) unsalted butter, at room temperature
1 teaspoon vanilla extract
3 tablespoons Grand Marnier or other orange-flavored liqueur, such as Cointreau

Combine the sugar and water in a heavy saucepan and bring to a boil without stirring. Cover and let boil until the sugar is completely dissolved, 3 to 5 minutes. Uncover and let the mixture boil until it reaches the soft-ball stage, 240° on a candy thermometer.

While the syrup is cooking, beat the egg whites with the salt and cream of tartar until very stiff peaks form.

When the syrup reaches 240°, pour ¼ cup of the syrup into the stiffly beaten egg whites, drop by drop, beating at high speed. Gradually add the rest of the syrup in a fine stream and beat for 8 to 12 minutes, or until the mixture is cool. There must be no heat left in the meringue or butter will melt.

In a separate bowl, cream the butter until light and fluffy. Add the butter to the cooled meringue mixture, 3 tablespoons at a time, beating well after each addition. The frosting should gradually become very thick and creamy. If it doesn't thicken properly, the meringue may have been too warm; stir over a bowl of ice until the frosting thickens. Beat in the vanilla extract and the Grand Marnier.

The buttercream should be used immediately. Keep the buttercream cool over a bowl of ice water, stirring often, but do not refrigerate it. Frost each layer with an undercoat, and refrigerate immediately.

The icing for this heart-shaped cake was piped on with a horizontal zigzag tip. Blue salvia, scabiosa, borage, and stephanotis were the garnish.

Croquembouche

Pastry chef Maurice Bonté does not like to make the croquembouche commercially because it is very delicate. But if the weather permits, or if you are entertaining in an air-conditioned space, this fantasy dessert is both romantic and extremely delicious. I often make these free-form, tall, cone-shaped mounds of pastry-cream filled cream puffs as a supplementary wedding dessert. Only rarely does a bride request a croquembouche as her sole wedding cake. I like to decorate this confection with full-blown pink roses and golden puffs of spun sugar.

PÂTE À CHOUX

MAKES APPROXIMATELY 60 PUFFS

1½ cups water
12 tablespoons (1½ sticks) unsalted butter, cut into small pieces
¼ teaspoon salt
1 teaspoon sugar
1½ cups all-purpose flour
6 large eggs

GARNISH: 1 egg beaten with 1 teaspoon water

CRÈME PATISSIÈRE (PASTRY CREAM)

6 egg yolks
½ cup sugar
½ cup sifted all-purpose flour
2 cups scalded milk
3 tablespoons unsalted butter
1 teaspoon vanilla extract
2 tablespoons Cognac
Pinch of salt

CARAMEL

2 cups sugar
⅔ cup water
2 tablespoons light corn syrup

GARNISH: spun sugar (page 340)

To make the puffs, put the water in a small heavy saucepan, add the butter, and bring the water to a boil. When the butter is melted, add the salt and sugar. Remove the saucepan from the heat and add the flour, stirring until smooth.

Return the pan to high heat and continue stirring until the mixture forms a smooth mass and the bottom of the pan is coated with a thin film. (This indicates that the flour is cooked.) Remove the pan from the heat and put the mixture into a mixing bowl. Let it cool slightly.

Add the eggs, one at a time, beating the batter until very smooth. Once the eggs have been added, the mixture can remain covered at room temperature for an hour or two.

Preheat the oven to 425°. Lightly butter or line several baking sheets with parchment paper.

Place the dough in a pastry bag fitted with a ½-inch round tip. Pipe the mixture onto the prepared baking sheets, forming mounds 1 inch in diameter and ¾ inch high. Lightly brush each with the egg glaze, gently smoothing the top of each puff. Bake for 10 minutes.

Reduce the oven temperature to 375° and continue baking until the puffs are golden brown, about 20 minutes more. Reduce the oven temperature to 325° and bake until the puffs are firm and the insides are not sticky or doughy. Let the puffs cool on a wire rack while you prepare the crème patissière.

Beat the egg yolks, gradually adding the sugar until the mixture is thick and pale yellow. Beat in the flour.

Add all but ½ cup of the scalded milk to the egg mixture in dribbles. Set aside remaining ½ cup of scalded milk. Return the mixture to the pot in which the milk was scalded, and stir over high heat until it comes to a boil. Stir vigorously; the mixture may become lumpy at first but will smooth out. Be careful, however, not to scorch the bottom of the pan. The cream should be thick, but if it is too thick to pipe, add a bit more scalded milk.

Remove the crème patissière from the heat and add the butter, a tablespoon at a time. Stir in the vanilla, Cognac, and salt, and let the pastry cream cool completely.

When the pastry cream has cooled, place it in a pastry bag fitted with a ¼-inch tip. Make a small hole in the side of each pâte à choux puff with the tip, and pipe the pastry cream into each one. Set aside. (Try to find a pastry-cream tip for filling the puffs for it makes the job easier.)

To make the caramel, bring the sugar, water, and corn syrup to a boil over high heat. Swirl the pan to dissolve the sugar, but do not stir or the mixture may become cloudy. Cover the pan to allow the steam to dissolve any crystals that might form, still boiling the syrup, for approximately 5 minutes. Uncover the pan and boil the mixture several more minutes, or until it turns amber colored. Reduce the heat to keep the syrup from hardening.

Dip the cream-filled puffs into the caramel syrup, one by one, and arrange in a cone shape to resemble a pyramid. Decorate the entire croquembouche with Spun Sugar. Garnish with flowers as illustrated.

NOTE: The croquembouche cannot be refrigerated because the caramel and spun sugar will soften, so it must be assembled as close to serving time as possible (2 to 3 hours). However, the pâte à choux puffs and the crème patissière can be prepared in advance. The puffs freeze very well and can be thawed the morning of the wedding and filled. Refrigerate filled puffs until ready to assemble.

The completed croquembouche—a fantasy of pâte à choux puffs, spun sugar, golden caramel, and delicate pink roses.

Chocolate Ganache Groom's Cake

This is one of my favorite cakes to assemble. I like working with the two textures of ganache—the creamy whipped undercoat, which covers and smooths the baked layers of chocolate almond cake, and the thin, shiny ganache, which can virtually be poured over the entire stacked cake and smoothed to perfection with a small metal spatula. When doubled, this recipe is enough to ice a 4-layer cake.

Layers of Chocolate-Almond Wedding Cake (page 351)

CHOCOLATE GANACHE

(MAKES 3 CUPS)

1 pound semisweet chocolate, cut into bits
2 cups heavy cream

GARNISH: Chocolate Curls (page 363)

Bake as many layers of the Chocolate-Almond Wedding Cake as desired.

To make the ganache, melt the chocolate with the cream in a heavy saucepan and cook over very low heat until the mixture is smooth and glossy.

Place half of the mixture in a mixing bowl and beat until it becomes thick. Use this mixture as the undercoat for the cake layers.

Stack the layers as desired, using straws for support, and pour the shiny, thin other half of the ganache over the entire stacked cake, smoothing with a metal spatula. The mixture must be relatively liquid to do this, but if it is too thin, gently stir over ice to thicken it slightly.

Top the iced cake layers with chocolate curls and chill the cake before serving.

LEFT: Before frosting, layers are trimmed with a sharp, serrated knife so they are exactly equal in height. ABOVE: The finished cake, garnished with chocolate curls and variegated ivy.

1. Applying the
undercoat of whipped,
creamy ganache to
make the layers ready
for the shiny coat.

2. Cutting the straw
supports for each layer.
I wanted no space between
the layers of this cake
so I cut the straws the
exact size of each layer.

4. Carefully pouring
the shiny, thin
ganache over the entire
stacked cake.

5. Smoothing the
shiny ganache with a
small metal spatula.
(The cake is
refrigerated
at this point before
it is decorated.)

3. Stacking the layers atop one another, placing them evenly. Each layer rested on a cardboard round cut exactly to size.

6. Decorating and garnishing the cake with chocolate curls and variegated ivy leaves right before serving.

Chocolate Curls

Melt finely broken chocolate (semi-sweet, sweet, or white chocolate) in a glass or stainless steel bowl placed in a very low oven (200° for dark chocolate, 95° for white chocolate). Dark chocolate can also be melted in a double boiler over barely simmering water. (If the chocolate becomes too hot, it will turn lumpy and cloudy. Adding a teaspoon of vegetable shortening or clarified butter may smooth it out.) When melted, stir until smooth. Using a pastry scraper or a large spatula, spread the chocolate evenly on a sturdy flat baking sheet. (I use heavy-duty aluminum or stainless steel sheets with no or very low edges. Very large curls must be made on large sheets.) The chocolate should be spread as thinly as possible while remaining opaque on the baking sheet; if applied too thickly, it will not curl at all. Refrigerate or freeze until hardened.

Remove the baking sheet from the refrigerator or freezer. Using a sharp metal pastry scraper held at a 45-degree angle (see below), scrape off a strip of chocolate from the pan; the chocolate will curl as it is scraped. Repeat until as much chocolate has been removed as possible. Chill or freeze the curls until firm and ready to use.

The type of curl you get will be determined largely by the temperature of the chocolate when you remove it from the refrigerator or freezer. If it is very cold, the chocolate will splinter when scraped and give you small "thatch." If the chocolate is a little less cold, you will produce tight curls. And if the chilled chocolate approaches room temperature (or if a lightly pressed finger leaves a slight print), you will have big, loose curls or sheets of chocolate, which can be used as "bark." The type of curl you produce will also depend on how you scrape the chocolate from the sheet. Just remember that making beautiful, perfect curls takes practice.